45

Social History of Canada

Allan Greer, general editor

In the Shadow of the Law: Divorce in Canada, 1900–1939

The sanctity of marriage and family life was virtually beyond question in the eyes of Canadian society during the early part of the twentieth century. Powerful elements within society had created these values and worked hard to maintain them. Assumptions about the family helped to shape the political, social, economic, and legal structures of Canada. The divorce laws served to maintain the status quo in familial values and gender-based attitudes, enforcing official standards of morality, family structure, and sexual conduct.

James G. Snell examines the divorce laws of this period and the efforts of those who confronted the social pressures and challenged the divorce system. In view of the considerable authority of the divorce environment and the broad social support for the status quo, their efforts are striking. An increasingly assertive group of Canadians, particularly women, defied the social taboos regarding divorce, claiming priority for their own marital needs. They manipulated the Canadian divorce process, taking advantage of existing loopholes in some instances and creating others where necessary. They insisted on the primacy of their own marital problems and in doing so resisted the immediate authority of the divorce environment while at the same time seeking the sanction of that authority. This was true not only for those using the formal divorce system, but also for many who resorted to informal processes of divorce.

These 'pioneer' divorces led the way in creating a modern Canadian divorce system, based on consensual dissolution of the marriage and relying on the courts less for arbitration between contending parties than for endorsement of a privately determined pact.

JAMES G. SNELL is Professor of History at the University of Guelph. He is co-author, with Frederick Vaughan, of *The Supreme Court of Canada: History of the Institution.*

In the Shadow of the Law

Divorce in Canada, 1900–1939

James G. Snell

UNIVERSITY OF TORONTO PRESS
Toronto Buffalo London

© University of Toronto Press 1991
Toronto Buffalo London
Printed in Canada

ISBN 0-8020-5889-2 (cloth)
ISBN 0-8020-6821-9 (paper)

∞
Printed on acid-free paper

Canadian Cataloguing in Publication Data

Snell, James G.
In the shadow of the law : divorce in Canada,
1900–1939

(The Social history of Canada ; 45)
Includes bibliographical references and index.
ISBN 0-8020-5889-2 (bound) ISBN 0-8020-6821-9 (pbk.)

1. Divorce – Canada – History – 20th century.
2. Divorce – Law and legislation – Canada –
History – 20th century. I. Title.
76924
HQ838.S54 1991   306.89'0971   C91-094048-7

Social History of Canada 45

This book has been published with the help of a grant from the Social
Science Federation of Canada, using funds provided by the Social Sciences
and Humanities Research Council of Canada.

Contents

Part 2: Divorce Behaviour

Tables

Acknowledgments

The staff at a number of archives have been particularly helpful in conducting my research for this project. I am grateful to Glenn Wright, Barbara Wilson, and James Whelan of the National Archives of Canada, Wendy Thorpe and the staff of the Public Archives of Nova Scotia, Cathy Shepard and Alix McEwen of the Archives of Ontario, and the staff of the McLaughlin Library at the University of Guelph, especially Lorne Bruce.

I also owe thanks to my research assistants: Mary Gibbons and Peggy Byrne helped a layman to understand the decisions of the Canadian and British courts; Greg Farrant laboured with impressive diligence and integrity on coding the parliamentary divorces; Roslyn Cluett checked newspaper reports. Others passed on information with a notable generosity: Alan Brookes, Ramon Hathorn, Gerry Stortz. Ann Malcolm efficiently entered the data on computer, and Sean Reynolds consistently met with both skill and support my requests for further manipulation of the data.

The Social Sciences and Humanities Research Council of Canada
provided a major three-year research grant and a leave fellowship.
At the University of Guelph, a Donald F. Forster Fellowship granted
release time, and research funds from the College of Arts paid for
programming help and for the conversion of my coding to machine-
readable form.

One of the most rewarding aspects of the scholarly community is
the readiness of colleagues to share their knowledge, ideas, and time.
I have been helped by many scholars from several different disci-
plines. I have heard some speak at conferences; I have read the work
of others. To those who have helped more directly, I must express my
gratitude explicitly: Alan Brookes, Neil MacKinnon, Marshall Fine,
and Joe Tindale gave me useful advice in the early stages of the
project. Many of my colleagues in the History Department, particularly Keith Cassidy, Clarence Munford, and Richard Reid, provided encouragement and help; Keith Cassidy was especially helpful in
introducing me to some of the now vast literature in the history of
the family, which has come to hold a great fascination with me.
Above all, I must thank those who took time out of their own busy
schedules to labour over earlier drafts of this study (in whole or in
part): Constance Backhouse, Susan Boyd, Keith Cassidy, Ellen Gee,
Rod Macleod, Wendy Mitchinson, David Murray, Emily Nett,
Veronica Strong-Boag, and Brian Young. Their comments and
suggestions were always helpful and often provocative. I am particularly grateful to Kathy Johnson for her skill as copy-editor. Her
attention to detail, her commitment to the clear and precise use of
language, and her conscientiousness have contributed immeasurably
to this book.

Finally, I owe an incalculable debt to my wife Leslie. Her support
has been constant and extensive. She, more than anyone else, has
helped me to think about and approach an understanding of marriage as an institution and as a constantly changing relationship. Like
all spouses, she has had to suffer the consequences of my mistakes
as I learned (and continue to learn) about marriage. To dedicate this
book to her is a very small gesture indeed in comparison with what
she has shared with me.

Glossary

Aggravated adultery   A legal result of the so-called sexual double standard; for the wife, a husband's adultery was an insufficient cause for divorce. The wife had to establish that the adultery had been compounded by some additional marital offence, such as legal cruelty, two years' desertion, or bigamy.

Cohabitation   The act by two persons of opposite sex, who may or may not have the capacity to marry, of living together for some duration without having gone through a form of marriage and thereby acquiring public status or recognition as a 'married' couple.

Collusion   A joint agreement between spouses to commit or to represent as having committed a matrimonial offence constituting ground for divorce, and subsequently appearing as adversaries in a divorce procedure.

Condonation   The conditional forgiveness, by means of the continuance or resumption of marital cohabitation, by one spouse of a known matrimonial offence by the other spouse, which offence would otherwise constitute a ground for divorce.

Decree absolute   The final court decree dissolving a marriage, usually granted after a waiting period following the granting of a decree nisi.

Decree nisi   A provisional decree warning that within a specified period of time a final decree will be issued dissolving a specific marriage, provided that no valid reasons are put forward in the meantime as to why that should not occur.

Judicial divorce   A divorce obtained through a judicial process (that is, through the courts rather than through Parliament).

Judicial separation   In earlier times referred to as a divorce *a mensa et thoro* (from bed and board); a contract of separation drawn up by the court, setting out the rights and responsibilities of each spouse to the other and to their children, and having the status of a court order. There are specific grounds in each jurisdiction for which alone the courts could grant a judicial separation.

King's proctor   An official of the state acting in a legal capacity to protect the alleged interests of society at large in a civil action.

Legal separation   A contract of separation drawn up and signed by the couple, usually with the assistance of legal counsel, and having the status of a civil contract. Normally, a contract of separation sets out the rights and responsibilities of each spouse to the other and to their children.

Parliamentary divorce   A divorce obtained from Parliament using the standard legislative procedures.

Watching counsel   In Nova Scotia, the king's proctor.

In the Shadow of the Law

1

Introduction

On 29 November 1920 John Taylor, a labourer in Pugwash, Nova Scotia, petitioned the provincial divorce court for a dissolution of his marriage of twenty-three years. Wed in Moncton, New Brunswick, John and Edith Taylor had lived together in Pugwash and Amherst for nineteen years, and had had four children, three of whom were still living. In October 1916 John and Edith had signed a separation agreement, soon after which Edith allegedly had begun an adulterous relationship with an Amherst factory worker. It was this that gave John grounds for his divorce action. But at the subsequent trial in March 1921, this rather pedestrian marital story took a number of remarkable turns. The watching counsel, on behalf of the state in this undefended divorce, examined John on his previous marital history and particularly on the dissolution of John's first marriage. His first wife, Millie, whom he had wed in Halifax in 1888, had left him after two years of marriage. She soon went through a form of marriage with another man in Halifax and was convicted of bigamy; having served her sentence of one month in the county jail, Millie left the area, and John did not hear from her again. Seven years later (a significant period of time in popular belief) John had married Edith. It became clear in the course of the testimony that John's marriage to Millie had never been legally dissolved. His 'marriage' to Edith was thus void, and the divorce action was necessarily abandoned.[1]

But the story was not over. Finding himself still married to Millie, John Taylor petitioned the court for a dissolution of that marriage. John had not seen or heard from his first wife for approximately thirty years. Yet others in the community were clearly in contact with her, since she learned of her husband's activities. From Welland, Ontario, she contested the action, counterclaiming for divorce on the grounds of John's cruelty to her and his adultery with Edith. John's petition was dismissed and he did not defend against her counter-claim, so Edith was granted a divorce in February 1922.[2] Here was a story of marriage, marriage breakdown, and remarriage, much of which occurred outside the sanction of the state and its legal system. Millie had chosen to end her marriage to John on her own terms and had entered into a new marital union in violation of the law. Punished for that violation, she nevertheless insisted that her first marriage had ceased, and ended all contact with her husband. John too took his marital status into his own hands, committing bigamy with Edith and maintaining a long marriage to her before the two jointly decided to separate. All of this was known to at least some elements of the local community; they tolerated John's bigamy and protected Millie from a cruel husband. Only in 1921–2, when John called on it for assistance, did the formal divorce process begin to play an active role in shaping the marital status of the persons immediately involved.

At about the same time Harriet McGill of Churchbridge, Saskatchewan, wrote to the minister of justice in Ottawa seeking help in resolving her marital situation. Because her story is set out in her own words, without the mediation of a lawyer (as in John Taylor's case), her letters are worth quoting extensively:

Dear Sir:–
I would like very much to know if you will kindly advise me what to do.
I was married to Angus McGill on Dec 16th 1914. We were only married 6 days when he was called up for the war. While in Yorkton, Sask. he came to see me every week or so then in Jan 1915 they were removed to Brandon Man. from there he came home to see me twice the last time being April 14th 1915 just one week later my baby girl

was born April 21 1915. he wrote to me regular unil Sept 6th 1916 then there was ten months or until June 6 1917 I never had one letter from him the he wrote saying our marriage was all a mistake, he still kept writing often and on. and he also stopped my allowance for three months in 1917. but I got that alright after I wrote to Ottawa He came home on March 1st 1919 from over seas but he never came back to me nor have I had a word from him since March 1st 1919. Now what I want to know is this is it Possible for me to get this marriage annuled so I could marry again. I can truthfully say I was faithful to him up to the time he came Back to Canada but after him coming home and not coming home to me, I had to go out and try to make a living for myself and little girl who is now almost seven years old and I have had to sell my little home (as I got it myself after he went over seas) to keep us living and what little I had saved is gone too.

Now I have no money for a divorce. I tried to get a divorce last spring but they could not locate him, and I also had a letter from one of his sisters saying he had died June 26th 1921 but this has been found untrue that he is alive, living somewhere in Saskatchewan.

Now I have met with a young man (a returned soldier), who wants to provide a home for me and my child who infact wants to marry me anyhow but I do want to know if I can get married under these circumstances.

I have no home nor no money and times are very hard alone and I can not get things for myself and Baby without help. as I said before I have never received any money from him since he came home to Canada, and to speak the truth I do not wish any I have done without any help from him for over three years now and I do not want his money. I have been with this other young man for two years now keeping house but now he wants me to be his homemaker so I will be very much obliged if you will kindly give your advice.

My mother says for us to get married and we were also advised in Winnipeg to get married so please do what you can to make us happy.

The Justice Department replied that, while it could not advise her in legal matters, she could not legally remarry without a divorce that would cost 'considerable expense.' Disappointed with the reply, Harriet wrote back, repeating her request for help and specifically asking for 'a written permission' to remarry.[3] There is no record of a reply.

Angus McGill, like John Taylor, had taken his marital circum-stances into his own hands with the help of his family, and had ig-nored the state. Harriet had established a new relationship which she hoped to regularize through remarriage. Blocked from doing so by her existing legal, though inactive, marriage to Angus, she turned to the state for help in obtaining a divorce. Given that Angus had failed to maintain the marriage and that she and her child were the innocent victims of his actions, surely the state could exercise its almost omnipotent powers and either annul her marriage or directly issue a 'remarriage permit.' Though Harriet herself had identified the desired result, she looked to the state for legitimation of that result.

Every story of individual marriage or divorce is unique, but these two accounts, like others analysed here, share a feature that is central to the argument of this book. Marriage, divorce, and remarriage were not straightforward matters for many early twentieth-century Canadians. Rather, they were matters of negotiation and compromise and accommodation of individual needs and expectations, family demands, and the rules and regulations of the community, of organizations, and of the state. The state, particularly through its control of the legal process, the local community, the family, and the individual all exercised varying degrees of power and authority in each marriage, as the stories of John Taylor and Harriet McGill suggest.

In this study of divorce in Canada I have gone beyond a chronological narrative of the political history of the subject. Even a brief examination of the history of divorce in Canada quickly demonstrates that a standard study, though useful, would be arid and not particularly revealing. Divorces were relatively infrequent for many years, and political and legal debates were limited in their scope. It did not take me long to realize that a merely political and legal study of formal divorce was not what I wanted to pursue; instead, I have attempted to explain why Canada maintained a distinctively restrictive divorce regime in the important decades of the early twentieth century and how Canadians behaved within that environment. Fundamental to that end was the defining of divorce behaviour to include those who obtained formal divorces and those who were denied access to the legal process.

On one level this is a study of the law and the family and the interaction between the two in the context of the history of divorce. The study of the law has moved far beyond the often arid examination of legal texts and appellate decisions from senior courts. Social historians and critical legal scholars have come to appreciate that the law is important not just in a separate arena of judicial disputes but in all aspects of society. E.P. Thompson, who has been among the most influential social historians in this regard, commented,

I found that law did not keep politely to a 'level' but was at *every*
bloody level; it was imbricated within the mode of production and
production relations themselves (as property-rights, definitions of
agrarian practice) and it was simultaneously present in the philosophy
of Locke; it intruded brusquely within alien categories, reappearing
bewigged and gowned in the guise of ideology; it danced a cotillion
with religion, moralising over the theatre of Tyburn; it was an arm of
politics and politics was one of its arms; it was an academic discipline,
subjected to the rigour of its own autonomous logic; it contributed to
the definition of the self-identity both of rulers and of ruled; above all,
it afforded an arena for class struggle, within which alternative
notions of law were fought out.[4]

The law is not an impartial process, representing a consensus concerning the dominant values and attitudes of the society and dispensing justice with an even hand. Instead, the law is a site in which
contending social forces – classes, sexes, generations – assert power
and struggle for ascendancy. Yet the law is more than just an arena
for struggle: the law itself is an actor in the contest, a vital conservative force that shapes the ideas of the contestants and helps to
maintain the existing social structure by inhibiting one's ability to
conceive of alternatives. R.W. Gordon has put this in especially effective terms: 'The power exerted by a legal regime consists less in
the force that it can bring to bear against violators of its rules than
in its capacity to persuade people that the world described in its
images and categories is the only attainable world in which a sane
person would want to live.'[5]
  It is particularly useful to examine the law from the perspective of
the family, for the family is a principal forum for the interplay of
classes, sexes, and generations. In the modern world the law plays
a fundamental role in shaping domestic lives and intimate relations,
in structuring daily lives and everyday experiences.[6] The form and
content of divorce law in early twentieth-century Canada presented
decidedly powerful images of the family, of marriage, of spousal roles
and relations, and of sexual behaviour and morality. In particular,
divorce law played a vital part in establishing the hegemony of what
I will call the ideal of the conjugal family. The notably restrictive
divorce laws in early twentieth-century Canada were simply one
element in a family law regime that articulated and legitimated a
particular form of the family. Other areas of family law were char-
acterised by similar attitudes and construction. Abortion, some
homosexual practices, and the dissemination of birth control in-

formation or devices, all of which were criminal offences, were perceived threats to the future of the family. It is striking that for all of these family-related issues in Canada (in contrast to the United States or the United Kingdom) there were no strong or well-organized reform attempts. The few Canadian attempts at liberal reform met concerted opposition from those who sought to defend and preserve a particular ideal of the family and the social structure that the ideal represented.[7] In Canada the political, social, and intellectual environment inhibited and even suppressed such reform and supported the existing legal regime.

Much of that law was articulated, elaborated, and upheld, either directly or through organizations, by representatives of the middle class. The ideal of the conjugal family, defined by them and sustained by the law, grew out of their middle-class perception of marriage and the family. Although paternal authority and wealth were dominant factors in the legal process, members of less powerful groups were sometimes able to bend elements of the law to their own ends. While those less powerful elements undoubtedly reshaped the divorce law and, even more, the legal process by operating within the boundaries of the law and the state, they were none the less required to conform to the basic values and ideas inherent in the legal environment. Thus, they absorbed some of the fundamental precepts of the family and marriage advanced by the middle class.

Divorce is a useful vehicle for an examination of this interaction, because tensions between men and women as well as between social classes were always present. Inheritance and the transmission of property were central to most divorces. A married man had a continuing legal obligation to support his wife, and she had a continuing claim on his assets and estate. Divorce was a vital means of defining and settling these claims and obligations and allowing men to reacquire unrestricted control over their property. Related to the question of property and inheritance was a second issue: the man's traditional need to be certain that he was the father of his wife's children. From this need came the historical insistence on adultery as the primary marital sin – in many jurisdictions the only sin that was serious enough to warrant dissolution of the marriage. In short, because property considerations were at the heart of the law of marriage and divorce, a fundamental issue of social class was inherent in divorce. Divorce served the material interests of those who had material assets to protect; the more assets a man had, the more potentially important was divorce. But divorce was not just about real assets and inheritance rights; it was also about the husband's property in his wife. The value of the husband's property in his wife was immeasurably diminished if she had sexual relations with anyone other than him.[8] That value was reduced not only because of the intrinsic loss involved, but because of the very real damage to the husband's certainty of the paternity of his wife's children. A contest for power was thus at the centre of divorce.

A study of divorce reveals both women's systematic inequality in marriage and their continuing struggles to alter that situation. At common law it was well established that at marriage the two parties were united into one entity with a single domicile, and that domicile was the husband's. Upon her marriage the wife lost her status as *feme sole*, and her independent rights at law were quite limited. For both women and men, marriage was an institution that fundamentally established their relative power and status. Any attack on marriage, either individually or generally, could be perceived as an attack on the distribution of power between the sexes or within the couple. In 1930 the minister of justice, Ernest Lapointe, defended the restrictive Canadian divorce environment as 'good law' because 'otherwise it would be too easy for many people' to take the law into their own hands.[9] Lapointe clearly saw divorce as a matter of the distribution of power between people and state and between husband and wife. A study of divorce can thus be used to inquire into the ways in which that power was asserted by all parties.

In Canada, divorce offers a particularly intriguing case study, for the formal law itself changed very little from 1857 (when England enacted important changes affecting the law inherited by those parts of the empire west of the Province of Canada) until 1968. In this study I have examined a forty-year period in the midst of that period of statutory stability. The years from 1900 to 1939 were selected for several reasons. First, they encompass the time when the number of divorces began to change dramatically. In the thirty-three years before 1900, there were only 213 divorces in all of Canada, an average of just over 9 a year.[10] In 1900 there were just 11 divorces throughout the dominion; by 1940 the annual total had mushroomed to 2,369 (see table 1). The great increase came towards the end of the First World War. The decade between 1900 and 1910, a period of relatively infrequent formal divorce, is included for contrast with later, more active, decades. Second, these four decades encompass a considerable variation in economic and social conditions. Third, the few legal changes enacted before 1968 all occurred within the selected period. Finally, there was the question of access to sources. An examination of divorce trial records was essential for this study,

TABLE 1

Divorces by process and province, 1900–1940

Year	PEI	NS	NB	Que	Ont	Man	Sask	NWT	Alta	BC	Sub-total judicial	Sub-total parliamentary	Total
1900	0	1	1	1	2	1		1		4	6	5	11
1901	0	10	0	0	2	0		0		7	17	2	19
1902	0	9	1	0	2	0		0		3	13	2	15
1903	0	8	4	1	2	1		1		4	16	5	21
1904	0	6	2	1	5	0		0		5	13	6	19
1905	0	6	2	3	2	2		2		18	26	9	35
1906	0	5	1	3	10	0	0		1	17	23	14	37
1907	0	8	3	1	3	1	0		0	9	20	5	25
1908	0	5	5	0	8	0	0		0	12	22	8	30
1909	0	8	5	4	8	2	1		1	22	35	16	51
1910	0	13	6	2	14	3	1		0	12	31	20	51
1911	0	10	6	4	13	3	0		2	19	35	22	57
1912	0	4	4	3	9	1	1		2	11	19	16	35
1913	1	0	4	4	20	6	1		4	20	24	36	60
1914	0	10	12	7	18	2	2		4	15	37	33	70
1915	0	13	6	3	10	1	1		3	16	35	18	53
1916	0	14	11	1	18	2	2		1	18	43	24	67
1917	0	8	6	4	10	0	1		2	23	37	17	54
1918	0	24	10	2	10	0	1		2	65	99	15	114
1919	0	36	13	4	46	88	3		36	147	318	55	373
1920	0	45	15	9	89	42	20		112	136	370	98	468
1921	0	41	13	10	96	122	59		89	128	452	106	558
1922	0	35	12	6	91	97	35		129	138	446	97	543
1923	0	22	19	10	102	81	44		88	139	392	113	505
1924	0	42	15	13	113	77	26		118	136	411	129	540
1925	0	30	15	13	119	79	43		101	150	418	132	550
1926	0	19	12	10	111	85	50		154	167	487	121	608
1927	0	29	17	13	181	101	62		148	197	554	194	748
1928	0	28	13	24	213	79	57		173	203	553	237	790
1929	0	30	21	30	207	89	71		147	222	580	237	817
1930	0	19	27	41	204	114	64		151	255	630	245	875
1931	1	36	20	38	91	94	55		157	208	661	39	700
1932	0	35	26	27	343	114	66		150	245	979	27	1,006
1933	0	27	12	24	307	116	48		138	258	906	24	930

TABLE 1 continued

Year	PEI	NS	NB	Que	Ont	Man	Sask	Alta	BC	Sub-total judi-cial	Sub-total parlia-mentary	Total
1934	0	33	17	38	365	126	67	170	306	1,082	40	1,122
1935	2	52	36	28	491	145	68	225	384	1,398	33	1,431
1936	0	41	38	40	519	179	84	218	451	1,530	40	1,570
1937	2	36	53	43	607	200	112	259	520	1,787	45	1,832
1938	2	51	39	83	824	205	126	271	625	2,141	85	2,226
1939	0	64	40	50	747	181	133	272	581	2,018	50	2,068
1940	0	60	52	62	916	206	125	274	674	2,307	62	2,369

SOURCE: *Canada Year Book 1921* (Ottawa 1922), 825; *Canada Year Book 1956* (Ottawa 1956), 230; Dominion Bureau of Statistics, *Divorces in Canada* (Ottawa 1923–41)

and it was early (if quite unofficially) hinted that the period before 1940 was far enough removed that access could safely be granted with little risk to the litigants' personal privacy; the clear implication was that to ask for more recent records might jeopardize the entire project. Since the first forty years of the century are a highly defensible period, I did not press the issue.

Formal divorce was an uncommon feature of the Canadian social landscape in the early twentieth century. To the extent that the divorce environment was structured to prevent marital dissolution, it can be argued that that environment was both powerful and successful. To paraphrase R.W. Gordon, the environment's essential power lay in its capacity to persuade people that the characteristics of marriage and of marital roles it described were the only sane and appropriate ones. When divorce did occur, the legal process transformed financial, emotional, and physical strains and conflicts within a marriage into sexual issues by insisting that adultery was the sole acceptable ground for dissolution. Nevertheless, the early twentieth century reveals some significant changes in Canadian divorce behaviour. Most striking is the pivotal importance of the First World War. The demographics of divorce began to change, and the number of divorces – though still quite low throughout the period – began to rise around 1917, and continued to rise during the next two decades. It was in the later stages of the war that important challenges and changes to the existing legal regime were initiated. The changes continued throughout the 1920s, and by the end of the 1930s the first major stage in the development of the modern Canadian environment surrounding the family had been completed: the legal regime had not yet caught up with societal changes, but a modern divorce system was in place. This was occurring at the same time that the birth control law was successfully challenged publicly. State control over two fundamental elements of family behaviour was being undermined by informal challenges broached by 'ordinary' Canadians.

By the end of the period under examination, divorce behaviour had changed considerably, though the divorce regime had changed relatively little. The law of divorce remained much as it had been at the turn of the century, although the process had changed to expand considerably the use of courts rather than Parliament. More and more people were turning to the state to dissolve their marriages. To a certain extent this reflected the greater pressures and new expectations placed on marriage.[11] But I would also argue that this enhanced use of state divorce facilities (both formally and informally) represents among all classes a diminution of the perceived legitimacy of community and family informal divorce processes and a parallel rise in the perceived authority of the state and its institutions. State control might have been weakening, but the role of the state in familial matters was growing.

In this study the sources structured the potential results. An explanation of the records used in this study and of the sampling techniques is contained in the Note on Sources, but some further points should be made here. First, a condition of access to the trial records was the protection of the privacy of the individual parties. This protection was extended to all those seeking formal or informal divorce. Where it was desirable for the sake of style or clarity, the parties were given fictitious names; their real names were used only if they were revealed in the published law reports. Second, the participants have been allowed to speak for themselves as much as possible; I have reproduced a number of extracts from law reports and correspondence. I have not emphasized spelling or punctuation 'errors' with '[sic]' or other interpolations. My intention was to reproduce accurately the views and character of the actors themselves, for this is ultimately their history. Finally, I have frequently used the terms 'formal divorce' and 'informal divorce.' Any study of marriage dissolution in a jurisdiction where divorce is legally highly restricted must acknowledge that those marriages that were dissolved through the formal or legal process represent only a fraction of the marriages that actually ended through human behaviour rather than death.

Both types of dissolution are discussed here. For sake of convenience, those that occurred validly through the legal process are referred to as formal divorces or formal petitions for divorce. Those that occurred invalidly through legal, quasi-legal, or extralegal processes are referred to as informal divorces or informal petitions.

Each of the primary sources used in this study has inherent strengths and weaknesses. Legislative debates and law reports reveal the ideas and the parameters of discussion of divorce and family in two of the most potent institutions of the period – Parliament and the courts. The ideas that circulated within those institutions demand examination because the institutions themselves were powerful and authoritative, not because the ideas were in any way necessarily representative of the society or elements of the society. The files of judicial divorces present their own problems. This material was produced through a complex procedure in which the demands of the judicial system, the views of the lawyers, and the actions of the parties all played a significant role. The files cannot be taken to represent fully the views of the parties, since the articulation of their attitudes and knowledge was being filtered through counsel and was potentially highly structured in response to the requirements of the judicial process. The process and the professional filter were male-dominated and class-bound, and severely restricted access and articulation for women and workers in particular. Though I have used the divorce files extensively, the reader should exercise caution in assessing the extent to which the parties were able or willing to expose to public examination their central beliefs or their knowledge of the history of their own marriages. The judicial system encouraged certain types of comments and complaints – for example, about adultery – whether or not these were of primary importance to the parties. The informal petitions for divorce that are discussed in detail in chapter 9 in part avoided some of these problems, but the petitioners were suppliants to figures of authority.

The divorce records themselves allow only a limited view of the individuals' social characteristics. The age of the parties was revealed only incidentally, though the length of the marriage was always reported (not necessarily accurately) in formal divorces and often in informal petitions. Occupations were often recorded, acting then, as now, as a useful labelling technique. This was the only consistent indicator of social class, and I have used it as such. The conceptions of class used here are discussed in the appendix. The sex of each party was always revealed, since it was fundamental to the divorce process, but ethnicity was a much more difficult problem. Place of birth or marriage was seldom revealed, and generally the only clue to ethnic origin, apart from the occasional racist remark from the bench, lay in a person's name. However, because of the variations in spelling and the tendency of individuals and officials to anglicize names, and because of the wife's adoption of the husband's name at marriage, surnames disguise ethnic origin too readily to be used in any reliable fashion. Consequently, no systematic analysis of ethnicity was possible.[12]

This is a study of divorce and of the patterns and techniques of marriage breakdown in all of Canada. But during the course of conducting this study I became increasingly aware that the behaviour of Quebec couples has not been effectively exposed through this research. While the Québécois used parliamentary divorce throughout this period, they did so only sparingly and at a rate much below other Canadians (see table 1). Although a few Québécois, both French- and English-speaking, used the informal petitioning process discussed in chapter 9, French-speaking residents of Quebec did so relatively infrequently. When marriages suffered problems in Quebec, spouses employed very different techniques from English-Canadian spouses in responding to such marital problems.

Marriage in Quebec operated under an entirely different legal environment. On the one hand, the Code civil forbade divorce, though after Confederation it was possible to override the prohibition by a federal statute granting divorce to any Quebec individual (a parliamentary divorce). On the other hand, the Code civil created the potential for some quite different legal forms of marriage. For example, judicial separation was a real alternative to divorce. As well, the law provided for both community of property and separation of property. Upon marriage breakdown, the wife could and often did petition the courts for separation of property (if she did not already have it); if her petition was granted, she could enjoy considerable economic independence from her husband. The rules of marriage and divorce were distinctive, particularly the rules establishing the hierarchy of sex. The contrasting character of both the marital regime and 'divorce' behaviour in the province of Quebec was tested in a specific study.

I have briefly examined judicial separation in Quebec. The petitions listed in the *Quebec Gazette* for 1900–39 revealed striking differences from Canadian divorces (see table 2). Only the class patterns in judicial separation followed approximately the class patterns found in divorce actions (as discussed in chapter 8); this was not true of other characteristics of those filing for judicial separation. First, the absolute numbers reflected a pattern quite the reverse of those

TABLE 2

Applications for judicial separation in Quebec, 1900–1939

Decade	By wives	By husbands	Total
1900–9	107	10	117
1910–19	89	9	98
1920–9	54	14	68
1930–9	50	4	54

SOURCE: *Gazette Officielle du Québec* (Quebec City 1900–39)

found in divorce throughout Canada, including Quebec. Rather than rising steadily over time, with a particularly significant increase towards the end of the First World War, the number of applications declined in each decade, though the number in individual years varied considerably. Second, wives dominated overwhelmingly throughout the entire period. Only in the 1920s did wives make up less than 90 per cent of the applicants, and that one deviation seems to be a statistical artefact. The patterns of behaviour in judicial separation reveal distinctly different timing and use patterns by sex. Thus, judicial separations in Quebec became less and less significant as a technique for coping with marriage breakdown, and at no time in the years 1900–39 was there a major shift in the applicants by sex. This suggests that the process of coping with marriage breakdown was quite different in Quebec. Divorce was little used by the Québécois, as was judicial separation. Marriage breakdown in Quebec was a distinct phenomenon, and demands a separate and more detailed study than is possible here.

Certain legal actions associated with divorce have generally been excluded from this study. First, I have not examined judicial separation and annulment. Similarly, I have not addressed legal separation in any systematic way, although it is clear that this couple-controlled device was often used, formally or informally, as a means of dealing with marital problems. Each of these three techniques is mentioned in the cases whenever their use was revealed, but they were not subjects of analysis because the records used did not lend themselves to that task. Second, although the division of property at marriage breakdown very much reflects and affects the distribution of power between spouses and between the sexes, I have not attempted an analysis of the division of property because of the difficulty in conducting such research. Divorce trial records very rarely included any evidence of the division of property or the level of support ordered, although at several points I was able to discuss the subject briefly. Regettably, the absence of an examination of property in this study has obscured an important element in the power and material relations of divorcing couples.

During the early twentieth century influential elements in Canadian society created and maintained important assumptions about marriage and family. Those assumptions permeated much of the fabric of society, structuring legal, economic, and social regulations and expectations. Within this authoritative environment, the various laws and legal processes associated with divorce operated on a day-to-day basis; they were part of the surrounding environment, and reflected the dominant social attitudes and values. The debate about divorce, the articulation and maintenance of divorce law in the legislatures and the courts, and the more subtle or indirect processes through which the state dealt with marriage and divorce combined to create what I refer to as the divorce environment. This term is meant to emphasize that the law is not something separate but is part of the broader social and political atmosphere, which give the divorce environment context and potency. The Canadian divorce environment intruded into and was enforced by many agencies of the state other than the courts, including private or informal law, such as that of the churches. It was also strikingly consistent. Though changes in some elements could certainly be detected over time, overall the formal divorce environment seemed on the surface remarkably impervious to pressures for reform.

Several scholars, aware of the adamant hostility of Roman Catholics to divorce and of the presence of a large bloc of Roman Catholic legislators in Parliament, have attributed the lack of further divorce reform to such basic political considerations.[13] They may be technically correct, for such factors were important and would in themselves have been enough to prevent meaningful legislative reform of divorce in those years. They were not, however, the root cause of the resistance to change. The absence of reform (or, to put it the other way, the continuing attraction of the existing restrictive divorce regime) was the product of something more fundamental to early twentieth-century society. The divorce environment took and retained the character and shape it did not just because it met the needs of Roman Catholics or French-speaking Canadians as such, but because it reflected a much more broadly based adherence to the prevailing familial ideal. Despite the greater popularity of divorce reform among

English-speaking Canadians and non-Roman Catholics, it was supported by only a minority. Most Canadians broadly accepted a restrictive divorce environment because it sustained familial values and gender-based attitudes. The maintenance of the existing divorce environment offered one way of enforcing official standards of morality, family structure, and sexual conduct.

Given the authority of and broad social support for the Canadian divorce environment, the actual behaviour of the relatively small number of divorcing Canadians is striking. An increasing number of assertive Canadians, particularly women, defied the social taboos against divorce and claimed priority for their own marital needs. They manipulated the Canadian divorce process, taking advantage of existing loopholes in some instances and creating others where necessary. They insisted, with surprisingly little regard for matters of social class, on the primacy of their own problems, and in doing so resisted the immediate authority of the divorce environment even as they sought the sanction of that authority. This was true not only for those using the formal divorce system, but also for many who resorted to informal processes of divorce. Both inside and outside the legal system, behaviour that was regarded as deviant was actually a rational response to the marital and familial needs of the individuals involved. These 'pioneers' led the way in creating a modern Canadian divorce system that was based on consensual dissolution of the marriage and that relied on the courts less for arbitration between contending parties than for endorsement of a privately determined arrangement.

Part 1

THE
DIVORCE
ENVIRONMENT

2

The Family and Canadian Public Culture

The ideal of the conjugal family was triumphantly popular at the beginning of the twentieth century. Conceived of as a single, uniform institution, it incorporated virtually all the principles and ideals valued by Canadian society. The family was the source of nurture and early training for children, of comfort and nourishment for weary men at the end of a hard day's work, and of women's true fulfilment as wives and mothers. This image of the family superseded the class and ethnic divisions that were becoming increasingly apparent in Canada's industrializing society. Central to the dominant ideal of the family was the assumption that its values were shared by Canadians of almost all ethnic and religious origins and engaged in almost any sort of occupation.[1]

The ideal of the conjugal family had replaced an earlier, nineteenth-century family ideal which emphasized hierarchy and the explicit recognition of male authority. The conjugal ideal contained several new elements, or at least placed greater stress on some aspects of family relationships. Wives and husbands still had their separate spheres, but there was a sense of greater equality between them; the wife and mother was entitled to as much respect and status in her work as the husband and father was in his. This belief in the near-equality of rights between the sexes was fundamental to suffrage reforms in the first decades of the twentieth century. Also important in the conjugal family was the place of romantic love in marriage. A husband's sexual infidelity was no longer tolerated; the new ideal was a couple-centred family in which both spouses were expected to share deep affection, emotional fulfilment, and sexual exclusivity. Marriage was inseparable from the ideal of the family and was seen to be equally at the heart of Canadian society. It was, wrote one Toronto lawyer, 'the very foundation of civilized society.'[2] Through marriage the state gave its initial imprimatur to a newly established union. Only within marriage were pregnancy and child-rearing socially acceptable. Both the nuclear and the extended family were legally and morally based on marriage. Sustained by the state, the churches, and public opinion, marriage was the bulwark of the social order.

The wedding, of course, symbolized much of the social construction of marriage. At the turn of the century, a wedding might take place in a church, in a clergyman's residence, or in the home of a family member. As the years passed, the use of the private home declined in popularity and the church became the usual location for the wedding. This change represented a stronger emphasis on community scrutiny and participation. Virtually all weddings in Canada were religious. Only in the four western provinces was civil marriage possible, and even there it was very uncommon. The wedding ceremony united church and state in sanctioning the ideal of the conjugal family. This union was reinforced by the interchangeable character of marriage licensing and wedding banns; either was sufficient for a wedding to take place.

Much of the wedding ceremony itself symbolized and ratified this family form.[3] The chaste bride, clad in virginal white, symbolized the prescriptive morality of the time, a morality reinforced by the ceremony's contrasting verbal emphasis on procreation within marriage and the public embrace by the bride and groom. The bride herself was 'given away' by her father as she passed from his protection to her husband's. The groom placed a ring on the bride's finger as a public token of her new status (double-ring ceremonies were uncommon), and the bride pledged to 'obey him, and serve him,' in the words of the Anglican service. He in turn pledged to 'comfort' his new wife, and both promised to love, honour, and keep each other. With the proclamation that the two were now 'man and wife,' both the asymmetrical character of the marriage and the distinctive roles of the sexes were underlined and legitimated.[4]

The romantic ideal pervaded the wedding. By the early twentieth century the capitalist and commercial spirit of the times was beginning to influence the character of the wedding ceremony. Gifts played a prominent role, and ready-made 'bride's books,' usually published in the United States, had successfully penetrated the Canadian market. These contained coloured prints of pastoral scenes and mawkish verses that expressed a sentimental vision of marriage. Such beliefs were perpetuated more broadly in the fiction of the day. In a story entitled 'The True Wife,' for example, the ideal man was said to have 'a sense of honour, an instinct of reverence for a woman simply because she was a woman, a desire to protect the weak against the strong.' But the husband in the story lacked those traits, and treated his wife with insensitivity and cruelty. The message was clear: a man's character was defined by his treatment of women. But the story's outcome made it equally apparent that a woman was to be judged by her commitment to her husband and to her marriage. Just as the heroine of the story was preparing to leave her undeserving husband for a better man, her husband was permanently paralysed as the result of a riding accident. True to her own selfless character and to the ideal of the conjugal family, the wife then gave up her fleeting 'self-indulgence' and returned to nurture her husband. For this the jilted man praised her as 'a true wife – a true woman.'[5]

This vision of marriage played a critical role in the contemporary culture, particularly in the values and beliefs derived or confirmed daily in the family. Most important in this regard was the family's role in defining and giving expression to modern womanhood. The doctrine of separate spheres – the public world of paid labour and government of men and the private domestic world of women – had been articulated in the nineteenth century and incorporated into the overlapping imagery of women and family.[6] The family was seen as the natural area of activity for women, a place where their biological and instinctual abilities could flower fully. Women's procreative capacity expanded into an all-consuming nurturing role, applying not merely to children but also to husbands and to kin, especially the elderly. The bond formed between mothers and children in pregnancy and lactation was seen as proof of a grand design that assigned women primary responsibility for child-rearing. Their special skill in nurturing and comforting complemented male aggression and competition in the public sphere. This sense of a female–male partnership, of a symbiotic relationship between the sexes, was basic to the dominant view of the family. Supplemental to this nurturing function, and increasingly important in the twentieth-century world, was the woman's responsibility for organizing and carrying out the day-to-day financial and domestic affairs of the family.[7]

The two spheres were held to be mutually exclusive. While young unmarried women were welcomed into the office and factory, their employment was expected to be temporary, since they were merely in a transitional phase in their life-cycle – between dependence on their family of origin and their coming junior partnership in the founding of a new family. Married women were expected to leave their outside employment and to devote their energy and skills to home-making. Women working in certain occupations – for example, civil servants and schoolteachers – were forced to resign when they married. For those in other occupations, informal pressures had the same result, as did the low wages paid to unmarried women. The underlying ideal was endorsed by many men and women; the Calgary Business Girls' Club petitioned the government in 1922 for a law 'compelling married women to stay in their homes where they belonged.'[8] Only in dire economic necessity was it acceptable for a married woman to undertake paid employment.

It was a woman's special responsibility to sustain her marriage. Her charge was the marital home, and she alone had the obligation to make it (and thus the marriage itself) happy and comfortable. Magazine articles and advertisements urged housewives to put greater thought and effort into running an efficient and successful home. A wife's paid labour outside the home was likely to destroy a marriage, but unpaid labour inside the home would sustain it.[9] Wives were expected to suppress their own 'selfish' desires and interests and to make sacrifices on behalf of their husbands and children. The glorification of motherhood reached new heights in the second decade of the twentieth century, when Mother's Day became a common celebration. The values appealed to were symbolized not simply in the woman as mother but also in 'the old home and its associations' with which she was so intimately connected.[10] No one wondered whether women might find a 'good' marriage or home unsatisfying or unfulfilling. From the incidence of sexual intercourse (it was legally impossible for a husband to rape his wife) to the amount of disposable resources committed to various family members, the wife and mother was expected to subordinate herself. The primary responsibility for a failed marriage, of course, was the wife's.[11]

But the man's place in the family was different. His primary work was outside the home, and while one of the ends of that work was certainly the support of his family, he also had his career to consider. A family or home could be too confining or too burdensome for a man in some circumstances. The serious problem of desertion was thus regarded as a male problem, so much so that it was normally called simply 'wife desertion.' Yet the question of a man's commitment to married life and its responsibilities was seen in the most positive light. The married man, it was argued, represented more than any other man the element of stability in Canadian society because he had 'given hostages to fortune' in the members of his family. His presumed commitment to them and their future meant that the man as head of the family would devote himself to ensuring the sort of society that was in his family's best interests.[12] This image of the husband was reflected in numerous middle-class accounts of the family. Rejecting any suggestion that cruelty was a common phenomenon in Canadian marriages, one female writer argued that any wife who allowed herself to be beaten or bullied deserved her treatment. 'In Canada the cad husband is rarely found,' she continued. 'The head of the Canadian household is usually an urbane and respectful husband, who gives his wife the desired allowance and is well-fed ever after.'[13]

If these gender prescriptions fell heavily on men in some instances, women were even more vulnerable to their implications at other times. It was the clear duty of the husband to be the breadwinner. But when he failed to fulfil this role, others were reluctant to step in and help out the deserted wife or children lest other husbands be encouraged to shirk their duty. The wife was caught in the middle – forced into a dependent role and then denied support when needed. For example, in 1937 the Montreal Unemployment Relief Commission removed several dependent classes of married women from its rolls as a means of cutting costs: those whose husbands were being held in provincial institutions, those whose husbands had deserted them, and those separated from their husbands where alimony had been awarded (the husband's failure to meet his payments was immaterial). Unmarried mothers were also cut from the rolls at the same time. Though contemporary studies recognized the problem caused by denying mothers' allowances to deserted women, it was considered more important to maintain the prevailing ideal of the family.[14]

The ideal of the conjugal family appealed to a number of genuine human needs and emotions. The image of an affectionate, emotionally supportive spouse and companion addressed powerful desires and hopes. Emotional and sexual intimacy with another person had great appeal, especially in the face of social change and disorder. Similarly, the desire for procreation was a strong emotional and cultural force, and was condoned only in the family. As well, the family offered 'a haven in a heartless world,' in Christopher Lasch's evocative phrase, a place where persons (allegedly regardless of class, age, ethnicity, or sex) could feel comfortable and protected from an increasingly alienating and competitive social environment.[15] The idea of the family home as a haven, apart from its obvious class bias, was primarily a projection of male needs, and helped to reinforce the family's systematic sexual discrimination. As the primary locus of female labour, the home could hardly have operated as a haven for women in the same way or to the same extent.

None the less, much of the female population in these four decades was socialized to find the vision of the conjugal family, grounded in very different roles for wives and husbands, both attractive and sustaining. It was, after all, a major improvement on the older ideal of a patriarchal family. Some women began to argue for a greater role for women in modern society. These maternal feminists, as they are called by historians, urged that women's reputed skills and special attributes be employed in the service of the broader public good.[16] At the same time these spokeswomen articulated some of the changing elements in the dominant familial ideal. It is clear that these early feminists recognized and sought to redress women's particular vulnerability in their domestic position and in their limited opportunities outside the household. As the idea of sexual equality increased in importance within the conjugal ideal, these spokeswomen fought to rearticulate outdated expectations and to rewrite now antiquated rules.

Though the ideal of the conjugal family was clearly established in the public sphere in Canada by the middle class, its hegemonic influence can be seen in the behaviour and expressions of the working class. Working-class men and women increasingly shared the bourgeois notion of separate spheres, and male workers came to be at least as assertive of their 'breadwinner' role as businessmen or professionals. A wife who was a full-time home-maker was a symbol of economic success and social status. Furthermore, labour unions supported the notion of the male breadwinner, and new legislation, such as workmen's compensation, was aimed at protecting him in that role.

The ideal of the conjugal family was central to contemporary images of the Canadian nation as a whole throughout this period. In

1938 a member of the Vancouver Provincial Normal School captured much of what the ideal family meant in Canadian society. The family played an important role as a symbol of certain values.

[Canadians] believe that a family means a nice marriage with children, a sacred institution and the fundamental one of our society; that the monogamous family is the outcome of evolution from lower forms and is the final, divinely ordained form; that men are more practical and efficient than women, and that as women cannot be expected to understand public problems, men should behave like men and women should behave like women; that a married woman's place is in the home and that any other activities should be secondary to making a home for her husband and children; that everybody loves children, that a woman who does not want children is unnatural and that married people owe it to society to have children.[17]

Such values made up the ideal of the family, which in turn was fundamental to Canadian society. Charlotte Whitton, the executive secretary of the Canadian Welfare Council, said in 1936, 'Family life is the cornerstone of our national life. British people have carried with them everywhere this basic characteristic. This perhaps accounts in some measure for the soundness and the stability of British nations to-day.'[18] By connecting the family to the British character of English-Canadian society, Whitton linked inseparably the fate of the family and the fate of the nation.

Because the family was at the centre of the nation, it was easy to attack and difficult to defend any phenomena that weakened this vital institution. The family in its traditional form became so closely associated with the state that to question its legitimacy was virtually tantamount to treason. The question of divorce was greatly influenced by this prior association of family and state. The same technique was used with other family-related issues, such as parenting, childhood, and women's suffrage.[19] The political system used this image of the home and family to its own advantage. In the 1937 Ontario election campaign, for example, the incumbent government of Mitchell Hepburn purchased full-page magazine advertisements headlined, 'Hepburn Safeguards Your Home!'[20] Social workers brought the state into the home on behalf of families in need of assistance. For several years the annual report of the London, Ontario, Children's Aid Society printed a list of 'moral truths,' including this one: 'The family is the unit of society, and most of the evils of society arise from a demoralized home. It is the duty of the state to co-operate with the family as long as possible and help to hold it up.[21]

The ideal of the conjugal family was far more than an ideological construct. It was sustained by – indeed, was a product of – both economic structures and dominant political relations. Over a vast area of authority and responsibility the state or its agents acted in various ways to support the idea of the family in its tangible expressions. Most directly these state activities were aimed at the maintenance of a particular form of the family: a family household dependent largely on men's wage labour and on women's domestic labour.[22] This state reproduction of the family was the complement of the economic reproduction of the family. What was present in Canadian society was an ideology of familism, defined by Michèle Barrett and Mary McIntosh as 'the propagation of politically pro-family ideas and the strengthening of families themselves.'[23]

This process of state reproduction can be seen in government policies on women and the family. Women, as Veronica Strong-Boag has effectively argued, were the targets of much state policy in the early twentieth century, policy that was largely a product of the dominant ideal of the family. Governments recruited female workers into domestic service to sustain middle-class households and to assist in the spread of family farms across the prairies. New educational policies of support for home economics and domestic science programs were aimed at developing girls' 'natural instincts' for housework and family care. School texts that depicted men in the paid workplace and women in their maternal role at home propagated the ideal of the family and were part of a broader process by which the educational system defined and restricted girls' visions of their future in the adult world. Women in the paid labour force were subjected to a variety of limitations as the state sought to protect the supposedly more fragile sex, even as it failed to protect women against discriminatory wage rates and dismissal because of marriage or pregnancy. Indeed, the essentially pro-natalist character of the wage labour system can be attributed directly to the familial perception of women's natural role. The state's activities can be seen, as Jane Ursel has argued, as one mechanism for the balancing of productive and reproductive relations in Canadian society. Women were singled out as legislative targets because of the emphasis on their role as reproducers within the family setting.[24]

Perhaps the legislative initiative that best illustrates the state's role in sustaining this ideal of the family was mothers' allowances. Beginning in Manitoba in 1916 and subsequently in all provinces except

Prince Edward Island, mothers' allowances were designed to assist married women with dependent children whose husbands were dead or unable to provide for their families. Aimed primarily at encouraging widows with dependent children to stay in the home rather than enter the paid workforce, the allowances in most provinces specifically excluded husbandless mothers who had attained that status through deviant behaviour. In most provinces, for example, deserted mothers were not assisted, on the ground that any such aid would encourage more husbands to desert. For the same reason, separated mothers whose husbands were delinquent in alimony and support payments were not assisted. In most jurisdictions never-married mothers and divorcées were also discriminated against. By emphasizing the support obligations of men and by discouraging women and children from accepting full-time paid jobs, the mothers' allowance programs sought to keep wives and husbands fulfilling their familial tasks and upheld the gender-based prescriptive morality of the day.[25]

Elsewhere, state regulations and policies were aimed at structuring the home environment and supporting the ideal of the family and the paternal role of the husband and father. Immigration policy favoured families. Indeed, the vital part of Clifford Sifton's description of the model immigrant is often omitted; his emphasis on the desirability of the family group and the family lineage was unmistakable. The federal government, he said, favoured not just agriculturalists but the 'stalwart peasant in a sheep-skin coat, born on the soil, whose forefathers have been farmers for ten generations, with a stout wife and a half-dozen children.' Despite the continuing protests of a number of women's groups, for many years Canada issued free homestead applications almost exclusively to adult males. When the first federal income tax was instituted in 1917, married persons were granted a personal exemption twice as large as that given to single persons, and there was considerable pressure in Parliament to expand the exemption on the basis of marital and family status. That same year military conscription was introduced; it excluded women and explicitly favoured married men, especially those with children. A number of provinces adopted parents' maintenance acts after the First World War, requiring adult sons and daughters to assume primary responsibility for dependent parents. In most jurisdictions this enforced family support took precedence over the means-tested, state-supported old age pensions of the time. Soldiers' allowances and veterans' pensions were determined in part by family status and family dependents; when a veteran's widow remarried, her pension continued for one further year as a sort of state dowry. Similarly, the reforms aimed at protecting married women's dower rights all occurred within a framework of reinforcing the husband's support obligations to his family.[26] Policy after policy conceived of adult men and women as living in an idealized family, and treated that family status as something to be encouraged and maintained.

The state agreed that the wife should be subordinate to her husband and dependent upon him for the necessities of life. At marriage the woman lost her separate legal identity and found herself subsumed within that of her husband; the legal doctrine of marital unity made clear the superiority of the husband. Women's inherently dependent character was reflected in what Diana Barker has called the state's 'repressive benevolence.' Not only was a wife required to adopt her husband's name, but her legal domicile and her citizenship became identical to his. Married women's property rights were still restricted, and a husband's responsibility for his wife was still reflected in the dower and maintenance laws. Like the mothers' allowances, much of the legislation imposed a moral code on married women's behaviour. In all provincial deserted wives' maintenance legislation, for example, a deserted wife was eligible for support only so long as she led a chaste life apart from her husband. Statute law explicitly articulated a husband's responsibility for the maintenance of his wife and children; only a wife could bring action against her spouse for alimony or for support in the case of desertion, but a wife's marital misconduct, such as adultery, was a legal bar to any claim on her husband.[27] While many of these state rules were products of the earlier patriarchal ideal, the legal environment failed to keep pace with the newer attitudes to the conjugal ideal.

The contemporary economic structure complemented the familial definition of women and the home. What little paid employment was available to women tended to incorporate and accentuate the family-related definition of womanhood. Various state programs directly and indirectly encouraged working-class and immigrant women to develop housekeeping skills and to accept domestic employment. Women who stayed at home often accepted piece-work, particularly from garment manufacturers. Other jobs replicated in the workplace women's nurturing and supportive role – teaching, office work, nursing.[28] In spite of this, however, women were participating more and more in the paid workforce. Employment opportunities, though usually for low-paid jobs, were expanding, and women took advantage of them in increasing numbers.[29]

The idea of the family wage – that a workingman's wage ought to be sufficient to support his family – had obvious appeal as an argument for raising the wages of some unionized workers. Indeed, male workers in general benefited, so much so that, by the end of the 1920s, for the first time the average male manufacturing worker's wages were sufficient to support an average-sized family.[30] But the real power of the idea lay in its implicit prescription that it was the husband's duty to be the 'breadwinner', to use the powerfully emotive idiom of the day, in the world of business and production. It was the wife and mother's role in the world of reproduction to sustain and comfort 'her man' when he returned home from work, and to bear, nurture, and raise his children. Though the idea of the family wage did not reflect the reality of many working-class families, it still served to perpetuate and strengthen men's claims to higher wages and more highly skilled work. On the same ideological basis, during the depression of the 1930s it was often said that married men, who were responsible for supporting a family, had a much greater right than women to paid employment; considerable social pressure was exerted on married women to give up their jobs so that married men could fulfil their primary familial responsibility.[31]

Complementing such structural features were the changing consumer patterns of the early twentieth century. Businesses whose economic prospects depended on a mass market of individual consumers appealed directly to the ideal of the family. Their advertisements pictured men at their place of employment or busy with home repairs and automobiles. Women were portrayed as being engrossed in fashion and cosmetics, food, children, kitchens and bathrooms, and housekeeping. The caption of one particularly evocative advertisement for a soap read, 'Careless little bride!' and described a young bride who, while giving her first party, was devastated by the grey appearance of her linens and clothes. The following morning she discovered the appropriate soap to use, and all of her marital problems were solved: she was portrayed as happily married with a prosperous and well-satisfied husband. It was that easy to create a successful marriage, and it was the wife's task to discover and use the means.[32] The world of business and capital thus played an essential role in the social construction of the family.

Yet for all its appeal, the ideal of the conjugal family had fundamental flaws. Basic to the ideal were its middle-class perspective, its sex-role prescriptions, and its adoption by English or French Canadians for specific ethnic ends. The norms governing the locus and character of women's work, the activities of children, and the cult of domesticity, for example, all failed to reflect the economic realities of many working-class families. Notions of the nation's use of the family to fulfil the messianic potential of English or French Canadians had little appeal to other ethnicities. Like gender, such factors as class and ethnicity fashioned the character of the family ideal, charging it with great vitality while circumscribing its appeal. Powerful forces in early twentieth-century Canada assumed that a particular form of the family and certain gender-based roles within that family structure were vital to the 'proper' functioning of modern society. Middle-class commentators were in no doubt that the fundamentals of their model of family behaviour and structure were crucial to the well-being of society as a whole. The ideal of the conjugal family defined and gave meaning to the conception and roles of all members of the society.

When this class- and gender-based ideal confronted the political and social reality of divorce, the ideal was threatened. The reaction of various social and political institutions reveals both the centrality and the relative rigidity of the prevailing ideology of the family. The conjugal family was not easily questioned or reconsidered, particularly among those who propagated the ideal. Elizabeth Pleck has argued in connection with domestic violence that the dominant idea of the family was 'the single most consistent barrier to reform.'[33] So too with divorce reform: the ideal of the family shaped debate, filtered reform proposals, and constructed behaviour.

The notion of the permanency of marriage is fundamental to any discussion of divorce. The vows exchanged by the bride and groom were to last until death severed the holy bond. The state and its agents were explicitly warned by the church not to consider terminating the marriage: 'Those whom God hath joined together let no man put asunder.' But if church and state were united in their support of marriage, they clearly parted company – at least to some degree – when it came to divorce. Every major Christian denomination in Canada at the turn of the century spoke out against divorce. Mandated Bible readings attacked divorce; church policies inhibited, if they did not prohibit, the dissolution of marriage. Divorce was evil. It violated biblical precepts and it could not be tolerated. The civil authorities were not so uncompromising. Divorce was a public and legal reality; divorce courts existed in several jurisdictions, and the power to legislate in connection with divorce was explicitly recognized and assigned to the federal Parliament in the Canadian constitution. Nevertheless, the continuing refusal of the various federal governments to enact general divorce statutes made it clear that the state did not look favourably on the dissolution of marriage.

Divorce was intolerable because of the crucial role of marriage in the family structure. To treat divorce as a possible response to an unsuccessful marriage not only undermined the foundation of the family structure but challenged the validity of the idealized notion of the family. Divorce was threatening because it drew attention to the gap between the ideal of the conjugal family and the reality of everyday life. A genuine acceptance of divorce required a fundamental rethinking of the nature of the family, and thus of the entire structure of gender and society, something most Canadians were unprepared to do.

What made the problem of divorce in Canada more complex was that the existing divorce regime was already outdated at the turn of the century, though many observers found it impossible to see this. Canadian divorce law, based essentially on English common law and on England's 1857 divorce statute, had failed to evolve with the changing ideal of the family. The sexual double standard that tolerated male adultery was sustained by the authority of the law. The legal status of married women reflected a much greater degree of subordination than ought to have been acceptable in the conjugal ideal. The grounds for divorce placed a single-minded emphasis on adultery; non-support, desertion, or (except in Nova Scotia) cruelty was no basis for dissolving the marital bond. The outdated character of the divorce regime was but one of a number of problems facing those seeking to use the process.

When politicians and other public figures began to discuss the possibility of divorce reform in the early twentieth century, they faced a number of almost insuperable barriers. The role of the familial ideal in Canadian culture and society was clearly a powerful one. The federal jurisdiction over divorce made reform difficult. The religious demography of the country reflected a high concentration of the population in churches that were formally opposed to divorce in most respects and that were comfortable with a close working relationship with the Canadian state. Issues that might jeopardize the delicate balance of religious and ethnic tolerance within the federal state were raised only very cautiously and infrequently. Finally, the character of Canadian public culture was vital. Dissident individuals or groups (or simply those with a fresh viewpoint) found it difficult to gain access to the Canadian public agenda. The result was that the 'debate' over divorce had its own particular shape and severe limitations. Significant change was to come from another direction.

Lynn Halem has argued that in the United States there was a series of overlapping stages in the way in divorce reform. In the last decades of the nineteenth century and the early part of the twentieth century divorce was overwhelmingly perceived as symptomatic of moral pathology. Liberal reformers (who favoured a loosening of divorce restrictions) and conservative reformers (who wanted stricter laws) disagreed on the cause of immorality and on solutions, but both groups were essentially moralistic. Sometime in the first decade of the twentieth century the monopolistic position of moral pathology was challenged successfully by social scientists. Increasingly, societal stresses rather than individual weaknesses were seen as the fundamental cause of marriage breakdown and divorce. Nevertheless, in the several decades following, exponents of this socio-cultural viewpoint still placed an emphasis on the individual, and advocated therapeutic 'treatment' of persons 'suffering' from a failed marriage.[34]

Although Canadian views of divorce followed a similar pattern of development, the major Christian churches occupied a stronger position of authority than their American counterparts, and in Canada the notion of moral pathology never relinquished its dominant position. Nevertheless, over time the socio-cultural perspective pushed its way forward in the public debate. Its impact was limited by several factors, not the least of which was the relative weakness of social science in Canadian universities and social-work agencies.[35] The debate about the competing points of view does reveal the slow growth of some new views of marriage and the family in Canadian society. But it is not at all clear that these signs were apparent to many of the moralists whose views still commanded much authority at the end of the 1930s.

The views of moral pathology were articulated throughout Canadian society. The inspector for a children's aid society reported in 1919 that the most important cause of neglected and dependent children was 'the wave of infidelity which is sweeping across the country.' Adultery was a factor in almost every case investigated, and 'families are broken up because no importance or sacredness is attached to the marriage vow.' Such behaviour called for a firm response to maintain 'the ideals of life,' including much more rigorous criminal laws.[36] Most Quebec commentators held similar views. *La Revue du Droit*, for example, consistently opposed reforms that would lead to more divorces; any changes in the law should aim at reducing or ending divorce. Setting out the Roman Catholic position on the issue, the journal labelled proposals to expand the grounds as 'foncièrement mauvais, antichrétien et antisocial.'[37] Awareness of such problems made the dominant ideology of the family even more attractive as a prescriptive model.

Many were willing to tolerate the existing divorce process, but were proud of its limited character and of the absence of change: the traditional standards of the past remained the standards of the day. The United States offered a frightening example of immorality run rampant as divorce reform was piled on divorce reform. In Canada, by contrast, divorce was difficult, and a 'healthy attitude' was evinced by a refusal to welcome divorced persons into social circles. Yet some were disturbed that this 'healthy attitude' seemed to be weakening in the early years of the twentieth century, at the same time that religious influence was declining.[38] Proposals for divorce reform were countered with suggestions for greater punishment of the 'guilty' party in divorce – for example, the denial of the right to remarry. It was casually asserted by many observers that 'the people of this country generally' were not inclined to view marriage as a mere matter of convenience between the parties. The religious and moral character of marriage was alleged to be widely supported: 'The sanctity of the marriage tie [is] accepted as something which admits of no question' among Canadians.[39] The state would act on behalf of those who failed to see marriage in this light: 'Preservation of the public interest in the binding nature of the marriage tie,' wrote the editor of the *Dominion Law Reports*, 'will in the end prevent more private suffering than will regard for the hardships of particular instances.'[40]

Other observers could be frustratingly imprecise about the nature of the divorce problem. The Toronto *Globe* described divorce as 'a great social evil,' 'an unmitigated evil that strikes at the root of home and family life, and saps the moral vitality of the nation.' Occasionally, however, the *Globe's* moral perspective penetrated its rhetoric, as when it commented that 'there is no individual sin that provides its own punishment as inevitably as does that related to sex.' No divorce reform should be accepted if it would tend to allow more divorces; this would simply take Canada down the well-worn path of the United States towards 'the breaking of the marriage tie and the overthrowing of marital obligations and responsibilities.' Any anomalies in the present divorce system must be dealt with without jeopardizing 'the sanctity of marriage and the moral life of the nation.'[41] The priorities, at least, were clear.

Fear of change and the socially threatening nature of divorce reform characterized much of the response among those dominated by the idea of moral pathology. Many observers took the absence of an organized or vocal movement for divorce reform as proof that reform was unnecessary and unwanted in Canada, thereby dismissing any individual calls for change. The editor of one law journal listed the dangers of divorce. Beyond the offence to religious denominations and religious principles, and beyond the disregard for the poor who could not afford divorce, any facilitation of divorce presented an 'admitted danger to the morals of the community, to the purity of domestic life, to the happiness of the home and welfare of the children.' Such concerns were genuine. The frequency with which divorce was discussed in popular literature and later in movies was disturbing, but enabled some to associate divorce with other societies, particularly the United States. When the total number of parliamentary divorces reached twenty-two in 1911, the *Canada Law Journal* entitled its discussion 'The Divorce Harvest,' and emphasized the strikingly high number. However much such an increase had to be tolerated by the state, the editor proclaimed his pride in the sterner stance taken by the various churches in defence of Christian principles. 'If it is made manifest to all that such [marital] offences constitute a recognized social blot ... there is less likelihood that people who have any regard for their reputation will perpetrate them.'[42]

In fact, social stigma played a prominent role in the community's attitude towards divorce. The most famous example of this stigma involved George Foster, one of Sir John A. Macdonald's cabinet ministers. In 1889 Foster had married his Ottawa landlady in Chicago, where she had obtained a divorce, having been deserted some years before by her husband. The 'marriage' was probably invalid under Canadian law, and both the prime minister's wife and the governor general refused to receive the new Mrs Foster. Many persons of lesser social status were similarly ostracized or otherwise discriminated against. After his divorce in 1933–4, the painter Lawren Harris and his second wife were hounded out of Toronto. Young single women from bourgeois families were forbidden by their parents to work for men who had been divorced. Divorced persons were excluded from 'polite' social circles, and children from 'respectable' families were often forbidden to associate with children of divorced parents. Children were sometimes told that the absent parent had died, so that they would not be forced to live with the truth of divorce. Divorced persons themselves often said that they were widowed. Nor was this phenomenon limited to the middle class:

when one worker's sister-in-law was called to testify as an innocent party in a divorce case, she spoke of the negative impact of even so indirect an association with divorce: 'And there may be two homes broken up on account of it because Don [her own husband] has changed, and I am sure we would separate after it was over, and I doubt if many people would have anything to do with me, as they think it is a disgrace to go into Court or have anything to do with it.' Stigmatization could have traumatic effects on the individual and the family, and expressed strongly held community standards and values.[43]

Others were unwilling to trust the deterrent force of social stigma. Divorce, it was argued, was a form of crime and warranted more direct punishment of the sort associated with crime. One letter-writer claimed that 'our whole social system is founded on marriage, and a violation of its obligations is not only a wrong to the individual, it is more or less a crime against the state, and if matrimonial offenders had the fear of a term of imprisonment, or fine, before their eyes, it might have a wholesome effect.'[44] Other suggested punishments were whippings for adulterers and prohibition of remarriage. To such observers marriage breakdown and divorce were simply the products of individual moral weakness. Violations of the dominant moral code must not be ignored lest the code and the social and sexual order that it represented be brought into disrepute and society fall into disorder. The issue was simple: divorce was wrong and should be restricted as much as possible. For these people the familial ideal offered both a secure model and a potent force to be used in counteracting the potential social impact of the realities of such marital behaviour.

Others, however, used the arguments of moral pathology to defend divorce. To deny people access to divorce was to force them to tolerate immoral living; innocent spouses would be forced to maintain marital relations with partners guilty of the most flagrant marital sins. Those who wished to find a new partner would be forced to do so outside of marriage, thus living a life of permanent adultery and bringing illegitimate children into the world. As one commentator put it, divorce reform 'is a question whether the spectacle of a married couple each proving untrue to the marriage vows and, colloquially, getting away with it [that is, being granted a divorce], is more likely to encourage immorality, than their being left in an enforced position where they must continue to live in immorality, or effect an utterly impossible reform.' Enhanced access to divorce on the existing grounds simply extended the attack on and punishment of immoral marital conduct.[45] This was an appealing argument to those who felt that minor reforms, largely in defence of equitable justice, should be adopted.

The idea of moral pathology persisted throughout the period under study. But some turned it on its head by subordinating the moralist viewpoint while retaining an emphasis on the individual. Should people be allowed no second chance at a happy marriage when their initial misery was caused by inexperience or momentary infatuation, asked one Torontonian in a letter to the editor? A marriage was a social contract based on mutual love, and the happiness of both parties its ultimate object. If it failed in meeting this end, then the unhappy parties should be released from their bond and allowed a second chance 'to better their sad conditions.'[46] Implicit in this, and developing over time elsewhere (especially in informal divorce petitions) was an emphasis on romantic love. There was a limit to how much unhappiness anyone should be called on to endure. Since marriage was increasingly seen in terms of personal fulfilment and pleasure, unhappy marriages ought to be ended and replaced with potentially happy ones. Why, asked the *Calgary Herald*, should a person be tied down for life to a spouse who calculatingly used cruelty to make his or her partner's life miserable? Why should spouses suffering alone because of desertion or non-support be forced to live for years without any hope of remarriage? Such men and women should be able 'to find relief and deserved freedom.'[47] This led logically to suggestions that divorce grounds should be extended.

In fact, in the years following 1918 a newer version of the familial ideal was being developed. In this depiction of marriage the stress was on ideas of equality, individualism, reason, and romantic love, in contrast to the earlier and still influential stress on hierarchy, morality, and the essential integrity of the whole family unit. But the differences in the pre-Second World War era in Canada can be exaggerated. The fundamental elements of the ideal remained unchanged; the wife's status had been further enhanced, and greater emphasis was now placed on a companionate ideal for spouses. There was still basic agreement, particularly among the middle class, on a gender-based, familial structure of reproduction.

After the First World War the socio-cultural analysis of divorce – Halem calls it social pathology – avoided the single-minded stress on morality and focused instead on the emotional and material quality of married life. This was the viewpoint adopted by the *Vancouver Sun* in 1929, for example, when it suggested that those concerned about the prevalence of divorce would do better to turn their attention to the marriage laws rather than tinker with the divorce laws. The entire solution to marital problems lay in the regulation of marriage: 'It is just as easy to get married today as it is to secure a dog license or a license to drive a car. And even the most optimistic will admit that the problems of matrimony are just a little more complex than the problems of keeping a dog or even of driving and paying for a car.'[48] The Montreal *Star* produced figures that indicated just how rare divorce really was in Canada. Once again using the family as a metaphor for society at large, the *Star* found great comfort in this fact, both for marriage and for the nation, and suggested that the northern climate and character was an important part of the explanation.[49] An environmental explanation was also adopted by the Dominion Bureau of Statistics. In attempting to account for the rapid increase in divorces at the end of the First World War, the bureau pointed to the psychological effects of the war, long periods of separation among soldiers' families, and the expansion of judicial divorce to the prairies. When the high numbers persisted, the bureau added, with less certainty, that there was also probably a more lenient view of divorce in some parts of the country. This combination of reasons continued each year after 1924 until 1932, when the bureau ceased its attempts to offer an explicit explanation for the rising divorce rate.[50]

Social workers realized better than most the complex forces leading to marriage breakdown. An unhappy marriage was usually the product of a number of factors, the executive secretary of the Ottawa Welfare Bureau told her colleagues in 1928. Early marriage, ill health, too-frequent pregnancies, an unsatisfactory sexual relationship, employment or financial problems, differences in age or nationality, interfering relatives, intemperance, and selfishness were all among the elements contributing to desertion among the working class.[51] Social workers found this explanation attractive because it justified their activity. In 1935, for example, Charlotte Whitton blamed the current disruption in family life on the strain of war and post-war conditions; at another time she blamed urbanization.[52] Others pointed to the depression of the 1930s.

These two predominant perspectives on the nature of divorce shaped the content and limited the boundaries of the debate over divorce reform. That debate centred on just two major proposals: the replacement of the parliamentary process with a judicial one, and the extension of the grounds for divorce. There was virtually no serious discussion of ending divorce entirely, because conservative reformers were generally content with the restrictive Canadian divorce environment.

In general, the bar was supportive of proposals to provide for judicial divorce. More extensive use of an effective judicial process was clearly in the self-interest of the legal profession, which helps to explain their attitude. Trained to turn to the law to solve problems, lawyers naturally advocated legal reform without having to consider the more fundamental implications for the prevailing ideal of the family. The major law journals maintained a continuous low-key campaign for divorce reform from 1910 on. Blanket opposition to divorce in principle was generally dismissed as selfish and unreasonable. Not only was divorce a necessary process in the modern world, best handled by a wise and dispassionate judicial process, but the grounds for divorce ought to be extended. The moralists' negative arguments were rejected as 'absurd,' and support was articulated repeatedly for an end to the sexual double standard and the necessary addition of new grounds. Many legal commentators were disturbed that Canadian divorce law was so unprogressive or rigid that it forced people to develop their own extralegal or illegal solutions, thus bringing the law into disrepute.[53] For some this frustration led to calls for constitutional reform that would give the provinces jurisdiction in divorce.[54] Others, including the bar, were disturbed by the lack of uniformity in Canadian divorce law. In the 1920s and 1930s calls were increasingly heard for a standardized law of divorce. Such calls were seldom accompanied by any explanation as to why uniformity was desirable – except that it was tidier, a quality that was considered inherently good in this period.[55]

The most influential commentators were religious organizations. Encompassing a considerable proportion of Canadians as active and inactive members, the major Christian churches each had a position on divorce. That position was usually articulated in the form of church regulations, and operated as informal or private law. This private law transposed doctrine into behavioural codes. The power of the law lay in its apparent consensual authority and in its ability to control membership and privileges in the church.

All of the major denominations were opposed to divorce, but that opposition took different forms and was of varying intensity. The Roman Catholic church had been unalterably opposed to divorce for a number of centuries; no member could divorce, much less remarry, and still remain within the Catholic communion. The Church of England in Canada was of the same belief. Members of both churches spoke out frequently on the issue, but Roman Catholics were noticeably more firm and forceful in their views. For Roman Catholics such as Henri Bourassa, divorce was simply a matter of Christian law and morality. Divorce should never have been allowed in Confederation in the first place, and reform attempts should aim at ending divorce rather than extending it.[56] Both churches accepted the annulment of voidable marriages; the Roman Catholic church had its own mechanisms for determining a religious annulment, while Anglican church courts had fallen into disuse elsewhere and had never been founded in British North America. In England the ecclesiastical courts had slowly been replaced by secular equivalents, but several of the North American colonies were left with neither.

The other Protestant churches were only slightly less rigid. Both the Methodists and the Presbyterians tolerated divorce, but only on very restricted grounds, and spoke out against any resort to divorce by their members. For Presbyterians, the Westminster Confession of Faith accepted divorce for adultery or irretrievable desertion only, and allowed the innocent party to remarry. By 1906 the Methodist church had articulated a similar position, but only for adultery; clergy were expressly instructed to investigate the marital history of all persons seeking remarriage and to refuse to remarry anyone whose divorce was granted on grounds other than adultery or who was the 'guilty' party in the divorce. The regional Baptist conventions in Canada addressed the issue of divorce infrequently; in one of the few discussions of regulations, the Maritimes Convention proposed that divorce grounds be limited to adultery or cruelty where life was endangered. There could be no doubt among the members of the denomination, however, about the condemnation visited upon the 'infidelity' and moral 'laxity' of divorcing spouses.[57]

Throughout the forty-year period under study here, the Roman Catholics and the Anglicans never altered their official stance on divorce.[58] But the other major denominations showed some flexibility. In the aftermath of the First World War some local presbyteries advocated a less rigid position. Church agencies also began to drop their defensive attitude and to accept that divorce was a modern reality that had to be dealt with rather than simply condemned. There was some support for the extension of divorce courts, but almost none for expanding the grounds for divorce.

One general body spoke for a number of denominations and social agencies. The Social Service Council of Canada (sscc) had been established in 1914 to co-ordinate the social reform and welfare activities of those groups touched by the social gospel movement.[59] The sscc was ambivalent about divorce. While it was not ready to accept that divorce was an appropriate solution to serious marital problems, the council was convinced that the issue was too fundamental to warrant simple dismissal. The First World War had revealed problems that were all too common. Official investigations of claims for dependents' pensions and spousal separation allowances had exposed a wide variety of marital practices and behaviour in Canadian society. As well, the tensions accompanying physical separation and economic distress during the war were both obvious and commonplace. A response was essential, and when a bill to establish divorce courts in all provinces was tabled in Parliament in 1919, the sscc was not willing to reject it. Although this might not be quite the right proposal, argued *Social Welfare*, a serious debate of the problem must take place.[60]

At the council's annual conference early in 1920 the Committee on the Family presented its analysis of the situation. While divorce was clearly on the rise, it was more accurate to say that the war had revealed rather than caused marital problems. It appeared that the solution to those problems was tighter marriage laws rather than easier divorce, but it was difficult to defend the financial barriers to divorce.[61] The following year the annual conference expanded on these views. Greater regulation of marriage, the delegates were assured, would contribute to 'the prevention of those factors which tend to disrupt family life.' To this end a number of proposals were made. At the same time the conference recorded its firm opposition to any extension of the grounds for divorce.[62] In the following years the sscc's position on divorce did not change, although the council was ambivalent on the question of sexual equality in divorce grounds.[63] At the 1922 annual convention a resolution was again adopted opposing any extension of the grounds for divorce. By 1938 the various denominations had altered their attitudes enough that the council, though no longer opposed to such a proposal, was unable to agree on any firm position.[64]

It was the United Church of Canada, newly formed in 1925 under the powerful influence of the social gospel and social democracy, that led the way in reassessing the official position on divorce. Its Board of Evangelism and Social Service devoted considerable attention to the problem. In an official restatement of the church's position, adopted by the General Assembly in 1932, divorce was depicted as a matter of forgiving past misconduct and making possible a new start in adult married life. Divorce on the ground of adultery was accepted and remarriage was permitted, provided that the projected remarriage had not been the cause of the divorce. Individual clergy were allowed to decide whether each remarriage conformed to the spirit of Christian marriage, but were encouraged to remember that the church discouraged remarriage during the lifetime of an ex-spouse.[65] In a separate report the United Church became the first major denomination to support birth control as a means of enhancing the quality of married life. At the same time, however, the church reasserted its support for traditional marriage. Counselling and educational programs were instituted for clergy and for lay members.

This was the extent of the change that occurred within private church law. The Presbyterians reaffirmed in 1930 their opposition to divorce, except in the case of adultery. Most churches adopted counselling programs in the wake of the United Church and American examples. But for the most part Canadian Christians heard a strong and consistent message from their church leaders: the sanctity of Christian marriage meant that the marital tie was indissoluble. There was a fundamental and unshaken belief that marriage was an institution ordained and sanctified by God and that marriage offered Christians a golden opportunity to live by the precepts handed down from on high. Most churches were unwilling to re-evaluate their stand on the family and therefore on divorce.[66] The private law's condemnation of divorce and matrimonial offences was repeated in other types of organizations. For example, the Orange Order could and often did expel members for such offences as adultery or marriage to a Roman Catholic.[67] The direct influence of private law is difficult to measure, but the negative message it proclaimed undoubtedly reinforced existing norms.

Like their male counterparts, female commentators on divorce demonstrated diverse points of view. In the 1909 meeting of the International Council of Women in Toronto, for example, one woman informed the delegates that in England most women were loyal to their marriages and never thought about divorce; only the 'smart set' of vulgar, fashionable women thought it *de rigueur* to run off with someone else's husband. In contrast, Dr Augusta Stowe-Gullen suggested that probably only 10 per cent of marriages were truly happy and should continue; for many wives unhappy marriages caused mental ill health or death.[68] For the most part women's organizations worked for greater influence in and liberal reform of laws concerning marriage and divorce. Suffrage groups certainly argued for such a voice, and many supporters saw women's suffrage chiefly as a means of strengthening the family by doubling its representation on public issues. Opponents of women's suffrage argued in turn that allowing women to vote would result in a revolution in traditional sexual relationships, a soaring divorce rate, and a plunging birth rate.[69] But women were as cautious as men about divorce. What women could agree on was that marriage could and should be made more equitable, and where divorce was available the most obvious forms of sexual discrimination should be removed.

Women's groups were ambivalent about divorce itself. The National Council of Women was apprehensive about divorce in general, but more positive about specific divorce reforms. As time passed, the council positioned itself more firmly in favour of divorce reform. Resolutions were repeatedly adopted at various levels of the organization in favour of divorce courts and sexual equality in divorce.[70] As the piece-meal legislative reforms of 1925 and 1930 occurred, they were applauded even as the need for further measures was proclaimed. The most important issue was the demand that men's and women's legal identities remain separate and unaffected by marriage. Some argued that women should be put on precisely the same ground as men when it came to divorce. This meant not only removing the double standard in grounds but establishing married women's separate domiciles. Though the reform would have significant implications for the nature of marriage, notably in sexual equality, this was not generally discussed in direct terms by the women involved.[71]

The idea of treating men and women equally in divorce law was widely accepted by early twentieth-century Canadians, who were unaware of some of the hidden biases in the legal system. Formal equality between the sexes was accepted within the ideal of the conjugal family because it was perceived not to challenge that ideal. Indeed, support for formal equality between the sexes helped to sustain the more fundamental inequities inherent in the familial ideal. Some Canadians bragged of the lack of overt discrimination in parliamentary divorces, compared with the statutory discrimination current in England.[72] Equality of the sexes in divorce could be agreed upon by most articulate Canadians of either sex. The stumbling-block to any such reform was the moralists' fundamental opposition to any change, no matter how fair, that would tend to make divorce more accessible. The reforms that were successfully adopted were those, such as sexual equality in grounds for divorce, that reinforced the ideal of the family.

That women's interests were inseparably linked with the issue of divorce was doubted by none. But defenders of the existing barriers to divorce argued in traditionally paternalistic terms that the divorce environment was in women's best interests. One 1910 writer in *The University Magazine* viewed contemporary monogamous marriage as an obvious product of the progressive development of the rights of women, since the institution had evolved from promiscuity through polygamy to its present state. Any relaxation of divorce regulations would be a step backwards in the protection of women, because outside marriage women had no secure place in society. 'The gifts and talents of most women, when all is said, form but a scanty equipment for any profession except that of a wife. If by nature, training and temperament they are adapted for this occupation at twenty: if they have spent ten or twenty years in its active practice, to what new career can they turn with any prospects of success?'[73] While implicitly realizing the dependency-creating character of marriage for women, that writer and many other men were unable or unwilling to conceive of women as other than wives who devoted their full attention to marriage and the home.

By the end of the 1930s a slow maturing could be detected in attitudes towards divorce. The suggestion that divorce was just possibly not the instrument of social and familial disintegration was expressed by a small minority of public voices. People were confused about what was happening to 'normal family life,' reported a west coast United Church minister. Not only was the number of divorces rising, but parental authority seemed to be waning and the position of women in the home changing. While such indicators were engendering confusion and even panic, in his words, this was probably an overreaction. Divorce statistics were misleading regarding marital estrangement or breakdown. The problem, he asserted, was that confusion prevailed concerning the purpose and ideals of marriage.[74] For him the key to ending this confusion lay in a reassertion of Christian values in marriage. Arguments such as this were important because they reinforced the growing tendency to focus on marriage as the means of understanding divorce, and because they conceded that fundamental changes were occurring within the family.

Other social gospel elements were important in articulating a positive standard and values for marriage in response to the divorce 'crisis.' While J.S. Woodsworth was busy in Parliament pushing for reform and reminding his colleagues of their broader responsibilities regarding the family, other social gospellers addressed the problem in a more positive way. A lead editorial in *Social Welfare* responded to the parliamentary divorce debate by considering the nature of a successful marriage. Marriage was a spiritual and physical union wherein husband and wife shared interests, information, and authority and recognized each other's preferences and wishes: the ideal marriage was a union of near-equals that accepted and tried to make more effective the gender-based ideology of the family. An adequate family wage was a means of reducing friction in the home and allowing the housewife to fulfil her role more effectively. While the husband was urged to take a greater interest in his children, the basic family structure was not questioned.[75] This viewpoint accepted divorce simply as the result of an unsuccessful marriage and urged couples to work harder at developing successful marriages. Indeed, this sense of the very real possibility of realizing the marital ideal of companionship and affection helped to make divorce more acceptable. One account of the United Church's re-examination of marriage in 1932 stressed the damage caused by spousal conflict: 'Where children are in the home the sight of constant parental conflict is so serious in its effect on young characters that, failing adjustment, separation becomes not only tolerable but obligatory.' Because the ideal marriage was one of the ultimate experiences of human creation, everyone had a right to strive towards it. Therefore, once a marriage had failed and the 'obligatory' separation had taken place, divorce and remarriage should be allowed.[76]

There was a great faith in education as a painless means of dealing with marriage and potential divorce. Spousal conflict in the presence of children would warp the children's social development and teach them incorrect marital values and behaviour. Educational programs were attractive techniques for inculcating existing values more effectively, thereby avoiding a more fundamental examination of the problems. Like so many other reform issues, education was given a new prominence in responding to divorce. 'Education must prepare young people both through constant emotional controls in childhood,' said a United Church official, 'and through constant social adjustments in home and society, for this richer and more delicate adjustment' in marriage itself. 'Society must provide clinics where spiritual re-enforcement will count for more than legal advice.'[77] Thus marital education and counselling programs began to play an important role in the new response to divorce in the 1930s in Canada. As organized education became a more popular response to divorce, conferences were held and programs set up. The wide-ranging implications of this were evidenced in one Toronto-area meeting of local sscc representatives late in 1934. In addition to adopting proposals for more marriage education, the delegates affirmed support for Christian marriage but agreed that adultery should not be the sole ground for divorce; they favoured the introduction of civil marriage, and they supported the establishment of birth control clinics.[78] Divorce was so central to the family as a whole that a rethinking of that issue necessarily entailed a reassessment of other aspects of family life. Clearly, as early critics of divorce had argued,[79] there was a link between a stronger idealism about marriage and a greater acceptance of divorce.

This new and more liberal approach to divorce was an aggressive response to those who were unwilling to abandon more conservative attitudes. Proposals to forbid the remarriage of divorced persons, for example, were vigorously attacked as regressive. Yet the 'liberal' reformers revealed their own conservatism in such attacks. Not only would a ban on remarriage force divorced persons to move to the United States, liberal reformers asserted, but it would bring the law into disrepute by encouraging widespread avoidance techniques. More important, moral standards would be jeopardized: some people would refuse to marry in the first place, and divorced partners would simply cohabit outside marriage. The ability to control marital behaviour in Canada would be seriously undermined, a result that disturbed all liberal reformers.[80]

It has been suggested that intellectual shallowness characterized the nineteenth-century English debate over divorce.[81] The Canadian debates in the early twentieth century were not only intellectually shallow, but strikingly orderless. In both the United States and England, for example, the contest over divorce reform produced significant lobbying organizations that helped to chart the agenda of the public and the political debate. In Canada there was no such movement, and interested individuals and groups were left to conduct themselves as best they might. Would-be reformers, such as the London solicitor G.N. Weekes, campaigned in relative solitude against the well-organized defenders of the existing system, with predictable results.[82] It may be that this absence of an organized reform movement is simply proof that the divorce contest was relatively peripheral. But it also suggests that the public culture of Canada was closed-minded, resistant to new points of view, and relatively stable. A serious debate over divorce and all the issues that debate entailed was strangled by a simplistic reaction in support of the dominant ideal of the family and marriage and by the authority that the ideal commanded in Canadian society. Most Canadians were unwilling to reconsider the fundamental issues involved in divorce, preferring to cling tightly to the sure and steady rock of the ideal of the conjugal family.[83]

3

Divorce Legislation: Resistance to Change

Writing in 1915, a distinguished legal counsel and future attorney-
general of Ontario complained that although the dominion Parliament had jurisdiction over the entire subject of marriage and divorce,
'the federal field remains almost wholly uncultivated.'[1] What was
unquestionably accurate in 1915 was still largely true in 1940. Despite a virtually unchallenged authority in the field and a vast expansion in the role of the state, successive federal governments chose
to avoid any major legislative activity in this area until 1968, when
the first unified divorce statute was passed. But this history of legislative inactivity, intriguing in itself, does not accurately reflect either the social or the legislative environment. There was in fact a
great deal of discussion and debate, some of which led to substantial, if relatively minor, legislation. An examination of the political
debate and the resultant statutes will help to explain the divorce
environment and to underline the contemporary support for the ideal
of the conjugal family.

At Confederation in 1867 jurisdiction over marital issues was divided.[2] The central government acquired responsibility for marriage and divorce under section 91 (26) of the British North America (BNA) Act, and the provinces were given authority over the solemnization of marriage under section 92 (12). In the following years the provinces exercised their jurisdiction by passing marriage acts; the central government was silent. None the less, divorce was available through two different methods. Residents of provinces without divorce courts had access to parliamentary divorce, a method of dissolving an individual marriage through passage of a private statute, without reference to any general legislation. In some provinces, though, judicial divorce had been established before 1867. England introduced judicial divorce in 1857 with the passage of the Matrimonial Causes Act,[3] but the established eastern and central colonies had by that time already inherited English (or French, in the case of Quebec) law, so that the English legislation had no direct impact. New Brunswick and Nova Scotia nevertheless both responded to the English statute by adapting their existing legislation. In 1860 New Brunswick, which had been active in this field as early as 1786, established a Court of Divorce and Matrimonial Causes; the grounds for divorce were adultery, impotence, frigidity, and consanguinity. In 1866 Nova Scotia founded a similar court; the grounds for divorce there were adultery, impotence, cruelty, and consanguinity.[4] At Confederation the BNA Act ensured legislative and legal continuity in section 129, which provided that in the various fields of the central government's jurisdiction, provincial law would remain in force until superseded. As a result, the Maritime provinces' divorce legislation and divorce courts remained in place in the years following Confederation, though surely no one would have predicted that they would continue in force until 1968. Moreover, this provincial legislation was frozen in time. After entering the Canadian Confederation, no province could amend or abrogate the divorce statutes; any such action was solely within the jurisdiction of Parliament.

In 1867 two provinces found themselves without divorce facilities. In article 185 of the Code civil Quebec had explicitly rejected divorce; Ontario was silent on the issue. As part of the United Province of Canada, Ontarians had participated in the adoption of Quebec's prohibition of divorce, but had failed to agree on any legislative provision for themselves.[5] Pre-Confederation Ontario thus best exemplified the irresolution that came to typify the national legislative response to divorce.

The circumstances and law relating to divorce were particular to each province, despite the clear intention of the BNA Act to facilitate a uniform law of marriage and divorce.[6] As new provinces joined the dominion after 1867 they added to this legal diversity. The British Columbia legislature had exercised jurisdiction in divorce at least since 1867, when the local Supreme Court was given authority to hear petitions for divorce on the ground of adultery. Prince Edward Island, which had not responded to the 1857 English initiative, had already established its own divorce court in 1835, though it had rarely been active and the statute was effectively a dead letter.[7] The Northwest Territories mimicked Ottawa (and a strong Ontario heritage) by doing nothing. Thus, by 1900 the legal apparatus connected with divorce was complex and varied. Three provinces actively provided facilities for judicial divorce, though the grounds varied in each, with adultery predominating overwhelmingly. In the other provinces and territories there was no divorce law. Divorces could be obtained only if a husband or wife applied for a private bill through Parliament. With no divorce law, there were no boundaries to the possible grounds for a dissolution, but in practice parliamentarians almost invariably insisted on evidence of adultery.

Canadian parliamentary procedure in divorces was first regularized in 1888. Before 1857 the House of Lords, as part of its judicial as well as legislative duties, had had primary responsibility for private divorce bills. This arrangement was copied in Canada, and the Senate accepted initial and primary supervision. The number of divorce petitions had been so low in the early years of Confederation that the Senate procedure had not been refined. When James R. Gowan, a former Ontario County Court judge, was appointed to the Senate, active leadership was available for the first time. Gowan wanted to put the Senate's handling of divorce on a formal, quasi-judicial basis, thereby adding legitimacy to the process. Under Gowan's influence a standing Divorce Committee was struck and special procedural rules established; the Canada Evidence Act was adopted as a guide to evidentiary rules.

An individual seeking a parliamentary divorce was required to submit a petition at least eight days before the opening of Parliament. A basic fee was payable immediately, along with a sum sufficient to cover the cost of printing the private bill; the costs of retaining counsel and presenting the evidence were additional. The divorce bill itself was dealt with in the same manner as all private bills, except that the bill began its parliamentary life in the Senate and after second reading was heard by a special Divorce Committee. It was necessary that all the essential evidence, including witnesses, be presented as if in a judicial proceeding, though the evidentiary rules of the committee were less stringent. If the bill was passed by the Senate, it was sent to the House of Commons, where the treatment was usually (but not always) cursory, the members generally relying on the senators' more intense scrutiny. If passed, the acts themselves had a standard form. They were always entitled 'An Act for the relief of' the petitioner; the details of the marriage and the reason for its breakdown were set out; the marriage was officially dissolved; and the petitioner alone was granted the right to remarry. The costs of the entire process – parliamentary fees, solicitor's fees and expenses, witnesses' fees and expenses – could vary considerably, but estimates placed the average between $800 and $1,500.[8]

This then was the situation in 1900: a diverse, complex legal framework accompanied by often cumbersome procedures was used to settle private marital problems. Divorce in Canada was squarely founded on a belief in innocence and guilt, which meshed nicely with the moral pathology of divorce. The process itself, through mandatory confrontation, always and with impressive assurance assigned those attributes to the participating parties. Few divorces were granted through either the judicial or the legislative process,[9] and the matter was not of particular concern in the dominion. There were only two aspects that bothered some observers, aspects that would cause increasing worry as the years passed. Some thought that the parliamentary procedure was entirely inappropriate and ought to be replaced by judicial divorce. Others were concerned about the undisputed fact of the rising number of divorces (see table 1).

Evidence of these perspectives was soon apparent. In March 1901 the member of Parliament for Kingston, Ontario, put forth a motion objecting to the parliamentary procedure in divorce as class-biased because of its high cost; he called for the exclusive adoption of judicial divorce. The issue of divorce, he argued, touched on the very foundations of society: 'It affects the well-being of society; the personal happiness of many in Canada from the Atlantic to the Pacific. It touches home-life. It involves the services of obedience to, or violation of law. Connected with it are parental duties, and the rights of innocent women and children; their rights to property, and their rights to social position and recognition.'[10] He clearly believed that the law could influence behaviour. That being true, it was inappropriate in a democratic society to frame a divorce procedure that was available to the wealthy but not to the poor. Divorce should be made more equitable and more consistent, but not easier.

The parliamentary responses to the motion reflected the attitudes that would prevail over the following years. It was an article of faith that the law was a vital instrument in the regulation of marital and familial conduct. One member suggested that permissive divorce laws were creating 'the greatest social discord' in the United States and 'more social disorder lies ahead of the [American] people.' Prime Minister Sir Wilfrid Laurier picked up this theme and effectively quashed the motion. The American example was a powerful one for Canadians, claimed Laurier: 'For my part I would rather belong to this country of Canada where divorces are few, than belong to the neighbouring republic where divorces are many. I think it argues a good moral condition of a country where you have few divorces, even though they are made difficult – a better moral condition than prevails in a country where divorces are numerous and made easy by law.'[11] It was a good thing that Canada discouraged divorces. Far better that a cumbersome procedure cause a little inconvenience than that divorce be made easier; in that regard, asserted the Liberal Laurier, 'I am a Conservative of the Conservatives.' There would be no tinkering with a system that worked well. All the speakers in this fruitless interchange agreed that through divorce, marriage breakdown was controlled by the law. And it followed that if divorce was restricted, so too – and this was much more important – would be the behaviour that constituted grounds for divorce in Canada.

While this attitude was shared by many, the practical question of the divorce process continued to be debated. Opportunity for comment was offered several times in each parliamentary sitting as private divorce bills were read – and reform-minded members took advantage of that opportunity. Objections were often made to the dissimilar procedures of the various provinces. The public character of the parliamentary process was unfavourably contrasted with the private character of the judicial process; the parliamentary debates and the evidence of the Divorce Committee produced 'a lot of low, nasty literature [that] finds its way to the public.'[12] Most common were criticisms of Parliament's ability to dispense individual justice. Members lacked judicial training; there was no divorce statute setting out clear legal boundaries; the proceedings in the House were casual and sometimes 'capricious'; and the system was potentially vulnerable to influence and partiality. Instances were cited of lobbying by members who hoped to protect relatives and by wealthy party supporters.[13]

In 1903 a more extensive debate took place when John Charlton, the Liberal member for Norfolk North in Ontario, introduced a motion calling for the establishment of divorce courts across Canada.[14] Proponents of reform had a difficult time making their case.

The real issue was not, as some opponents would have had it, whether to allow divorce. That question had already been decided in principle by the BNA Act, by the passage of private divorce bills, and by the existence of judicial facilities for marital dissolution in several provinces. But many politicians and observers felt that to support divorce reform was tantamount to supporting divorce itself, and this they would not do. Also, any suggestion of legislative change was easily associated with the reputation of easy divorce and loose morality in the United States. As one member put it, 'One of the strongest objections to any change in our divorce laws is the fear entertained by the ordinary domestic people of the country that any change may lead us to fall into the other extreme of the too great freedom of divorce which prevails in the great republic to the south of us.'[15] Such arguments, based on morality, prejudice, and fear, were proof against all rational assaults.

Charlton's motion failed. The prime minister once again spoke out against any reform, citing the divorce environment as proof of a good moral climate. Of more political importance was Laurier's unchallenged assertion that there was no popular demand for change; not one petition for divorce reform had been received by Parliament. In the absence of popular pressure, most politicians were content to evade the problem. As one member put it with masterly understatement, 'There is no great zeal on the part of members generally to deal with this question.'[16] Indeed, most members tended to absent themselves from debates on divorce bills, (both in the House and in committee), indicating lack of interest, moral aversion, or politically astute avoidance of the issue.[17]

The status quo was thus maintained, and parliamentarians presented themselves as defenders of the family. Divorce facilities remained available for at least some Canadians, and the politicians' hands were still clean. Sporadic debate occurred over the next few years, but the issues were generally superficial and the arguments slight. At a time when the country was experiencing rapid economic development and considerable social change, the family seemed a secure, stable institution, and a restrictive divorce law offered one way of maintaining that stability. One Ontario parliamentarian linked economic change and social stability, citing the traditional distinction between the public world of business and development and the private world of the family:

We may build all the Grand Trunk Pacifics we like, we may debate free trade or protection, we may grant autonomy to all the provinces from

Vancouver to Halifax, we may pass all the laws on a business basis we like, but if we interfere unnecessarily or recklessly in the relations between man and wife, we will go a long way towards undermining the morality of this country, and if our laws tend to produce such a result and break up homes we had better repeal them and build up a system of laws more suited to a sound condition of public and private morality.[18]

Change in the economic sphere was to be balanced by continuity in the home. Others made clear the link between the family and social stability. Attacking a proposed divorce, a senator reminded his colleagues that 'this country is not given to breaking up the family ties and social conditions.'[19] These speakers and others like them were convinced of the power of the law to structure familial relations and behaviour. They were not prepared to take any action that they or their supporters could construe as undermining marriage or the family.

Indeed, there was considerable sentiment in favour of making divorce decidedly unattractive. In 1906 an amendment was moved to a private divorce bill, presumably as a test case and an example. The proposed amendment emphasized the retributive character of Canadian divorce by explicitly denying the guilty husband the right to remarry during his ex-wife's lifetime. The amendment failed, but the idea of punishment had been advanced, and not for the last time. In 1908 Senator H.J. Cloran sponsored a bill 'to restrict the evils of divorce,' by explicitly denying the guilty party in a parliamentary divorce the right to remarry. The issue ought to be approached from 'the interests of the fatherhood and motherhood of the nation of Canada, on grounds high and holy.' The guilty party in a divorce was 'a scoundrel, knave and debauchee.' Surely such a person ought not to 'have the right to do further damage elsewhere.' 'Not one of us would permit a divorcee to enter our homes, and if we would not allow him into our own homes, why should you let him into the homes of people less acquainted with his character? You brand him as a man unfit for ordinary society, yet give him equal privileges with the poor woman over whom we spend so much sympathy in granting a divorce.'[20] The bill was defeated, but not because of a lack of sympathy with its stance. Rather, there was a more powerful fear that such legislation would force people into cohabitation and other extramarital practices.[21] Although senators demonstrated continuing concern with divorce, or at least the divorce process, in these years, it was not until early 1914 that the House of Commons was once again presented with a motion for divorce reform. The motion itself emphasized the restrictive costs of the parliamentary process, but the debate concentrated on the ineffectual character of the process, on the absence of a general divorce law, and on the evil nature of divorce. As before, no politicians in a position to do so were willing to take concrete action towards reform; the motion was talked out. It was left to the courts and individual citizens to initiate change.

Early in 1917 Catherine Walker petitioned the Manitoba Court of Queen's Bench for a declaration that her fifteen-year marriage to Edgar Walker was null and void on the ground of his impotence. Not long after, but independently, William Board petitioned the Supreme Court of Alberta for a divorce from his wife Mary on the ground of her adultery. Counsel in both cases argued that the superior courts of these provinces had jurisdiction in matrimonial causes. At trial level the Manitoba court declined to support the claim to jurisdiction; the decision was overturned on appeal. In Alberta the trial and appellate courts held that such jurisdiction did exist. The cases reached the Judicial Committee of the Privy Council in May 1919. When argument for the appellants had been heard, the committee did not bother to call upon counsel for the respondents; the case was relatively straightforward. Writing for the committee, Viscount Haldane followed the reasoning of the provincial appeal courts in finding that the prairie provinces and territories had acquired English law as in force on 15 July 1870.[22] The law and procedure of divorce as established by the 1857 English act were thus part of the law of Manitoba and Alberta; it followed that the same was true for Saskatchewan.

The *Walker* and *Board* cases were products of the wartime environment which had placed new strains on individual families and on society at large. The First World War was a cathartic experience for English-speaking Canadians. Many were persuaded that Canadian society would be purged by the 'war to end all wars'; a better life was possible in the future.[23] One response at the individual level was to demand release from a failed marriage. The cases of Catherine Walker and William Board challenged the procedural status quo regarding dissolution of marriage. Even more indicative of an evolving local climate of opinion was the intervention of the provincial governments in support of the claim to jurisdiction; further, local members of the legal profession were outspoken in their support. An important change in the divorce process had been achieved, but it was a limited change: it involved the process rather than the substance of the law. The superior courts of the prairie provinces now were recognized as having jurisdiction in divorce on the ground of adultery. There was an immediate jump in the number of divorces in the region. Over the past decade the three prairie provinces together had averaged 5.2 parliamentary divorces annually; but in 1919 alone there were 127 divorces, all but 5 granted through local courts (the Saskatchewan Court of King's Bench exercised its jurisdiction too late to be reflected in the 1919 figures in table 1).

Only three provinces – Ontario, Prince Edward Island, and Quebec – were left without a divorce law and dependent on parliamentary facilities. Of those, Ontario made the heaviest demands on parliamentary time. Prince Edward Island had sent just one successful divorce petition to Ottawa since joining Confederation; Quebec had averaged only 3.4 divorces each year in the past decade, and Ontario 13. But the number of completed divorces, both in Parliament and in the courts, rose markedly beginning in 1918. In the British Columbia courts the number of successful divorces rose from an annual average of 16.8 in the previous ten years to 65 in 1918 and 147 in 1919. In Parliament the number of petitions also began to climb: for Ontario alone 46 divorces were granted in 1919 and 89 in the following year. When these figures were combined with the results of the court challenges emanating from the prairies, the evidence was clear: divorce was entering a new era.

Faced with this new situation, the Union government of Sir Robert Borden began to signal its support for new legislation, probably in the form of a bill to establish judicial divorce in all provinces. When the *Board* and *Walker* cases were raised in the House in 1918, the prime minister commented that 'it would be a very desirable consummation' if divorce could be referred to the courts. As he had a number of times in the past, Borden mentioned Nova Scotia's favourable experience as an example of the advantages of judicial divorce.[24] But the government remained cautious. That the central government, despite prompting by the opposition, chose not to intervene in the cases before the Judicial Committee of the Privy Council is a further sign of the delicate political nature of divorce.

Nevertheless, by early 1919 the federal cabinet was considering proposals for government divorce legislation. Cables flew back and forth between Ottawa and Paris, where Borden was attending the peace conference. Concerned about the domestic situation facing many returning soldiers and their wives, the ministers in Ottawa proposed 'unanimously' to establish a federal divorce court. Arthur Meighen, the leader of the cabinet on domestic issues, privately expressed his opinion that the time was right for action: 'I think the feeling in favour of a more rational divorce system has grown to considerable proportions.' That, combined with the judicial pressure for change, made this the appropriate time for divorce reform. But the ministers in Paris were quickly made aware of the political sensitivity of the issue, particularly by Charles Doherty and other Roman Catholic cabinet members. After fumbling for a compromise, the parties agreed that the legislation would be introduced, but not as a government measure; no cabinet ministers or government supporters would be obliged to vote for it.[25]

Thus, in April 1919, before the final opinions had been rendered in *Board* and *Walker*, W.F. Nickle, a Conservative Unionist back-bencher for Kingston, Ontario, introduced a private bill to reform Canadian divorce law. Nickle, who had originally intended to introduce a motion in favour of judicial divorce, claimed to have received so much encouragement from various sections of the country that he had decided to push for legislation instead. The bill itself was wisely very moderate. All divorce proceedings would be transferred from Parliament to provincial superior courts and the Exchequer Court, and a general divorce and matrimonial causes law would be promulgated for all of Canada – a law in which adultery would be the sole and common divorce ground for both men and women. Nickle openly admitted that the bill was designed to 'facilitate' divorce, thus badly misreading the political atmosphere.[26] The bill failed, not because it was defeated, but because as a private member's bill it did not receive sufficient time for passage. The measure had the open support of the prime minister in the House, and on a recorded vote a motion quashing the bill was defeated 35 to 68.[27] The typically cautious members seem to have preferred to allow the bill to die a natural death rather than kill it outright.

The debate on the measure reveals contemporary attitudes to divorce in Canada. The first opponent to speak to the bill demonstrated many of the fears associated with any such legislation, making clear in particular that both the restrictive grounds and the difficult process were equally appealing and important. A.E. Fripp, a Conservative Unionist member for Ottawa, raised the spectre of vastly increased numbers of divorces. He predicted that within five years divorces would multiply by a thousand, producing the same conditions in Canada as in the United States. Difficult divorce was not only good for Canada's moral environment, he claimed, but also of lasting advantage to individual couples. Divorce was simply an easy way out of marital problems: 'Hundreds of people consult me [as a lawyer] about their problems at home. When you explain to them the present difficulty of getting a divorce, they are perfectly satisfied, and I never hear any more of them. I fancy they return home and by the exercise of a little forbearance are able to live together as man and wife should.'[28] From such a perspective it is easy to see how many could believe that divorce caused broken marriages, rather than simply reflected unions that had already ruptured.

The many arguments in support of enhanced access to divorce could not really shake the members who shared that view. The weaknesses of the parliamentary process were again enumerated, and the bias in favour of the wealthy was underlined. The efficiency and privacy of the judicial process were pointed out, and the British precedent in favour of the legislation was discussed. More immediate arguments were also put forward. The war had left many wives and children in serious trouble; soldiers had deserted, committed adultery, or entered bigamous marriages. It should be made possible for these women, most of whom were poor, 'to begin life again under new and better circumstances.' A prairie representative made the same contention for returning soldiers, whose 'rights' now included the right to divorce an unfaithful wife.[29] But if these arguments lacked political influence, they nevertheless reflected a decidedly new and growing attitude to divorce. Divorce was not a shameful end to a marriage; it was the start of a new life that would reaffirm the ideal of the conjugal family. In the opinion of some, society had a duty to make divorce available to its faithful citizens.

The year 1920 witnessed similar, if less intense, legislative activity. Rumours of government sponsorship of a bill were raised in the House. Any such measure was not only 'anti-Christian' but would contribute to the social disorder and 'the spirit of bolshevism.'[30] Nevertheless, two bills were indeed presented, this time in the Senate, and together they encompassed the major features of reform proposals for the next decade. Both were introduced and ushered through the Senate by the Conservative W.B. Ross, a Nova Scotia banker and business executive. The proponents of one bill tried to overcome perceived objections from Quebec by making the bill applicable only to Ontario and Prince Edward Island. They sought to establish judicial divorce in the two provinces by declaring that, as in the prairie provinces, the law should be that of England as of 1870. The second bill proposed for all of Canada, except Quebec, a uniform divorce law, including the removal of the sexual discrimination in adultery and in domicile (where desertion had occurred). Both bills received the Senate's approval, but did not move beyond first reading in the House because of technical problems. The Prince Edward Island legislature responded by unanimously objecting to any such action as it affected that jurisdiction – first, because the people of that province had not requested the legislation, and, second, because 'the establishment of such a court will tend to destroy the stability of the home and encourage the dissolution of the marriage tie.[31]

Though no substantial change had been made in Canadian divorce law, some observers were concerned that the increasing discussion of divorce was itself having very undesirable effects. 'The newspapers are discussing the question, and there is talk of legalizing in Canada this social cancer which is eating the heart of other countries,' lamented one Quebec member of Parliament. The principle of the indissolubility of marriage 'conforms with the natural law' and was important 'from a social and a national standpoint'; the social unrest in Canada could be directly attributed 'to the dire ravages caused by divorce and the reduction of the birth-rate.'[32] Obviously, such thinking underlined the need to conserve and support traditional familial structures and behaviour as a means of dealing with broader societal problems.

Similarly, the moral concerns that permeated the divorce debates and inhibited reform were emphasized by a 1923 bill that would have made it a criminal offence to publish evidence in parliamentary divorce proceedings. Though only 450 copies of the evidence were printed for the use of members and senators, some parliamentarians were disturbed that such material might circulate beyond the walls of Parliament; indeed, one unnamed journal was accused of publishing in its entirety the proceedings of or evidence taken before the Divorce Committee.[33] Newspaper coverage could expose young people in particular to very undesirable material, given the proclivity of some journals to emphasize the salacious. The bill passed the Senate but not the House of Commons. Nevertheless, the proponents of liberal change persisted in their efforts. Instead of proposing more general reforms, they began to concentrate on specific aspects of the legal environment which they thought inappropriate or, better still, unfair. The first target was the blatant sexual discrimination in the grounds for divorce. The English act of 1857 had given a legislative imprimatur to the sexual double standard. A husband applying for divorce had to prove only that his wife was guilty of adultery. A wife, had to prove what was often called aggravated adultery: she had to show that her husband was guilty of adultery and of some additional marital offence, such as cruelty, incest, bigamy, or desertion of at least

two years' duration. Since the English law was the divorce law of the four western provinces, this bias was entrenched there alone. This legal discrimination had ended in England in 1923, thus making it politically safer for the colony to follow suit. Canadian women's groups and representatives cited this precedent as just one of many reasons for abolishing such an offensive law.

Not surprisingly, the legislative initiative for change came from the west. Early in 1924 Joseph Shaw, the Independent Labour member for Calgary West, introduced in the House of Commons a motion to place wives and husbands on an equal footing in grounds for divorce. His supporting argument emphasized several points – the 'patchwork' character of Canadian divorce law, the present inequality, the 'very narrow' nature of the change he proposed, and the English precedent. Again, the response in the House concentrated on the morality of divorce itself rather than on the specific issue at hand. Nevertheless, Shaw was encouraged by the government to work out the details of the proposal in the form of a bill, and was promised that the bill would be given sufficient time for debate. But the government reneged and the bill died at the end of the session. Undeterred, Shaw reintroduced his bill in 1925. The issue of sexual equality again received little direct attention in debate. Instead, discussion focused on the weaknesses of the existing law or on the evil of divorce. Opponents of liberal divorce reform simply viewed the issue from a totally different perspective, one that prevented any meeting of minds:

> [Would it not be better] that the evil of divorce, with all the wickedness it implies and all the wretchedness it entails, should wither away like the short-lived, fraudulent affections that foster it and linger only as a memory of what was once a mockery of Christian faith ... Think of the harm that infects the divorced home, the deceit and defection, the misery without measure, sorrows innumerable, wasted lives, perverted careers, children bereft, their sacred rights of parents' united care parceled out or denied them, husband and wife divided.[34]

How could anyone support a bill which destroyed the home and replaced the sanctity of marriage with 'legalized lechery' (or, alternatively, 'legalized adultery')?

The discussion took place on two different planes. One approach sought to grapple, however weakly, with the perceived reality of a social problem; the other wanted to use legislation to defend an ideal. It is not surprising that the debate resolved little. But on a recorded division, the bill passed second reading by a vote of 109 to 68, immediately moved into Committee of the Whole, and was passed there.[35] Opponents, however, were not yet finished. An attempt was made to cripple the bill by adding a clause denying any divorced person the right to remarry. This, of course, brought the House back to the issue of the immorality of divorce. Biblical and ecclesiastical pronouncements were quoted at length, but to no avail; the frontal attack on divorce was defeated by a vote of 60 to 73. A second amendment to bar remarriage during the ex-spouse's lifetime also failed by a vote of 63 to 106. On third reading the bill was adopted, 112 to 61, and the Senate followed suit.[36]

Post-Confederation Canada had passed its first public divorce statute.[37] The act failed to discuss process, and it did not set out the grounds for divorce; it simply stated that in petitioning for a divorce a wife was required to furnish proof of her husband's adultery. The basic ground for divorce was thus left unaltered. The issue was one of sexual equality rather than more liberal divorce, though establishing grounds for divorce now became somewhat easier for wives in western Canada. Yet, as in the ideal of the conjugal family, sexual equality was limited. As protesters pointed out later, a clause in the legislation singled out wives in negative ways. Condonation or collusion by the wife invalidated her divorce petition, and the 'clean hands' concept (the petitioner could not be guilty of marital misconduct) was restated to apply to wives only. In short, as Ruth Roach Pierson has said in connection with a different issue, contemporary commentators saw no contradiction between the idea of sexual equality and the notion of the conjugal familial ideal in which married women should remain dependent upon their husbands.[38]

An analysis of the voting patterns in the House is suggestive of the kinds of divisions caused by the issue of divorce in the period. Three of the four votes were remarkably similar in numbers, suggesting a relatively stable set of opponents and proponents. Regionally, strong support for liberal reform came from British Columbia and the prairie provinces. Those Ontario members who voted were strongly disposed in the same direction, but there was a noticeable absentee rate, approximately double the rate among prairie members. This suggests that it was politically important in some Ontario constituencies for a member to avoid taking a public stance on the issue. Quebec members were equally strongly opposed to liberal reform, although they too had an absentee rate almost as high as that of the Ontario members. For Maritimes members, support and opposition were fairly even. There was a deceptive correlation between voting and party affiliation. Both Conservative and Progressive members tended strongly to vote in favour of liberal reform; on the various divisions, approximately 90 per cent of those members supported the proposed reform. The Liberal representatives, however, evinced much greater disagreement, which is perhaps why the Liberal government hesitated to take any decisive stand on divorce; about 75 per cent of the Liberals voted against liberal reform. But the most revealing factor in voting was religion, and it is this factor that explains both the regional and the partisan voting patterns. In the four recorded votes on this bill Anglicans, Baptists, Congregationalists, Methodists, Presbyterians, and other Protestants tended to vote in support of limited divorce reform. Roman Catholics voted overwhelmingly against any such reform. Only the Liberal party had large numbers of both Catholics and Protestants, and only that party showed a major split. The same explanation largely accounts for the regional variations.[39]

At first glance it seems that once the resistance to general divorce legislation was overcome, further activity could reasonably be anticipated. Two more statutes were enacted in 1930, and the debate on one measure, at least in part, fed on the other. The less controversial was a proposal to deal with another aspect of sexual inequality. It was well established that jurisdiction in divorce was determined by the legal domicile of the couple;[40] at common law and in Quebec civil law, it was equally well established that at marriage the two parties were united into one entity with a single domicile, and that domicile was the husband's. Upon her marriage the wife lost her status as *feme sole*, and her independent rights at law were quite limited.[41] This was of vital importance in determining jurisdiction in divorce. By law, application for divorce could validly be made only in the court where the applicant had domicile. While this rule is perhaps most famous for its impact on the validity of Canadian divorces in the United States, it had a much more basic effect on women in general. Because of the legal fiction of a single marital domicile, wives could apply for divorce only in the court having jurisdiction in their husband's domicile.

This was true no matter what the husband's domicile. If, for example, a husband had been born and raised in Alberta and continued to live there, his wife in Edmonton would have no problem in gaining access to the Alberta Supreme Court because his domicile of origin remained intact and unchallengeable. If that same husband had deserted his wife and had fully established himself in a new life elsewhere, by Canadian law his wife could petition for divorce only in her husband's new jurisdiction – whether he now lived in Vancouver or Los Angeles. In a much more difficult position was the Alberta wife who had married an itinerant Hungarian who had never settled down in any one place; if she could not persuade the court that her husband had acquired and retained a domicile of choice in Alberta or some other North American jurisdiction, her domicile would be her husband's domicile of origin – Hungary. If the rule of domicile effectively prevented this wife from gaining a valid divorce, the position of a deserted wife of an adulterous husband who had disappeared was equally invidious; because she did not know where her husband was, it was difficult or impossible to determine his domicile, and she too was denied access to divorce.

This problem could have been solved in a number of ways. It is surely instructive that of all the possible solutions Canadian divorce reformers favoured the one that would least disrupt the existing legal view of marriage and spousal relations and would best sustain the dominant familial ideal. The first proposals would have given deserted wives separate domicile. But when these ran into vigorous opposition, the reform was severely modified: there would be no separate domicile for married women, and only wives' access to divorce would change. The basic legal view of the married couple was unaltered.

Legislative leadership came from W.J. Ward, a Progressive member from Dauphin and a farmer who was active in the Manitoba farmers' movement. He introduced his bill in both 1926 and 1927, but on neither occasion did it receive any consideration beyond formal acceptance at first reading. Though Ward sponsored no similar bill in 1928, possibly because of all the attention that was being paid that year to parliamentary divorce, the proposal returned to the floor of the House in 1929. For the first time the private member's bill reached second reading, and Ward had an opportunity to put forward his argument. Known as the Divorce Jurisdiction Act, the bill provided that a married woman, who was living apart from her husband or who had been deserted by and had lived apart from her husband for two years, could acquire a separate domicile and could commence action for divorce in a court of proper jurisdiction. Ward emphasized, correctly, that he was not altering the present divorce law; the grounds for divorce were not being added to. All that he sought to do was to replace 'an obsolete rule of law' so that women would be treated the same as men in access to divorce; this was simply 'a matter of common sense, reason and fair play.' For liberal reformers the attractiveness of the bill's acknowledgment of the idea of sexual equality was proof against the reality of a wife's continuing inequality – she, for example, had to establish desertion of two years' duration to gain access to the court, while the husband suffered no such onus.

Here indeed was an issue that could play on liberal sensitivities and appeal to a middle-class image of women. By the 1920s some forms of formal sexual inequality were no longer acceptable. The bill's supporters made clear their views of the proper roles and behaviour of wives and husbands. When a husband 'grossly deserted' his wife, she was 'the victim of his evil propensities. That is undoubtedly an injustice to the decent womanhood which finds itself in that position.' This was not a question of divorce; personal conscience was distinct from a 'sense of justice and duty to the womanhood of Canada with regard to its right to equal treatment with the men of Canada.'[42]

As usual, the response of the opponents of liberal reform reflected apprehension and moral constancy. Any bill that enhanced access to divorce made divorce easier; no one who objected to divorce in principle could in good conscience do anything other than vote against such legislation. If wives were free to establish their own domicile, they could simply move to a province with judicial divorce and then apply for dissolution of their marriage. The result would be to turn any such province 'into a Reno.' To allow a married woman to acquire a domicile separate from her husband was to threaten the institution of marriage; the total union of wife and husband must be maintained if the stability of marriage and the family was to be preserved. One must not dismiss as fictitious 'the idea of unity as between man and wife,' argued one member. 'It is not merely saying that husband and wife shall be one; it is more than that. It is a question of the very existence of the family.'[43]

Opposition to the bill was such that Ward sought to save it by introducing amendments that would limit even further the effect of the proposed reform. Instead of allowing a married woman to establish her own domicile, the amendment defined her domicile as that of her husband at the time of desertion. This restriction of the abandoned wife to her husband's former domicile met at least some of the objections of more conservative reformers, and was adopted by a vote of 36 to 28. Shortly thereafter, the bill passed the House by a vote of 80 to 32.[44] But in a Senate that was contemplating the reform of the divorce process, the bill ran squarely into formidable opposition to any change in the substantive law – particularly to an aspect of the law as basic as the concept of marital domicile. To give a married woman a separate domicile, or even a limited semblance thereof, was a 'radical departure' from established legal principles, according to the chairman of the Divorce Committee, and was clearly undesirable. The bill was defeated by a vote of 12 to 18.[45]

Undeterred, in 1930 W.J. Ward introduced the same bill as amended by the 1929 House. Most of the arguments were the same as before, but those of Minister of Justice Ernest Lapointe bear repeating for their emphasis on caution and restraint. Severance of the matrimonial domicile was a dangerous development, he argued: 'Surely everyone will admit' that the rule of a single matrimonial domicile 'is a good law.' 'Mere' desertion did not dissolve a marriage bond; 'otherwise it would be too easy for many people to do so.'[46] In other words, the rule of domicile was one of the myriad ways in which the law attempted to support a particular form of family structure; any acceptance of desertion as an exception, in however minor a form, to this legal environment threatened the substance of the law by allowing individuals to determine the result by their own actions. There was a basic fear that changing the law would allow and perhaps even encourage changes in marital behaviour. While the attitudes implicit in Lapointe's arguments received wide approval in Canada at the time, they were not in this case powerful enough; for many, the debate was not about preserving the family but about overt sexual equality. Indeed, it is revealing that the minister of justice was immediately caught up in a debate with Agnes Macphail, the Progressive member for Grey South East and the first and only female member of the House, over the paternalistic protection of women through legislation. Once again the divorce jurisdiction bill passed the House.[47] Senators expressed some of their earlier concerns about the ability of married women to acquire a separate domicile, but were not disposed to stand in the way of the will of the House. The bill became law.[48]

In the meantime a much more intense debate had been taking place regarding reform of the divorce process. Since the end of the First World War the number of parliamentary divorces had been increasing fairly steadily. Having jumped from 15 in 1918 to 55 in 1919, the number rose to 237 in each of 1928 and 1929. Much of this total emanated from Ontario, which averaged 132.2 divorces annually in the 1920s, in comparison with an average of 16.8 in the previous decade (see table 1). Each of these divorces, it must be remembered, required the passage of a separate statute, and each statute had to pass through all the usual legislative procedures in both houses of Parliament before receiving royal assent. It was a lengthy process. Not surprisingly, under pressure of so much private divorce legislation, Parliament found it essential to adjust the process. A second Divorce Committee was struck in the Senate in a conscientious attempt to cope with the new demands. Members of the House of Commons, however, demonstrated a growing reluctance to deal responsibly with the bills, and deflected an increasing proportion not only of the work but also of the supervision of the legislation. In the 1921 session, for example, the Private Bills Committee of the House deviated from past practice by failing to appoint a subcommittee to attend the evidentiary hearings of the Senate Divorce Committee. The House thus became increasingly dependent on the work and the judgment of the Senate committee. By the late 1920s the number of divorce bills passing through the House was making a mockery of parliamentary procedure. Late in the 1926 session some members suggested an almost total abdication of House responsibility, though it is only fair to say that examination of the bills in the House had already become so cursory as to be virtually non-existent in most cases. On the evening of 8 June 1926, for example, forty-seven divorce bills passed through second or third reading without debate; it was suggested that all divorce bills for each session be covered by one motion, thus preventing the House's spending so much time on 'this nuisance.'[49]

The following year the House's treatment of the bills was even more perfunctory. 'In order to save time,' announced the Speaker, the bills would no longer be read by name, and a single motion was carried to give third reading to bills 4 through 40. For the rest of the session this procedure was adopted repeatedly. In the interest of 'facilitating the passing' of private divorce statutes, batches of bills began to be given both first and second reading at the same time; this measure was made part of House procedure by a suspension of the governing rule.[50] While the interests of efficiency were thus well served, there is a striking contrast between such procedures and members' purported concern about familial values and ideals. But a hint of the approaching debate was given by the future antagonist of these ad hoc measures, J.S. Woodsworth, the Independent Labour member for Winnipeg North Centre. His description of the practice of the House is revealing:

> As a member of the private bills committee I know the practice there is simply to receive the bills as they come from the Senate. The evidence is submitted to us in pamphlet form, but it is rarely read, and bills go through the committee and the House without any consideration whatever. Occasionally bills that are controversial are

held up, but that is very seldom. This session we have between 100 and 150 divorce bills going through all the stages of parliamentary procedure without any real consideration from this House.[51]

This method of conducting business had become a 'public scandal.' The time had come, suggested Woodsworth, to deal with the basic problem and to put an end to temporary solutions. The House ought to look seriously at a bill that had just arrived from the Senate, a bill that would give the courts of Ontario responsibility for divorce in the province.

The bill received only first reading in the House late in the 1927 session. Supporters of the bill decided not to press it on the House so as not to imperil its future passage. The measure returned early in the 1928 session, again from the Senate, which bore the burden of the growing number of divorce petitions. This time, however, the senators were willing to exert some pressure on the Commons. When it became clear that the bill was stalled in the House, the opposition leader in the Senate issued a warning: if the bill was considered and defeated in the House, Conservative senators would ask the House of Commons to take over the basic work on half of the divorce petitions next year; if the House failed to deal with the bill, Conservative senators would refuse to serve on the Divorce Committee, except to hear petitions from Quebec.[52] At first, neither threats nor protests resulted in any significant change.

The battle was just beginning, however. When private divorce bills next came before the House, the member for Winnipeg North Centre rose to launch a devastating attack on the process of parliamentary divorces. Woodsworth's first tactic was to obstruct any device designed to alleviate procedural unwieldiness; if the House insisted on continuing to handle private divorces, members would be made to suffer for doing so. Woodsworth refused to consent to a blanket motion covering a large number of divorce bills, and instead demanded individual treatment. When the first bill came forward, he insisted that the bill's sponsor speak to its contents. As was often the case, the sponsor was not even in the House, and at any rate probably would not have been familiar with the details. Several members agreed with Woodsworth that the bill establishing judicial divorce in Ontario should be discussed, but they were unwilling to support any obstructionist tactics. Undeterred, Woodsworth and a fellow member of the so-called Ginger Group, William Irvine, continued to raise procedural obstacles to private divorce bills in the following days. Members were so accustomed to automatic passage of most such bills that when any attempt was made to discuss the contents of a bill charges of filibuster were immediately raised. In the face of these early tactics, the prime minister remained adamant that the divorce court bill would receive no special treatment. A motion by Woodsworth to consider that bill forthwith was defeated, with the Liberal government seemingly marshalling its votes against the motion.

Woodsworth tried to make it clear that he was not simply being obstructionist; he was trying to expose the intolerable character of the parliamentary divorce process. To make this point he selected for detailed consideration two of a batch of eighty bills. Woodsworth focused on an aspect sure to appeal to contemporary sensibilities and perceptions of the prevailing ideal of the family: neither of the bills made any provision for support or child custody, both of which were matters of provincial jurisdiction. The first petitioner was a woman who had married in Ottawa in 1924; she and her husband had one four-year-old son. Her husband, a clerk, had committed adultery, and in doing so had contracted venereal disease, which he had passed on to his wife. 'If the woman has been so wronged the least we can do is to see that she be given something to maintain her during the years that she may remain unmarried,' suggested Woodsworth. The emotive elements of the case having been raised, the amendment gave the wife custody of the child and five hundred dollars' annual maintenance along with two hundred dollars for child support. In a proper judicial process, he pointed out, such issues would be dealt with effectively and fairly, taking into account (as he was unable to do) the wife's needs and the husband's means, and providing for methods of payment and penalties for non-payment. Further, in an appeal to contemporary concern about nuptiality and eugenics, Woodsworth proposed a clause forbidding either party to remarry until he or she was pronounced free of venereal disease by a physician.[53]

The second petitioner was a woman who had married in England in 1924; her husband, a manager, had committed sodomy. In this case Woodsworth's amendment awarded her maintenance of five hundred dollars and child custody, and explicitly prohibited the husband from remarrying. Whether this was a calculated emotional appeal for support or a matter of personal abhorrence is unclear, but Woodsworth's argument was strikingly strong: 'I submit that we should hesitate to grant the privilege of remarriage to a man who has so cruelly mistreated his wife and who has committed a crime for which he is liable to life imprisonment. Are we going to tell this man he can go scot free and leave him in a position to abuse another wife? I would hope that the time might come when, in cases of sexual perversion of this kind, there might be some sort of surgical operation.'[54] Despite his determined effort to appeal to the members' and the public's sensitivities, Woodsworth's amendments were defeated, both bills passed unaltered, and the divorce court bill failed to receive consideration in the House.

In 1929 the same bill giving Ontario courts jurisdiction in divorce was quickly passed in the Senate and introduced in the House. The following day debate began on second reading; Woodsworth's tactics of the previous session had begun to produce results. And Woodsworth and Irvine kept up the pressure, insisting that for each private divorce bill the sponsor be present and that details of the divorce be explained. Throughout the session the two members repeatedly used the issue of support and child custody to remind their colleagues of the weaknesses of the parliamentary process. The immediate result was that the process in the House began to be somewhat more responsible; members were at least showing an awareness of the character of each divorce bill. The bill to give Ontario courts jurisdiction in divorce received extensive debate which often carried over into discussion of private divorce bills. By now, the arguments were familiar to all: the weakness of the parliamentary process; the perceived effectiveness of a judicial procedure; the evil of divorce; the fear that any change would encourage marital breakdown. Only one new argument was raised: there was no evidence that the people of Ontario wanted the proposed legislation, and divorce courts were thus being imposed upon them. The bill passed second reading, and then disappeared among numerous other private members' bills. Through it all the government remained silent and offered no leadership on this politically delicate issue. The most that the prime minister was willing to do was to promise that the government was considering the problem and hoped that some solution could be arranged by the 1930 session.[55]

In 1930, when the bill was introduced once again, it was met with a direct challenge. Henri Bourassa, the Independent member from Labelle, sponsored a bill that would amend marriage and divorce law by reverting to the situation before 1925. Although the bill had little chance of passing, it did give opponents of reform an additional opportunity to attack the changes, both real and proposed, that legitimated and facilitated marital dissolution.

For his part, J.S. Woodsworth was quick to remind the government of its promise that a solution to the problem of parliamentary divorces would be forthcoming. The bill to give Ontario courts jurisdiction in divorce was again introduced from the Senate, and the government finally showed its hand. True to his word, Prime Minister Mackenzie King and his cabinet had reconsidered their stance on the bill and had decided to ease its passage; to minimize political damage, the bill would remain a private member's initiative. As Senator Raoul Dandurand said privately, 'that plague – the Divorce Bill' would finally be pushed through Parliament.[56] But tacit government approval did not reduce the contentious character of the proposal. The usual arguments were raised for and against the bill. Opponents emphasized the absence of strong support from Ontario; more Ontario members had voted against the measure than for it; several amendments to make the bill take effect only after some indication of support by the Ontario people or legislature were defeated. After considerable debate, the bill passed through the House by a small margin and received royal assent. The voting patterns in the House of Commons on both of these 1930 reforms reflected the same tendencies as in the 1925 legislation. Denominational affiliation was the single most important element in determining a member's response to these proposals.

The new statute gave the Supreme Court of Ontario jurisdiction in divorce and annulment.[57] The law to be applied by that court was defined as the law of England of 15 July 1870 as amended in Canada – that is, the same law that was now applied by the courts of the four western provinces. The change had been very contentious, but it was very limited and decidedly cautious. The government continued to decline to draft its own divorce law, and chose to rely instead on the outdated law of England. The administrative problem of the vast number of Ontario divorces clogging the parliamentary machinery had been solved, but that was all. Judicial divorce was now available in seven provinces; only petitions from Quebec and Prince Edward Island continued to pass through Parliament.

These three statutory changes encompassed the legislative initiative and reform of divorce in Canada before 1968.[58] Thanks to judicial decisions and new statutes, access to divorce had been expanded in the first few decades of the twentieth century. There was little doubt among any of the participants in these debates that the changes in process would result in more divorces, and this proved to be the case. The number of divorces in the three prairie provinces increased greatly after the court decisions of 1919; in Ontario the annual number had more than doubled by the end of the 1930s. Parliament was relieved of what was becoming an intolerable burden, but continued to deal with divorce petitions from Quebec and

Prince Edward Island (and from Newfoundland after 1949). The two reforms aimed directly at women were important for their intent, but their impact in law differed. Removing sexual inequality in the ground of adultery undoubtedly made it easier for wives to establish proof of the charges against their husbands. But the new definition of domicile in the case of desertion helped relatively few wives, to judge from the trial cases examined. These particular reforms were probably only a small factor in the rising proportion of female plaintiffs in divorce cases after the mid-1920s.

After several years of intense debate on the principle and law of divorce, the second half of the 1930s was relatively quiet. Conservative reformers still advocated retribution and punishment. In 1935 and 1936 the Senate considered a bill to prevent the guilty spouse from remarrying during the lifetime of the innocent spouse. Late in the decade, however, the divorce issue resurfaced once more. In 1937 England amended the Matrimonial Causes Act by expanding the grounds for judicial divorce; added to adultery were desertion of at least three years' duration, cruelty, and incurable insanity of at least five years' duration. As in the 1920s the Canadian response again partially reflected a continuing selective reliance on British precedent. A bill to much the same effect passed through the Senate in 1938 after several amendments. The bill purported to give Canada its own law of divorce and matrimonial causes, however derivative its nature. Grounds for nullity were enumerated; a procedure was established for a declaration of presumption of death; clergy were expressly relieved of any obligation to perform a marriage of a divorced person; and the three new grounds for divorce were listed, though the minimum duration of desertion had been raised to six years. Some clauses tried to appeal to opponents of liberal reform. The courts were given greater powers to inquire into collusion, connivance, and condonation; so-called hasty divorce was addressed by preventing any divorce in the first three years of marriage, 'thus affording the parties an opportunity of straightening out their difficulties.' But members of the House of Commons were uninterested in such attempts at compromise; the bill was soundly defeated without debate.[59] That the debate over the grounds for divorce never reached a serious level in Parliament in this period is further evidence that the moral pathology of divorce remained the pre-eminent focus for Canadian legislators.

Canadian divorce law in the early twentieth century can best be described as restrictive, unequal, diverse, derivative, and fundamentally conservative. The social and political climate was such that there was no strong political impulse to alter the situation. Governments, both Liberal and Conservative, shied away from direct involvement in any action aimed at reform. All proposals for legislative reform, liberal and conservative alike, were made by private members and received no overt support from the government of the day. Politically, the sure and safe ground of the status quo was more attractive than any alternative. The actual reforms that passed into law were marked by their limited nature and a conservative frame of mind. The British influence was still strong, both in colonial structures such as the Judicial Committee and in the broader culture. Changes in the divorce process were easier to achieve than changes in the substantive law, where virtually any reform proposal was seen in terms of the dominant ideal of the conjugal family.

It is striking and somewhat misleading that reform was apparently easiest in the area of sexual equality. The sexual double standard had, of course, been under attack for several decades in the Western world, and idealized womanhood had been a powerful stereotype even longer. What better way to reassert the values and attitudes that these concepts represented than to enshrine them in legislation? The new laws undoubtedly redressed, at least partially, women's legal disabilities. Yet, as a number of feminist writers have reminded us, such reform can be deceiving. The removal of overt discrimination legitimated a legal regime that retained much covert discrimination; the reforms appealed to a protective impulse among many male legislators to defend members of the 'weaker sex' left vulnerable by husbands and society. The statutes confirmed the dominant gender-based view of womanhood. In short, legislative initiatives were successful when they reformed divorce by taking marriage closer to the dominant familial ideal and by enforcing an altruistic ethic. Frances Olsen has pointed out that such reforms have historically tended to support sexual hierarchy.[60]

Social class was also a prominent factor in political attitudes to divorce. Liberal reformers frequently complained that the existing divorce regime excluded the poor because of the costs of parliamentary divorce and the limited grounds. Using egalitarian rhetoric, they sought to reduce the costs and to widen the grounds to allow greater access to members of the working class. While their arguments and proposals were undoubtedly well intentioned, something equally basic lay behind their attitudes. What disturbed these divorce reformers was that the working class appeared to be excluded from the marital and divorce regime defended and advanced by the law;

members of the working class were perceived to be operating outside the prescribed norms of the institution of the family. In the 1938 debate on extending the grounds for divorce, Senator Walter Asseltine, a Saskatchewan lawyer and farmer, made this point directly: if new grounds were added, he argued, 'the poorer classes – who were formerly unable to afford the luxury of a divorce where adultery had to be proven by the hiring of detectives or other persons, sometimes at great expense – will be greatly benefited, and instead of illicit unions there will be valid divorces and remarriages.'[61] By reforming the law, a greater number of working-class people would be brought within the operation of the state-condoned familial ideal as expressed through the divorce process. As was the case elsewhere, the perceived plight of the working-class family became a focal point for interaction with state authorities and middle-class social leaders.[62]

Politicians confronting the divorce question shared certain basic assumptions about the dual institutions of the law and the family. Both played a vital role in maintaining social stability. The family was 'the central institution of the state,' commented one politician in 1930, echoing a central tenet of the ideal of the conjugal family. In the interests of the state and of society at large, what action and measures by the state best secured and supported the family? Politicians answered this question in a variety of ways, but with respect to divorce there were only two basic answers. One, as expressed by a politician in 1928, saw divorce as wrong in principle: 'Divorce strikes at the very foundations of the State. The [primary] unit of the State is the family, and there is no other social evil that so demoralizes or injures the family as the evil of divorce.'[63] The state should do all it could to prevent divorce, and nothing to facilitate it. If the state refused to pass divorce laws, marriages would remain whole and families would remain stable. The second answer was that divorce was evil, but there were even greater evils. To refuse or inhibit divorce was to force individuals, whose marriages were already broken, into deviant, immoral, and illicit behaviour. Rather than drive such people into illegal divorces, bigamous or common law marriages, or adultery, rather than promote circumstances in which illegitimate children might be brought into the world and raised in immoral environments, surely it was better to accept legally the reality of the broken marriage and allow the succeeding relationship to be brought within a regulated environment – that is, within the law and within a socially acceptable family – through the state's reasonable provision for divorce.

Both answers rested on the vital position of the family as the

than one scholar has argued that in both England and the United States a dual law of divorce evolved: the statute law, which in many states was restrictive, and a jurisprudence, which was much more flexible in adapting the law to the perceived needs of families and couples.[1] In an examination of American family law Michael Grossberg has placed an even more direct emphasis on the role of the judiciary. His study of nineteenth-century American case law revealed a judiciary that saw itself as the preferred 'guardian of the American hearth'; here was a judiciary that not only filled a void but actively substituted its own view of the family for that of the legislatures.[2] Constance Backhouse has confirmed some of these findings for nineteenth-century Canada in a series of articles dealing with women and the law. In her analysis of the reported cases, Canadian courts, though they did not support the sweeping decisions of the American courts, actively asserted, defended, and maintained gender as a vital criterion in Canadian law; in particular, they reinforced a patriarchal view of marriage and of appropriate relations between the sexes. Most attempts by legislators to develop a more egalitarian family law were not supported – indeed, were knowingly thwarted – by the judiciary.[3]

Because the judiciary was active and the legislatures relatively inactive, an examination of the Canadian jurisprudence is essential in any attempt to understand the legal environment regarding divorce. In this chapter, I have limited this examination in two ways. First, only the reported cases will be discussed; while this approach reveals the reasoning of the bench and the precedents that were handed down, it ignores the day-to-day handling of matrimonial causes in Canadian courts, where those precedents may or may not have been followed. I will examine this latter type of court involvement in later chapters. Second, I will discuss only those legal issues most important to early twentieth-century Canadian divorce law.

Knowledge of divorce law was very limited among much of the Canadian bar in these years. The federal Department of Justice received numerous queries from lawyers, particularly those in jurisdictions with little local experience of divorce, revealing a disturbing lack of awareness of governing legal principles. Early in 1920 Chief Justice T.G. Mathers of Manitoba lamented that the recent transfer of jurisdiction in divorce had 'found us with a knowledge of the subject that was extremely nebulous.'[4] This environment produced two responses in the legal community: first, as might be expected of those with little experience or knowledge, judges tended to rely strictly on traditional or established rules, particularly when those rules operated to confirm the dominant familial ideal; second, judges tended to fill any voids in legal information with existing extralegal rules or principles of behaviour; when the rules conferred judicial discretion on them, they tended to exercise that discretion in ways that reinforced governing British legal principles and societal norms, especially those regarding gender. Canadian jurisprudence on divorce confirms the ideal of the conjugal family and offers a window on the ideology of the dominant legal culture of the period.

Domicile

It was a well-established rule in British (and thus Canadian) law that the current domicile of the married couple was the only true test of jurisdiction.[5] This followed from the common law principle that legal disputes ought to be settled in and judged by the standards of the community in which one lived. But there was also more than one element of control in this rule. If the community's marriage and divorce standards were to be upheld, people had to be prevented from going wherever they wished to deal with their marital disputes. As well, the very concept of community standards, with the associated implication of consensus, permitted the views of limited social sectors to be enforced as the standards of all members of the society. The rule of domicile was basic to the maintenance of any regime ordering marital behaviour; it was also vital in determining a court's jurisdiction in divorce and the validity of any resulting judgment. The extent of the courts' adherence to this rule was a matter of great importance. Because only a few provinces had divorce courts for much of this period, a flexible judicial application of the rule of domicile would have met some of the social pressure for access to divorce facilities by allowing Canadians access to courts in other provinces or in the United States. A second area of possible flexibility was that of the definition of the unified domicile, in which the couple was regarded as having only one domicile – the husband. Any relaxation of this definition would have been important to wives seeking divorce. An examination of each of these areas is instructive.

There were no simple rules for determining legal domicile; it was a matter of interpretation. In construing domicile, the surrounding circumstances, particularly intent, were crucial. The courts tended to use their discretion to uphold two premises: that a person, particularly the husband (given the nature of the rule), should not be allowed to flout local community standards, and that the law and courts ought to assist the innocent party, particularly the wife (given the ideal of womanhood), by incorporating aspects of equity or natural justice when common law rules were insufficient.

This tendency can be seen very early in the period. In *Bonbright* v *Bonbright* (1901),[6] a husband challenged the jurisdiction of the Ontario court in a petition for alimony. Born in the United States, the man had moved to Ottawa as an adult and had owned a store there. After marriage he and his wife had lived in Europe and the United States for short periods before returning in 1891 to Ontario, where they purchased a summer home; they kept this home, though they lived and worked in the United States for several winters. In 1899 the husband moved to California and instigated divorce proceedings there; he sold all his Ontario property. His deserted wife sued for alimony in Ontario. The Ontario court, both at trial and on appeal, refused to find that he had abandoned his domicile of choice in Ontario, and held that he had gone to California merely for the temporary purpose of obtaining a divorce and remarrying. Thus, an 'innocent' deserted wife could benefit from the sympathy of the court. But if the wife was seen as the guilty party, she could expect no such support. The case of *Cutler* v *Cutler* (1914)[7] is a good example of this attitude. Married in England, the Cutlers had moved to Manitoba, where Mrs Cutler had eventually committed adultery and deserted her husband. While she continued to live in Manitoba with another man, her husband moved to British Columbia, where he eventually applied for a divorce. The question was whether the local court had jurisdiction, and whether local community standards could apply to a woman who had never been in the province. The bench showed no sympathy for the wife, and Justice Clement readily dismissed the fact of the husband's failure to attempt a reconciliation: 'He [the husband] very frankly informed me that he had never asked his wife to join him in this province; in fact, he has had no communication with her since she ran away from him. Under the circumstances the most censorious could scarcely blame him.' Nor was the court disturbed by any infringement of natural justice: 'There is nothing of merit on the wife's part or of undeserved wrong suffered by her in holding her strictly to her husband's domicile.' The contemporary concept of deserving and undeserving poor was clearly matched by that of deserving and undeserving spouses, accurately reflecting the dominant moral pathology of divorce. In 1914, of course, there was a distinct advantage to having a domicile in British Columbia rather than in Manitoba. British Columbia offered a judicial divorce process; couples on the prairies could seek redress only through Parliament. According to the reported cases, the local courts were aware of that advantage and were cautious in allowing a petitioner to assert a local domicile of choice.[8] Jurisdiction had to be established,[9] but additional factors could sway the court's response.

One further case will serve to underline this and to emphasize the discretionary nature of the rule. An English-born man, Charlie Thornback, had moved to Canada in 1907 at the age of fourteen; Ontario-born Margaret McCarter was living in the Yukon Territory before their marriage in England in 1916. After the husband's demobilization in 1919, the couple moved back to the Yukon, where they intended to live permanently. One year later the husband deserted his wife and two children, and moved with Ruth Thomson to various towns in the United States. Mrs Thornback petitioned the local court for divorce. The central issue was whether the court had jurisdiction. Holding that a domicile of choice in the Yukon had been acquired and not abandoned, the trial judge commented in this undefended action, 'After the lapse of a year spent in immoral living ... this respondent should not be permitted, merely by his evil conduct, to deprive the petitioner of her established domicile within this jurisdiction and to "set up his iniquity for a stumbling block" to that end.' The court found that it had jurisdiction, but went further. In a comment that articulated the growing sympathy for deserted wives, Justice Black stated, obiter, that even if it were true that the husband's domicile of choice had been abandoned, he would have held that an exception to the rule of domicile should be made in this case, on the ground that it would be absurd to require an innocent deserted wife to follow her husband around the globe to get a divorce.[10]

In a similar case the court went further and held that a deserted wife had maintained a separate domicile from her husband. The English-born husband and wife had moved to Alberta in 1910 and acquired a domicile of choice there. In 1920 the husband moved to Montana temporarily; the following year he returned to Montana, obtained a divorce, and remarried. The Alberta trial court held that although the husband had abandoned his Canadian domicile, the wife's Alberta domicile continued. The court thus had jurisdiction, and the wronged wife was granted a divorce.[11]

This clear-cut support for the wronged wife and antipathy towards the violator of the marital ideal was developed further by other courts. In *McCormack v McCormack* (1920),[12] the Supreme Court of Alberta seriously considered moving beyond these artificial determinations of continuing domicile to the recognition of a wife's separate domicile. The existing rule of domicile put wives at a 'disadvantage,' said Justice C.A. Stuart; surely the American rule of separate domicile was preferable. Since English law admitted the possibility of exceptions to the basic rule, why should not 'this Court also be privileged to develop the law according to principles of natural justice and to lay down a rule to fit the justice of the case ... where the facts present very special circumstance of injury and wrong.' In this case an English war bride had joined her Scottish-born husband in Lethbridge, Alberta, where on demobilization he had preceded her and had begun working for a railway company. She found him cohabiting with a war widow, and he took his bride to live with himself and this widow, the wife thus being placed in the 'shocking' position of being 'the actual witness of their adulterous intercourse.' After a few months the husband, in the company of the widow, deserted his wife and moved to Montreal. Justice Stuart concluded, 'I cannot fully see the justice of denying her, a British subject, access to the [local courts] ... where by the gross wrongs of her husband, she has been left stranded and alone. But no doubt any rule will at times work injustice in individual cases and it is perhaps well we should in the general public interest go carefully in any attempt to enlarge jurisdiction.' Although he drew back from such judicial innovation, it would not be long before he became more assertive.

In *Cook v Cook and the Attorney General for Alberta* (1923),[13] the wife's petition for a divorce was rejected at trial because the husband was now domiciled in Ontario. On appeal, however, the Supreme Court of Alberta held by a majority of 4 to 1 that because a judicial separation had been granted in 1921 the wife had acquired a separate domicile. The judges in the majority, led by Justice Stuart, said that in view of the trend towards equal rights for women in other areas, such as separate property and suffrage, it seemed both convenient and just that in the special circumstances of a judicial separation the wife should be able to have a separate domicile. This should be an exception to the general rule of domicile, it was said, following the British cases that established an exception in suits for nullity; the principle of a united domicile under the husband continued 'where the ordinary relationship of husband and wife has not been modified.' Thus, while the decision altered the rule of united domicile only in a limited way, it was nevertheless important. On appeal to the Judicial Committee of the Privy Council, this judicial innovation was firmly quashed. The law lords of the empire reviewed the precedents and found that none supported the notion of a separate domicile for the wife. The rule of a united domicile was founded both on the wife's obligation to live with her husband and on the union of husband and wife as a result of marriage; this was a concept that should be maintained.[14] So the imperial judicial structure put a stop to any Canadian, or at least any western Canadian, tendency to judicial creativity in this area of family law.

But the western attempts to modify the rule of a unitary domicile did not end. In *Harris v Harris and Harris* (1929),[15] a wife's petition for divorce on the ground of adultery and desertion was dismissed because the husband was found to have abandoned his Saskatchewan domicile of choice and to have acquired a new domicile in California, where he had committed bigamy. A majority of the judges of the Saskatchewan Court of Appeal followed *Cook* and upheld the lower court, although they expressed sympathy for the 'great injustice to the wife' caused by their decision. Chief Justice Haultain, in dissent, argued in favour of a finding that would allow the wife to bring action in the couple's last domicile before the desertion. This, of course, was the rule that was currently being debated in Parliament and that was enacted in 1930.

Support for the wronged wife was again emphasized in *Nelson v Nelson and Andrews* (1930).[16] The Nelsons were married in Ontario in 1910, and began farming in Saskatchewan that same year, acquiring a domicile of choice there. In 1919 the husband deserted his wife and moved back to Ontario permanently; he eventually cohabited with a woman by whom he had a child. By the time Mrs Nelson petitioned for divorce, almost a decade had passed. In dissent Chief Justice Haultain again evinced a strong desire to find some way to help such women. Since grounds for divorce had been amply proved, and since the wife could not gain relief in the Ontario courts (which still had no divorce jurisdiction), such instances ought to be considered exceptions to the rule of united domicile; Haultain would accept the jurisdiction of the Saskatchewan court and would grant the divorce. His fellow justices, however, were not able to find an acceptable way around the husband's clear abandonment of his domicile of choice in Saskatchewan. But they made it clear that their personal sympathies lay with the 'unfortunate' Mrs Nelson; one judge referred to an innocent wife's dependent domicile as a 'medieval form of bondage.' The 1930 Divorce Jurisdiction Act was designed to deal with just such problems.[17]

Two other cases will serve to establish the limits of that legislation, however. In 1926 the Jollys had married in Saskatchewan and taken up residence in North Battleford. Three years later the husband abandoned his wife and child to live with another woman. In 1934 he moved to Sherridon, Manitoba, found work as a miner, 'and continues to live in adultery with Mrs Anna Woods'; in the same year Mrs Jolly moved to Vancouver. A few years later she petitioned the courts of British Columbia for divorce, and was successful at trial level. The decision was overturned on appeal, 'however much one may sympathize with the petitioner.' Mrs Jolly had no separate domicile; she could sue for divorce in the domicile at point of desertion (Saskatchewan) or in her husband's current domicile (Manitoba), but not in British Columbia.[18]

Porkolab v *Porkolab and Fazekas* (1941)[19] made apparent the numerous difficulties facing a married woman who sought redress through the courts. Albert Porkolab, a Hungarian-born baker and itinerant labourer, had emigrated to Canada in 1929, residing in Alberta until 1936. In 1937 he married in Regina, where he and his wife lived until he left for Ontario in November 1938, to follow to Hamilton the co-respondent, Rosie Fazekas, by whom he had already had one child. There he took up residence with Fazekas, and in September 1940 Mrs Porkolab commenced action in Saskatchewan for divorce. The court rejected as of no value the defendant's self-serving statements designed to substantiate a Saskatchewan domicile and thus assist his wife's suit. The divorce petition was dismissed on two grounds. First, the Divorce Jurisdiction Act required that the wife be deserted for two years continuously; the full two years had not elapsed when she commenced the action. Second, Albert Porkolab's domicile was not Saskatchewan. Though the court did not say just where his domicile was, it is reasonable to suggest that it was Hungary: he had abandoned his domicile of choice in Alberta, and until he acquired a new domicile of choice, jurisdiction reverted to his domicile of origin. It is not surprising that Canadian women's groups were becoming increasingly vocal in their pleas for legislative attention to this problem.[20]

There was one exception to the general tendency of the law of domicile to operate to maintain a wife's legal dependence on her husband. According to article 207 of the Code civil of Quebec, upon a judicial separation a married woman could establish her own domicile. This provision was upheld by the courts,[21] and was just one more element in Quebec's distinctive marital regime.

A study of domicile reveals several features of Canadian courts and jurisprudence in this period. Sexual bias and a desire to defend prevailing gender stereotypes of both men and women strongly influenced judicial findings. The courts were willing to exercise their discretion in favour of those conforming and against those violating these stereotypes. While there was some evidence of a judicial willingness to move beyond the mere exercise of discretion to develop new precedents, those attempts were limited in their scope and were quashed by an imperial judicial structure.

Foreign Divorce

Foreign divorce was a fundamental reality in a Canada, where divorce was restricted and sometimes inaccessible. Many American jurisdictions had relatively permissive divorce regimes and a strikingly different definition of domicile, and the American divorce courts were attractive to many Canadians (this topic is discussed in chapter 9). For some, American divorces posed a threat to the integrity of the strict Canadian divorce environment and therefore to the fundamental familial ideal. Though American divorce behaviour and Canadian use of American courts were often commented on in Canadian legislatures, it was primarily the courts that had the task of responding formally to foreign divorces on behalf of the Canadian state.

Nevertheless, there was one explicit statement from Parliament on the government's position. In 1892 the new Criminal Code had extended Canadian courts' jurisdiction over bigamous marriages by making anyone who had committed bigamy outside the dominion liable to conviction if the person, being a British subject and a Canadian resident, had left Canada with the intent to commit the offence. In 1897 the validity of the extraterritorial character of this clause came before the Supreme Court of Canada, where the legislation was upheld.[22] Justice John Gwynne, in the majority, held that control over such matters was essential if the central government was to play an important role within the framework of the Canadian constitution. Furthermore, 'bordering as Canada does upon several foreign States, in many of which the laws relating to marriage and divorce are loose, demoralizing and degrading to the marriage state, such legislation as is contained in the above sections of the Criminal Code seem[s] to be essential to the peace, order and good government of Canada, and in particular to the maintenance within the Dominion of the purity and sanctity of the marriage state.'[23] Protection against bigamy was an essential element in the defence of marriage and the family.

For the Canadian courts the test of validity in divorce was whether the court issuing the decree had jurisdiction and the essential test for jurisdiction was the domicile of the parties. Many American states did not distinguish between residence and domicile, and many had

a law of separate domicile for married women; both of these factors
tended to undermine the validity of any American divorce in the eyes
of Canadian courts. A strict application of the rule of domicile regarding the validity of foreign divorces was already well established
by the beginning of the twentieth century. Binding British precedents
made it clear that domicile was the appropriate test of validity.[24]
Finally, the Canadian Parliament, though its finding had no judicial
authority, had decided in 1887 that American divorces acquired
without legal domicile were invalid.[25]

It did not take the Canadian courts long to affirm that these rules
would be upheld. In *R. v Brinkley* (1907),[26] both spouses had accepted an American divorce as valid. Married in Huron County,
Ontario, in 1897, Rosa Mary Brinkley had always been domiciled in
Canada and her husband had always been a British subject. After six
years' marriage she deserted her husband Jasper, and moved to
Michigan with no intention of returning. Three years later she obtained a divorce there on grounds of extreme cruelty; her husband
was served no notice of the action, though he obviously knew about
the decree. Within three months Jasper Brinkley, having been advised
by a lawyer that the divorce was valid in Canada, travelled with Emily
Florence Picot to Detroit to remarry, and returned immediately to
Goderich, Ontario. He was charged with bigamy and convicted by
the trial judge, who left for the appellate court the issues of the validity of the Michigan divorce decree and of the absence of mens rea,
or guilty intent. The conviction was upheld; the Supreme Court of
Ontario held that the Michigan court lacked jurisdiction in divorce
because Rosa Brinkley's domicile continued to be that of her husband. Bigamy was an exception to the general principle of mens rea,
and the purpose of that exception was to avoid 'divorces while you
wait' or easily obtained divorces in neighbouring countries; it was no
defence that the defendant 'honestly believed in the existence of a
non-existent divorce.' And certainly mutual acceptance of a marital
dissolution was insufficient for validity. The interests of society in
general as articulated through the state made it imperative that local
divorce restrictions be maintained.

The courts' insistence on the dubious validity of American divorces
obtained by Canadians forced Canadian couples into often extensive
litigation. In *Yates* v *Yates* (1924),[27] the husband not only went
through the legal formalities of divorce in the state of Washington,
but also defended against his wife's action for divorce in Manitoba
and carried the case to appeal. Mr and Mrs Yates had been married

in Winnipeg in 1912; both spouses were British subjects and domiciled in Manitoba; they had one child, a daughter, born in 1916. In December 1919 Mrs Yates insisted on leaving for England for an extended visit, and her husband, a department supervisor for the Grand Trunk Pacific Railway, reluctantly paid for the trip. Two months later, while she was still overseas, Mr Yates moved permanently to Seattle, where he consulted a lawyer almost immediately about getting a divorce. As soon as he had completed the one-year residency, Mr Yates applied for and received a divorce in Seattle on the basis of his own testimony and affidavits, in which he alleged desertion by his wife. Two days after receiving his divorce, he married a woman who had been a stenographer in his Winnipeg office.

Clara Yates, however, was not prepared to accept the American process or the result. Forced to rely at first on the reluctant support of her parents-in-law in Winnipeg, she soon obtained employment at Eaton's department store and supported herself and her child. She commenced divorce proceedings in Winnipeg, and Mr Yates contested the divorce there (perhaps in an attempt to legitimate his subsequent conduct in the United States). He charged his wife with various types of misconduct – desertion; forcing him to go into debt to pay for her passage overseas; violent and quarrelsome behaviour; and, since 1920, adulterous association with 'immoral, vicious and unsavory persons.' None but the last charge was a ground for divorce, or for undermining a divorce action, in Manitoba. The Manitoba Court of King's Bench chose to believe the wife's testimony: 'The evidence shows that she has been a good and faithful mother to her child.' The husband was found to have left Manitoba for the sole purpose of obtaining a divorce, which was invalid in Canada: 'The respondent has deserted both the child and the mother, and already has married again and has another child.' The Manitoba court granted the wife a divorce from her husband on the ground of his adulterous remarriage and awarded her custody of their child. This case illustrates more than the rules of law or the costs and effort of litigation. Divorce involved a labelling process; spouses were publicly designated guilty or innocent. Presumably to avoid this stigma, and to protect his claims to the marital assets, Mr Yates returned to Winnipeg to defend his own conduct and to castigate his wife; more was at stake here than personal freedom.

Many of the reported cases involving foreign divorces centred on petitions for a declaration that a succeeding marriage was null and void because a previous divorce had been invalid.[28] Some revealed the potentially tangled character of marriage. In *Holmes* v *Holmes* (1927), the wife brought an action in Alberta for alimony from her fourth husband on grounds of cruelty. Mrs Holmes's first husband had died. She had divorced her second husband in South Dakota in 1906; at the time, that husband had been domiciled in Iowa, but the Alberta Supreme Court held that the validity of that divorce was not relevant to the present case. Her third marriage had been dissolved in the state of Washington in 1913, while that husband, J. Lloyd, was domiciled in Alberta. Under Canadian law the Washington court lacked jurisdiction in the case, so the divorce was invalid; Mrs Holmes was still married to her third husband. Her action for alimony against her fourth husband therefore failed, but he was entitled to a declaration of nullity, for which he had counterclaimed. Mr Holmes was thus free of his 'marriage' and of any obligations to his 'wife.' She, having long ago severed all but her legal ties to her third husband, was left with nothing. Her attempts to claim payment for rent and for her services as housekeeper while Mr Holmes had lived in her home were easily dismissed.

As with the issue of domicile, courts tended to exercise discretion punitively against violators of gender stereotypes. In *Fields* v *Fields* (1925),[29] the husband filed for dissolution of his second marriage in the Nova Scotia Court of Divorce and Matrimonial Causes. He had been married for the first time in 1895 in Nova Scotia; his first wife had deserted him within a year and had gone to Massachusetts. Mr Fields followed her there in 1898, establishing domicile, and she obtained a divorce in Boston in 1902. He later returned to Nova Scotia, where he remarried in 1906 at Truro, but his second wife soon left him for another man. When he petitioned for divorce almost two decades later, his wife explained her desertion by claiming that she had discovered that his previous divorce was invalid and that he was thus already married. The legal issue centred on whether he had received sufficient notice of the 1902 proceedings; the emotional issue focused on the second wife's desertion and adulterous conduct. The decision of the trial court was overturned on appeal. The Nova Scotia Supreme Court held that, where jurisdiction was valid, there was a presumption in favour of the validity of the proceedings in foreign courts. The prior divorce was thus valid, and Mr Field's second wife could be publicly chastised for her unacceptable conduct.

In *Brown* v *McInness* (1927),[30] a wage-earning carpenter lived for ten years with his wife in Prince Edward Island; they had five children. He then deserted her and moved to British Columbia. Undaunted, Mrs McInness followed her husband west with her children.

She found him 'passing himself off as a single man and keeping company with a young girl.' Mrs McInness persuaded him to set up housekeeping with her again in Vancouver in 1897, but after a year the marriage broke down again. There was no evidence as to where McInness then went, but four years later his wife found him in Seattle and soon filed there for divorce. The Washington court issued the final decree in 1903, and four years later Mrs McInness remarried. Her second husband now sought relief from that marriage on the ground that the first divorce was invalid. The British Columbia Supreme Court evinced considerable sympathy for Mrs McInness and the treatment she had received from her first husband: 'He bitterly contested the [divorce] case and, in my view, he did so from a fear that some such [support] order would be made rather than from any desire to retain the respondent as his wife. The evidence is all against the view that he valued her as a wife.' On extremely slight evidence the court found that a Washington domicile had been established and that the divorce was therefore valid.

Similarly, in *Chatenay* v *Chatenay* (1938),[31] infringement of prescriptive gender roles was punished. A twenty-nine-year-old farmer, a native of Switzerland, had married in British Columbia. He and his wife had lived there and in Alberta for eight years. In 1934 he returned to Switzerland and obtained a divorce there on grounds unavailable in Canada. There were adequate grounds for the Alberta court to find in favour of either a Canadian or a Swiss domicile in this case. What stands out in the reasons for judgment is the evidence of behaviour unbecoming a husband. There was evidence of violence on his part; after sending for his future wife to come to Canada, he had broken into her bedroom to have sexual relations with her; after having made her pregnant, he waited to marry her until just before the child was born. He slipped off to Switzerland 'without a word' to his wife and gave false testimony to the Swiss court. After obtaining his decree, he sent her a 'peremptory' letter ordering her to leave the farmhouse and to take nothing with her. The Swiss divorce decree had deprived the mother of their child, whom the husband seized forcibly, injuring his wife; only the intervention of the local police stopped him, and the child was returned to its mother. In short, Mr Chatenay's conduct, all of which was discussed by the court in the judgment, earned him no sympathy from the bench. The divorce was held to be invalid because his domicile was now Canadian; despite the wife's participation in the Swiss proceedings (she had denied Swiss jurisdiction), she was not prevented (as she normally would have been)[32] from challenging the validity of the divorce in Canada. The wife was awarded the judicial separation for which she had petitioned, as well as custody of her nine-year old daughter.

The Canadian courts were more uniform and less sympathetic in their responses to the issue of foreign divorces than they were to the issue of domicile. There was no sign of judicial creativity, no evidence of an attempt to facilitate access to American divorce courts. There was instead a consistent support for the restrictive and limited Canadian divorce environment and an insistence on maintaining the jurisdiction of Canadian courts. The courts were part of a broadly based attempt on the part of the state to preserve the ideal of the conjugal family. The few indications of judicial initiative, such as occurred in *Fields* and *Chatenay*, were aimed at upholding the prescriptive roles of the sexes.

Bigamy

As is apparent from some of the cases discussed above, foreign divorce raised the spectre of bigamy. The criminal offence of bigamy was not the state of being married a second time or more, but the act of going through two or more forms of marriage.[33] Thus, although a divorce and a remarriage in the United States might be invalid, the act of going through the form of marriage was an offence, and the individual was liable to prosecution in Canada. Here the state had the powerful weapon of the criminal law at its disposal to enforce marriage law, though that weapon was subject to strict evidentiary rules and a heavy burden of proof.

An important common law defence against most criminal charges is that of honest belief. That is, a person must be shown to have knowledge or intention that a criminal offence was being committed (mens rea). The Criminal Code set out four instances in which this defence was specifically invited in cases of bigamy: (1) if in good faith and on reasonable grounds the accused believed his wife or her husband to be dead; (2) if his wife or her husband had been continuously absent for the last seven years and the remaining spouse could not be proved to have known that the absent spouse was alive at any point during that time; (3) if he or she had been divorced from the first marriage; and (4) if the former marriage had been declared null and void.[34] The defendent bore the burden of proving honest belief on reasonable grounds; it was for the judge or jury to decide whether the proof was sufficient.

This defence usually became a legal issue when the defendant claimed an honest belief that a previous marriage had been validly dissolved. On this question the courts were not entirely consistent. In *R.* v *Haugen* (1923),[35] the Saskatchewan Court of Appeal held that the well-established principle of mistake of fact was a valid defence where the husband had remarried in good faith and on the reasonable grounds that his first wife was already married at the time of their marriage. Johanna Johnsen had first married in Norway in 1910, and had legally separated from her first husband in 1919. In June 1921 she married Mr Haugen in Saskatchewan; when this marriage broke down, he remarried in the belief that the 1921 marriage was null and void, but without obtaining a declaration of the court to that effect. Charged with bigamy, Mr Haugen successfully appealed his conviction. The Saskatchewan court was willing to show some leniency to a spouse who had been duped into an invalid union.

But such sympathetic treatment was not common in the reported cases on bigamy. Consider, for example, the treatment accorded Jasper Brinkley in the 1907 foreign divorce case discussed earlier. Here was a man whose wife had deserted him, taken up residence in Michigan, and obtained a divorce there. Wishing to remarry, he cautiously sought legal advice and was informed by counsel that the Michigan divorce was valid in Ontario; as a further precaution, for the marriage ceremony itself Brinkley took his prospective bride to the state in which his wife had obtained her divorce. Surely he had no intention of violating Canadian criminal law, and took every reasonable precaution against doing so. Nevertheless, on appeal the Ontario Court of Appeal held that this was no defence and that Brinkley was guilty of bigamy.[36] Justice Meredith wrote a forceful judgment on the social importance of the law of bigamy in maintaining the moral order and in defending the jurisdiction and authority of Canadian law:

The wrong struck at was an evasion of the law of Canada, in favour of peace and morality, by the simple expedient of stepping over an international boundary line, to go through a form of marriage. How can it be said that the punishment is for a crime committed beyond the territorial limits of the Dominion? Or that there is any infringement of any such principle as that 'crime is local'? The purpose of the enactment was to compel residents of Canada, who were also British subjects, to obey the laws of Canada in respect of marriage and divorce.

If this enactment be a dead letter, what is there to prevent the indulgence, without limit, in duality or plurality of wives or husbands in Canada ... Such a state of things would obviously be against the peace, order and good government of Canada.[37]

With the spectre of a widespread breakdown in monogamy threatening peace, morality, and social order, it is no wonder that the courts were sympathetic to attacks on foreign divorce through the criminal law.

If someone who had taken as many precautions as Brinkley had was guilty of bigamy, it is not surprising that the less cautious were readily found guilty. An invalid foreign divorce was plainly no defence against bigamy. Domiciled in Ontario, Mr and Mrs Woods married in Windsor in July 1897. Fourteen months later the husband moved across the river to Detroit; Mrs Woods followed one month later. They lived separately, and as soon as they met the residency requirements, they obtained a divorce and then returned to Ontario. In November 1900 Mrs Woods remarried in Toronto, and within a year was convicted of bigamy.[38] It mattered not that the second marriage was invalid; the punishable offence was going through a second form of marriage.

The courts did insist, however, that the first marriage be strictly proved. This requirement was usually easily met, although a presumption of the validity of the first marriage was not incorporated into the Criminal Code until 1953–4. It was necessary to establish not merely that the marriage had taken place, but also that it was valid – that it had been celebrated in accordance with the formalities of the law between consenting parties who had the capacity to marry according to the law of their domicile.[39] In general, marriages performed in Canada were rarely subjected to a heavy burden of evidentiary proof because the courts were well acquainted with the requirements of provincial law. Foreign marriages were held to much more stringent evidentiary requirements. The second marriage was subject to lower evidentiary standards, however, because it was necessary to prove only that the accused had gone through another form of marriage. People wanting to remarry sometimes sought to protect themselves against a future charge of bigamy by obtaining a declaration of presumption of death of the first marriage partner. The courts generally refused to issue such a declaration, except when required to do so as part of another action; a simple petition for a declaration of death would usually be rejected. (This topic is discussed further in chapter 5.)

Overall, an examination of bigamy in the reported cases adds a dimension of complexity to the picture of the courts' activities and attitudes. While the evidentiary burdens and obstacles of criminal law were not relieved in any attempts at stricter enforcement of prescribed marital behaviour, the bench repeatedly made clear its support for a law that was seen as essential in protecting social order. That law was interpreted and applied in such a way that individual Canadians were left vulnerable and uncertain, perhaps in the hope that in such circumstances they would err on the side of caution with respect to the law of marriage.

Adultery

Since adultery was the basic and almost sole ground for divorce in Canada in these years, the offence was of fundamental importance in the law. The sexual double standard in adultery that existed in law until 1925 in the four western provinces helped to legitimate and encourage a gender-based perspective on this and other divorce-related issues. The courts complemented this legislation by using class and sex as important criteria in dealing with adultery. The definition of adultery was not a matter of much dispute; most of the reported cases turned on the admissibility or sufficiency of evidence. Three cases did help to set the limits of what constituted adultery; they offer an insight into judicial attitudes towards 'immorality.'

In *Babineau* v *Babineau* (1924),[40] a married woman in New Brunswick petitioned for divorce on the ground that her husband practised bestiality. Justice Grimmer of the New Brunswick Court of Appeal could find no precedents that would allow him to broaden the definition of adultery to include such sexual activity as bestiality: 'I have with great reluctance come to this conclusion, and would have been very glad if I could possibly have ... found any possible reason, to authorize entering the decree asked for, and had the Divorce Court found it possible to have made the decree sought I would have had still greater reluctance, in case of an appeal against the same, in forming any conclusion to disturb it.' While any form of sexual activity other than 'normal' sexual intercourse between husband and wife was highly objectionable, the definition of adultery was not so broad.

The bench frequently took advantage of its position to comment in this way on marital and sexual practices, even (or perhaps especially) when the legal result would not directly condemn the practice involved. In a 1905 Manitoba case, for example, a woman who was already pregnant as a result of 'seduction by another man' married a local lawyer who was not informed of her condition until after the marriage. He left her, but with 'a kindness and consideration nothing short of chivalrous' he continued to support her and offered to take her back after the birth provided that she gave up the baby. When she did so and returned to him, he announced that he needed another nine months to decide whether to take her back, and in the meantime gave her twenty-five dollars for support each month. When he finally decided not to take her back, she sued for alimony; her husband put forward a defence in which he attempted to characterize her actions as adultery. The court agreed that adultery and cruelty were valid defences against a petition for alimony. However, the adultery had to occur after marriage, and deception was not legal cruelty. Therefore, the wife was entitled to alimony, although she was publicly chastised by the judge: she had 'inflicted on her husband one of the greatest wrongs a woman could do to a man. She [had] humiliated him in the eyes of the world and rendered the marriage rite between them disgraceful in place of sacred.'[41] A man's honour had to be upheld, as did his procreative rights in his wife.

Orford v *Orford* (1921)[42] made it clear that there was at least some latitude in the definition of adultery. While living separate and apart from her husband, Lillian Orford had given birth to a child conceived through artificial insemination. She claimed alimony from her husband, which he contested on the ground that she had commited adultery. The court appeared to have little difficulty in concluding that artificial insemination did amount to adultery. Emphasizing the procreative purpose of marriage, Justice Orde of the Supreme Court of Ontario defined adultery as the 'invasion of the marital rights of the husband or the wife ... the essence of the offence of adultery consists not in the moral turpitude of the act of sexual intercourse, but in the voluntary surrender to another person of the reproductive powers or faculties of the guilty person; and any submission of those powers to the service or enjoyment of any person, other than the husband or the wife comes within the definition of adultery.' Any form of sexual intercourse, including artificial insemination, could be adultery, 'because in the case of the woman it involves the possibility of introducing into the family of the husband a false strain of blood.' When the wife's counsel suggested that artificial insemination would not have been adultery if she had still been living with her husband, the bench was truly offended: 'A monstrous conclusion surely. If such a thing has never before been declared to be adultery, then, on the grounds of public policy, the Court should now declare it so.' The *Orford* decision served a number of functions. The definition of adultery acquired some flexibility; the limits of acceptable reproductive behaviour shrank; and a husband's reproductive rights in his wife were underlined, thus reinforcing a gender-based hierarchy of power within marriage.

One cannot help but speculate about the influence of the wife's 'deviant' marital behaviour and of her failure to meet her husband's sexual expectations. Three years after emigrating from England to Toronto, Lillian met her future husband; a few months later, in August 1913, she married him. On their honeymoon they journeyed to England, presumably to visit her relatives. Trouble began early, for despite several painful attempts the marriage remained unconsummated owing to Mrs Orford's physical problems. Eventually, Mr Orford left for Toronto in early November, while his wife remained in England with her parents. Thus began a six-year separation. By 1917 Lillian Orford had established a friendship with George Hodgkinson, and this relationship evolved to the stage where she was able to tell him of her sexual difficulties – 'her affliction and her inability to have sexual intercourse with her husband.' By this time she had consulted a local doctor, who had refused to undertake corrective surgery without her husband's consent; according to the doctor, the only way she could otherwise conceive was 'artificially.' Hodgkinson exhibited a good deal of interest in Lillian's problem, and arranged to supply his own semen, to retain a doctor, to pay for all expenses connected with the procedure, pregnancy, and birth, and to adopt the child. Mrs Orford agreed to undergo the procedure. She was met at Hodgkinson's apartment by Hodgkinson himself and an unnamed doctor; there she undressed, went to bed, and was rendered unconscious by anaesthetics. On regaining consciousness, she saw that the doctor had gone. Hodgkinson explained to her what had transpired. By the time of the second such session, in May 1918, there was evidence to indicate that Lillian's physical problems had been overcome and that she was having 'natural' sexual intercourse with Hodgkinson. Indeed, Justice Orde was more than a little suspicious of a much greater sexual relationship: 'It is difficult to avoid the conclusion that from some time in the latter part of 1917, perhaps as early as July, she had entered upon a course of conduct with Hodgkinson which, if all the facts were known (and I feel that she has failed to disclose them all) would establish that she had become Hodgkinson's mistress.' In February 1919 a male child was born to Lillian Orford and George Hodgkinson, and by December Lillian's relationship with Hodgkinson had ended. She returned to her husband in Toronto, but he refused to take her in as his wife. She immediately sued for alimony, charging him with numerous acts of cruelty during their honeymoon, unnatural sexual practices, and adultery.

While Mr Orford's conduct could certainly be seen as 'callous and inconsiderate' (to use the judge's words), it was Lillian Orford's actions that so grievously offended against the ideal of the conjugal family. She had not followed her husband back to Toronto; she had developed a close and possibly sexual relationship with another man; she had allowed her body and her reproductive capacity to be violated and used by men other than her husband. Worse, she showed no remorse; Justice Orde spoke directly of her 'very slight appreciation of the gravity of what she had done.' Such behaviour and attitudes were not designed to evoke the sympathy of the court, and it is striking that all of this information (and more) was recited in the court's judgment against Mrs Orford.

The case served to articulate the courts' concerns about acceptable marital and sexual behaviour and to reinforce the proscriptive role of the law, but the issue of artificial insemination was not prominent either socially or legally. Much more important, at least legally, were the evidentiary concerns related to adultery. Direct evidence of adultery in divorce cases was not required; the nature of the offence meant that it was seldom available. However, there had to be circumstantial evidence from which the inference of adultery flowed as a necessary conclusion. The standard of evidence was the civil test of the balance of probabilities or the preponderance of evidence, rather than the criminal standard of 'guilt beyond a reasonable doubt.'[43] When it was available, direct evidence could of course be very persuasive. Conception at a time when the husband could establish lack of access was clear evidence; similarly, either partner's contracting a venereal disease could be evidence of adultery, although, because the disease was often communicated to a spouse, it was important to establish timing.[44]

But the courts were very careful with confessions of adultery. They were well aware that some husbands and wives wanted to escape from their marriages and might fabricate evidence. Collusion and connivance were bars to divorce, and the bench tended to watch for these and to guard against them. Divorce by consent would not be tolerated; the dissolution of marriage was a matter for the courts to decide, not the individual couple. Confessions of adultery were admissible, provided that a warning had been issued about self-incrimination, but they were usually held to be insufficient in themselves.[45] On occasion, though, the court was impressed with the demeanour of the spouse making the confession (was he properly contrite?) and accepted an otherwise unsupported admission of adultery.[46] In one crucial case the courts distinguished between collusion to commit adultery and a statement made to facilitate proof. In *Parry* v *Parry and Tench* (1926),[47] the only evidence of adultery, in this instance extending over a five-year period, was the wife's written admission to the partner of her husband's solicitor. The trial judge dismissed the case on the ground that the admission represented collusion. On appeal it was held that confession of adultery made simply to facilitate proof was not collusive and was therefore admissible. This decision became important in allowing couples to simplify their divorces.

Other jurists were intent on maintaining a much more prominent supervisory role for the courts. A Saskatchewan trial judge characterized the introduction of a wife's confession as suggesting collusion and divorce by consent: 'There is little use in requiring a presiding Judge to exercise vigilance to protect the public against arranged divorces if we are met at the outside with a rule of law which shackles the exercise of any discretion by the presiding Judge.'[48] In another case, where a vulnerable woman had provided evidence of her own adultery, the trial court rejected the evidence as pre-arranged and collusive: 'I am satisfied that there was an agreement between the husband and wife for a divorce, an arrangement settling such matters as would naturally be in dispute between them other than the mere decree for divorce, and an arrangement as to the testimony which should be offered to establish the claim for divorce ... and that the evidence she gave was in accordance with the arrangement previously arrived at between them.' The wife's story was 'mostly untrue,' but she was held not responsible because her 'mentality [was] below normal.' Such collusion ought to be a bar to divorce, and the judge refused to be bound by *Parry*. In marriage, he wrote, the home and family were protected, and the state's interest was superior to that of the individuals involved.[49] While *Parry* introduced some evidentiary flexibility, other judges remained on guard lest their colleagues go too far.

Confessions were not required to establish adultery, however. Direct evidence had been found to be unnecessary; it was enough to show familiarity and opportunity from which the inference of adultery could be drawn.[50] For example, adultery could be inferred from witnesses' evidence that a couple had been seen in a 'compromising position' or from evidence of a long and intimate friendship combined with the couple's having spent the night together in the woman's room.[51] In an unreported Nova Scotia case, Justice J.J. Ritchie of the Court for Divorce and Matrimonial Causes at first held that insufficient evidence of adultery had been adduced, but gave counsel for the petitioner an opportunity to introduce further evidence. When this had been completed, Ritchie found that the allegations were sustained:

> There is no direct evidence of the act of adultery, but it is a case of familiarities and constant and very ample opportunity. It is generally difficult to establish by direct evidence the fact of adultery, and this may be one of the reasons for the rule that evidence of familiarities between the parties coupled with opportunities for sexual intercourse is sufficient to establish the fact of adultery. This rule is fully supported by the authorities and I act upon it in this case, as I think the inference of adultery is strong.[52]

Thus were the rules applied.

The cases reveal the delicate balancing act that the courts were expected to perform. While preserving the public interest in social order and family stability, they also had to punish those who violated the normative moral and behavioural standards of the day. Actions or words that transgressed those norms influenced the court's response to individual cases. In one instance a husband's general conduct, his excessive drinking, and his frequent physical abuse of his wife were taken by an appeal judge in Saskatchewan to suggest that chastity on the husband's part was improbable; this was sufficient to corroborate other evidence and thus establish adultery.[53] In another trial a married woman's stated views on marriage (if she cared for any man, she was free to go out with him and to have sexual intercourse with him) were held to be contributory to proving adultery.[54] In *Wright* v *Wright* (1928),[55] the wife deserted her husband more than once and lived 'in open adultery with a negro.' On her husband's petition a decree nisi had been entered at trial. Before the final decree was issued the king's proctor intervened with evidence of the husband's alleged adultery (he had visited a brothel several times). The Alberta Supreme Court held that an inference of adultery was inappropriate here, because as a taxi driver the husband could be taken to have been at the brothel on business. As well, such conduct paled beside that of his wife, whose behaviour was 'particularly inexcusable ... and thoroughly disgusting to a sense of decency.' It was therefore in the interests of 'sound public policy' to grant the husband a divorce, thereby chastising the wife. Whether the judge was more disturbed by the sexual or the racial elements in the case is unclear, but it is certain that they combined to influence his findings.

At times, stereotypes and expectations could operate in an individual's favour. For example, in a 1918 New Brunswick case a married woman, whose husband was still overseas, had gone out for an evening drive with two men. She knew only one of them, a doctor. The threesome had broken into a golf club and had stayed there drinking for hours; after the doctor had fallen asleep, the wife and the other man, a banker, stayed together; later all three returned to her home. The trial court held that an inference of adultery was reasonable and granted the husband a divorce, but the appeal court ruled otherwise. 'It is extremely improbable,' said Chief Justice Hazen of the New Brunswick Court of Appeal, 'that any woman except a common prostitute would commit the offence charged with a man whom she had only known a few hours.' As an otherwise respectable member of the middle class, the woman had remained with the men only because to have summoned help would have attracted attention and created a 'public scandal.'[56] Thus, class and gender stereotypes worked to protect some people, while presenting a façade of consistency regarding marital behaviour.

Cruelty

Legal cruelty was an issue of importance for several reasons. Before 1925 in western Canada, married women seeking judicial divorce had to prove aggravated adultery on the part of their husbands; cruelty was one of the major forms of aggravation. In Nova Scotia, cruelty was an independent ground for divorce. As well, cruelty was a ground for alimony or judicial separation in Canada. What constituted legal cruelty was clear in this period: on the basis of the English cases of *Evans* (1790) and *Russell* (1897), the victim must suffer physical illness or mental distress that seriously impaired bodily health or endangered life. Legal cruelty was thus something more than ordinary cruelty, and the leading cases emphasized that 'casual' cruelty was insufficient. In *Evans* the court stressed that justice took precedence over simple humanity in such questions, and broader interests had to be considered: 'It must be remembered that the general happiness of the married life is secured by its indissolubility. When people understand that they must live together, except for very few reasons known to law, they learn to soften by mutual accommodation that yoke which they know they cannot shake off ... In this case, as in many others, the happiness of some individuals must be sacrificed to the greater and more general good.' Evidence of legal cruelty had to be 'grave and weighty, and such as show[s] an absolute impossibility that the duties of married life can be discharged.'[57] The courts focused not on the marital conduct itself, but rather on the result of the conduct.[58] This judicial emphasis tended to frustrate individuals who sought to use the divorce courts to articulate new standards of marital behaviour. It also tended to ignore more recent English and particularly American decisions that established a standard for cruelty reflecting a more companionate ideal of marital behaviour.[59]

A conservative judicial culture imposed a particular conception of legal cruelty, one with which many local jurists were comfortable. Again the courts were expected to measure the needs of the individual against the needs of the broader community, with special weight being given to the latter. Nevertheless, it was well established that the test for legal cruelty was subjective and depended upon the individuals and circumstances. Canadian jurists had a good deal of discretion, which they apparently exercised frequently.

J.M. Biggs has argued that judicial discretion in applying divorce rules is essential in permitting the legal process to take into account the wide variety of individual standards, values, and behaviour.[60] But this allowed the judges to use their discretion to incorporate or maintain sexual and class discrimination within the jurisprudence. Given the power of precedent in the Canadian judicial culture, this incorporation had a potentially broad influence. The problem is to try to discern patterns in the exercise of judicial discretion.[61] The reported cases reveal a growing tendency on the part of judges to accept evidence establishing cruelty. Types of incidents and proofs that had earlier been rejected were increasingly being found sufficient by the end of the 1910s, if not slightly earlier. A 1905 case, for example, emphasized the couple's potential advantages and harmony. The wife was described as attractive and as having natural force and ability; her husband of twenty-six years was strong, healthy, sober, active, and a prosperous businessman. The wife sought alimony on the basis of her husband's violent rages and adultery, which she claimed amounted to cruelty and had caused her ill health of four years' duration. The trial judge, however, found no evidence showing either legal cruelty or that her illness had been caused by her husband's treatment; the judge pointed out that she was not afraid of her husband. Here, it seems, was a couple that conformed in many ways to the middle-class ideal, and the trial judge was not willing to assist in separating them. 'A good deal of valuable time has been lost,' he commented, 'but if the parties will accept an intimation to let all that is past be buried, they may live very happily together yet.'[62]

In 1916 a second case suggested that while some change was occurring, the forces of stability were still strong. On the basis of previous acts of cruelty and a single incident of assault and battery by her husband, for which he was criminally convicted, a wife brought suit for alimony. The trial judge found sufficient evidence to establish cruelty, but unsuccessfully sought to encourage a reconciliation. The decision was reversed on appeal. The appeal court unanimously held that a single specific incident was not enough to establish cruelty. One appeal justice pointedly disagreed with the trial judge's statement that it was up to the wife to say whether or not she should return to her husband; 'it is her duty to return,' and any failure to do so would not be condoned by the court or supported by her husband. While agreeing in the result, another of the judges regretted that the law of cruelty had not been changed and thought it inappropriate that the trial judge's attempted reconciliation was taken to demonstrate that the couple could continue to live together.[63]

A decade later a married woman, a stenographer, petitioned for divorce in Saskatchewan, charging adultery and cruelty. The adultery was readily proved, but was there evidence of cruelty sufficient to establish aggravated adultery? The wife was described as being frail and depressed, and her health had suffered because of her husband's adultery. The court found that the husband's adultery had injuriously affected his wife's health and that he nevertheless pursued the affair; the husband had since deserted and moved to the United States. While acknowledging that there were no legal precedents and that he was extending the law, the judge found that the adultery itself constituted serious mental cruelty, and a divorce was appropriate. After an extensive review of the case law, the judge chose to move beyond the established precedents to include new ideas. 'It must be borne in mind that we now have a better understanding of the effect of misery and pain and anguish of mind in its relation to health.' Jennie Jones sought and deserved relief, he concluded, 'from a marriage which to her was intolerable, and would be to any decent woman.'[64]

Though the three cases do not fully establish the pattern, they do illustrate several trends found in the judiciary's general treatment of cruelty. Concern for marital stability and the public interest, as articulated in *Evans* and repeated in several Canadian cases, while still present, was increasingly balanced and even overcome by an urge to reinforce gender roles. Nevertheless, judges continued to hope that marriages could be 'repaired' and spouses reconciled to one another; there was a sense that some couples brought to court problems that could and should be solved privately. More and more it was regarded as a function of judges to attempt or at least to facilitate reconciliation. Judges commonly pointed out the possibilities of reconciliation and criticized the grounds and evidence presented as morally insufficient to dissolve a marriage; they seemed to believe that the complaints and proofs were the sum total of couples' problems, rather than being legal constructs. Judges altered alimony payments from lump sums to monthly amounts in the hope of encouraging the couple to resume cohabitation. At other times simple admonitions were offered; when some spouses tried reconciliation unsuccessfully, the attempt was not seen as condonation but as an attempt to do one's duty by living with one's spouse. In short, the concept of 'matrimonial duties' was alive and vital.[65]

But gender was a more and more powerful factor, at least as far as women were concerned. Married women who were perceived to be frail, high-strung, nervous, or vulnerable tended to be offered a degree of legal protection that was denied stronger women, though given the health-related test for cruelty this is not very surprising. In *Correll* v *Correll* (1919),[66] for example, the spouses had quarrelled for nine years; in one recent fight both spouses had been injured. The wife sued for alimony; her claim was dismissed because she was the stronger of the two (her husband was physically disabled) and she had been the aggressor. In another case an elderly woman was found to deserve protection from her husband's deviant sexual habits; his practice of oral sex led her to claim mental cruelty. The judge found that while she owed her husband natural coition, her obligations did not extend to such 'disgusting,' 'perverse,' and 'vicious' practices. It was natural that not only the plaintiff but 'all women with the sense of modesty and decorum which she has' would feel such 'abhorrence and disgust' as to damage her health and to be 'dangerous to life itself.'[67]

The weight attached to factors such as class or gender often depended on the individual judges. A judgment of Justice Meredith, then a member of the Ontario Court of Appeal, offers a good example of the subjective nature of legal cruelty. Meredith argued powerfully for broader social interests in the preservation of marriages in Canada. One of his dissenting judgments led off with a succinct statement of his attitude to marriage:

There is one thing that ought to be certain in cases such as this, and that is, that the Courts ought not to encourage any such notions as, that the marriage tie is not unlike some shoe-strings, easily broken and not much good anyhow; that a divorce, even a divorce a mensa et thoro [a judicial separation], can be obtained for anything less than the gravest causes. The Courts may not be concerned in the secret [private] nature of the tie, but must be deeply concerned in the binding character of the contract; and must not let individual sympathy or individual notions of gallantry, false or true, misguide their footsteps. Nor is it to be forgotten that the evidence of the parties, and their relatives, should be scrutinized with the utmost care, and properly discounted, for there is no other kind of case in which they, consciously or unconsciously, the more exaggerate, marshal and concentrate, their grievances so as to give them a spectacular, and over real, effect.[68]

With this conservative philosophy and sceptical eye, Meredith commented on a number of important cases dealing with cruelty.[69] He consistently defended an earlier familial ideal based on a hierarchy of sex; he would accept no modifications to reflect changing attitudes.

For Meredith, incidents of marital cruelty and violence were just that – incidents. All it would take to solve such problems was good will on both sides. There is no evidence that it occurred to him that the incidents might be symptomatic of more basic problems in the marriage; he saw no reason to suppose that the couples would not go forth from his court with good intentions and a desire to repair whatever damage had been done. For him the appeal court was as useful an instrument in mending strained relationships as the domestic relations courts that were beginning to be discussed. Justice Meredith was intent on exercising his discretion in support of marital, family, and social stability. He balances our view of jurists, such as Justice Stuart of Alberta, who were equally intent on moderate innovation. Between these two extremes were jurists such as R.H. Graham of Nova Scotia who, though not opposed to dissolv-ing a marriage that had irredeemably broken down, was unwilling to grant a divorce unless the evidence met the existing legal tests.[70]

Developments in the law of legal cruelty repeat some of the themes already detected in other areas of the law. Where change occurred, it was slow and cautious. Where no change took place, the bench exercised its often considerable discretion in defence not of the formal rules of law, but of the informal and equally powerful ideal of the conjugal family and the rules of gender and class. The potential scope of discretion was widened in the case of divorce, as in much of family law, because of the absence of juries.[71] The law reports operated both directly, through jurists such as R.M. Meredith, and less formally, through jurists such as C.A. Stuart, to protect the individual and public interest in familial and moral stability. As Constance Backhouse has found for much of nineteenth-century Canadian family law, the courts acted to defend their notion of the patriarchal family. The continuing power of such ideas as gender roles combined with the increasing influence of case law and a constricting legal culture to present an authoritative jurisprudence.[72]

There is little evidence that Canadian judges acted to develop the law of divorce when Parliament failed to do so. While there were occasional calls from the bench for legislative action, judges tended not to accept direct responsibility for developing the law in new directions. The exception was the law of domicile, but even those new steps were limited and were soon ended by the imperial judiciary. This lack of judicial assertiveness stands in considerable contrast to Michael Grossberg's findings for the United States.[73] In Canada the judiciary confidently asserted and maintained traditional notions of the centrality of marriage, family, and gender in society. The conservatism of Canadian judicial culture reinforced existing middle-class rules, both formal and informal, for spousal behaviour. Indeed, that judicial culture tended to operate as a force against change, even within the broad parameters of those rules. It was not the role of the courts to initiate change; that was the responsibility of legislatures. If legislators declined to act, Canadian judges generally did not perceive themselves to have acquired any additional responsibilities. But more than that, the judiciary was neither passive nor neutral in its ideas about the family. Judicial paternalism was an active and important factor in divorce-related issues, particularly in connection with the judicial defence of the 'weaker sex' within the broader protection of the prevailing ideal of the family. This paternalism was paralleled by a punitive response to the violation of gender roles, especially by women.

5

The Role of the State

One other broad area of the law played a vital role in establishing the legal environment surrounding divorce. More than the formal legislative debates about divorce and more than the precedents set and maintained by the judiciary, a cluster of legal elements – the divorce process, the criminal law, the police, family agencies, and statutes regulating familial behaviour and duties, many of them strengthened by the expanding role of the state in the early twentieth century – affected the treatment of those who sought to deviate from stable marital behaviour. Both the divorce process itself and a variety of complementary laws inhibited divorce and articulated an important set of norms for society at large. Gail Savage has recently described these elements as a major part of the explanation of the differing incidence of divorce in England and France in the late nineteenth and early twentieth centuries.[1] Most of her statements about the restrictive English environment apply equally to Canada.

Of obvious importance were the procedural rules governing divorce in the one parliamentary and seven provincial jurisdictions that granted marital dissolutions. The nature of the various stages through which a petitioner was required to pass and the ease of access contributed significantly to the communication of ideas and attitudes. Delay was one of the most prominent, consistent, and expensive features of all Canadian divorce procedures. Persons petitioning Parliament were required to give at least six months' notice of action in the *Canada Gazette*; the vagaries of parliamentary sittings and legislative procedure could add many more months. Of course, if a divorce bill failed to pass all the legislative hurdles in one session, it was necessary to begin proceedings all over again in the next session. The most common cause of delay was the two-stage decree, which had been copied from English practice. Once a court had formally decided to dissolve the marriage, the petitioner was granted a decree nisi. The decree nisi did not end the marriage, nor did it grant the petitioner any new privileges. Only after at least a further three or six months (depending on the jurisdiction) had passed could a decree absolute be issued dissolving the marriage. But the decree absolute was not automatic; the petitioner had to apply for it. Many people, usually out of ignorance, neglected to take this last formal step in the process; others were unwilling to wait for the final decree before remarrying.

Access to divorce was also geographically restricted. Any Canadian desiring a parliamentary divorce had to seek it in Ottawa; many could not afford to travel that far. Similarly, the provincial divorce courts were not easily accessible. In Nova Scotia the Court of Divorce and Matrimonial Causes sat only in Halifax, and petitioners had to conduct their legal business there. Provincial supreme courts tended to go on circuit, but even then access could be quite limited. In Ontario, for example, a Supreme Court judge would sit in most counties only twice a year. Cases filed in one county could be heard in another, and many divorce causes were transferred for trial to nearby counties because of the timing of the local sittings; nevertheless, this procedure necessitated more filings before the court. Furthermore, no matter where the trial was held, the application for and the granting of the final decree in Ontario were centralized in Toronto. Difficulty of access thus contributed to delay in inhibiting divorce.

Implicit in this emphasis on delay was the belief among legislators and the judiciary that parties seeking divorce often did not really mean it; they were using divorce as an easy solution to marital problems, problems that could be readily settled by means that would not end the marriage. Many observers regarded divorce as the beginning, not the end, of a process of marriage breakdown. In making that beginning less accessible, legislators and judges truly believed that they were helping to prevent marriage breakdown. Also inherent in this attitude was the belief that divorce was not merely a private affair between two spouses; the courts and Parliament had erected explicit barriers to any mechanism of 'self-divorce.' Most obviously, no form of collusion was tolerated. Procedural rules insisted that the petitioner swear that there was no collusion or connivance between the plaintiff and any defendants; the petitioner's counsel had to attest not only that he had credible evidence that the alleged acts had occurred, but also that he had carefully investigated and believed that no collusion or connivance existed. Because the ideal of the conjugal family made marriage the cornerstone of society, both the public in general and the state on its behalf were considered to have their own (and overriding) interests and rights in divorce actions. Thus, notice of the parliamentary petition was required to be given not merely to the defendant spouse, but to the public at large through the *Canada Gazette* and two local newspapers for five successive weeks.[2] As Justice Graham of Nova Scotia commented in a 1926 trial, 'In weighing evidence ... the Court must keep in mind that marriage is a basic and essential part of the social system, and that its duty is to uphold the married state, if it can justly do so.'[3] For the same reason state officials had a right and in some circumstances a duty to intervene in divorce proceedings.

The central figure in the state's intervention was the king's proctor. Not all Canadian jurisdictions officially appointed such a person, but most had an official who performed similar duties. In England the king's proctor acted on behalf of the Crown to ensure that justice was done both individually and collectively in matrimonial causes. In the case of divorce his foremost obligation was to ensure that, particularly in an undefended action, justice had been served and the parties had not colluded or connived in the evidence. In the 1920s and 1930s, as each new provincial jurisdiction in divorce was established, the need for such an official was debated and usually confirmed. (This was at a time when the office of the king's proctor was falling into increasing disrepute in England.)[4]

In Canada, Nova Scotia led the way in the use of the equivalent of the king's proctor. In every undefended divorce action a local lawyer was appointed as watching counsel; the title itself is instructive and somewhat suggestive of intimidation. For a set fee this officer attended all proceedings and intervened whenever he felt it appropriate. The trial records contain a number of examples in which the watching counsel was quite active and aggressive in bringing out evidence that undermined the petitioner's case, such as collusion or the petitioner's own misconduct. On the rare occasion when watching counsel was not present, the judge pointedly took up the responsibility of cross-examining those giving evidence. 'The watching counsel was not present,' wrote Justice Longley of the Supreme Court of Nova Soctia on one occasion, 'but I put the whole of the witnesses to such a thorough cross-examination that I am perfectly satisfied that the divorce proceedings are not the result of collusion.' On another occasion the respondent's counsel abandoned the case in the middle of the trial, whereupon R.H. Murray, the watching counsel, took over the defence with considerable vigour. He submitted a typewritten copy of the evidence and a decision in an earlier unreported Nova Scotia case that discredited the petitioner. In a 1933 case a watching counsel and trial judge combined to badger the female petitioner about her original reasons for marrying, repeatedly suggesting that she had simply sought a loose sexual relationship from which she expected an easy escape. On other occasions the judge expressed his suspicion of collusion but pointed to the lack of resources required to impeach the evidence presented.[5] Nova Scotia leaders were so committed to the principle behind the king's proctor that they repeatedly urged other jurisdictions to employ a similar official.

Other provinces supported the principle, but shied away from so extensive an involvement.[6] When Ontario implemented judicial divorce in 1930, the first rules of procedure drawn up by the judges in June made it mandatory that the attorney-general be named a defendant in the actions. He was to be served with copies of writs and affidavits, and had a right to participate in the action. A department official was assigned to examine each case and to certify that the petition was in order and that, on the basis of the file, there was no apparent collusion. The procedure was unsatisfactory, since evidence of collusion was unlikely to surface in this bureaucratic way (as the official himself noted at times), and it was certainly cumbersome and expensive. In November 1930 the Ontario judges adopted new rules: the attorney-general would no longer be a party to each action. He would still have the right to intervene at any stage of the proceedings, and the petitioner was required to serve him with a copy of the decree nisi within one month of its issue. The rules of the Senate Divorce Committee contained a similar provision. The committee was explicitly invited, in the case of suspected collusion or connivance, to ask the minister of justice to intervene and oppose the divorce bill in 'the interest of public justice.' There is no evidence that this procedure was ever used.[7]

A number of contemporary observers argued that a king's proctor should be appointed and given considerable authority. At the heart of their plea was the conviction that the state had an important interest in a divorce action. Lawyers and government officials pointed to the king's proctor in England as the sort of officer needed to take on investigative duties. One Ottawa counsel suggested that every case in which a decree nisi had been granted should be checked: 'Several of the Judges had said to me that the present practice of delaying for six months in the granting of a decree absolute seemed practically useless, in the absence of some official whose duty it would be to make an independent enquiry into the facts and circumstances of each divorce action.'[8] Such an investigation would ensure that the state rather than the couple controlled the process of divorce.

The actual practice of the Ontario officials is instructive. They were reluctant to intervene; as the deputy attorney-general described the practice, 'so far as possible we follow the practice of the King's Proctor in England, and do not as a rule actively intervene unless facts are brought to our attention.' Elsewhere he defined the official's functions as preventing collusion and seeing that all the facts were before the court. In England the king's proctor usually relied on the judge to draw attention to suspicious cases, but there is no evidence that Canadian judges adopted this practice.[9] Nevertheless, despite their being limited to a reactive policy, the attorney-general's officials were prepared to intervene when sufficient evidence was shown.[10] And in cases of action for nullity, where the Ontario attorney-general became a mandatory defendant as of 1927, officials were quite active. Indeed, in one 1932 case, ministry officials attempted to restrict the definition of nullity by arguing that sexual intercourse before marriage constituted consummation.[11]

No such responsibilities for divorce were assigned to officials in British Columbia, Saskatchewan, or New Brunswick. But Alberta had a king's proctor, who was always an official of the attorney-general's department, and the first provincial rules of practice in divorce, published in 1919, required that notice of application for a decree absolute be filed with either the king's proctor or the attorney-general.[12] In 1928 Manitoba followed suit by appointing the deputy attorney-general as king's proctor. Saskatchewan was content with a practice rule that allowed a judge to permit the attorney-general of the province to intervene. This authority was used on occasion. In 1921, for example, after issuing a decree nisi, the trial judge directed that the pleadings and papers be sent to the attorney general so that he might intervene; he did so, and had the decree set aside by arguing before the trial judge that the plaintiff had deserted the defendant. This result was upheld on appeal.[13] Such a rule placed the initiative for state intervention even more explicitly on the shoulders of the judiciary. But state officials had limited resources, and their other and more pressing responsibilities meant that relatively little time was devoted to the duties of king's proctor.[14]

Indeed, if the Ontario attorney-general's office is representative, civil servants appear to have been much less enamoured of such work than those who did not actually have to carry out the duties. The deputy attorney-general objected that 'there is already sufficient ill-advised and ill-informed meddling' without expanding such work. A king's proctor could labour at a great many 'ill-advised and futile interventions ... without any very beneficial result.' In a 1933 Ontario action for divorce and alimony, counsel for the petitioning wife sought to force the provincial Liquor Control Board to testify as to her husband's liquor permit and his purchases in the previous year. The trial judge was sympathetic to the request; he felt that the Crown should assist as much as possible in matters such as this, where the husband might be spending on alcohol the money that should be going to his wife and children. But the ministry officials dissented: 'I entirely disagree with him, as I cannot see that it is the duty of the Crown to either assist or hinder any parties in private litigation, especially in cases where matrimonial disputes arise.'[15] Unanimity was not a feature of the state's role in such matters.

Divorce litigation, like other civil cases, was subject to the adversarial process. Dissolution of a marriage was not something to be worked out between the parties to the marriage; rather, a neutral arbiter would take into account not only the positions of the parties and the circumstances of their marriage, but also the needs of society at large.[16] The insistence on spousal confrontation was one means of trying to ensure that the ultimate decision in such cases rested with the state on behalf of society. Thus, when the applicant for a parliamentary divorce was required to advertise the application in two local newspapers, the locale referred to was the applicant's rather than the respondent's. Public involvement was solicited at least as much concerning the one party as the other. As well, the adversarial process was a symbolic means of maintaining the fiction that one party was innocent and the other guilty. This was reinforced by the 'clean hands' rule taken from English divorce practice, which held that the 'innocent' petitioner must not be 'guilty' of any other marital misconduct.[17] This enforced confrontation at the individual level was inhibiting – a result undoubtedly welcomed by those who sought to limit divorce. It was not easy for an offending spouse to avoid becoming at least a nominal antagonist. The courts were diligent in searching out missing respondents; if a respondent could not be found, family members in the area were served with a notice of action, and newspaper advertisements were placed in likely locales. The Senate rules required that anyone requesting substitutional service (that is, newspaper advertisements in lieu of notice) should provide evidence that attempts had been made to determine the respondent's whereabouts through his or her friends and relatives. It was thought that involvement of one's family and the possibility of public humiliation would encourage respondents to appear.

An adversarial process added to the stress involved in divorce, as did the procedural requirement that a co-respondent be named. In Nova Scotia this requirement was not enforced; none of the divorces examined in that province showed a co-respondent as a party to an action. In Ontario, however, the rule was sternly enforced, and a court order was needed to waive the requirement. By naming the co-respondent publicly in the style of cause, several purposes were accomplished. Pressure was exerted on respondents to defend their honour if the allegations rested on trumped-up evidence; the alleged adulterer was publicly chastised; and the point was made that this was more than merely a matter between the two spouses. It is ironic as well as tragic that a requirement aimed at enhancing marital stability disrupted a number of additional marriages that had either co-existed at the time of the adultery or had been established since.

The original English legislation of 1857 had required a male plaintiff to name the co-respondent as a party to a suit, but female plaintiffs were required to do so only if the judge so directed. Thus a different form of the gender-based double standard was articulated in law. Two of the western provinces adopted similar rules. While the Saskatchewan courts required that all co-respondents be named, Alberta declined to include co-respondents in the suits, despite the pleas of the provincial chief justice. The Manitoba rules of 1919 were modelled on the English rule. In 1925 British Columbia adopted a similar practice. Where the naming of a co-respondent had not previously been required, it now became compulsory, but only if the third party was male. If she was female, a sealed copy of the pleading containing the allegation was delivered to her; similarly, if a respondent husband answered his wife's petition by charging her with adultery, her alleged partner in adultery was also to receive a sealed

copy of the charge.[18] The strengthening of a gender-biased procedure was thus combined with a desire to protect individual privacy.

In judicial divorce in all provinces it was possible to take evidence
on commission, thus avoiding the expense and inconvenience of
forcing witnesses to travel long distances. This procedure was not
available in parliamentary divorce, where the petitioner had to bring
all the witnesses before the Senate Divorce Committee to testify.
Given the costs and the possible difficulty of persuading witnesses
to travel, this requirement can be seen only as a deliberate obstacle
to divorce.

But it was not only the divorce process that reflected and reinforced certain norms. The same was true of the legal system as a
whole. The notion of presumption of death offers a useful example.
If one's spouse was dead, one had an absolute right to remarry; but
where a spouse had been missing for a long time, death was uncertain (and practically unknowable) and legally unprovable. By law
the remaining spouse could remarry without being liable to prosecution for bigamy if the missing partner had been unheard of for at
least seven years. But this was a far cry from being able to contract
a valid second marriage. Not only did remaining spouses have
trouble obtaining a licence to remarry,[19] but, if the missing spouse
returned at any time, the second marriage would be invalid and the
first would continue undissolved. Understandably, deserted spouses sought to ensure the validity of any remarriage, and some petitioned the courts for a declaration of presumption of death.

Though there was some inconsistency in practice across Canada,
in general the courts refused to issue such rulings for that purpose.
The Ontario courts consistently declined to issue declarations of
presumed death unless the declaration was incidental to another
action; a direct request for a declaration was held to be improper. A
series of Ontario decisions upheld this stance.[20] One case will serve
as an example. Before 1933 a Mr Irvin left his wife 'in circumstances which would not preclude the possibility of his communicating
with her.' Neither she nor his family heard from him. He failed to
attend his mother's funeral or to keep in touch with members of his
family despite his being on friendly terms with them. Advertising and
inquiry at the place of his disappearance and in his home town failed
to produce any information. 'The facts as disclosed in the material,'
said the judge, 'would indicate that this man is probably dead.'
Nevertheless, when Mrs Irvin applied for a declaration of the presumption of death, the judge refused to comply.[21] The Ontario courts
declined to offer a means of solving her dilemma.

The reported decisions suggest that western courts were more flexible, though it was not until the 1940s that such jurisdiction acquired an explicit statutory basis. While the practice in British Columbia and Alberta was inconsistent, at least some petitioners were granted declarations of presumption of death.[22] Manitoba courts were ambivalent. Justice Adamson of the Court of King's Bench pointed out in 1927 that such an order would have no authority regarding remarriage if the missing spouse eventually returned, and suggested that a declaration 'may do harm by misleading some innocent person who might rely upon it.' This is precisely what was happening, but other judges were sometimes willing to assist the individuals involved in gaining that sense of security.[23]

The dilemma created by a negative decision is illustrated by a Manitoba case. Sometime before the First World War the Morgans married and lived in Winnipeg until June 1924, when they separated. Two weeks later Mrs Morgan departed from Winnipeg, leaving behind her husband and two young children. She was not heard from again, and inquiries by her family and friends produced no information about her fate. Fifteen years later her husband Alfred, who wanted to remarry, applied for a declaration of presumption of death so that he might obtain a marriage licence. The trial judge refused to issue the declaration. Admitting that sufficient evidence had been adduced to establish a legal presumption of death, the Manitoba Court of Appeal could find no authority upon which to issue such a declaration and dismissed the appeal.[24] By 1937 the English legislation provided for such declarations, and calls began to be heard from the bench and the legislatures for a similar provision in Canada. None the less, the problem remained unsolved until the 1940s. In the meantime a serious obstacle inhibited Canadian spouses from setting aside a dead marriage and regaining whatever benefits they sought from that institution.

Complementing the divorce process was the most potent weapon in the legal arsenal – the criminal law. Its use in the regulation of marital behaviour is further evidence of the role of the legal environment in reinforcing normative values. The criminal law can impose penalties directly, and has great indirect coercive authority. The federal Criminal Code was the source of many powerful injunctions regarding marital behaviour in this period, and it was also the target of many middle-class reformers.

At the turn of the century the criminal law already contained several relevant prohibitions. In New Brunswick an unrepealed pre-Confederation statute that criminalized adultery was still enforced.[25]

As well, section 310b of the Criminal Code, which was enforced by the courts, declared cohabitation to be illegal when it involved conjugal union with a person who was married to someone else or who lived with someone else in a conjugal union. The section did not apply to adultery without cohabitation or to cohabitation by unmarried persons.[26] In the following two decades efforts were made to extend these laws to cover adultery and extramarital cohabitation throughout the country. In the years before the First World War national and local assemblies of several Christian denominations, branches of the Women's Christian Temperance Union and the Young Women's Christian Association, and the Moral and Social Reform Council of Canada, as well as individual clerics and members of the judiciary, urged the government to strengthen the legislation. While the government consistently resisted this pressure on the ground that such activity was not criminal, it was willing to amend the law to attack some more specific forms of adultery and extramarital intercourse. Thus, the Criminal Code sections dealing with offences such as seduction and prostitution were reinforced.[27]

In the years following 1914 the pressure continued. In 1918, for example, a Roman Catholic priest on Cape Breton Island supported the government's rumoured intention to make it a criminal offence for two unmarried persons to register at a hotel as man and wife:

> However, I ask you whether it be not possible to give us legislation to deal with offences more common and more productive of public scandal than that you propose to legislate against. I refer to the open violation of marriage vows which, I am afraid, has increased alarmingly during the past few years ... I feel sure you will appreciate the importance of this matter, from the standpoint of public decency as well as of religion. It is hard to calculate the harm which the multiplication of such scandals ... will work. It will be fully apparent in another generation.[28]

The Criminal Code continued to be used as a means of attacking adultery indirectly. But by the mid-1920s the lobbying for a direct attack on adultery had come to an end.[29]

In the meantime local magistrates began to use non-criminal legislation to punish some adulterers. Statutes such as the Ontario Children's Protection Act and the federal Juvenile Delinquents Act made it an offence to imperil a child's morality or to contribute to his delinquency. Adultery was defined as doing just that, and in the absence of criminal legislation these lesser statutes were used to punish such deviant marital behaviour. This is demonstrated by the case of Mabel Curtis and Reg Warden. Mabel married John Curtis in April 1905, and left him in July. She had since supported herself and her child; by 1913 her means of support was a boarding-house in Toronto. Reg Warden left his wife and their two minor children in late 1914, and became one of Mabel's boarders. Reg's wife soon laid a charge against Mabel. Accused of contributing to the delinquency of Warden's two children by knowingly keeping company with Warden and thereby depriving the children of proper parental control, Mabel was convicted in Toronto Juvenile Court and sentenced to three months in jail.[30] In this case the law was used to punish desertion as well as adultery.

In 1918 a new clause was added to the Criminal Code making it a crime to contribute to the corruption of a child 'by indulgence in sexual immorality' in the child's home. This provision was given more force in 1933 and 1935, when a further amendment reduced the burden of proof on the Crown: the new legislation made it 'an irrebutable presumption' in any prosecution for corrupting children 'that the child was in danger of being or becoming immoral, its morals injuriously affected and its home rendered an unfit place to be in, upon proof that the person involved did in fact, in the home of such child, participate in adultery, in sexual immorality, in habitual drunkenness, or in any other form of vice.'[31] Local courts were inconsistent in their findings under such legislation; sometimes unmarried persons who lived in a stable conjugal relationship were exempted. But on the whole the purpose of both the statutes and the court decisions was to strengthen the legal environment in defence of the prevailing familial ideal.[32] During the 1920s and 1930s over half of the cases heard by the Toronto Women's Court and the family courts involved persons charged with contributing to the delinquency of a minor.[33]

Similar pressure was exerted to use the law as a means of preventing desertion and non-support. It was already a criminal offence at the turn of the century to fail to provide the necessities of life to one's wife or minor children if the failure resulted in death, danger to life, or permanent injury. A number of associations, particularly charitable agencies dealing with urban welfare, soon began to push for a broader definition of non-support. By 1913 tangible results were apparent. The Criminal Code was amended by removing the onus to establish death, danger, or permanent injury, and the definitions of 'wife' and 'husband' were expanded to include 'common law' relationships; summary conviction for the offence was now possible.

Social workers were urged to use the law against negligent husbands.[34] Not content, reformers continued to press for further changes. The secretary of the New Westminster Benevolent Society, for example, described its members' findings: 'The ladies while investigating the condition of parties requiring relief have frequently found that the father or husband is worthless and won't try to support his family, and sometimes leaves them without anything to subsist on, returning when there are some supplies in the house furnished by the Society to help consume them. In other cases men have spent their wages in drink, leaving their families destitute.' The society suggested that the answer was legislation to force support or to have the men's wages paid to the wives for the benefit of their families.[35] Since many deserters were thought to use the international border to avoid their obligations, concerned Canadians began to press for the inclusion of desertion in the extradition treaty with the United States. The Canadian government passed an order in council to this effect in 1915, and the treaty was eventually amended late in 1922.

Provincial law was also used to enforce certain standards of spousal behaviour. The Ontario Deserted Wives Maintenance Act of 1888, the first such Canadian legislation, allowed a wife to take her husband to court for a support order, using a summary conviction procedure before a local magistrate in a civil proceeding; by the beginning of the twentieth century this act had been strengthened by defining as 'deserted' a wife who had left her husband because of his failure to support her or because of his cruelty. Other provinces soon adopted similar statutes, so that by 1912 all provinces west of Quebec, except Alberta, had such legislation. New Brunswick joined this group in 1926, as did Nova Scotia in 1941.[36]

The provincial maintenance acts are among the most prominent pieces of legislation accepting and reinforcing gender roles within the ideal of the conjugal family. As befitted her status as her husband's dependent, the wife alone was entitled to support from her spouse, and that entitlement was related entirely to her status as wife rather than to her need, except in the British Columbia legislation. The right to support was closely linked to conduct. To retain her entitlement the wife had to present herself as an innocent party in her matrimonial behaviour; proof of adultery would disentitle her. It was necessary to establish that the husband lacked sufficient reason to abandon his matrimonial obligations. The husband was recognized for his role as the wife's protector and as the family breadwinner; the wife was seen as an economic dependent required to remain in the home, except where conditions were legally and demonstrably intolerable; she was entitled to support only if she remained sexually faithful to her husband before and after separation. In some jurisdictions later amendments gave local authorities the right to take action on behalf of the wife against her husband.[37] Matching legislation established or reinforced married women's dower rights; in the prairie provinces in particular new dower statutes protected married women's rights in their homesteads. Other legislation, such as the 1920 Testator's Family Maintenance Act in British Columbia, tried to ensure that male testators provided adequately for their wives and children.[38] The husband's responsibility for his wife and children was underlined, while the wife's rights and benefits were consistently defined in terms of her husband. Indeed, the state enforced matrimonial obligations even when the couple had tacitly or formally ended them. In the public interest the state prevented couples from controlling their own circumstances by insisting on the overriding necessity of their maintaining spousal obligations to one another. In a British Columbia case in which the couple had signed a separation agreement ending the husband's support obligations, the court ruled on appeal that the husband's duties were absolute and could not be dispensed with: as dependents, wives had to be protected against manipulative and irresponsible husbands.[39]

Maintenance legislation was regarded as having been designed to protect marriage and its incumbent duties and responsibilities. A Saskatchewan judge made it clear that desertion was not defined in some narrow physical sense, but rather involved the failure to recognize and discharge 'the common obligations of the married state.' But at the same time the courts were careful not to go too far in giving effect to a statute that accepted, and thus implicitly condoned, the separation of the married couple. In a 1923 case, for example, one British Columbia judge articulated this concern, while finding for the wife: 'I don't think wives should be encouraged in leaving their husbands for insufficient cause, and offering to come back when it suited their convenience to do so.'[40] In quite different ways this legislation attempted to structure the behaviour of both spouses.

The jurisdictional contrast between desertion law and divorce law is striking. The desertion legislation was generally given a rather expansive jurisdiction. It was not domicile that was important, but the place in which the desertion had occurred, in whole or in part. This is apparent in almost all of the statutes and in the case law. In Re Hanlan, for example, the wife had left her husband temporarily with his permission and had then refused to return; the court held that the jurisdiction was determined by the wife's location, since that was the place in which he had failed to provide for her.[41] The contrast with the rather strict interpretation of domicile is most easily explained by the laws' different functions. While the maintenance acts were designed to enforce marital obligations, divorce law dealt with the termination of those obligations. Both operated to reinforce the ideal of the conjugal family.

But for many husbands the maintenance acts probably played only a directive or educational role. Enforcement was a major problem. If a man refused to accept responsibility for the support of his family, no law could change that. At best the man could be shamed into modifying his behaviour; at worst he could simply be punished. Welfare agencies spent a good deal of energy and expense in pursuing negligent husbands and fathers and bringing them to prosecution but the exercise was costly and often fruitless for the family involved. Even if prosecution was successful, there was no guarantee that the husband would continue to obey a support order. In any case, support orders were not binding in any other province (much less outside the country). Nevertheless, the agencies were actively discussing the problem and looking for legislative solutions.[42] It was recognized at least by the late 1920s that the pursuit of deserting husbands was not cost effective, since the costs of finding the deserters was greater than the money subsequently given to their deserted families. But state and quasi-state agencies decided to pursue deserting husbands in spite of the policy's ineffectiveness. To do otherwise would have questioned the power of the law and the relative importance of prescribed marital roles, and this was something most of Canadian society was unprepared to do.[43]

The difficulties of attaining any practical results are exemplified by a 1930 case. When a Massachusetts district attorney applied to the Brockville, Ontario, police for the arrest of a local man for failure to provide, the application was forwarded to Toronto. The deputy attorney-general pointed out that extradition proceedings must be instituted and that by Canadian law there must be proof that those deserted had been left in destitute or necessitous circumstances. The alleged deserter was held pending application by the American authorities, but when more than a month had elapsed without action, the deputy attorney-general complained strongly. It was 'ridiculous' to spend so much time on such a case; 'in fact I think it was a great mistake to have added the offence to the Extradition Treaty. In the experience of this office extradition is quite futile for offences of this nature and we never attempt it because, as you know, the accused is returned and an order made against him for payment, which is usually ignored and the accused goes away again and the extradition proceedings might have to be repeated half a dozen times.'[44] The law officers reiterated the tension between the ideal and the practicable; yet these same officers searched for techniques to make desertion laws more effective.[45]

Nevertheless, various local welfare agencies pursued their responsibilities by making use of the legal processes. In Montreal, for example, the Family Welfare Association (FWAM) and the Society for the Protection of Women and Children (MSPWC) worked together on cases of desertion and non-support. Within the umbrella association of Protestant charities in Montreal, each organization had distinct but complementary duties. The FWAM was the basic family welfare and casework agency; its aim was 'to conserve and develop family life as the foundation of human society.' Individuals were of interest primarily because they were members of a family. The MSPWC lobbied both for the enactment of suitable laws for the protection of women and children and for the subsequent enforcement of those laws. Agents of the society had the authority to act not merely as social caseworkers, but also as commissioners of the Superior Court, justices of the peace, and special constables of the provincial police.[46] These bridging institutions were designed to supplement and encourage state agencies in their protection of the family and their enforcement of marital norms.

The MSPWC was particularly concerned about 'the problem of troubled and disturbed conditions of family behaviour, where the causes appear traceable to the neglect or delinquency of responsible parties.' Within this broad area, 'behaviour arising out of ignorance of, or open disregard of, the obligations arising from a contract of marriage,' such as neglect, cruelty, or immorality, was singled out for attention.[47] This perspective made the society especially sensitive to the problem of desertion and non-support. In 1920 the society acted as the voice for a group of thirteen city agencies seeking a more assertive Criminal Code. It urged Parliament to enact legislation making it an offence for a husband and wife to live apart without reasonable excuse and without the consent of a magistrate or judge.[48] When this initiative failed, the society's agents used their quasi-legal status and their knowledge of individual cases to assist or re-establish many marriages in Montreal. The society handled the tracing of deserting husbands on behalf of the Montreal Council of Social Agencies, and did so rather aggressively. Caseworkers tracked down husbands in various cities in Canada and the United States, negotiated support settlements, and, where necessary and advisable, paid to have the delinquent arrested and returned to Montreal, where he was taken to court. The society's annual reports boasted of the number of husbands pursued and the types of solutions employed. In 1933, for example, the society accepted 822 new cases. Of those, 306 simply involved matters of legal aid. Of the remainder, 222 (43 per cent) involved desertion, non-support, or neglect. The society reported satisfactory adjustment or rehabilitation in 69.9 per cent of those cases. In 61 cases of desertion, 26 absent spouses were located; in 163 non-support cases, 97 husbands (59.5 per cent) were persuaded to begin making support payments. If the husband could not be persuaded to meet his familial obligations of support, the society often swore a warrant against him; in the 13 such cases in 1933 in which court action had been completed, convictions were obtained in all but one case. This court work represented an absolute decline from previous years, the society bragged in its annual report, and was proof of the growing effectiveness of its agents' ability to win voluntary acceptance of the behavioural standards.[49]

Despite this alleged success, the process of coercion of deviant spouses was frustrating to social workers. The Montreal Council of Social Agencies objected that such problems were not taken seriously enough by governments. 'Social agencies in Montreal are handicapped through failure of public authorities to enforce desertion and non-support laws,' said the executive committee in 1931, 'and inadequate financial provision for the pursuit and apprehension of deserters or the prosecution of those, who, without lawful excuse, fail to provide their families with the necessities of life.' At other times agencies were not certain that such responses would be adequate in the absence of even broader legislative activity. In 1929 the FWAM complained that the pursuit of deserters 'often reveals the inadequacy of present methods, and the need for strengthening inter-provincial legislation, as well as the ties of family life. To return a man to the home from which he ran away is only to court recurrence of the deed, and it is part of our Visitors' work to find the causes that brought disruption into the home.' One of the basic causes, said the FWAM, was the inegalitarian character of marriage. Too many men looked on their wives 'as something to devour and destroy,' and it was hard to convince them that 'the only human relations that have value are those that are rooted in mutual freedom, where there is no domination and no slavery, and no tie except affection.'[50]

But it is unclear just how many observers perceived such a basic flaw in the contemporary character of marriage. More often commentators felt, as indeed did the FWAM and the MSPWC, that more effective laws were the answer. In a study of broken homes in the 1920s, the secretary of the Social Welfare Commission of Winnipeg suggested that more stringent marriage laws, the establishment of courts of domestic relations, and tougher desertion laws might solve the problem. The secretary agreed that existing laws and enforcement were ineffective, but 'so long as a law is on the Statute Books it should be enforced, if for no other reason than to uphold the majesty of the law.' What was needed was more rigorous enforcement. Therefore, responsibility for desertion should be placed in the hands of the Royal Canadian Mounted Police, who had a nationwide jurisdiction and a reputation for always getting their man.[51]

The demand for tougher marriage laws was echoed many times across the dominion in the second and third decades of the twentieth century.[52] Action was taken in all provinces to establish and enforce stricter licensing procedures, greater regulation of the marriage ceremony in terms of official and of place, and more parental control over minor children. In some jurisdictions medical or eugenic standards were articulated. In the Winnipeg study the first solution offered was a greater state control over nuptiality: 'Marriage is too easy. It will be seen that marriage is entered into by girls of tender years, without realizing what is before them, and often on the spur of the moment. Surely we could by proper publicity make some of these youngsters pause, so that they may realize that the only basis of marriage is mutual understanding.' To this end four practical steps were recommended. First, the authority to issue marriage licences should be given to a local public official in each community. Second, there should be a waiting period between the application for and the issuance of a marriage licence. The recommended period was two weeks; elsewhere the period was often closer to one week. The idea was the same: to stop hasty marriages through legal devices. Third, the names and addresses of the parties to the application should be published, and the public invited to disclose information as to why the licence should not be issued; the publicity would prevent 'clandestine' unions. Finally, 'in view of the appalling number of sex factor cases, involving the physical ruin of both men and women,' both parties to the application should be required to produce medical certification of good health.[53]

Time and again arguments and proposals such as these were voiced by individuals and organizations. The legislators listened, and cautiously enacted those regulations that were practicable. Parental control was reinforced by the demand for affidavits of consent. The authority to issue licences was given to local officials with no direct commercial interests, and taken away from the jewellery and furniture stores that had been using licences as a means of attracting business. Clergy were approved individually, and the ceremony itself increasingly became a public event. It was hoped that these changes would thwart attempts to use weddings as commercial attractions in depression-era walkathons and dance marathons. Finally, in the 1930s British Columbia, Alberta, and Saskatchewan imposed medical requirements on licence applicants.[54]

The Winnipeg study proposed to reinforce the statutory changes by the institution of specialized domestic relations courts. These courts of domestic relations were to be judicially distinctive. A product of sociological jurisprudence, these forerunners of the family courts were first established in the United States. Rather than simply adjudicating and enforcing the law, courts of domestic relations functioned as 'social clinics.' They were designed to explore sympathetically the problems that were disrupting the life of individual families and to mediate solutions rather than to impose punishments. Such courts would use indirect coercion by persuading family members to abjure deviant behaviour, with the threat of more direct coercion by other courts lurking in the background: as one Montreal observer put it in 1914, 'The maintenance of the little home by strenuously forcing the husband to work and to provide for the home is better than breeding criminals by the wholesale' through simple incarceration.[55]

By the beginning of the 1920s the idea had gained considerable popularity among reformers. The Canadian Council on Child Welfare commissioned a pamphlet discussing the proposal. This support from social work organizations illustrates one of the primary characteristics of the domestic relations court: the court's 'true function,' explained the pamphlet, would best be met by utilizing 'those forms of social service which are helpful in healing breaches and allaying misunderstandings.' Social workers would be essential components of such courts. And because the emphasis was on solving family problems and healing breaches, it would be inappropriate to give domestic relations courts any jurisdiction over divorce or annulment. 'The very power to undo the marriage tie might, and probably would, insidiously tend to weaken the all-important emphasis on conservation of family values.' Instead the courts should be limited to providing constructive services designed to 'contribute to the permanence and efficiency of the marriage relationship on the basis of helpful home life' and to defend the ideology of the family.[56]

A new and potentially intrusive judicial office was thus proposed.

Social workers, as officers of the court, would conduct personal interviews and examine the home environment, acting as 'any wise and impartial friend.' Private hearings were considered essential. A process of conciliation, in which legal and evidentiary rules were dispensed with to the extent possible, and the use of non-incarcerative techniques were of prime importance. A new group of state officials would assist in the maintenance of family and marital stability by offering advice, articulating higher standards of behaviour, and ultimately using the threat of legal coercion to achieve their ends. Slowly, such institutions began to appear in major Canadian cities. At first this happened informally; for example, a separate Women's Court was established in Toronto shortly before the First World War, and domestic cases were heard separately beginning in the early 1920s in Ottawa. Then, in 1929, the Ontario government authorized the first Court of Domestic Relations in Toronto as an adjunct of the local juvenile court.

Deputy Judge Hosking, who handled all of the judicial work of the Toronto court, described its practice. Reconciliation attempts were technically optional, he explained, but were made in virtually every case; only in cases of serious spousal assault or perhaps a case of long-standing and seemingly irreconcilable differences was a summons issued immediately. Normally, when a spouse (usually the wife) came to the court with a complaint, a letter was sent to the husband by the probation officer, who then heard both parties and attempted a reconciliation. If he succeeded, a local social agency might be asked to supervise the couple, since the court itself had no personnel available for this task: 'We find them very co-operative and willing to assume the supervision of these cases,' said Hosking. If the attempted settlement failed, the social worker then got in touch with the court and, if necessary, returned the case to the court. Though no statistical record of case dispositions had been kept, Hosking was confident of the efficacy of the process: 'Personally, I know of many [cases] that are successes, and of some that are not.'[57] The new courts were established slowly and on only a limited basis; by the end of the 1930s there were domestic relations courts in Toronto, Montreal, Ottawa, Hamilton, and York County, Ontario. Vancouver and Winnipeg were added to the list by the mid-1940s.

Despite such slow growth, the family court structure had an impact on the disposition of cases. Dorothy Chunn has tabulated the operations of the Toronto Juvenile and Family Court in this period. With the founding of that court in 1929 the number of cases handled under the various statutes rose markedly. In the period between 1920 and 1928, when there was only a Juvenile Court, an annual average of 6,719 cases had been dealt with; in the 1930s the new court heard 12,594 cases. What was more, nearly all of the increase was accounted for by occurrence interviews – that is, cases that did not reach the stage of formal court hearings. In the 1930s probation officers and social workers attached to the court handled 75.2 per cent of all cases.[58] This was not unplanned: when the court was organized in 1929, the senior judge was explicit about his expectations. Occurrence interviews would allow the Domestic Relations Court to operate as 'really a clinic where parents could come with their difficulties without any stigma or stain of a Court action and have adjustments made and difficulties settled, while preserving and capitalizing the good name of the various parties affected.' To ensure the effective carrying out of this extrajudicial procedure, the judge arranged for the appointment of a chief probation officer skilled in occurrence interview techniques.[59]

What is more, senior government officials wanted this new judicial system to operate in just such an informal yet supervisory fashion. In 1934 the deputy attorney-general of Ontario described his view of the family court:

> The head of a Family Court settles many difficulties of a domestic nature. He gets the people in before him and deals with the case, usually, if possible, without the necessity of the laying of any Information, or bringing the matter into Court. It is a gradual process of plain talking and the working out of the best system possible, to prevent many matters which disrupt a home (such as adultery, drunkenness, quarrelling, etc.). That is the main idea behind the establishment of a Family Court – not to have this by legislation, but by moral suasion and supervision.[60]

This was precisely the system instituted. But that was not all. Like the judges in the juvenile courts, the magistrates in the early domestic relations courts 'shut our eyes to legal technicalities and rules of evidence in the interest of domestic peace,' in the words of H.A. Burbridge, the police magistrate of Hamilton, 'without any harm having been done to anyone.' What was more, these courts could do an even more effective job if their authority was expanded. Burbidge encouraged the government to expand the powers of the domestic relations courts: they should have the power to subpoena third parties who might be interfering in or disrupting the stability of the family; greater use should be made of recognizances; and the courts should be able to hear cases involving drunkenness and adultery. In short, as Dorothy Chunn has argued, these new family courts operated in much the same way as the police courts had long done in upholding middle-class standards of morality and family life, and among the same class of clients.[61]

Nor was the judiciary in such a role limited to family courts. There is clear evidence in some of the divorce records that judges, magistrates, and even counsel saw it as their duty to preserve existing marriages and to defend the marital ideal. In a 1921 Nova Scotia trial, the petitioning wife testified that after she had learned of her husband's adultery, she went to a justice of the peace for a dissolution of the marriage. Instead he drew up a separation agreement, which 'he said was as good as a divorce.' Only later, when her neighbours told her that divorce was a more complex procedure, did the woman suspect that she had been given something less than what she sought. Other magistrates promoted the dominant familial ideal by coercing young men to marry pregnant young women; occasionally they pointed a finger at the wrong man.[62]

The courts were not the only institution devoted to maintaining this divorce environment. The law enforcement agencies worked closely with the other participants in the justice system towards the same end. Police at all levels of jurisdiction were directly involved in the maintenance of the ideal of the conjugal family as expressed in the criminal and civil law and by the courts. At the national level, the Justice and Immigration departments instructed the police to investigate individual family disputes. At the local level, police departments worked closely with magistrate's, juvenile, and family courts in dealing with family-related disputes. The informal adjudication and counselling provided by family and juvenile court social workers was matched by similar work on the part of police officers. One section of the Toronto Police Department, for example, operated as a family complaints bureau: domestic settlements were informally negotiated and support payments for deserted wives were collected. That this section of the police force was called the Morality Department communicated an underlying message to those who came in contact with the office.

As Greg Marquis has pointed out, the police force's social service function assumed major proportions in early twentieth-century Toronto. The Morality Department had a vested interest in co-operating with social agencies to regulate the marital behaviour of the working class. Indeed, the police officers, both men and women, were 'far more important interpreters of family law than were the courts' on a day-to-day basis. Marquis has estimated that the number of domestic disputes reaching the courts represented only 1 to 3 per cent of the total in any given year. Urban residents, particularly women, who feared or could not afford the formal legal process called upon the police to settle family disputes. The number of Morality Department cases doubled after the First World War, and the amount of money collected in support payments from husbands and fathers rose even faster. The police may have been relied on by women and members of the working class, but they were not a neutral force; Marquis has argued that the Toronto morality officers 'projected a strongly traditional view of the family' in their work.[63]

Particularly in rural and smaller urban areas, the police sometimes became directly involved in individual divorce cases. Occasionally, police officers were called as witnesses to family disputes or to acts of immorality. More often a local constable or some similar official acted as a process server, giving notice to the respondent or co-respondent of various stages of a divorce action and serving the associated petitions and affidavits.

This police involvement at the local and federal levels gave the legal process and the civil dispute an authority that was important to the sanction claimed for divorce. One example of the federal use of the police occurred in 1910. An Austrian-born male had come to Canada in 1904–5, promising to send for his wife once he was settled and had accumulated enough money. Finally in 1909 she gave up waiting, sold all her property in the old country, and emigrated. Once in Canada she could not find her husband, who was no longer at his last known residence in Manitoba. But eventually she heard that her husband was 'remarried' and working in Ottawa under a different name. In a letter to the minis-ter of justice, the wife described her desperate economic circumstances: 'Therefore I beg very kindly your Excellency to enquire into this matter, force my husband to gave me support or let he release me from being his wife and then I will work for my living or marry another man.' The minister asked the Dominion Police to verify the report. Within two weeks they reported that the husband was living at 287 York Street as Harry Krochak with a woman and two children who were known as his wife and family; the police were careful to point out that Krochak's was a stable and economically successful family situation. The minister conscientiously passed all of this information on to Krochak's first wife, and advised her that she had a right to undertake proceedings to compel him to support her.[64] There are many similar instances of the department's use of the police.

In the same way, police were available to king's proctors in their investigations. In one Alberta case the king's proctor, acting on a suspicion that a female plaintiff had herself committed adultery, ordered a police constable to investigate. The constable visited the apartment of the wife's alleged lover at 9:00 AM and found the wife and her lover in dressing-gowns. The lover admitted to the constable that they had been cohabiting for several months. The king's proctor called the constable to give evidence, and used his testimony to persuade the trial judge to refuse a decree absolute.[65]

The records of the Royal Canadian Mounted Police also reveal the extent of that force's activities in connection with marital behaviour. The Mounties regularly answered inquiries about lost friends and relatives on the prairies. Missing persons notices and investigations were used by spouses, families, and police to track down deserting wives and husbands. Where a husband's support payments were insufficient or non-existent, local constables took action. In one instance, for example, a husband was retrieved from Calgary, where he had been working, and taken to his family sixty-five miles away. There the constable took the family and husband to a local store, where 'a complete outfit of food' was purchased. The officer was pleased to report that the husband had decided to stay on with his family.[66] Officials of the Royal North-West Mounted Police were inclined to moralize. In a case of foreign desertion and non-support, for example, the commissioner thought it unlikely that there was any legal provision by which the husband could be forced to provide for his family, 'but I think it might be well, if he can be located, to have him interviewed and ask what provision he intends to make for them. The desertion by fathers of their wives and families is becoming so frequent now that it is receiving attention at the hands of those in charge of Legislation with a view to the adoption of some measure which will have the effect of restricting the practice.'[67] Such attitudes were often tempered by a sympathetic awareness of local and individual circumstances. Officers were willing to condone desertion, for example, if it had occurred as a result of a spouse's serious misbehaviour. In 1912 a Glasgow electrician asked the RNWMP to investigate his wife, who was living in a small Saskatchewan town. After leading an adulterous life in Scotland, she had, he charged, deserted him and their two 'helpless' girls (aged eleven and nine), and left for Canada with their six-year-old. Bragging of 'her intentions of passing as a dashing young widow and taking the first chance of the first good husband she got,' she had recently sent to Glasgow for her two girls, whom the husband had had to place with the local Parish

Council. It was a 'gross injustice' that the colonies should be used as a refuge for such people; would the police please quietly inquire about the life she was leading? The police constable found that the wife and her son were living in a small house on the outskirts of town, where she supported herself and the boy by nursing and taking in washing. The boy attended school, and local reports had it that she was 'a hard working and respectable woman.' According to the wife, her husband was an alcoholic who had abused her and had refused to support his family; he had been incarcerated at least four times for these offences; during the last incarceration the two girls had been put in charge of the Parish Council, and the wife had left. The wife now wanted to bring the two girls over to Canada. The officer's total acceptance of the wife's version of the story is apparent throughout his report. Here was a woman who was behaving properly, according to the prevailing ideals of womanhood; she deserved support and protection. 'Not one person had a word to say against Mrs Jackson in any way,' he concluded. 'All speaks well of her.'[68]

This sympathetic police treatment is important, but not surprising. Both the commissioner of the RNWMP and the local officers, in their policies and actions reinforced the same norms that the reformers sought to enshrine in legislation. In doing so the police added the weight of their authority to those ideals, aiding and protecting those who conformed and chastening those who did not.

It is possible to view this legal environment as a product of and a means to social control. There is unquestionably a negative or defensive character to a good deal of the debate and the law. Social class was an important motivating factor, as middle-class reformers and officials sought to find ways to change the marital behaviour of some members of the working class. This attitude pervades the discussions of marriage law by social workers, clergy, social reformers, legislators, and judges. It unquestionably affected the application of the law and legal process. One early example of this must suffice. In August 1904 an American immigrant homesteader deserted his wife and six children near Estevan, Saskatchewan; he was reported to be working as a hired hand on a North Dakota farm. The reaction of the investigating officer is instructive: 'Findley is a lazy good for nothing fellow. He will only work for a time and he drinks a good deal. It appears to me that Canada is getting [to be] the dumping ground for all the worthless characters from the States who come here and take up homesteads and have no means to support at all when they arrive.'[69] Findley's shortcomings as a husband and father were inseparably connected with his provenance and his work habits.

The legal infrastructure that permitted investigation of the family life of the deviant has been depicted by some scholars as exceedingly intrusive and manipulative.[70] As far as it goes, that interpretation has a good deal of validity. But there is more to the creation of the environment surrounding marriage and the family than the defensive impulse to control the lives of others. There was a desire for real improvement in marriage and family life. This was more than mere rhetoric; delay was at the heart of the divorce process because of the very real belief that marriages could and ought to be saved. Courts and police were active in translating that belief into real terms; through counselling and advice, their informal pressure on individual family members offered alternative solutions to divorce. Organizations associated with social reform, such as the Young Women's Christian Association and the churches, matched this concern by offering their own alternatives, and in the early 1930s these groups began to give marriage counselling and marriage preparation courses.

Nevertheless, these attempts to offer positive alternatives were limited in scope and number. Far too many observers and participants relied naïvely on the law and the legal process to protect the institution of marriage and to reform deviant marital behaviour. The efforts to regulate marriage, and through it the family and society, faced some intractable problems. They failed to address in any substantive way the realities of marital problems among early twentieth-century Canadian couples – problems such as cruelty and spousal violence, and desertion and non-support. As one British commentator observed of similar reforms in England, 'reforms of the marriage law without change in [working class women's] economic position may be of little use to many whose lives are being ruined by marriage.' Legislation that was not accompanied by an increase in the available social support systems was unlikely to lead to any overall improvement in Canadian family life.[71] The creation, elaboration, and maintenance of the legal network of support for particular types of marital behaviour was deceptive. Social reformers and legislators thought they were responding to the changing needs and demands of the institution. But in reality their responses were largely negative and, as will be seen in later chapters, ineffective in direct terms.

The first four decades of the twentieth century saw the acceptance of a number of measures designed to enhance and protect a particular form of marriage and marital behaviour as part of the prevailing familial ideal. The importance of these developments lay only partially in their limited legislative achievements. Both the continuing debate and the statutory results of the movement to control marriage had important indirect (or extralegal) results. The law played a major educational role, showing Canadians through its rewards and punishments and through its public and symbolic activity what was acceptable in marital, familial, and sexual behaviour. In this way the extended discussion of these various marital problems as much as the different legal solutions contributed in a major way to informing the public regarding marriage and marital behaviour. Some practices were condemned, others were legitimated. Norms were rearticulated and reinforced. Nowhere is this more evident than in the case of traditional gender roles. When men and women conformed to their prescribed roles, they could expect the full weight of the legal apparatus to support them; those who violated the prescriptions could expect no sympathy and no support. Indeed, the defence of gender roles at times took precedence over the policy of marital unity and stability, as was apparent in the case of the Scottish woman who had left her husband in Glasgow. The perception of the roles of men and women shaped the law and its application. A single sexual standard was beginning to be advocated by middle-class observers across the Western world, and men, as the beneficiaries of the 'double standard,' were naturally the targets of much of this reform. Adultery, desertion, and non-support were all seen to be chiefly the result of male activity which created problems for passive females. Those problems deserved serious attention. Middle-class men could agree with women on this issue because their class perspective allowed them to distance themselves from the problem.

United to a considerable extent in their beliefs regarding gender and class, men and women and reformers and legislators, of the early twentieth century created a legal environment that both complemented and helps to explain the divorce environment in those years.[72] Where divorce reform was very limited, reform of the broader marriage law was more extensive and much more active. Marriage law reform was a substitute for divorce reform, and reflects the importance of stability in marriage and the family. The mere presence of a considerable number of Roman Catholic legislators and voters in Canada does not explain the absence of divorce reform. Those who produced the legal environment surrounding marriage also participated in a significant and continuing debate about the place of divorce in a modern society.

Part 2

DIVORCE
BEHAVIOUR

6

The Demography of Marriage and Divorce

If the divorce environment in Canada in the early twentieth century was restrictive, manipulative, and conservative, it remains to be seen just what impact that environment had on the behaviour of couples intent on dissolving their marriages. There is considerable evidence that individual Canadians were seeking to gain greater control over marriage, and a more extensive use of divorce was one means of accomplishing this. By the end of the 1930s, long before the formal divorce rate had reached its pre-1968 peak, the basic demographic characteristics of modern divorce – to the extent that they can be examined with the available data – were present in Canada. Women were now the predominant initiators of formal and informal divorce; they used a variety of methods to defend their interests and to gain a marriage that met their own needs, or to end one that no longer did so. To gain an understanding of this behaviour it is important first to discuss the demographics of marriage, some aspects of which have received a much more detailed historical examination than divorce.[1]

Canadian men and women followed the Western European tradition of relatively late marriage. During the second half of the nineteenth century this pattern was intensified as the singulate mean age at marriage showed a marked and steady rise.[2] The increase reflected changing economic circumstances. The declining supply of cheap agricultural land in eastern and central Canada led to a significant migration of young people from the rural areas there to urban centres, the prairie provinces, and the United States. This reordering itself tended to delay marriage, and produced an imbalance in sex ratios in both rural and urban areas. The result was a significant rise in the age at first marriage. For males the average moved from 26.1 years in 1851 to 29.1 in 1891; for females the comparable figures were 23.0 and 26.0. By 1921 the figure had dropped for females to 24.3 before beginning to rise again; it reached 25.1 in 1931. For males the changes were slower and less marked; the age at first marriage was slightly higher in 1911 (29.2) than in 1891. Not until 1921 was there a decline (to 28.0). During the 1920s the figure began to rise as it had for females, and reached 28.5 by 1931. Ellen Gee suspects that a trend towards a younger age at first marriage was already underway for both sexes, but was hidden by the effect of immigration on the figures.[3] Certainly both sexes experienced an almost identical sharp drop in age at first marriage during the 1930s, and the drop was common to all provinces (see table 3).

These figures reflect some basic characteristics of nuptiality in Canada. Women have consistently married at a younger age than men. In the decennial figures for 1851–1931, the sex difference in singulate mean age at marriage was never less than 2.6 years (in 1861), and rose in the early twentieth century. In 1911 and 1921 it was 4.3 (almost twice the difference in 1971 – 2.2), and fell to 3.4 in 1931. Since modern studies of divorce have found that the age differences between spouses correlate directly with the divorce rate,[4] this development may be important. Beyond that, the relatively late age at first marriage for females was of potential importance to marital fertility.

Marriage was, as always, a highly popular institution.[5] The marriage rate rose when economic conditions were favourable and declined when the economy slowed. But overall the proportion of people marrying was high. Nevertheless, the relatively low incidence of nuptiality in the early twentieth century, particularly among males, is striking, and perhaps reflects the great tide of male-dominated immigration at the time and the strong adherence to endogamous

TABLE 3

Average age at first marriage, 1891–1951[1]

	1891	1911	1921	1931	1941	1951
Males						
Canada	29.1[2]	29.2	28.0	28.5	26.3	24.3
PEI	31.1	31.0	30.0	29.7	26.4	25.1
NS	30.1	29.5	28.7	28.7	25.6	24.8
NB	29.4	28.8	27.7	28.2	25.6	24.4
Quebec	27.5	27.4	27.3	28.5	26.8	25.1
Ontario	29.3	28.8	27.7	28.0	25.8	24.4
Manitoba	29.8	29.5	28.5	29.3	26.5	25.0
Sask.	–	30.6	29.1	29.2	26.3	25.2
Alberta	–	30.7	29.2	29.0	26.3	24.8
BC	32.7	31.5	28.5	29.1	26.8	24.9
Females						
Canada	26.0[2]	24.9	24.3	25.1	23.0	22.0
PEI	27.9	27.8	26.5	25.7	22.8	21.6
NS	26.4	25.7	24.8	24.9	22.4	21.6
NB	26.3	25.4	24.3	24.7	22.0	21.0
Quebec	25.3	25.1	25.1	26.4	23.9	22.6
Ontario	26.6	25.8	24.7	24.9	22.7	21.9
Manitoba	23.8	24.2	24.0	25.2	23.0	21.9
Sask.	–	22.3	22.4	23.8	22.4	21.7
Alberta	–	22.8	22.6	23.6	22.2	21.6
BC	22.3	23.7	23.8	24.8	23.3	22.1

SOURCE: Ellen Gee, 'Fertility and Marriage Patterns in Canada: 1851–1971,'
168, 221

1 Figures for 1891–1931 are computed singulate mean ages at first marriage; figures for 1941–51 are median ages at first marriage.
2 Excluding the Northwest Territories

marital norms regarding racial, religious and national groups. In the
second half of the nineteenth century, the percentage of single (that
is, never married) males aged 45 to 49 varied between 6.7 and 10.3;
but by 1911 that percentage had jumped to 15.1 and remained high
for the next three decades (the figure was 14.2 per cent in 1941).
Markedly fewer men were marrying in the early twentieth century,
but this pattern is less apparent among females. The figures for the

second half of the nineteenth century vary between 7.3 per cent and 11.3 per cent; in 1911 the percentage rose to 12.0, fell to 11.1 in 1921 and 10.3 in 1931, and rose again to 11.2 in 1941. While marriage remained the norm for an overwhelming proportion of the adult Canadian population, a small and slightly growing minority did not participate in the institution. The nuptial behaviour of this minority can be explained in part by the sex ratio. In the second half of the nineteenth century the number of males of marrying age was consistently lower than the number of females.[6] But early twentieth-century immigration reversed that imbalance. By 1911 there were 116.5 such males for every 100 females; thereafter the numbers tended towards an even balance, so that by 1941 the ratio of males was 99.6.

While these aggregate figures are illustrative of the overall picture nationally, they mask some of the basic factors that influenced the demographic patterns. For example, there are some important geographical differences whether one discusses these phenomena in terms of provinces or of an urban-rural dichotomy. The proportion of young adult males to young adult females was far higher in the four western provinces than elsewhere in the early twentieth century. In 1911 the number of young men per 100 young women was 197.9 in Saskatchewan and 251.9 in British Columbia.[7] Given the relative scarcity of women in the west, it is not surprising to find that the singulate mean age at marriage was lower than the national figure for females and higher for males. This in turn would have tended to increase the age difference between spouses in those provinces. The other regions reflect their own patterns (see table 3).

Similarly, the marriage patterns in rural society contrasted with those in urban Canada. In 1931 there were 81.8 young marriageable males for every 100 young marriageable females in urban Canada.[8] In rural Canada the imbalance was reversed – 100 females to 171.9 males. This demographic fact affected marriage in both locales. The singulate mean age at marriage for females was 23.9 years in rural areas, 26.0 in urban. Females were more likely to marry, and to marry earlier, in rural Canada. In 1931 only 7.1 per cent of rural females aged 45 to 49 were single, compared with 12.4 per cent in urban areas.

Ethnicity was another factor in demographic patterns. In 1931 11.6 per cent of females of British and French origin were single between the ages of 45 and 64. Women of both ethnic groups showed a similar tendency to marry at a later age: 65.4 per cent of British and 66.8 per cent of French women aged 20 to 24 were single. Among females of other Western European origin, 56.6 per cent were single at ages 20 to 24, and just 6.2 per cent at ages 45 to 64. In the same year, 41.4 per cent of females of other European origin were single at ages 20 to 24, and 1.5 per cent at ages 45 to 64. The native peoples of Canada had their own demographic pattern: 34.0 per cent of females were single at ages 20 to 24, and 2.7 per cent at ages 45 to 64.[9] A somewhat different pattern is revealed for the cohort of married women born between 1887 and 1896. In 1941 married women of British origin aged 45 to 54 had married at a later age than women of other ethnic groups. Just 57.9 per cent of British women had married at or before age 25, in contrast to 62.8 per cent of those of French origin and 65 per cent of those of other ethnic origin.

Ethnicity was important in another way. There was considerable debate in early twentieth-century Canada about 'mixed' marriages between persons of different races, nationalities, or religions. At times the debate was heated; the mixed marriage became a metaphor for the ubiquitous and unending question of relations between French- and English-speaking Canadians.[10] That 'mixed' marriages were the subject of much discussion, which sometimes became quite nasty, is of no doubt. But just how common exogamous marriages were in the early twentieth century is uncertain.

However, the rate of endogamy / exogamy has received relatively limited attention to date, despite its potential for revealing much about the character of interrelationships in Canadian society. Little information can be retrieved from the aggregate census figures, though two studies of 'interfaith' marriage suggest that the rate of exogamy in the early twentieth century was very low. The *Canada Year Book* sets out, by province, aggregate data showing that women were consistently more likely than men to wed in their province of birth and that both sexes in the longer-settled portions of the country had high rates of homogamy. More recently, Lucia Ferretti has examined levels of exogamy in a francophone working-class Montreal parish in the first few years of the twentieth century. In a detailed investigation of the published banns, she reveals that the level of exogamy was quite low, particularly for females. Spatially, 95.9 per cent of the females married in their own parish, compared with 41.4 per cent of the males. But most males (90.4 per cent) came from Montreal, compared with 99.0 per cent for females, so that the extent of geographical openness for males can be easily exaggerated. While only 4.2 per cent of the marriages were between members of different ethnic groups, social class was almost as powerful a factor – 92 per cent of females married within their own class of origin.[11]

There can be little doubt that social class was an important variable. Studies elsewhere confirm this,[12] though in Canada the aggregate data do not allow direct testing for this factor. Nevertheless, it is possible to draw inferences from some of the data. For those ever married, for example, the 1941 census makes it clear that level of educational attainment directly correlated with age at first marriage. The lower the level of school-leaving, the lower the age at first marriage. Similarly, heads of households with higher incomes tended to have married later. Such factors expose important variations in the patterns of nuptiality in early twentieth-century Canada.

The nuptial behaviour of Canadian men and women was changing in significant ways. That this affected marital behaviour is undoubted, but the manner and extent of that effect remain to be examined. One demographic effect that can be measured is fertility. If all other factors remain constant, a drop in female age at first marriage will have a positive impact on fertility. But in Canada, as in much of the Western world at this time, fertility did not increase in spite of earlier marriages. During the period from 1891 to 1921 the general fertility rate remained relatively stable, after a rapid decline at least since the mid-nineteenth century.[13] Since 1851 the general fertility rate had fallen precipitously from 206.5 in the province of Canada to 131.4 for the dominion as a whole. But for the next three decades the change was only marginal, as a continuing decline in fertility was counterbalanced by increasing nuptiality; by 1921 the fertility rate was still 128.1. During the 1920s and 1930s the decline increased markedly, particularly during the 1920s. By 1931 the general fertility rate was 99.5; it fell to 89.1 by 1941. To put it another way, Canadian women gave birth to an average of 6.8 children in 1871, 4.7 in 1911, and 2.6 in 1937.[14] This change is equally evident if female first-marriage cohorts are studied. J. Légaré has calculated that the average number of children ever born per woman fell steadily from 4.46 for the 1910–14 cohort to 3.29 for the 1935–39 cohort.[15]

Those same marriage cohorts that passed through the divorce environment under study here were altering their nuptial behaviour and their family size. For females, a lower age at first marriage increased potential fertility. Despite this, fertility rates fell in the early twentieth century. It is clear that Canadian couples were controlling and even reducing their fertility. For individual couples on an aggregate basis, marriage was changing not merely in terms of attitudes and expectations, but in very real and substantial ways.[16] There were also important changes in fertility patterns. The rate of change differed for various age groups. For females in their 30s and 40s, the decline in fertility was greater than for those aged 15 to 29; that is, in the 1920s and 1930s it was less and less common for older females to give birth, a pattern that is typically found when marital fertility declines.

If the spacing of childbirth was compacting, so too was the average family size. The number of large families (that is, families with six or more children) was falling noticeably. Of those female birth cohorts who had completed their fertility by 1941, each succeeding cohort showed a marked reduction in the number of large families. While 42.3 per cent of the 1861–76 cohort (of those ever married who had borne children) had had six or more children, the figure for the 1877–86 and 1887–96 cohorts was 35.7 per cent and 31.7 per cent, respectively. For all three cohorts, the number of families with five children showed a similar pattern. But for families with one to four children the pattern was reversed; each succeeding cohort showed an increased tendency to have that many children. At the same time the incidence of childlessness remained fairly constant. Couples were again altering their marital behaviour, not by rejecting parenthood but by reducing the number of children in any one family. As well, the average household size was shrinking considerably. In 1851 the average household had contained 6.18 persons, but by the turn of the century that number had shrunk to 5.03. That decline continued steadily in the early twentieth century, reaching 4.55 persons in 1931.[17] Again, the changes in fertility and household size differed for various groups. The urban fertility rate, for example, was markedly lower than the rural rate. Those of British origin had a lower total fertility rate than those of other European origin. Educated women had fewer children than those with less education. The average Ontario household in 1931 was smaller than the national average (4.2 persons); in the Maritimes (Nova Scotia, 4.67 persons) and Quebec (5.32 persons) the average household was larger.

Nuptiality and fertility were changing in significant ways in the early twentieth century. Influenced by a variety of factors, couples tended to marry earlier and, once married, to have fewer children. Women and men individually were altering the character of marriage and family life. Not surprisingly, some of these changes were reflected in divorce.

This general demographic picture serves as a useful background for a discussion of the character of divorce in this period as derived from an analysis of a sample of divorce documents. The nature of the

TABLE 4

Proportion of divorcing women pregnant at marriage

	Marriage cohort							
	1867–79	1880–9	1890–9	1900–9	1910–19	1920–9	1930–9	Total
Percentage	0	21.4	8.9	7.2	12.3	14.5	21.3	14.5
N	4	14	56	111	268	484	254	1,191

SOURCE: Sample of judicial divorces in Nova Scotia and Ontario, 1900–39

sample used is outlined in the Note on Sources. In the general discussion here the overall sample was used as much as possible, but the paucity of information for both parliamentary and, frequently, the informal divorces forced me to rely on the subsamples of judicial divorces in Nova Scotia and Ontario. The frequency of reported information also varies according to sex. In divorce documents, for example, wives were almost invariably defined by their marital status at marriage, whereas husbands were defined by their occupations. Nevertheless, much can be learned from the documents.

Throughout the entire period the vast majority of women and men were single (that is, never married) at the time of marriage. In the overall sample, less than 4 per cent (n = 3,605) of the women were other than single at marriage, and most of those (2.9 per cent) were widows. Men had a slightly greater tendency to have been previously married (or at least were more willing to admit it); a little over 6 per cent were no longer single: 4.1 per cent were widowed, 1.9 per cent divorced, and 0.4 per cent already married.[18] In the judicial sample, however, one further characteristic at marriage is revealed. A generally rising proportion of the women were pregnant at marriage (see table 4). The considerable variety in cohort premarital pregancies may reflect a constant characteristic of premarital sexuality, or some other factors may be involved. Peter Ward's analysis of nineteenth-century premarital pregnancy rates in English-speaking Canada shows a range of such behaviour very similar to that set out in table 4.[19] Whatever the cause, a marriage founded on a premarital pregnancy may have a poor long-term prognosis.[20] Here, the divorce patterns for such marriages followed closely the patterns found in the total sample. Overall, 57.6 per cent (n = 964) of the divorce petitions were initiated by the women involved, and 85.9 per cent (n = 932) were uncontested. Only in one aspect did such marriages differ significantly from others in which a spouse was seeking divorce: the median length of initial cohabitation was 5.2 years, a much shorter period than for the other marriages in the sample.[21]

Marriage based on premarital conception reflected some basic values and prescribed roles of the period. If the result of extramarital sexual activity was pregnancy, the man was expected to marry the woman. As Ward makes clear, the law exercised its influence in favour of this result. The man was thought to be doing his duty in marrying the female and giving her and the child his name. It is clear that families often intruded to encourage the couple to wed. One man facing such a situation, a cooper from Owen Sound, emphasized the coercive nature of his marriage as well as the couple's basic incompatibility: 'We didn't quarrel when we separated at all. We just never got along from when we got married, in fact we never had what you might call a real serious quarrel at all. You see we had to get married in the first place. It was through her Mother and my Mother that we got married.'[22] Such marriages reveal the values of the time. The idea of marriage rather than the substance was held by many to be crucially important. It was not uncommon to find among the divorces studied a 'shotgun' marriage in which the man had simply appeared at the wedding ceremony but had never cohabited with or supported his wife or child. Subsequently one of the spouses would seek a divorce, charging the marriage partner with violation of marital norms.[23] Such 'marriages' are important reminders of the cultural power attached to the idea of marriage and 'legitimate' birth.

An eastern Ontario marriage followed the typical pattern suggested by Ward. A twenty-five-year-old Michigan schoolteacher found herself pregnant by a twenty-six-year-old small-town Ontario butcher in the summer of 1934. When he failed to respond positively to her predicament, she applied for a filiation order in Brockville, whereupon he agreed to marry her. Cohabitation was delayed for three months until the wife brought her husband to court under the Deserted Wives' Maintenance Act. The magistrate was able to persuade the husband to fulfil his prescribed duties, and the couple finally took up residence together in Morrisburg. After one month he deserted her for two weeks. They resumed cohabitation for a further two weeks at the home of his parents, who were apparently less than welcoming. During this period the husband allegedly 'adopted a course of calculated cruelty and abuse toward the Plaintiff, resorting to obscene language, physical violence, refusal to support ... and unjustified desertion.' Finally, she left her husband and returned to Michigan for the birth of her child two months later. When the child was two years old she initiated divorce proceedings in Cornwall,

Ontario, and was granted an uncontested divorce just over four years after her marriage.[24] The marital values of the time had compounded one 'error' – extramarital pregnancy – by coercing two young adults into a series of unhappy and emotionally damaging experiences.

By the 1930s the judiciary began to comment upon the number of 'shotgun' marriages ending in divorce. Justice R.H. Graham, the sole judge of the Nova Scotia Court for Divorce and Matrimonial Causes, had particular opportunity to notice this phenomenon. 'Most women' who come into divorce court, he wrote in one 1936 judgment, were pregnant at marriage. In a case where a nineteen-year-old woman had married her stevedore husband in Halifax because she was pregnant, he emphasized the weakness of such marriages: 'As is usual, in three weeks they parted, and have not lived together since. ' Graham went out of his way to point out the parties' 'improper' premarital sexual activity. In one case he wrote that 'the parties married with undue haste, following a period of sexual intercourse which began according to the evidence of the respondent [husband] on the second night after he began to go with the petitioner. He says he was never engaged to marry her, but did so because she was pregnant, and he considered that he should do so.'[25] For Justice Graham such premarital behaviour was all too common among young people, and the resultant marriages were inherently unstable. Yet he too upheld the practice and the values inherent in it. When a twenty-one-year-old farm manager appeared before him as a corespondent who had impregnated another man's wife, both Graham and the king's proctor browbeat the young man into a reluctant agreement to marry the woman after a divorce had been granted.[26] The rising number of marriages based on premarital pregnancy may partially explain the tendency towards a young age at marriage among divorced persons.

Divorced persons tended strongly to have married at a relatively young age. The parties reported age infrequently (in approximately 30 per cent of the judicial sample) and with only enough detail to allow calculation of age in full years. Some parties were willing to falsify their ages at various times. To permit marriage without parental consent, young couples often lied about their ages when they applied for a marriage licence. Later in life older adults might lower their ages so as to appear closer to the age of a prospective younger partner, just as younger persons might raise their age in similar circumstances. Some of this imprecision can be attributed to the relative unimportance of accuracy regarding age in the society in

TABLE 5

Median age at marriage for divorcing couples

	Marriage cohort						
	1867–79	1880–9	1890–99	1900–9	1910–19	1920–9	1930–9
Female age	19	19	21	20	20	20	21
N	4	5	28	49	120	186	102
Male age	19.5	27	25	23	24	23	23
N	2	10	26	46	104	190	100

SOURCE: Sample of judicial divorces in Nova Scotia and Ontario, 1900–39

general. While the figures are thus suspect, they nevertheless suggest that divorcing couples tended to have married much younger than the singulate mean age at first marriage as calculated by Gee (see table 5).

What is surprising about these figures is the strikingly different patterns for women and men. The median age for men, which was some five years below the reported singulate mean age for all men in the two provinces, did show some of the same decline being experienced by the male population as a whole. For women, however, the figures are remarkably consistent; this is largely accounted for by the legal barriers to early marriage (one had either to meet the minimum age or lie about it). When this is taken into account, the age for women was very likely close to the same number of years below the mean for the total population as it was for men. For both sexes early age at marriage was probably a significant factor leading to divorce, reflecting the findings in the current literature on modern divorce.[27]

Unfortunately, a lack of information made it impossible for me to use ethnicity as a variable, but I was able to examine religion. Religious affiliation was very infrequently recorded, but the religious character of the wedding ceremony was given often enough to offer some suggestive evidence.[28] While the proportion of Baptist weddings in the overall sample declined over time, Roman Catholic weddings made up a reasonably consistent 9 per cent (n = 1,012) of the reported cases in the overall sample. This is a distinct under-representation of Roman Catholics, of course, but it is interesting, given the church's strict views on discipline in general and divorce in particular, that the pressures of failed marriages were unpleasant enough that so many persons found it necessary to flout the church's rules. As well, this information is tempered by the finding elsewhere that while Roman Catholics were less likely than Protestants to divorce (thus obeying their church's strictures), they were significantly more likely than Protestants to deal with an unsatisfactory marriage by resort to desertion and non-support.[29] This is suggestive both of the behavioural impact of law, either informal (as in this case) or public, and of its capacity for influencing results. (This theme will be taken up in later chapters.) Members of the Church of England in Canada made up an increasing proportion of divorced persons. Fourteen per cent of the 1890s marriage cohort, 33 per cent of the 1910–19 cohort, and 39 per cent of the 1930s cohort petitioning for divorce had been married in an Anglican church, and this despite the church's condemnation of divorce. Internal discipline clearly varied among the different denominations.

Perhaps the most interesting figures are those concerning members of the United Church of Canada. The United Church altered its stance on divorce in the early 1930s and publicly accepted the necessity of divorce for some couples. This seems to have had a major impact on the 1930s marriage cohort. While members of the Presbyterian, Methodist, and United churches had consistently made up some 35 per cent of divorcing couples, for the 1930s cohort the figure was 52.6 per cent (n = 95). It is possible, of course, that 1930s couples contemplating the possibility of divorce chose to wed in a church that would accept divorce, but this sort of premeditation seems unlikely. Instead, the figures suggest that while some couples felt compelled to seek divorce in spite of their church's opposition, other couples were dissuaded from divorce by religious sanctions and admonitions. Once those strictures were weakened in the United Church and divorce became less unacceptable, church members more willingly sought this form of marital dissolution. This does not, of course, account for the changes in Anglicans' divorce rate in spite of their church's continuing strictures.

Divorce is often viewed as an urban problem.[30] Among the evils of urbanization, according to contemporary critics, was a lack of commitment to the prescribed ideals and behaviour of traditional marriage; this lack of commitment led ultimately to adultery. While the rhetoric is dubious, the environment of urban centres, particularly large cities (those with a population of more than 25,000), may have played a significant role in the rise of divorce in the early twentieth century. Throughout the life of the marriages in this study, from the wedding to the initial breakdown to the location of the divorce petition, rural and small communities were underrepresented. This was increasingly so over the forty-year period. While 78.9 per cent of the national population in 1891 lived in communities of fewer than 5,000 people, only 40.9 per cent (n = 298) of the weddings of the 1890s marriage cohort took place in communities of that size. By 1931, when 58.4 per cent of the national population still resided in such communities, they were the locale of only 21.0 per cent (n = 324) of the weddings of the 1930s marriage cohort. Marriages ending in divorce in this period were thus increasingly likely to have begun in urban centres. This may be explained by a stronger tendency in smaller communities to use informal mechanisms of forming and dissolving marriages, but the size of the urban centres was also a factor. While small (5,000 to 24,999) and medium-sized (25,000 to 99,999) cities were somewhat overrepresented in the sample, it was the cities with populations of more than 100,000 that played a dispro-portionately greater role. While 8.3 per cent of the national popula-tion in 1891 lived in communities of more than 100,000, fully 16.4 per cent of the weddings of the 1890s marriage cohort took place in communities of that size. By 1921 19.4 per cent of the national population lived in small communities, but 54.7 per cent (n = 1,059) of the weddings of the 1920s marriage cohort in this study (and 44.1 per cent of the 1930s cohort) took place there.

The same pattern is apparent in the spouses' location at the time of petition. For those escaping an unwanted marriage or trying to start a new life, the city offered the best opportunity to leave behind an unhappy past and to look forward to a better future. The city also offered anonymity; the story of a past divorce could be covered up, and, especially for men, new matrimonial opportunities abounded. To put it another way, behavioural controls exercised by neighbourhoods and local communities were relatively strong in rural and small communities; in large cities such controls were relatively weaker. Since divorce violated those controls, the large city accepted divorce more readily and offered a haven for those escaping tighter controls elsewhere. In the first decade of the twentieth century divorcing wives were somewhat more likely to be found in large cities and divorcing husbands in rural areas, probably because of the differing economic opportunities for the sexes. But by the second decade of the century this difference in location had disappeared.

It is debatable, however, whether the geographical differences can be attributed to the urban environment. It is clear that economically motivated rural-to-urban migration in this period had a distinct age bias; young adults tended disproportionately to leave rural

TABLE 6

Length of initial cohabitation for divorcing couples

	Year of divorce petition							
	1900–4	1905–9	1910–17	1918–19	1920–4	1925–9	1930–4	1935–9
Years	6.3	5.5	4.8	3.8	4.9	4.8	5.1	4.2
N	62	77	163	93	161	113	376	608

SOURCE: Sample of judicial divorces in Nova Scotia and Ontario and unofficial divorce petitions submitted to Ottawa, 1900–39

communities to seek urban employment. This movement produced an age-skewed demographic profile in both urban and rural societies. Rural communities had a disproportionately large number of older adults, an age group less inclined to divorce, while urban societies had a disproportionately large number of younger adults, an age group more inclined to divorce.[31] Whether the higher frequency of divorce in urban centres was a product of the environment or of the demographic profile is a question that this study cannot answer.

It is clear, however, that divorcing couples lived together for shorter and shorter periods before separating for the first time (see table 6). Whereas those seeking divorce in the first years of the century had initially cohabited for 6.3 years, by the early years of the second decade the figure had dropped to 4.8 years. This level of initial cohabitation was maintained throughout the 1920s and early 1930s, until it fell to 4.2 years in the late 1930s. What is most interesting, however, is the aberrant situation in 1918 and 1919.

Those traumatic years were of peculiar significance in Canadian society. By the time the First World War ended in November 1918, the nation had suffered severe stresses in its ethnic, economic, and class relations. And while international peace returned relatively swiftly, domestic peace did not. The conflicts evident during the war continued, and were particularly apparent in class animosity and distrust. Soldiers came home from overseas slowly because the government wanted to avoid rapid demobilization in an atmosphere of economic and social uncertainty. Labour unrest increased, culminating in the Winnipeg General Strike of May 1919. A new era in politics seemed imminent with the electoral success of the United Farmers of Ontario in 1919, which (along with other signs) suggested the disintegration of the old-line parties and a realignment of political forces in Canada.

It was in this atmosphere that Canada came as close as it would until 1968 to its first national divorce law. In 1918 the number of divorces began to rise dramatically (see table 1), paralleling developments in England and elsewhere in the Western world,[32] and the number of applications received in the Senate made it clear that this trend was continuing. As well, in Alberta and Manitoba the parliamentary monopoly on dissolving marriages was challenged in the courts, resulting in the extension of judicial divorce to the three prairie provinces. Divorces were becoming more common and easier to obtain, and there was considerable pressure to recognize these circumstances in a general federal divorce statute. The federal cabinet seriously considered such legislation and rumours circulated in the press and among interested parties that government action was imminent, and that at least for soldiers access to divorce would be improved. A better world was possible, and so too were better marriages; and in the opinion of some no one had a greater right to better marriages than those whose domestic happiness had been irretrievably damaged by military service. One veteran from St Thomas, Ontario, inquiring about the imaginary 'soldiers' divorce statute,' played on the pathos of the soldier returning to a broken home: 'Have we fought in vain. We were in mud slime and blood fought our way through, shook hands with ourselves to think we go[t] through, but for my part after coming back and finding things in such a condition it took all the morale and spirit out of many of the boys. We cannot seem to get justice at all. I have been to our Magistrate and Crown Attorney but they say from a thousand to fifteen hundred dollars is the cost of a divorce.' He complained that it was impossible to bear such costs on a soldier's pay, and concluded: 'Now sir do what you can for us. There is in St. Thomas a score of cases of unfaithfulness and it almost seems as though we are deprived of the liberty and justice we went to fight for as we have neither the privilege of a single or married man as the case now stands. Hoping I can get some satisfaction from you.'[33] Encouraged, or perhaps confused, by the new policies of the English government, some soldiers believed that the Canadian government had established special procedures 'to help deserving soldiers to get divorces' by reducing or eliminating costs. Others cited specific legislation, such as 'the Soldiers' Divorce Act,' or said that officials had recommended taking advantage of the 'new law.'[34] While such reports were false, they showed remarkable vitality.

Those who did obtain divorces during 1918 and 1919 demonstrated a number of statistical differences from those who came before and after them. Most striking was the length of initial co-

TABLE 7

Percentage of female and male divorce petitioners

			Marriage cohorts				
	1867–79	1880–9	1890–9	1900–9	1910–19	1920–9	1930–9
Female	66.7	52.8	52.1	48.2	52.5	65.5	67.3
Male	33.3	47.2	47.9	51.8	47.5	34.5	32.7
N	15	72	305	745	1523	1228	349

SOURCE: Overall divorce sample

habitation: these couples had cohabited for just 3.8 years before separating for the first time, a full year less than divorcing couples in the years immediately before and after. Similarly, they waited the shortest time after the final breakdown before filing for divorce – just 0.4 years. Given these figures, it is not surprising that these marriages in which the partners were seeking dissolution were of a shorter duration than at any other point in the forty-year period under investigation. Men (particularly those whose marriages had initially broken down in large urban centres, to judge from the Nova Scotia sample) led this charge against the divorce barricades.[35] The percentage of husbands petitioning for divorce peaked in 1918–19 at 62.2 (n = 90) in the judicial sample. Not surprisingly, in view of the shorter duration of these marriages, both spouses tended to be relatively young at the time of petition. In the judicial sample the median age for husbands among the 1918–19 petitions was 31.5, in contrast to 41 during the earlier years in the decade; wives recorded the lowest median age at any time in the period under investigation – 27, in comparison with 34 during 1910–17. The years at the end of the First World War were traumatic not just for the national polity and economy; apparently the strain of the wartime environment and changing individual expectations resulted in a new demand for personal freedom and for release from unhappy marriages. That demand was heard at the political level and in the divorce courts.

While husbands may have led the way in 1918–19, overall it was wives who increasingly took the initiative in divorce. For every marriage cohort except one, women made up the majority of petitioners in the sample (see table 7). Only in the 1900–9 marriage cohort did men constitute a majority of divorce petitioners. At first women's domination was relatively slight, as wives consistently initiated between 52 and 53 per cent of the divorce petitions. But in

TABLE 8

Median age of divorce participants

	Year of petition							
	1900–4	1905–9	1910–17	1918–19	1920–4	1925–9	1930–4	1935–9
Female	28	27.5	34	27	29	29	32	31
N	11	10	25	12	29	41	113	250
Male	35	42	41	31.5	31	33	35	34
N	15	11	19	12	19	41	109	248

SOURCE: Sample of judicial divorces in Nova Scotia and Ontario, 1900–39

the last two marriage cohorts under investigation a significant change occurred, and soon wives outnumbered husbands two to one as petitioners. (This topic is discussed in more detail in chapter 7.)

In 1923 the Dominion Bureau of Statistics began to publish an annual bulletin analysing divorces for the previous years. This was not just a reflection of the growing awareness of and concern with divorce in Canada; it was also one of the early attempts to understand the components of divorce. The bulletins were superficial; the sex of successful petitioners was the only personal characteristic analysed during the 1920s.[36] Nevertheless, the figures are helpful. In the first year of reporting, 41.9 per cent (n = 544) of successful petitioners were female. Two years later, in 1924, women for the first time made up more than 50 per cent of successful petitioners, and from 1926 on divorce was a predominantly female process. For the period 1922–9 as a whole, wives were the petitioners in 50.4 per cent (n = 5,100) of divorces. For the 1930s women made up 62.8 per cent (n = 13,649) of successful petitioners.[37]

The initial surge of additional divorces at the end of the First World War and into the early 1920s found a disproportionate number of younger participants, to judge from a rather limited number of cases (see table 8). The median age of divorced persons rose slowly thereafter, but again there were noticeable differences for the two sexes. For men the median age was in the early to mid-thirties, and never returned to pre-war levels, which were surprisingly high (and may simply be a product of the small sample size). For women the median age not only rose to the late twenties and early thirties, but may well have exceeded pre-war levels. Certainly the difference in ages between spouses shrank considerably over these years. By the

TABLE 9

Median duration of marriage at point of divorce petition (years)

| | Year of petition | | | | | | | |
	1900–4	1905–9	1910–17	1918–19	1920–4	1925–9	1930–4	1935–9
Duration	12.7	9.0	12.0	8.4	10.3	10.3	10.7	9.6
N	44	47	111	86	134	93	391	666

SOURCE: Sample of judicial divorces in Nova Scotia and Ontario, 1900–39

1920s and 1930s the age gap reflected that of the national mean for first marriages. An analysis by the Dominion Bureau of Statistics of 1933 Ontario divorces generally confirms the data in table 8. In 75.6 per cent of all Ontario divorces granted that year, a median age of thirty-one for wives and thirty-four for husbands was reported.[38]

While the gap thereafter remained relatively stable, the median age of women and men at divorce did not. Indeed, these early figures stand out in contrast to post-1968 figures. In the 1970s and 1980s men divorced at an older age (around thirty-six years), as did women (around thirty-three years) than in the 1920s; only in the 1930s did the median age for both sexes approach that of the modern era, if one accounts for the additional time consumed by the divorce process itself by adding one to one and a half years to the earlier figures.[39] How can the relatively youthful character of the parties in the early surge of divorces be explained? It may be that part of the social conservatism of aging was a greater reluctance to challenge the norms of the day, norms that by definition were a product of the attitudes of older rather than younger persons. Only as divorce became more tolerated did older men and women feel ready to participate in the public spectacle. To put it another way, there was a youthful bias among those ready to challenge the norms of the day. But this is not meant to imply that by the 1930s most elements in Canadian society had come to accept divorce as an unhappy necessity. Such acceptance was still some years away, certainly among the middle class and many religious groups. The 1920s, the age of jazz and of 'flappers,' was a time of cultural and sexual experimentation, and it may be that the young age of divorced persons in that decade is simply one more manifestation of a generation's rebellion.

With age at marriage falling for divorcing couples, the duration of the actual marriage lessened somewhat over time (see table 9). Individual petitions in the judicial sample reflected a great range in the duration of the marriage at the time of petition.[40] In the forty-four divorces sought between 1900 and 1904, for example, the duration of marriages ranged from 1.4 years to 32.8 years. Nevertheless, the aggregate figures do suggest a pattern. In the pre-1918 petitions the median marriage lasted some 12 years before one of the spouses initiated divorce proceedings. In 1918–19 this figure dropped precipitously. Thereafter the figure rose, hovering around 10.5 years for the next fifteen years, and never returning to pre-war levels. In the second half of the 1930s the median age of marriage began to drop again, probably as a result of the economic pressures of the period and of evolving attitudes towards marriage and divorce. But here again the extreme variation in individual experience must not be overlooked. The petitions for the period from 1935 to 1939 dealt with marriages that were as short as 3 months and as long as 40 years, 8 months. However, the overall pattern appears reasonably clear.

The average duration of the marriage by the 1920s and 1930s had already reached the levels found in judicial divorce petitions in the 1970s and 1980s. If one allows a further year or year and a half for the petition to make its way through the judicial process to an absolute decree, the duration of the marriage in the 1920s and 1930s is similar to that in the present day.[41] What was different was the longer duration of marriages in 1900–4 and 1910–17 and the shorter duration in 1905–9, 1918–19, and 1935–9. A longer duration would be hypothesized in an era when divorce was less frequent and much more deviant; it is the shorter time span that calls for explanation. The later two periods have already been discussed, but it is unclear what forces may have produced the low figure for 1905–9, though this period coincides approximately with the height of an economic boom that may have contributed to marital instability. But other features can be discussed with more certainty. It is of interest that the median duration of marriage at divorce (rather than at time of petition) in the United States was much lower than in Canada – just over six years in 1932.[42]

The overall pattern of family size in the divorce petitions is also clear. The proportion of childless marriages is well above the national average (see table 10), which is consistent with the historical evidence available for other Western societies.[43] This partially reflects a prevalent attitude that couples who were unhappy ought to stay together 'for the sake of the children.' The proportion of marriages with no dependent children at the time of petition rose a further 10 per cent on average throughout the time period,[44] indicating that up

TABLE 10

Number of children ever born in marriages seeking divorce (%)

	Year of petition							
Number of children	1900–4	1905–9	1910–17	1918–19	1920–4	1925–9	1930–4	1935–9
0	33.3	32.6	35.8	34.9	38.8	30.1	30.8	37.0
1	15.4	26.1	22.9	27.7	21.6	34.4	35.6	35.9
2	15.4	21.7	10.1	13.3	10.4	14.0	17.9	17.3
3	7.7	6.5	11.9	9.6	9.0	8.6	8.7	5.3
4	12.8	2.2	7.3	8.4	7.5	5.4	2.8	2.1
5+	15.4	10.9	11.9	6.0	12.7	7.5	4.1	2.4
N	39	46	109	83	134	93	390	660

SOURCE: Sample of judicial divorces in Nova Scotia and Ontario, 1900–39

to 10 per cent of divorcing couples may have waited until their children had grown up before beginning the divorce process. The large number of childless marriages may also reflect a cause of marriage breakdown. Given the powerful pro-natal attitudes in the period, marriages that failed to produce children were more likely to be judged as failures, both by the couples involved and by others.[45] Couples who were voluntarily childless clearly were willing to ignore the pro-natal norms; and if they were willing to ignore those norms, they may also have found it easier to ignore normative attitudes towards divorce.

While the proportion of childless marriages is reasonably consistent, patterns of change are evident for those marriages with children. One-child marriages make up a significantly greater proportion of the marriages from the later 1920s onward. Equally, marriages with four or more children are much less common. This pattern reflects both the shorter average duration of those marriages in the divorce sample and the changing fertility rates in the country as a whole.[46] Although the sex of the children had no apparent effect on the proclivity towards or timing of divorce petitions, on the basis of a limited number of cases in the early years of the period under study, the age of the children was of some importance (see table 11). While the average age of the oldest child remained stable at around ten years, that of the youngest child rose somewhat over the period. This raises the possibility that there was a tendency to listen to the common stories about how hard divorce was on children and to

TABLE 11

Mean age of children at time of divorce petition[1]

	Year of petition							
Child	1900–4	1905–9	1910–17	1918–19	1920–4	1925–9	1930–4	1935–9
Oldest[2]	11.6	8.0	11.2	8.7	10.6	9.8	10.2	9.5
N	16	7	29	21	34	23	86	114
Youngest	7.1	4.9	5.7	5.3	6.5	6.8	7.2	6.6
N	22	20	54	42	64	53	224	330

SOURCE: Sample of judicial divorces in Nova Scotia and Ontario, 1900–39

1 Age was coded in completed years only for dependent children (ages 0 to 15).
2 A single child was coded as the youngest.

TABLE 12

Respondent's defence, by sex (%)

Defence	1867–79	1880–9	1890–9	1900–9	1910–19	1920–9	1930–9
Female marriage cohort							
Defended	100	27.8	17.4	13.8	22.5	16.4	13.1
Undefended	0	72.2	82.6	86.2	77.5	83.6	86.9
N	1	18	46	109	182	195	99
Male marriage cohort							
Defended	55.6	31.6	27.4	15.1	19.1	10.1	9.2
Undefended	44.4	68.4	72.6	84.9	80.9	89.9	90.8
N	9	19	62	86	183	327	163

SOURCE: Sample of judicial divorces in Nova Scotia and Ontario, 1900–39

delay divorce until the youngest child was at least of school age and thus less dependent.

Clearly, the decision to resort to the divorce process was a calculated one, and children were only one element taken into account. This calculation is particularly apparent when one examines the responses of the defendants in the proceedings (see table 12). Most divorces in this period were uncontested, a tendency that increased over time. But there are some interesting differences in spousal behaviour. In the marriage cohorts from 1867 to 1909, a husband was consistently more likely to defend against his wife's petition, and in all but one case simply to seek to maintain the marriage. But the marriage cohorts from 1910 to 1939 showed an opposite tendency; a wife was more likely than her husband to defend against a divorce petition. While the female patterns were somewhat erratic, males demonstrated a relatively consistent pattern of increasingly deferring to their wives' divorce proceedings. This seemingly passive acceptance of the process is confirmed in the type of defence chosen by each sex. In challenging the petition only 8.1 per cent of the husbands counterclaimed for divorce; but fully 24.3 per cent of wives entered counterclaims. The figures and the process obscure as much as they reveal, however, and will be more fully discussed in chapter 8.

When the Dominion Bureau of Statistics began in the 1930s to extend its analysis of divorce, the first category added was remarriage. This inclusion acted as a reaffirmation of marriage, and was thus reassuring (whether intentionally or not) to readers. Remarriage was common, as it is today. In 1939 over two thousand divorced persons remarried; this 'interesting sidelight,' as the bureau put it, reflected a marked increase in the number of remarriages.[47] Even though this increase in the number of remarriages was simply a product of the increase in the number of divorces, it helped to put a silver lining in what was otherwise considered to be a rather dark cloud. So too did the bureau's constant reporting of the much higher number of divorces in comparable jurisdictions elsewhere.

An analysis of the grounds for divorce must proceed with caution. First, the legal environment naturally shaped the allegations made. Since adultery was the one major ground for divorce (except in Nova Scotia, where cruelty was also a ground) it is only reasonable to expect that allegations of adultery would have a prominent place in divorce petitions. Similarly, allegations of cruelty or non-support or alcoholism could be influential in any contest for child custody. Thus, allegations by petitioners undoubtedly were shaped by the legal requirements of their situation. Second, the petitions were written by solicitors and therefore expressed only a second-hand version of the complaints of wives and husbands. Nevertheless, through the cant of legal terminology, some of the emotions and attitudes of the righteous, wronged, and calculating spouses are evident from the documents. To control both factors, the judicial petitions are reported separately from the informal petitions for divorce, since the latter would have been subject only to informal restrictions and would be more likely to reveal the concerns of the petitioning spouse.

I have divided the charges into two artificially distinct categories – causes of breakdown (such as adultery, cruelty, or ill health) and results (such as bigamy, desertion, or foreign divorce). Legally, there was no difference in importance between the two. Most of the results simply confirmed the basic charge, particularly adultery. Thus, if a petitioner sought to establish a spouse's adultery, proof of bigamy, of foreign divorce and remarriage, or of cohabitation with a new sexual partner firmly established the veracity of the charge. Nevertheless, this information provides the initial evidence for a theme of central importance in this study: how discontented spouses asserted their own control (at least temporarily, in the case of desertion) over the way in which the marriage was severed.

In petitioning the courts for divorce it was essential to establish that cohabitation had ceased. Otherwise the courts could infer that 'normal' marital relations continued and that the offences complained of had been condoned. Petitioners used several phrases to describe this disengagement. Two involved mutuality to a degree that cannot be determined. Legal separation was mentioned in 15.4 per cent and 23.2 per cent of judicial and informal petitions respectively. Others used the phrase 'ceased cohabitation,' a non-pejorative term that is taken here to be distinct from 'desertion.' 'Ceased cohabitation' includes the possibility of some mutual consent, and was present in 27.5 per cent and 7.1 per cent of the same groups of petitions.[48]

The grievances of wives and husbands (see tables 13 and 14)[49] clearly show the impact of the legal environment. For both sexes, for example, adultery played a very prominent role in allegations presented to the courts, and this is as expected. But the striking drop in relative importance among the unofficial complaints by both wives and husbands gives some indication of the true weight placed on sexual infidelity, although even unofficial petitions must have been subject to some influence from the formal legal environment. Similarly, allegations of economic inadequacy (including non-support) played a much larger role in women's perceptions of their marriages when the legal constraints were removed. Legally, such allegations would be significant only when custody of children was at stake, but informally it is well established that economic problems are a fundamental cause of marriage breakdown.[50]

Wives and husbands clearly valued different elements of marital behaviour. Men were particularly disturbed about sexual infidelity; even the greater concern for criminal conduct among the unofficial petitioners was a reflection of this, and often was manifested in stories of wives' conviction for prostitution. This may also explain

TABLE 13

Wives' complaints about their husbands (%)

Judicial petitions	Issues	Unofficial petitions
	Causes of breakdown[1]	
44.4	Adultery	9.9
4.3	Alcoholism	5.3
2.6	Criminal conviction	10.9
26.5	Cruelty	15.2
0.2	Ill health	1.3
2.5	Inadequate support	1.8
0.3	Incompatibility	0.2
0.0	Insanity	2.0
17.6	Non-support	52.5
1.3	Sexual problems	0.8
0.3	Other	0.3
100.0		100.2
	Results of breakdown[2]	
5.4	Bigamy	12.8
37.0	Cohabitation	12.0
55.8	Desertion	65.8
1.8	Foreign divorce	6.8
0.0	Migration	2.6
100.0		100.0

SOURCE: Sample of judicial divorces in Nova Scotia and Ontario, 1900–39, and unofficial requests for divorce submitted to Ottawa, 1900–39

1   N = 1,594 for judicial petitions, N = 396 for unofficial petitions
2   N = 505 for judicial petitions, N = 266 for unofficial petitions

husbands' relative concentration on the results rather than the causes of marriage breakdown. For husbands, complaints dealing with the results of breakdown accounted for 49.1 per cent and 68.7 per cent of judicial and informal petitions respectively, in contrast with 24.1 per cent and 40.2 per cent for wives' petitions. Or was it that the male's pride and his socialized sense of marital dominance were particularly affronted by demonstrations of female independence, particularly sexual independence?

Overall, wives articulated many more complaints than did hus-

TABLE 14

Husbands' complaints about their wives (%)

Judicial petitions	Issues	Unofficial petitions
	Causes of breakdown[1]	
83.9	Adultery	66.9
1.3	Alcoholism	2.3
3.0	Criminal conviction	10.0
5.4	Cruelty	5.4
0.5	Ill health	3.9
0.8	Inadequate support	0.8
1.8	Incompatibility	3.1
0.3	Insanity	6.2
2.6	Sexual problems	1.5
0.3	Other	0.0
99.9		100.1
	Results of breakdown[2]	
6.0	Bigamy	8.7
34.6	Cohabitation	26.3
50.3	Desertion	48.1
5.8	Foreign divorce	10.9
3.2	Migration	6.0
99.9		100.0

SOURCE: Sample of judicial divorces in Nova Scotia and Ontario, 1900–39, and unofficial requests for divorce submitted to Ottawa, 1900–39

1   N = 608 for judicial petitions, N = 130 for unofficial petitions
2   N = 586 for judicial petitions, N = 285 for unofficial petitions

bands, and were concerned about a broader range of behaviour, following patterns observed in the decades since the Second World War.[51] Abusive conduct, whether physical or mental, was an important and relatively common charge, although the judicial system may have exaggerated its occurrence in marriages. Criminal conviction was often a disruptive factor in marriages from women's point of view. But most vital were economic problems. If the male's prescribed role in marriage was that of breadwinner, then economic failure could easily be laid at his doorstep – and was. When unconstrained by the judicial process, this was the cause on which most marriages foundered as far as wives were concerned. For the same reason, and because non-support and desertion often went hand in hand, wives placed greater emphasis on simple desertion by their husbands.

Neither wives nor husbands gave much weight to other issues: incompatibility was a concept virtually unthought of; apart from adultery, aberrant sexual behaviour (such as impotence, incest, or non-consensual continence) was not particularly important; ill health was not regarded as a major cause of marital problems, although insanity became a ground for complaint in unofficial petitions, particularly by husbands (this undoubtedly reflected the notion, already adopted in a number of American jurisdictions, that insanity was an appropriate ground for divorce).

What is most striking about the demographic and attitudinal characteristics of divorce reported here is their similarity to modern divorce. While many Canadians would date the beginning of modern divorce in this country from 1968, when the first general divorce statute was enacted, the demographic evidence suggests that the transition to modern divorce began in the years following the First World War and was complete by the 1930s. Divorce by then had become, at least on the surface, a device by which women predominantly sought to control their marital circumstances. The divorces examined in this study follow the modern patterns in terms of the age gap between the sexes, the normal duration of a dissolving marriage, and expectations of marital behaviour for both sexes. This in turn is suggestive of the extent to which law can control familial behaviour, and it is to this that we now turn.

Marriage was an economic necessity for almost all women, and for some men. One group of men especially depended upon stable marriages for economic survival. Canadian agriculture during these years was dominated by the family farm; the male head of the household had overall direction of the enterprise and was responsible for the field work and the heavy machinery; only he was called a farmer. Married women's productive and reproductive tasks were extensive. Wives were usually responsible for maintaining the home and children, for cultivating the vegetable garden and sometimes helping in the fields, for tending the poultry and small animals, and for preparing food.[1] The subsidiary character of the woman's role was reflected in her title – farmer's wife. The importance of her contribution and the extent of the farmer's economic vulnerability became readily apparent when that contribution was withdrawn. The farmer found himself economically crippled – and this seemed to be the critical point – when his wife abandoned farm and marriage for some more satisfying opportunity.

A 1931 informal divorce petition revealed the conflict between the traditional patriarchal family unit on the one hand and the farmer's dependence on his wife's economic partnership on the other. A farmer living near Formosa, Ontario, sought the assistance of the minister of justice in obtaining a divorce, hoping to play on the minister's sympathy for a fellow male whose authority had been undermined. Married in 1927, the couple had stayed together for just fifteen months before separating. During that time the farmer had, by his own admission, continually asserted his authority over his wife. He refused to give her money to visit her family; when the wife countered by asking her mother to come to the farm, he refused on the basis that the couple should concentrate on the development of their young marriage. While his refusal held, the wife and her family were able to retaliate: 'I was a brute bye her & all her people were against me as well.' When a sickly baby was born and the wife's sister was summoned to help, the farmer sought to assert his authority over the sister, warning her that she would be sent home. The wife countered by threatening to leave if that happened. When it did, the wife returned permanently to her parents' home in Hamilton. The husband's attempts to persuade her to return were rebuffed. Though he asserted that he was heartbroken and wished he were dead, what he really wanted was a divorce and economic security: 'Now what is worrying me is supposing I apply for a divorce & get it or not is it possible after this long of her being away & supporting herself if I should be compelled to pay allimony. Allso how much a divorce should cost. I have a farm here & without her I cannot run it to a paying proposition nor can I sell it or even put a mortgage on it to get money to pay for a divorce.'[2] Both the structure of farming and the legal system constrained his behaviour and underlined his economic vulnerability.

That vulnerability was common to farmers whose wives had left. Some were quite open about their need for a housekeeper rather than a helpmate. One Nova Scotia farmer bought another farm and moved to it, leaving his wife behind at their old farm; as she recounted it, 'he sent for me to go out and I went out and I asked him if he wanted me to come and live with him; he said, no, only to clean the house; and after I cleaned the house he told me to take the children and go home.'[3]

Men in most other occupations tended not to see themselves as quite so dependent on a female partner, despite the reality that women were the sole purveyors of what the courts called wifely services. A wife was expected to manage her husband's home, to prepare his meals, to purchase the necessary consumables, and to raise his children. Sexual intercourse was normally included in the services, but it was not necessarily the most important. A locomotive fireman in Truro suspected his wife of adultery in 1919. Not wanting to lose her housekeeping skills, he expressed his disapproval by withdrawing from their sexual relationship and moving to a separate bedroom; they also stopped exchanging Christmas presents. But she stayed on for a further year as mother and housekeeper before the husband brought his divorce action. In southwestern Ontario a London optician sought a Michigan divorce because his wife insisted on running her own business, refused to keep house for him, and thus 'denied him the wifely services to which he was entitled.' Many husbands cited their wives' refusal to perform housekeeping and cooking duties as a cause of marital breakdown. Wives who failed to perform such services were publicly chastised by the courts and were given little protection.[4] A husband's, and indeed the broader society's, expectations of a wife made clear the essential nature of her work in the home on behalf of her husband and family. In truth, most adult men probably could not conceive of their living without women to look after them. A Nova Scotia husband, who had long since deserted his wife and children, justified his living with a young woman who had taken his name: 'He was going to live with her; he would have to have a housekeeper.'[5]

Women's association with housekeeping and nurturing skills combined with familial expectations to place considerable strain on some marriages. One farmer in the Owen Sound area described his wife's departure: 'Well her people, her brothers were after her to go and keep house for them and that they would pay her wages. They had [had] a woman for 8 years. They were after her; she went for this other lady was not staying. They came in to get her, her brother Bill offered to pay her wages, and said she would never want for a thing, and she would have a good home there.'[6] Women were often called on to come to the long-term aid of siblings, parents, or other family members. A London-area housewife recounted a common story. After eight years of marriage she was called home to care for her mother during an illness; thereafter she never returned to full-time cohabitation with her husband, managing only occasional weekends with him until he deserted a year later.[7]

Both husbands and wives demanded loyalty and accountability. In 1901 a Halifax plumber complained not just that his wife had 'totally neglected her domestic duties.' but that she went out (particularly at night) 'without his knowledge or permission,' often remaining out for considerable periods of time and refusing to account for her activities. While many husbands clearly expected obedience of their wives, both sexes were offended by spouses who went out alone and clandestinely.[8]

In defending themselves against charges that they had failed to fulfil their wives' expectations, men used gender prescriptions to underline their wives' own similar and more egregious failures.[9] A Nova Scotia farmer in 1900 countered his wife's allegations of cruelty by pointing to her own unwifely behaviour. He objected to her preparation of meals (too salty, too hot, impure and putrid), to her morose and sullen temper, to her laziness, and to her unaffectionate nature. But most of all he charged her with violating the ideal of domesticity by turning their home into a battleground and teaching their children to hate and despise him. She sought to exclude him from 'the intercourse and affection which should exist between a father and his children and ... from any part or share in the home life of his family and she has enticed his children away from him.'[10] According to the husband, no proper wife or mother would behave this way, and she had no claim to the protection of the court. In 1918 an Alberta farmer complained that his wife had deserted him in 1910, after less than two months of marriage, and he had not heard of her since. He had persevered and built up his farm, but without a wife he could go no further. Indeed, the lack of a wife, he estimated, meant fifty-five fewer acres under plough and considerably fewer animals being raised. The divorce law was standing in the way of his economic development: 'Now I want to get the right to marry again. I cannot go to town but my hogs run away and coyotes steel my chickens and I have to do fours hours work out of twelve in the house and that cut down my crop acrage. if I hire a woman the people around they make all kinds of noise. so what can I do can I marrie again leagley or ... will I have to marriey illlagley and stand the trouble afterwards.'[11] His plea was echoed by other deserted farmers. There was community pressure to control the use of female housekeepers other than wives, and it is in this context that women's vulnerability is underlined.

Marriage, of course, was fundamentally a source of economic security for women. The economic dependence of most women on their marriage was self-evident. One of the ways in which this was emphasized was the avenues of resort sought by women after formal or informal separation. Without any doubt some re-entered the job market successfully, though the range of employment open to 'married' women was limited. Indeed, at least some married women were forced to conceal their marital status so as to avoid some of these restrictions and to increase their employment opportunities, although some businesses that refused work to married women would employ them once separated.[12] Job opportunities for women were expanding rapidly throughout the early twentieth century. The great increase in employment in such professions as teaching and nursing was more than matched by the opening up of the wage labour market to women in manufacturing, and even more in the white-collar clerical and service sectors.[13] These changes potentially altered women's economic dependence on marriage, strengthening the possibility of employment. But, to judge from the evidence in the divorce records, the impact of these changes may have been long-term. In the 1920s and 1930s many divorced women found themselves with few marketable skills and limited employment opportunities. Many women were forced to take refuge in their family of origin or in remarriage (whether legally or illegally), and thus to repeat the cycle of dependence.

Women were generally best trained and most experienced in one skilled occupation – housekeeping. Those who returned to their family of origin often accepted room and board in return for performing various household tasks. Others (if they had enough money) could run boarding-houses in urban areas. There was a demand for boarding facilities among blue-collar and white-collar workers, migrants, single people, and young adults. However, one needed a house and furniture; the house could be rented, which required a cash deposit, and most furniture could be acquired on credit. Women who had been deserted by their husbands often had the advantage of unchallenged control over furniture and household goods accumulated during the marriage. If there were enough of these, they could be used to start a boarding-house. Bettina Bradbury effectively emphasized the importance of access to such limited capital goods for the boarding business, but her data do not facilitate a separate analysis of this occupation among female-headed households.[14] The reported divorce cases suggest that deserted wives may have been disproportionately present in the business. Women who had no access to such assets could work as domestic servants or housekeepers. The pay was usually low (women who brought children with them might be paid nothing), and they had little or no control over their work, but housekeeping was an obvious and common means of support. Two 1936 cases in Sudbury, Ontario, offer interesting examples.

Dan and Carol Donnelly were a Roman Catholic couple who had married locally in 1931 while still quite young. For the first three weeks of their marriage they had lived with Carol's parents for a week, then with Dan's parents for a week; they finally moved to the back of Dan's barber-shop for a week before Dan left for Toronto for four weeks to complete a barbering course. They then resumed their nomadic residential habits. Dan was forced to continue in this mode of living only by threat of court action for non-support. Dan's lack of interest in maintaining the marriage became increasingly apparent from his indifference towards Carol, who finally left him ten weeks after the wedding to return to her parents' home. Carol's parents were aging, however, and could not easily support her. It is not clear how Carol supported herself over the following two and a half years; she was unable to get a job and had a child thirteen months after leaving Dan. But in 1934 she reached an arrangement with a Copper Cliff miner, Henry Sawchuk, who testified, 'I am staying at [mining] camp and paying $40.00 for my board and room and I can't afford that [since] I am only getting 30 cents an hour so I said to Carol I get a place and you keep my house, keep my clothes clean and my meals and I will pay you wages.' Carol moved in with her baby. She worked as Henry's housekeeper, and earned twenty dollars a month. At Dan's divorce trial Henry was named co-respondent, but Henry fought hard to defend his own and Carol's honour – much harder than Carol, who presumably had already been labelled by the birth of her child. Henry assured the court that he slept in a bed in the kitchen while Carol and the baby had the bedroom, and that Carol was known in the neighbourhood as Mrs Donnelly, not Mrs Sawchuk. Dan received his divorce, but had his wrists slapped by the court, which refused to issue an order as to legal costs.[15] Carol's punishment had already been somewhat harsher.

A second couple, Pyotr and Polly Zaduk, had married in 1922. They resided most of the time in a small town near Sudbury, where Pyotr was a section hand for the Canadian Pacific Railway. After eleven years of marriage and with five living children, the couple signed a separation agreement in 1933. The older three children stayed with their father and the younger two left with their mother. Polly moved first to Sudbury. Pyotr, who was so alienated by her alleged sexual misconduct that he forbade her to call herself Mrs Zaduk, cut off her support. Within seven months Polly moved to a small town in the Algoma district, and began to work as housekeeper to a railway section foreman. She admitted to a sexual relationship with her new provider, though she insisted that they had separate bedrooms. Locally she had adopted her provider's last name, because, as he said, 'it looks better in the country.' Polly provided sexual and house-keeping services in return for board and complete support for her two children. Like Carol Donnelly, Polly openly admitted her infringe-ment of the moral code, while her new provider declined to supply the court with any such evidence. Indeed, Polly co-operated in the divorce process, and sought only limited access to her other children. This request was ignored, the divorce was granted, and legal costs were levied.[16]

Married women often had few skills to sell other than their home-related experience. One Polish woman had lived with her husband in their homeland for two years before he emigrated to Canada. When he failed to send for her after two years, she sold their assets and emigrated on her own initiative. They lived together unhappily for four years in London, Ontario, while he worked as a moulder and she took in as many as six boarders. Finally they separated, and within a short time she began to live with another Polish man, for whom she also ran a boarding-house. Her responses to counsel's questions are revealing:

Q Do you live there [with the second man] as man and wife?
A We are, because he supports.
Q Was there any other way in which your husband conduced or connived in this adultery other than you accuse him of abusing you?
A He was refusing me a home, and he told me to get out, that is why I did it; it was the best thing to do.[17]

Women, especially working-class women, who usually lived close to the poverty line, could view marriage in very hard terms: an exchange of sex and home management in return for support. Viewed in such terms, marriage in some form was very much an economic institution for women, usually essential for their daily survival.

The cases reveal an additional aspect of the boarding or housekeeping business. For some young to middle-aged women – that is, for those in their childbearing years (which were perceived to be their sexually active years) – neither housekeeping nor boarding-house keeping was looked upon favourably by the middle class. Rural townspeople seemed to prefer that a woman living in the home of a man adopt the man's last name; presumably this offered reassurance that some important elements of a traditional family structure were in place and that a stable relationship had been established. But others were not so willing to condone such arrangements: one resident of a small town in Nova Scotia complained of the 'notoriety' of a local man and his housekeeper. Another housekeeper, who had been feeling some community pressure, sought reassurance from the police that her arrangement did not infringe community standards. A Saskatchewan farmer, left to cope with two children and a farm after his wife had been committed to a mental hospital, complained that whenever he took his housekeeper into town or to a community dance, 'neighbours talk and make it unpleasant. Where shall I apply for a divorce? or must I go on living like this all my life?'[18] A deserted Owen Sound wife and mother regarded housekeeping as an obvious means of economic support, but informally petitioned for a divorce before accepting such employment: 'I would like to be of some service to some one needing a woman for housekeeping or a dutiful wife, which I was before, but consider myself much to efficient to take a chance on housekeeper without being free.'[19]

Any man or woman who was a party to a housekeeping or boarding arrangement and who was otherwise suspected of improper conduct found his or her living arrangements used as grounds for assuming improper sexual behaviour.[20] The divorce cases did offer ample evidence that such arrangements created considerable opportunity for adulterous conduct; it would not have been too difficult for counsel and judges to develop a jaundiced view of boarding-house life. It is therefore not surprising to find court officers searching for possible misconduct in boarding-house arrangements. Since the plaintiff in a divorce case had to be innocent of marital misconduct (the 'clean hands' concept), defending and watching counsel often challenged any plaintiffs who were in a boarding-house or house-keeping situation.

In Nova Scotia the watching counsel were particularly careful to investigate such plaintiffs. There was no sexual discrimination in this; boarding-house landladies were challenged as often as men who lived with housekeepers. A Lunenberg farmer, for example, had hired several housekeepers in the five years since his wife had left him and their three children. By the time of the divorce none of the children lived at home, and he had found it difficult to retain a housekeeper longer than two or three months. The result was a steady stream of housekeepers, often local girls from the neighbourhood, possibly in their first stage of independent employment. The farmer explained that he had finally started the divorce action because it was 'pretty hard for a man to get anybody to keep house' and he was therefore thinking of remarriage. A wife was simply an alternative to a housekeeper. The watching counsel closely questioned the farmer and other witnesses regarding possible misconduct with the housekeepers.[21] In a 1935 application by a thirty-two-year-old line-man for the Nova Scotia Light and Power Company, the trial judge was most disturbed by evidence that in the three years since the couple had separated the husband had had a thirty-year-old housekeeper caring for himself and his two children. It was not only their ages that aroused suspicion; their sleeping arrangements also upset the judge. While the husband shared a bedroom with his two sons, the housekeeper had her bedroom on the same floor. The judge instructed counsel: 'Get all the facts out of this man so that it can be investigated; who he works for, and what church he goes to, to whom you can apply for information. It may be all right, but he assumes great responsibility when he takes a young girl in for housekeeper and lives with her two or three years and afterwards comes here for a divorce. It must be cleaned up before I can consider it at all ... I am not prejudging it; he has the onus of proving it.'[22] The reverse onus is an indication of the social importance attached to the issue.

Spouses, particularly husbands, to whom sexual misconduct had a much higher priority, used such suspicions to attack one another. One Pictou, Nova Scotia, husband had been guilty of frequent physical and mental cruelty over a ten-year period before his wife finally left him. She supported herself by running a boarding-house in Truro. Incensed at this assertion of her independence, the husband wrote a threatening letter to her brother challenging his manliness just as the husband obviously felt his own manliness had been publicly challenged: 'Ar you a man or not if you ar put a stop to that man living with Betty your sister as she was my wife once ... put a stop to it now John A McGregor or you soon will see me there and I will soon stop it, I will make a Hell of a Racet when I go I am not afraid of any of you death or life ... I am going furs to the preachers and deacons of the Churches tell her to be ready to meet me in this Racet for she will have to leave truro.'[23] Clearly, he felt that he had a powerful weapon to wield against his wife and her family in the community.

If both sexes were vulnerable to such allegations, it was women who were much more open to actual sexual and economic exploitation. Husbands could and did sever all economic links to their wives and cut them off from all support. This could be done informally at any time, but there were also several formal mechanisms. One that was particularly demeaning was known colloquially as 'advertising.' In order to protect himself legally against continuing financial responsibility for a wife who no longer lived with him, a husband could insert an advertisement in a local newspaper announcing, usually because of the wife's alleged desertion, that he would no longer be responsible for her debts. Such announcements appeared regularly in newspapers across Canada, and, to judge from those referred to in divorce cases, male plaintiffs and male respondents used this tactic in their struggles with their wives.[24] These notices were powerful declarations of the husband's position. They also tended to ratify the breakdown in the marriage by appealing to the power of community opinion. One Annapolis County woman was working to support herself because her husband was unable to do so. He collected her wages from her employer and then inserted the standard notice in the local paper. 'I asked him what he advertised me for ... he said his father told him to advertise me; I said, "what did he tell you for"; he said "because I might bring some trouble on him" ... I told him I did all I could for him; if he wanted to advertise me he would have to; I could not live with him after he advertised me to the world.'[25] Once the wife had been publicly shamed, the community knew of the depth of the couple's problems, and the final blow to this marriage had been struck.

The advertisements had several results in addition to their immediate legal purpose. A public notice to the effect that 'my wife has left my bed and board without just cause' went well beyond a mere labelling of the woman, albeit at some cost to the husband's reputation. By terminating the husband's financial obligations as a result of a wife's deviant behaviour, the notices confirmed the husband's role in marriage. The husband was able to exercise his considerable economic authority to ensure his wife's submissiveness, and the notices in the local press served as warnings to wives and as reminders of their economic dependence. At the same time, however, the advertisements conjured up images (and reflected genuine male fears) of wives' using their husbands' credit to do serious damage in retaliation for various marital grievances.

Many couples arranged a partial dissolution of their marriages through mutually agreed-upon legal separations. A legal separation was usually drawn up by a lawyer in consultation with the couple, but occasionally the agreement was drafted by the spouses themselves. The contract spelled out the continuing obligations of each spouse to the other and to their children, and divided the couple's property and income. While the terms of these contracts varied greatly, the small number found in the divorce records frequently gave expression to the husband's continuing authority. The wife's dependence on his income was often underlined, and husbands sometimes bartered away their claims to child custody in exchange for economic release. Where alimony or child support was pledged, there was usually a clause that limited the husband's obligation to the period in which the wife remained chaste and unmarried. In one agreement the husband's control was extended so as to dissuade his wife from considering remarriage: if she remarried and left her parents' home, she would lose custody of her children. In another, custody was exchanged for an abandonment of any claim to support and on condition that the child would never be allowed to live with the wife's mother.[26] Thus the husband's authority was extended beyond the active marriage, in much the same ways that nineteenth-century wills extended husbands' influence from beyond the grave.[27]

The husband's economic power could, of course, be exercised in other ways to underline the wife's vulnerability. A miner and his wife had lived in various Nova Scotia towns after their marriage in 1913. After seven years the wife began to look to other men for emotional and sexual fulfilment. Finally, after nine years of marriage, she deserted her husband and consulted a lawyer. She quickly learned that because she was the 'guilty' party at law she could not be the one to petition for dissolution of the marriage. Her letter to her husband reveals her legal and economic vulnerability, since her husband refused to support her any longer: 'I write to you to get a disvorce paper you the one that have to get them I cannot get them you got to get them and send them to me that what the lawyer tell me so I want to know what your intention to do your got to do one thing or another you are not giving me no suport so I can be lefte alone all the day of my life. I want a clear understanding from you so I know just what to do.'[28] It is indicative of a theme (to be developed in the next chapter) that within six months the husband complied by filing for divorce. But that did not alter the wife's essential position as a suppliant dependent on his economic support or his legal initiative. Legal rules thus often contributed to the dependency created by the economic structure of marriage.

Many of the rules centred on the sexual behaviour of both spouses. This emphasis reflected male concerns about marital behaviour, and minimized or completely ignored female concerns about economic support and abusive behaviour. The divorce process, and thus the divorce records used here, concentrated on adultery, often to the exclusion of all else, undoubtedly distorting the actual concerns of each spouse and the individual history of each marriage. The contrast between women's complaints (see table 13) and the divorce rules and procedures reflect the striking extent to which male concerns defined the divorce system and the ways in which women struggled within that system to meet their own needs.

The rules of divorce required a spouse to cease cohabitation upon learning of the other's marital offence; otherwise he or she could be charged with condonation of the offence which removed it as a possible charge against the 'guilty' spouse. Women's economic dependence on marriage made cessation of cohabitation difficult, something that was generally ignored by the legal system. The courts did not often acknowledge the wife's vulnerability, and the rules of law generally reinforced her dependence on her husband. A 1939 ruling by a temporary judge of the Nova Scotia divorce court is unusual in its sensitivity to a wife's vulnerability, and draws attention to the dependency-creating tendency of the legal rules. A wife had married her labourer husband in 1928. She followed him to his various jobs in Nova Scotia and the United States, enduring a good deal of mental and physical cruelty. Finally in 1936 she left and took a job as a domestic servant. She maintained tenuous links with her husband. He turned to other sexual partners; in 1938 he fathered an illegitimate child, whose birth the wife learned of almost immediately. The wife nevertheless took up residence in a boarding-house paid for by her husband and for a short time cohabited with him before leaving him once again; by this action she had apparently condoned his adultery. The judge spoke directly of a wife's vulnerability:

Condonation is forgiveness with a knowledge of the facts. In the present case there was knowledge of the facts ... The question as to whether there is forgiveness in the case of a wife is not always a simple one. If a woman is living in the same house with a husband whom she finds to be guilty of adultery, she may not always be able to leave the house or even to withdraw herself from intercourse and consequently she may not have condoned the offence by conduct which under similar circumstances would be conclusive proof of condonation in the case of a husband.

But in this case the wife had voluntarily returned to her husband. She had therefore condoned his adulterous conduct and could not use it as a ground for divorce.[29] In cases where finances were of no direct concern, the legal rules tended to assume an economic equality among the spouses that was almost always far from the truth and highly discriminatory against women.

As well, the legal emphasis on adultery to the practical exclusion of all other grounds (except cruelty in Nova Scotia) placed women at an evidentiary disadvantage. Given the greater social control over women's sexual behaviour and the fewer opportunities for adultery available to them, it is likely that fewer women than men participated in adultery. Nevertheless, a woman's adultery was more likely to be detected. If a pregnancy resulted from a sexual liaison, it offered incontrovertible proof of her behaviour, provided that the husband could establish his own lack of access to his wife. Husbands operated under no such threat; although they could be named in paternity suits, those suits could be contested legally and remained open to doubt informally. Not so for a wife's adulterous pregnancy.

One pathetic case illustrates women's economic, legal, and biological vulnerability. A Lunenberg County couple lived together for five years before separating in 1932. Although the husband earned good money from rum-running, he refused to support the wife, thereby violating their separation agreement and a court order. The wife found employment as a housekeeper to an elderly couple and eventually gave birth to a child in the fall of 1934. When her husband used this birth as the basis of a divorce petition, she attempted to cover up the evidence by writing a fraudulent and anonymous letter to the court:

This letter I have written as I understand that Mrs Edward Johnston or Marion Watson as she was before marriage was in the fault of having a baby girl, it was I. I used her name and her clothes and also her rings and she also helped me out with the money to pay the Doctor

and hospital bill at Yarmouth ... So if it is two persons in the world
that look alike it is she and I. So why not send your smart man out
and look for me as now I am at Upper Blanford. I see you are not in
favour of the Bootleggers but here you gave one a divorce without
hearing the wife's side of the story. pretty smart and stupid.

> From an unknown friend.

do not write to her as she does not know I wrote this letter.[30]

Involved in civil litigation that sought to punish her sexual misconduct, Marion Johnston expressed her frustration at society's
tolerance of her husband's own illegal conduct – bootlegging and
non-support. Not only was the story totally improbable, but she had
already written several other letters of inquiry in which the hand-
writing was unmistakably the same. Marion Johnston had been
caught up in the discriminatory machinery of legal, moral, and
economic processes and suffered the predictable consequences.

By insisting on adultery (an extramarital offence) as virtually the
sole ground for divorce and, in many jurisdictions, on the naming
of co-respondents as parties to the proceedings, the legal system
pitted members of the same sex against one another. Every wife who
charged her husband with sexual misconduct was required to charge
another woman as well. This made systematic what was already an
informal tendency to blame women more than men for sexual
misconduct. The sexual double standard still enjoyed a good deal of
popular currency: men's sexual urges were thought to be so strong
that they were difficult to control; it fell to women to maintain sexual
propriety, and it particularly fell to wives to satisfy their husbands'
sexual needs within marriage. For their part, husbands were expected
to maintain their authority over their wives and to control their
behaviour. Husbands who could not do so were singled out for
community disparagement as cuckolds.[31]

This community pressure and the divorce process itself served to
articulate and reinforce gender expectations. Wives lashed out at men
who could not control their own wives and at women who had
'stolen' their husbands. One wonders, for example, at the vindic-
tiveness of a Kingston wife who petitioned for divorce from her
Sudbury husband and selected as the site of the trial Cornwall, where
the co-respondent resided.[32] Delia Ortico, the fifty-two-year-old wife
of an Annapolis Valley contractor, was outspoken in her bitterness
towards her husband's partner in adultery, Ellen Darnton, and at
Ellen's own husband. On the back of two photographs of Ellen, Delia

wrote, 'Just an old *Sow* that can't get enough' and 'The free for all *Cow* Always ready. waiting for black and white All kind welcome.' To Ellen herself Delia sent a clipping from Dorothy Dix's column about married women who destroyed marriages, on which Delia wrote, 'This is you Ellie Darnton. You rotten old dirty bitch.' A letter from Delia to Ellen after the divorce proceedings had begun took the same tone: 'Listen, every morning I wake, I wake with a deeper hate in my heart for you, and I can hardly wait to get my hands on you. And I'll lay in wait for you, if I have to wait till I'm an old woman. I'll get you, you dirty liar. Don't you ever think of anything else except getting other womens husbands, and breaking up home. You dirty low miserable wretch Ellie Darnton We were happy. But it can never be again, and you are going to suffer for it.' Ellen's husband received a letter calling him a 'cuckold' for failing to control Ellen. He was called lazy, 'soft,' and 'a God dam fool,' and was blamed for bringing a person such as Ellen into the community and for allowing the destruction of 'innocent' families.[33] In such cases the popular response to marriage breakdown and divorce was based on and helped to reinforce the prevailing gender-based ideal of the family.

Husbands had to protect their reputations too. While the English practice of requiring the husband to sue his male competitor for criminal conversation was not followed in Canada, men could still exhibit considerable animus towards co-respondents, albeit much less frequently than wives. One Toronto-area labourer complained that he had 'suffered great humility and distress and damage to his marital honor and prestige and to his family life, and … further loss of honor and prestige in his home' because of the co-respondent's adulterous activity; he asked for damages of $25,000 against the co-respondent in his petition.[34] This was an unusually public admission by a husband of his suffering. More common among husbands was the considerable shame of their being unable to control their wives' behaviour. Worse still, however, was a husband's tolerance of his wife's misconduct. To minimize the damage to reputation and community standing, husbands had to dissociate themselves from their wives. Two years after a Lunenburg County wife left her husband, she asked him to take her back. She was pregnant and obviously desperate for help or support, but her husband flatly refused to get involved because 'it will only ruin my character as well as my people.'[35] A returning soldier felt compelled to file for divorce when he discovered his wife's infidelity; not only was his home 'smashed up,' but 'people are throwing it in my face.'[36]

Perhaps this partly explains the stronger tendency of a minority of husbands to defend against their wives' petitions for divorce (see table 12). A divorce action threatened a husband's reputation and his finances, and also challenged his position of authority in the family. When a husband had not informally taken the initiate to end the marriage or agreed to dissolution, the wife's initiative was an affront to 'the head of the family.' One way of responding was to fight back in court, and there was clearly community pressure to do so. Only as the ideal of the conjugal family began to alter slightly in the 1920s and as divorce became somewhat more common did husbands become less likely to defend against wives' petitions.

The divorce process itself played a vital role in placing gender roles at the heart of individual spousal confrontations. Nowhere was this more apparent than in the divorce trials themselves. Not only had some of the assumptions of the gender-based familial ideal been systematically incorporated into the law, but individual parties were judged directly by their conformity to the prescribed model of behaviour. This was particularly noticeable in parliamentary debates of divorce bills that moved beyond committee to a more than perfunctory study in the House.

The 1905 divorce bill of Mrs Clara McDermott offers a useful example. The debate in the House was an argument about the moral character of the wife and the husband and their relative compliance with the prescribed family ideal rather than a quasi-judicial analysis of whether the legal tests for divorce had been met. Supporters of Mrs McDermott pointed out that her merchant husband George had been separated from his wife and 'three little children' in a small town in Ontario for two years before he went to British Columbia for some fourteen years; in all that time he sent her only four hundred dollars for support. She was 'one of the most respectable [women] in the whole country and [had] raised a nice respectable family.' Another member informed the House that he had known Mrs McDermott since she was a child: 'She belongs to one of the best families in our country, I never heard a word of reflection cast upon her. She has raised these three children for fourteen or sixteen years ... Her three children are as nice girls, as well behaved girls, as well brought up girls as there are in the country of South Ontario. Mrs McDermott is as fine a woman as there is anywhere. There is not a word to be said against her, she has the sympathy of every person there.' When opponents of the divorce pointed out that none of this was relevant to establishing a legal ground for divorce, Mrs McDermott's chivalrous defenders called out: 'Do you think it is right to stay [away] for fourteen years and let your family shift for themselves?'

The opponents replied by asking why she had not gone to live with him for all those years. After marrying in 1881, the couple had spent their first seven years living with Mrs McDermott's parents. When George sought to establish his own home, his wife 'had insisted on living with her parents and would not follow her husband to his own home' in the same town. 'Her duty, when she married that man, was to stay by him as long as he was true and faithful to her. She preferred to disregard the obligation she took and she went to live with her father.' Attention was drawn to the evidence of her clergyman, who said that when he tried to persuade her to join her husband she had been able to offer no substantial complaint about the husband's conduct – she simply chose not to live with him. The opponents of the divorce suggested that this ought not to have been her choice to make, and that Clara had in effect driven George away and was thus at least as guilty as he; she had never made a move to join him in the west. Only after her disregard of her wifely duty were there any allegations about George's adulterous conduct.[37]

Who had deviated more from the ideal of the conjugal family? The members of the House decided that the husband had. But the decision, like the debate, tended to confirm the informal yet powerful rules of that familial ideal. Members of Parliament, it was asserted, were meeting an obligation of their claim to manhood; in chivalrous fashion they were defending a woman when her rightful protector failed in his duty.[38]

As time passed and divorce bills became more frequent, much less time could be devoted to their consideration in open debate. From time to time, however, the fundamental criteria on which the parliamentarians based their judgment were hinted at. In a 1917 debate the male petitioner for a divorce was attacked for having 'so little parental love' that, despite his ample income, he had not attempted to take custody of his children from his allegedly immoral wife. Moreover, the husband had failed to make court-ordered support payments. Another man was attacked in the House for his 'ruffianly conduct' and for seeking a divorce to relieve himself of his financial obligations to his wife and children, which he had already failed to meet. Gender-based characterizations were commonplace in the debates. A wife deserving of a divorce was a 'poor little woman,' her husband a 'brute.' When a wife was named as a respondent in a divorce action she was charged with 'the worst offence of which a woman can be guilty, disloyalty to her husband.'[39]

The divorce courts were just as vulnerable to the influence of gender-based assumptions. Where adultery was involved (as it was in almost all divorce cases), the courts were particularly vulnerable because the offence could properly be inferred from circumstantial evidence. Evidence tending to show infringement of normative rules in other respects could thus be used to imply sexual behaviour, particularly the violation of sexual codes. For example, as seen earlier, a failure to exchange Christmas presents was offered as proof that a husband and wife had withdrawn from a full marital relationship to one in which housekeeping was exchanged for support. In a 1901 case, one piece of circumstantial evidence cited by the judge in his finding that the wife of a prominent Halifax merchant had committed adultery was that she and the co-respondent were on a first-name basis with one another.[40] Wives and husbands should be on a first-name basis with only one non-blood relative of the opposite sex – the spouse – and they should certainly not appear socially with partners other than the spouse. Only by the enforcement of such rules could the integrity of a marriage be assured.

Socially inappropriate behaviour could be interpreted by the courts to signify adultery. After seventeen years of marriage, the wife of a police official in Digby County left her husband in 1909, apparently having fallen in love with a local tinsmith. She moved to a local boarding-house, and her landlady and others testified that the couple took walks together, sat together on a local hill (he sometimes with his head in her lap), and had been seen kissing. After several months the tinsmith began to visit the wife in the boarding-house, spending considerable time in her room behind a closed door. One witness had entered and seen her sitting on his lap, and she had been heard to declare her love for him. Two witnesses were anxious to point out not only this unseemly conduct but the twenty-year disparity in the couple's ages (she being older). While there was no direct testimony to indicate an adulterous relationship, the judge found that the evidence of opportunity together with the obviously inappropriate conduct was sufficient for him to infer adultery. The husband was granted a divorce – just as, one suspects, the wife wished, since she had openly flouted the rules.[41]

Men were also vulnerable. Husbands found that their failure to support their wives or to remain in communication with them was accepted in court as support for allegations of adultery. A man's character could easily be painted as immoral with evidence of his use of birth control devices or of his prompting his wife to use abortifacients, though women were at least as likely to face the latter charge.[42] Indeed, as Robert Griswold has made clear, the prevailing assumptions about marriage and the divorce process itself tended to place the individual judges in a position where they were being appealed to on behalf of ideals and assumptions founded in class, gender, and morality.[43] In defended divorces, each spouse battled to wrap himself or herself in the cloak of righteousness and propriety while denigrating the behaviour of the other. The 1913 trial of Flora and Donald McLean is a typical example.

Married in 1899, the couple had resided in New Glasgow, where Donald was a merchant, and had had one child. Flora's divorce petition fourteen years later was a litany of Donald's failures to meet his responsibilities as a husband. He had failed to provide sufficient funds to clothe his family, so that Flora had found it necessary to establish her own millinery store to earn the money needed. As well as running their house, Flora had helped in Donald's store. Her selfless devotion to the family had been met on his part by mental cruelty, in the form of violently abusive language, public charges of unfaithfulness, and his refusal to allow her to take her meals with the family. Flora responded by leaving him for several months, though she eventually returned to her wifely duties. But Donald's improper conduct continued, encompassing alleged sexual perversion and cruelty that expanded to include physical attacks. Flora's response was to end her sexual relationship with Donald in 1912. Three months later, after Donald threatened to expel her from their home, she left with her child on the basis of Donald's pledge to continue to support them. Donald immediately opened their home to a housekeeper, who began a sexual relationship with him. After this string of charges, little remained of Donald's good reputation.

But Donald McLean answered in kind. Flora had never behaved as a husband had a right to expect. From the very start of their marriage she, being 'lazy and slothful,' had refused and neglected to perform the ordinary household duties 'of a woman in her station of life,' forcing Donald to add the management of the house to his many other duties. She frequently rejected homemaking and mothering responsibilities, and sought instead an independent business career. Flora was quick-tempered and quarrelsome, and was continually irritating and abusive in her language and demeanour. She showed a further lack of respect by frequently absenting herself from their home day and night (Donald referred to this sore point four different times in his answer) and refusing to account for her whereabouts, taunting him with her possible misconduct with other men. It was Flora, he alleged, who refused to eat her meals with him in spite of his entreaties, and over time as she withdrew from his company she became increasingly 'slovenly and unclean in her person and apparel.'

Not only that, but her sexual attitudes were improper; Flora, he said, 'is a woman of extremely passionate and amorous disposition and often taunted the respondent with alleged physical inability to satisfy her sexual desires.' Finally she had deserted Donald, taking their twelve-year-old daughter for whom she was unfit to care. When they wanted to, men could appeal to the prevailing norms as effectively as their wives; whose appeal was more persuasive depended on the evidence adduced.

When combined with the overt racial discrimination so common at the time, this sexual bias could be devastating. A native Indian couple came to divorce court in 1939 at the husband's petition. His wife, he claimed, had been guilty of repeated adultery, and he was not the father of the last two children born to his wife. She had absented herself from their home outside London for long periods of time and had 'failed in her duty as a faithful wife and housekeeper.' Eventually his wife had gone off to live with another man, taking the children with her. The husband, a locomotive engineer, asked for custody of the two children he had fathered, because his wife 'since her desertion ... has been residing on an Indian reserve in a home where they would not be in good moral surroundings.'[44] Forced to appeal to the dominant attitudes of the local society and the legal system, this man was induced not only to articulate the gender assumptions of the time but also implicitly to denigrate his own racial background.

Class was also a vital element. A London businessman objected to his wife's insistence on running her own beauty parlour. Because he operated his own local business, 'her working wouldn't look good for me ... I was a professional man in business there, and I had it put to me different times by friends, why did I want to corral all the money in London, my wife working and myself working; my business decreased.' The community pressure affected the husband's treatment of his wife, and was expressed by counsel during examination of the wife:

Q I take it, Mrs Arthur, you would rather be in business than be a housewife, is that the case?
A No, I don't think I would; I would rather be a housewife.[45]

Though the trial formally centred on allegations of adultery, the actual argument focused on the more fundamental issues: the distribution of power between the spouses and the particular pressure of gender expectations.

Even those who could not defend themselves against their spouses' charges nevertheless sought to appeal to the moral sensibilities of the court. A railway gateman had been cohabiting with another woman for over a decade and had had a child by her when his wife finally sought a divorce. His lack of opposition to the divorce was explained by his desire 'to put himself right as far as possible with society' by marrying the other woman. In another case, a woman clearly guilty of adultery was quick to point out what a good mother she still was to her young daughter.[46]

Because the responsibilities for maintaining a marriage that conformed as closely as possible to the ideal of the conjugal family fell so heavily on women, there was a much stronger onus for wives to preserve the marriage, 'to bear the burdens' of their husbands' foibles and weaknesses. As in the past, wives were expected 'to suffer and be silent.' Socialized as they and their peers were to believe that woman's special duty was to maintain the marriage and to keep her husband happy and content, even a husband's misconduct could be laid at his wife's door. Under such constraints it was arguably more difficult – on this ground alone, and ignoring the many other constraints – for women to petition for divorce. When that psychological barrier had been surmounted, wives still had to justify to themselves and to their community (and to the court) the abandonment of their fundamental responsibility. As a result, where men's divorce petitions tended simply to meet the basic legal requirements, women's petitions often went well beyond that. Wives felt constrained by the dominant familial ideal to respond to the much broader societal conditions for divorce. While a majority of women included more than one characterization of the spouse's personal conduct, fully three-quarters of the male petitioners offered only one such description. Similarly, women were much more likely to attribute to their husbands more than one manifestation of marriage breakdown. Women's need to establish a claim to alimony accounts for some but by no means all of the additional allegations and evidence submitted on their behalf. One example will help make the point effectively.

In September 1930, soon after federal legislation awarded jurisdiction in divorce to the Ontario Supreme Court, Mildred Newton filed her petition. Her husband Wilbur had been arrested with the co-respondent a year earlier and had admitted his adulterous relationship to officers of the Toronto police court. Because evidence was available from respectable sources, Mildred's petition had to deal with nothing more than Wilbur's adultery and the time at which she had ceased to cohabit with him. Instead, she complained of Wilbur's frequent disregard of his husbandly duties. shortly after their marriage in 1926 Wilbur, an eighteen-year-old painter and welder, had lost his job. The sixteen-year-old Mildred, a factory worker, had supported them both until Wilbur deserted her six weeks after the wedding. When Wilbur returned several weeks later, the couple took up residence with Wilbur's mother. They argued frequently and Mildred still had to work. When Mildred rented a small apartment for them, Wilbur's authoritarian behaviour caused Mildred's health to fail. Mildred recuperated at her grandmother's home. When she recovered she had to go back to work. Wilbur not only failed to support his wife, but also continued to harass her so that she was forced to seek the protection of the Toronto police. All of this was laid at Wilbur's doorstep in Mildred's petition.[47] Mildred resisted the tendency of the divorce process to focus on sexual issues. For her it was important to establish that her husband was not merely guilty of occasional sexual misconduct. He had never accepted responsibility and seemed incapable of forming a stable marital relationship.

It was fundamental to this additional female onus that the double standard was still popular, and the mere passage of the 1925 legislation that legally abolished the double standard in divorce grounds could not end the prevalence of the idea. Neither women nor society at large had fully absolved wives of the extralegal need to establish the greater transgressions of their husbands. This simply reflected the imbalance in power and benefits within marriage itself. The divorce documents are windows on the male exercise of their authority within the marriage. Much of the power exercised by husbands was a product of their economic position and was thus a structural element rather than one based on a conscious decision to dominate. When the husband moved to a new job, the family moved with him. The money he earned was his and he handed it over to his wife at his discretion. Even when agreements and court orders obliged him to support his wife and children after separation, enforcement was difficult and costly; in practical terms the husband's support payments were voluntarily made by him, and his wife remained dependent on him.

Some husbands had no qualms about exercising their economic power. Though its legal purpose was of primary importance, the process of 'advertising' was, of course, the most prominent example of husbands' assertion of their economic control over their wives. Other husbands would informally stop their wives' credit at local stores; some went so far as to rent the family house while the wife was still living in it.[48] In an undefended 1916 Nova Scotia divorce case, a wife charged her master mariner husband with adultery, with insufficient economic support, and with physical and mental cruelty to her and their children. Before the trial (and in anticipation of a successful outcome) the husband and wife signed an alimony agreement that was filed with the court. When he read it, Justice J.J. Ritchie was shocked at its one-sidedness: the agreement was 'so improvident ... that it has given rise to a suspicion in my mind that there may be collusion between the parties.' Ritchie declined to render judgment until he was persuaded of the parties' good faith. In explanation, the couple's eighteen-year-old daughter testified that her father had forced the agreement on her mother. He had presented his wife with a take-it-or-leave-it proposition: if she waited for the court to determine the alimony, he would simply go to sea, thereby escaping the court's jurisdiction so that she would not be able to enforce the order. To courts that were insensitive to the exercise of this sort of power by husbands, such an explanation was insufficient. Ritchie refused to grant the divorce.[49] A number of cases gave evidence of husbands' attempting to coerce their wives into accepting unfair settlements.

On other occasions husbands used their power – whether economic, legal, or physical – to coerce their wives to act as the husbands wanted in the divorce action. One plaintiff husband refused to sign over the insurance policy to the benefit of the children in his wife's custody unless she agreed to co-operate in the divorce. A respondent husband had tried repeatedly to have his wife file for divorce; finally, he seized their twelve-year-old daughter and pledged to send her home only if his wife promised to proceed with a divorce.[50] Some respondent husbands attempted to use whatever leverage was available to them to gain advantages; in one case there was evidence that the husband tried to get money from his wife in return for his co-operation in the divorce action.[51]

Men's economic power in marriage and divorce was reinforced even further by the law of matrimonial property. While women had already won or were in the process of winning the right to control the property they had brought with them at marriage and the wages or income earned by them during the marriage, husbands still owned most of the matrimonial property and assets. When a wife worked at home caring for her husband and children, the family's major source of income was the husband's wages, and thus the major assets acquired during the marriage were normally in his name. His control of those assets was legally limited only by the wife's dower right in most common law provinces (a rather weak right of a widow to a lifetime use of a one-third portion of the husband's freehold estates) and by her right to support while she remained chaste and unmarried. But ownership – and thus the power to sell – rested with him. A wife's welfare depended on his judicious management of the matrimonial property and on his willingness to share at least some of its benefits.

Norma Basch has pointed out that the law's insensitivity to the disadvantaged position of women was structural: 'Despite – and probably because of – concessions to women, one way the law functioned to sustain the subordination of women in the nineteenth century was in maintaining a fundamentally asymmetrical system of marriage and marriage property that continued to disadvantage wives.'[52] This feature of the law was not limited to the nineteenth century. The law, along with other forces in early twentieth-century society, operated 'to disadvantage wives' because the dominant societal views of marriage expressed through the law did not yet proclaim a familial ideal in which wives were seen as the true equals of their husbands. The marriage system that it protected was indeed asymmetrical, and the overwhelming economic power of husbands continued to be confirmed by the courts, which merely reflected the dominant view of the way in which marriage ought to function.[53]

Nevertheless, in the face of such discrimination and power early twentieth-century Canadian wives were active in asserting their own demands and in trying to shape marriage to meet their own needs. In the absence of family or kin to provide temporary (and often long-term) support (with all of the reciprocal obligations that this created), a woman who wanted a divorce had to tolerate an otherwise intolerable marital situation. In the face of this, the number of wives who deserted their husbands and the increasing number of women who were willing to seek a divorce is even more impressive.

Women's systematic inequality in the divorce process may provide part of the explanation for the obvious discrepancy in the figures for female-initiated divorce. The number of successful divorces originated by women rose to a majority of all divorces in Canada in the mid-1920s, reaching 62.8 per cent for the 1930s, as reported by the Dominion Bureau of Statistics (see table 15). This contrasts with the figures generated by this study, which show that women in every marriage cohort (except 1900–9) filed a majority of divorce petitions, whether formal or informal (see table 7). Both sets of data agree that women's divorce behaviour changed noticeably in the 1920s and 1930s; wives became much more assertive of their right to file for divorce. In table 7 the sex-based petitioning is organized by marriage

TABLE 15

Percentage of divorces granted to wives[1]

				Jurisdiction					
Year	PEI	NS	NB	Que	Ont	Man	Sask	Alta	BC	Overall
1922	–	45.7	50.0	66.7	38.9	42.3	21.6	38.0	50.0	41.9
1923	–	36.4	47.4	63.6	57.1	39.5	39.0	33.3	53.2	46.5
1924	–	52.4	53.3	61.5	57.0	54.5	21.4	44.9	54.4	51.2
1925	–	56.7	40.0	69.2	49.6	54.4	35.7	42.6	52.7	49.4
1926	–	68.4	58.3	80.0	61.1	48.2	43.8	48.7	55.1	52.0
1927	–	51.7	35.3	46.2	64.8	54.9	33.3	44.6	53.8	52.5
1928	–	42.9	57.1	72.0	59.2	44.3	50.9	46.4	50.7	52.0
1929	–	56.7	47.6	53.3	55.3	51.7	47.8	48.3	59.5	53.9
1930	–	36.8	40.7	55.0	62.3	59.7	45.2	57.6	62.4	58.4
1931	00.0	50.0	60.0	81.6	50.0	57.5	52.9	55.2	61.1	57.8
1932	–	45.7	46.2	75.0	51.3	65.8	54.1	55.7	63.3	57.0
1933	–	63.0	16.7	60.9	58.9	66.4	52.1	58.5	68.2	61.7
1934	–	70.0	52.9	80.6	71.0	69.8	62.9	63.1	68.6	68.5
1935	–	59.6	55.6	77.8	63.9	47.6	56.7	64.6	62.8	61.6
1936	–	41.5	65.8	72.5	66.1	56.4	50.6	64.6	68.1	64.0
1937	50.0	50.0	57.4	81.4	65.6	60.5	59.6	57.7	65.2	63.4
1938	100.0	62.8	61.5	78.3	64.3	60.0	65.9	60.5	62.6	63.5
1939	–	65.6	47.5	78.0	65.5	62.4	54.1	60.3	70.6	65.2

SOURCE: Dominion Bureau of Statistics, *Divorces in Canada* (Ottawa 1923–40)

1 The percentage for husbands can be gained by subtracting from 100 the figure for wives; *N* can be derived from Table 1.

cohort; however, if that same information is presented chronologically, the results for the divorces in this study come much closer to those of the bureau. For the two decades before the 1920s, husbands predominated as petitioners; not until the 1920s did wives become a majority. This suggests that women in the early marriage cohorts were much slower to resort to divorce, though they eventually did so. This delay can be most readily explained by women's vulnerability, and at least some of that disadvantage was lessening by the 1920s.

There are several other possible explanations for the differences between the two sets of statistics, assuming that those reported through the bureau are accurate and that this study's sample is representative. Most obviously, it is possible that women, because of their economic and legal vulnerability, were more likely to petition unsuccessfully. The failed action could have been the result of outright dismissal by the court, but it could also have been caused by the wife's withdrawing the petition or failing to proceed. This in turn could have been the result of coercive action by her husband or the community, or because she could not pay the legal fees. A wife had the right in a divorce action to petition the court for the necessary funds from her husband; but this emphasized her dependency, and there is inferential evidence that at least some wives refused to put themselves in such a position. It is also possible that wives initiated action in the hope that their husbands would be frightened into changing their behaviour, and that they never intended to proceed with their petitions. For several years at the turn of the century, for example, a Yarmouth merchant had been attempting to persuade his wife to sign a separation agreement specifying his commitments, but she had refused, seeking a more attractive settlement. He in turn withheld all support until she filed for divorce, whereupon the two worked out an arrangement and the divorce petition was withdrawn.[54]

Wives were increasingly willing to challenge publicly their husbands' marital behaviour. It seems reasonable to suggest that such challenges were occurring at least at the same rate privately, and the informal divorce petitions bear this out. Marriage was far more important to women than to men. While only a portion of most men's daily lives were directly affected by their marriages, most women's lives were overwhelmingly shaped and directed by their marriages and their choice of marriage partners. It was thus natural that women tended to have a more fully developed view than men of the marital ideal and of their own expectations of marriage. Marriage (and family) was the most important institution shaping the daily lives of most Canadian women. Their dependence on that institution forced them to tolerate a great deal of unattractive behaviour on the part of their spouses. It is thus even more striking that when their marriages failed to live up to their expectations, women were increasingly willing to consider formal dissolution. Divorce and the prospect of a second marriage that might come closer to fulfilling their expectations were particularly attractive to women because of the centrality of marriage in their lives.

Yet at the same time it is important to view this development with some caution. W.J. Goode made a useful distinction between those who decide to divorce and those who formally file for divorce. Sociological studies agree that the decision to divorce is seldom a joint one, and that there is little, if any, correlation between the nominal plaintiff in a divorce action and the spouse who actually initiated the divorce. Most recent studies have found that wives take the initiative in a large majority of divorce decisions (as distinguished from applying for divorce).[55] But was this true in the early twentieth century? It is useful to examine the distinction between the decision to terminate the marital relationship and the actual filing. It is certainly possible that one spouse had a greater tendency to take the initiative in ending the marriage de facto while the other spouse responded by seeking formal dissolution. One way of testing for this is to examine the divorce petitions for evidence of initiatives to establish de facto termination of the marriage. To this end I have singled out those judicial petitions in which one of the spouses had already resorted to at least one of the following devices designed to put an end to a marriage: bigamy, foreign divorce, desertion, and cohabitation (see table 16).[56] The figures followed much the same pattern, with one exception, as the divorce petitions. In each marriage cohort women predominated in the use of informal techniques for ending the marital relationship. This was true until the 1920s, when men became the primary users of these strategies in the 1920s and 1930s marriage cohorts. This helps to account for some of the changes in women's divorce petitioning for those cohorts. Overall, women used informal divorce as much as men, so that neither sex can be said to have acted merely passively or reactively to deteriorating marital situations. The techniques used by women and men differed, however. Women tended somewhat more often to use strategies leading to a new heterosexual relationship: bigamy, foreign divorce (including divorce with subsequent remarriage), and cohabitation. Although men also used these techniques, they tended more strongly to resort to desertion. Indeed, it is desertion that accounts for the rise in the overall use of informal divorce by men in the last two marriage cohorts.

Despite the power exercised by men in marriage, there is clear evidence that women asserted their own power and influence. Many wives refused to accept passively their husbands' ill treatment or misconduct. Nor was wives' resort to formal divorce a mere reaction to their husbands' decision to terminate the marital relationship. Wives responded to their husbands' conduct both formally through the Canadian divorce process and through strategies of informal divorce, and asserted their independence from one spouse even as they moved on to a new relationship.

TABLE 16

Spouses' use of extralegal divorce strategies

	Marriage cohorts						
	1867–79	1880–9	1890–9	1900–9	1910–19	1920–9	1930–9
Wife's bigamy	0	0	5	8	8	7	1
Husband's bigamy	0	0	4	4	5	9	2
Wife's foreign divorce	0	0	2	6	10	13	2
Husband's foreign divorce	0	0	1	1	2	2	0
Wife's desertion	0	9	9	32	39	48	17
Husband's desertion	2	6	11	16	47	72	41
Wife's cohabitation	0	5	10	24	58	60	27
Husband's cohabitation	2	3	9	23	48	73	25
Wives overall	0	14	29	68	115	128	47
Husbands overall	4	9	27	44	102	156	68

SOURCE: Sample of judicial divorces in Nova Scotia and Ontario, 1900–39

Nevertheless, despite this evidence of wives' agency in marriage, it is reasonable to suspect that husbands influenced female-initiated divorce. Access to divorce by wives was in the best interests of many married men, who could thereby divest themselves not only of an unhappy marriage but also of the accompanying economic responsibility. All too often they ignored their legal and moral duty to support their children and ex-wives. Women could be persuaded to end an unhappy marriage and to risk the loss of economic benefits by the prospect of personal freedom (and the possibility of a better second marriage) and by the hope of receiving some support from their ex-husbands. Women knew that they would probably go hungry if their husbands simply left; if they chose to file for divorce, they could implicitly co-operate with their husbands and could seek to use the law to reinforce their claims to marital assets and support. For their part, husbands who deferred to their wives' formal initiatives in divorce conformed to the gender prescriptions of the day. The potential damage to a woman's reputation was certainly thought to be greater; allowing the wife to file as the 'innocent' party may have been part of the husband's recompense to his wife in exchange for the divorce.

While there is, then, some evidence to suggest that the sex imbalance in divorce petitioning is somewhat deceptive, it is important to emphasize that wives were active in the process of determining their marital environment and status. Their increasing public activity in the 1920s and 1930s corresponded with their enhanced civil status in Canada as they received the vote and were elected to public office. Vulnerability and the authority of husbands are prominent themes in women's experience of divorce, but the process was by no means one-sided. Wives found ways of asserting themselves in spite of the biases of the legal system and their limited power within marriage.

Although husbands had much more economic power and used it far more often than women did, some wives sought retribution by using the devices available to them. Divorce was for some women a matter of revenge, a means by which the husband was publicly shamed and his authority bluntly challenged. This was presumably an element in those cases where the husband chose to defend against the divorce. Other wives took matters into their own hands, seeking retribution in ways that would hurt their spouses closer to home. Preparing to desert her husband, a travelling salesman, one rural Nova Scotia wife sold their livestock, farm implements, and personal property, including notes for debts owing to the couple; their farm was burnt down and she collected the insurance before she left. Her husband returned from his sales trip to find most of their assets either sold or in ashes.[57] There were a number of cases in which wives claimed what they regarded as their fair share of the marital assets before leaving. The alienated wife of a Cape Breton miner sold $250 worth of his furniture when she left him. The wife of a Hants County machinist sold household goods valued at $550 and ran up debts of over $200, which her husband was forced to pay. In the north of Wellington County, Ontario, a farmer's wife of eleven years engaged a trucker to remove the furniture (except the husband's bedroom furniture) from their home, took the children, and left her husband for four months. Fifteen years later she decided to leave her husband again. This time, according to the farmer, she 'sought to damage his reputation in the community by imputing selfishness, unfaithfulness and adultery to him ... and caused a public radio broadcast to be made asking for prayers for him' that he might repent his sins.[58]

Other wives asserted their sense of independence and their authority over their husbands in more positive ways. In fact, the Cape Breton wife was simply withdrawing from the marriage her share of the accumulated property. During the active years of the marriage she had frequently asserted her authority within the relationship. According to the husband's divorce petition, she had threatened him with physical violence unless both the farm and the house were bought in her name; he complied, and almost all the assets, including the livestock and implements, were registered in her name, to a total value of $4,000. While the husband was off on sales trips, the wife would sell off some or all of the moveable property, keep the proceeds for herself, and refuse to show her husband her accounts. When he returned, he restocked the farm only to find after his next trip that more goods had been sold. As well, he complained bitterly, she had twice in their twenty-three-year marriage deserted him for periods of two to three years, always refusing to account for her whereabouts when she returned.[59] At least some wives wielded a great deal of power within individual marriages. While this power could be exercised in a wide variety of ways, such accounts make it particularly clear that many women considered the household effects to be theirs – the tools of their domestic trade. At the same time, however, men's control over the house itself was generally accepted. Whenever they chose, husbands were able to order their wives out of the house, and the order was usually obeyed. Husbands, that is, usually controlled the occupancy of the house, while wives governed the domestic environment.

In spite of their economic and legal vulnerability, some women were able to assert their own influence and authority in the marriage in many subtle and not so subtle ways. Divorce actions were not designed to disclose the small, daily examples of women's influence; as legal processes usually do, they focused on the most prominent forms of confrontation. But some wives simply refused to perform their 'wifely services' – withdrawing from the sexual relationship, not cooking the meals, not cleaning the house. Others challenged their husbands' authority by going out at night without their spouses. A few achieved economic independence by running their own businesses. For example, a ship-rigger's wife in Lunenburg took in boarders despite her husband's objections. She allowed one of them to run a hairdressing business in the parlour, and the wife kept all the rents for herself.[60] As these examples indicate, there was a continuing contest for power, particularly economic power, in these marriages, a contest that led to conflict and sometimes to divorce.

Other wives used their housekeeping skills for leverage. One wife was unable to persuade her husband to support her. Their only remaining asset was an insurance policy; she alone had paid most of the premiums. To get him to sign over the policy to her, she cooked some meals for him because 'I thought I was entitled to something.'[61] Much more elaborate was the scheme devised by a woman in Musquodoboit Harbour. When they were first married the couple had lived with the husband's mother. They eventually separated. Six months later the elderly mother became ill and frail and needed constant care. The husband effectively hired his wife to take on this task, but the wife protected herself with a rigorous agreement. The husband was forced to convey title of a property to his wife, to pay her four hundred dollars for her recent legal and medical expenses, and to assume responsibility for all household debts incurred before their separation; further, the husband, who was to live apart from the wife, was to provide all the household needs for his wife and mother, to construct a picket-fence around the house, and not to interfere with any repairs to the house arranged by the wife. Finally, the husband had to agree 'not to object to, insult or interfere with any friends which may visit or be invited' to visit his wife and 'will on all occasions properly respect his wife and his wife's rights and her guests.'[62] At times wives had considerable leverage and were clearly willing to exert it.

Many women deserted their husbands, either temporarily or permanently, for the prospect of a better life elsewhere. Some went to the United States to get a divorce before remarrying. Under Canadian law, these divorces were usually invalid, but they were certainly not so regarded by some of the women involved. When her husband of ten years, a shop foreman, refused further cohabitation, an Amherst, Nova Scotia, woman moved to the United States. She obtained a divorce in Reno, Nevada. There she married an Amherst dentist and took up permanent residence. When her Canadian husband needed her signature for the sale of some property, she refused to respond to any inquiry that referred to her by any name other than that of her new husband. She wrote to the Nova Scotia lawyers, 'My name is not Macdonald neither am I his wife, as you have put it in the deed, and I cannot sign by that name. If there is any document for me to sign disclaiming any interest in the property I am only too willing to do so but I can't sign any but my own name. If there has to be a deed signed by me, make it in my name & I will sign it.'[63] No Canadian legal process would be allowed to besmirch the validity of her remarriage if she could prevent it. Some women in similar circumstances simply refused to co-operate.[64]

Other deserting women, such as Millie Taylor, described in the introduction to this book, simply 'remarried' bigamously or took up cohabitation with a new partner. A 1915 divorce action in Halifax, for example, made public one woman's marital career. First married in 1906, she had deserted her husband in 1914 and soon 'married' a second Halifax man. A police officer discovered this first bigamy when he arrested her second 'husband' for theft, shortly before the man joined the Canadian Expeditionary Force and went overseas in 1915. The woman soon formed a liaison with a third man, whom she was planning to wed until the legal system caught up with her. Instead, she brought a paternity suit against him.[65] Some women simply took refuge with their parents or siblings, and a few established an independent existence.

In fighting back, wives had a number of possible tactics at their disposal. Some wives resisted their husbands' authority by taunting them about the wives' interest in or behaviour with other men.[66] The wife of a Nova Scotia fisherman played on her husband's vulnerability to charges of cuckolding, by publicly announcing to the townspeople that she was deserting him permanently.[67] Others retaliated by turning children against their fathers.[68] Some attempted to extort money from their husbands in return for not opposing a divorce action.[69] When the wife of an elderly Colchester County farmer sought a divorce and alimony, he denied all her allegations and cried poverty. But after enduring his cruel treatment for over a decade, she was determined to stand up to him from the safety of her new situation in Massachusetts. When her lawyer informed her of her husband's offer of a $200 lump-sum payment, she rejected it indignantly: 'If he dont give me considerable more than that, I will trust my case to the Law in your hands. I think God will help me. For I have been terribly wronged by him. If he will put another cipher to the end of the 200, and make it 2000 I will begin to talk to him. He must give up the idea now that I am the silly soft timid woman that I was when I lived with him. He could frighten me then with his fists. But no so now. I am braver now than I was then.'[70] Despite the intimidating nature of the law and the divorce process, some found in it the strength to grow and to establish their own self-worth.

Most of the female petitioners sought no alimony or child support from their husbands. In every marriage cohort in the judicial sample less than one-third (overall 28.1 per cent, n = 907) of the petitioning wives formally asked for some form of continuing aid for themselves or their children. For many, the absence of a claim seemed to represent both a statement of their own sense of independence and a recognition that they were unlikely to receive any payments ever regardless of the courts' orders. As one wife from Prince Rupert commented, 'I am not looking for any money from this man because I know he would never pay any but would move about from place to place.'[71] Wives sometimes used their potential claims for alimony as a bargaining chip. Some offered to forgo alimony if their husbands would not oppose the divorce. Others asserted their claims and then used them to persuade their husbands to comply with an agreed-upon portion of the court judgment. For example, one Nova Scotia wife in 1931 waived her claim to alimony or custody of their three children (ages six to three) in return for her husband's agreement to pay her legal costs in her divorce action; the court nevertheless awarded her custody as the 'innocent' party.[72]

At times the courts found it difficult to understand why these women would not press their claims for support. Most women were not required to explain their failure to assert their legal claims or to behave in a prescribed manner. However, in 1939 Justice R.H. Graham of the Nova Scotia divorce court was particularly distressed by a truck-driver husband who had failed to support his wife and child since 1930 and had been having an active sexual relationship with another young woman for some time. Graham refused to issue the divorce decree until the husband made provision for his child. To this the wife replied, 'I am engaged in employment and hope to continue such and I wish to feel under no obligation to my husband in any way and would not desire that he should be compelled to contribute towards my support. His employment is such that I feel that any provision whereby he would be obliged to support me would be almost incapable of fulfillment and the effort to collect from him would not be worth the amount which he could conveniently give from his very small earnings. I do not desire anything further from him in any way.'[73] Graham accepted her decision and issued the decree. Perhaps this woman spoke for many who saw divorce as finally ending a difficult and unhappy relationship and as allowing women to make a new start. Ties to or claims on an ex-spouse perpetuated a relationship, particularly when the legal system made it difficult to convert those claims into steady and substantial support.[74]

In this regard the rising number of female petitioners for divorce must be seen in a positive light. Whatever the influences of their husbands, women were asserting themselves and their rights in filing for divorce. Women described themselves as gaining their freedom or 'getting free,' thereby suggesting their own sense of liberation. As Nancy Cott has pointed out, for over a century this had been an element in wife-initiated divorce elsewhere. In contrast to the experience of American women, Canadian women's freedom was long delayed. American women initiated a majority of divorces from the 1870s on. The fifty-year delay reflected in the Canadian statistics was very likely a product of the narrow parameters of Canadian divorce law and the absence of a developing egalitarian family jurisprudence. For Canadian women divorce was an assertion of their own rights, but it was also, in Linda Kerber's words, 'the gambit of the desperate.'[75] Many Canadian wives were too vulnerable economically, socially, and legally to see divorce as anything other than a last resort.

But the increasing use of divorce by Canadian women allows us to glimpse some of the ways in which they fought to reshape their marriages in the early twentieth century. As Veronica Strong-Boag has suggested, Canadian women spent far more time and effort struggling in the privacy of their families for a 'working feminism' than they did fighting in the public arena for women's rights.[76] Wives looked first to themselves and their family and neighbours to alter or sustain the rhythm of their daily lives. They used the informal problem-solving resources of the local churches and community agencies. Only when they failed in these venues did they take their private problems to the public arena, where men set the rules of the game. Divorce was a public part of a private fight by women.

That public struggle was constructed in such a way that it did not cast doubt on the idealized visions of family, femininity, and masculinity; in fact, it served to reinforce those ideals. At the turn of the century the chairman of the Senate Divorce Committee received a letter from Lord Dufferin commending him for his work. 'I am quite sure that your 14 years as President of the Divorce Tribunal, in spite of whatever may have come before you,' vouched the former governor-general, 'have not undermined your faith in the general goodness of womankind.'[77] While individual marital behaviour fell far short of these ideals at times, gender occupied too central a place in Canadian beliefs to be reconsidered seriously.

8

Making the
Divorce Process Work

Women were not the only group to exert a growing influence on and through the divorce process. The authoritative and restrictive formal divorce regime was consistently tempered by a number of social forces. At times the local community and family values could be even more restrictive than those of the state, though there was a greater flexibility in the enforcement of locally based rules. Community and family perceptions of marriage and divorce were articulated through mechanisms much less formal but at least as powerful as those of the state. The customary rules of marriage and divorce coexisted with the formal divorce regime and interacted with the needs and position of individual couples and spouses to produce a strikingly complex divorce environment. Always operating within the constraints of that environment, divorcing couples in early twentieth-century Canada were able to turn the system back on itself, using it to meet at least some of their own ends. Mutual consent was the most prominent characteristic of a process in which couples took advantage of loopholes in the formal divorce process, thus forcing the system to operate (to some extent, at least) as the participants desired. The most important of these loopholes was a long-standing rule, confirmed by the Saskatchewan Court of Appeal in *Parry* v *Parry and Trench*,[1] that there was no collusion if 'guilty' spouses provided evidence of their adultery after the commision of the offence. Although spouses could not agree that one of them would commit adultery so that they could obtain a divorce – that was collusion – an offending spouse could nevertheless effectively present his or her partner with ready-made evidence after the fact. In a variety of ways Canadian spouses took advantage of this loophole and turned an adversarial, state-controlled process into a co-operative, couple-controlled one.

Most often, as in *Parry* itself, one spouse simply informed the other of existing evidence of adultery. In 1934 the wife of a Guelph teamster received a letter from her husband, who had deserted her two years earlier. Writing from Kingston Penitentiary, the husband sought to put an end to the marriage:

> You shall be somewhat surprised in hearing from me at this time. I thought I would drop you a line to let you know in case you have not the following information.
>
> I was convicted of Bigamy on the 7th of June, & since I have given you grounds for a divorce. Will you? please put in application for the same. As to myself as you already know, there is not any affection on my part for you & I am not believing for a moment there is any on yours.
>
> So let's consider it a terrible mistake we ever met. We are both young & there is a lot of happiness in the future for you I presume.
>
> Let me wish you all the happiness & success in the world. I sincerely hope you shall answer this letter & let me know just what you are going to do. If there is any papers to sign send them in care of the Warden here at Kingston.[2]

In less than two months the wife began proceedings for divorce on the basis of the evidence adduced at her husband's bigamy trial. Though the evidence was already in the public domain, she apparently had been unaware of it until her husband informed her.

Usually, a spouse would provide evidence that was not in the public domain and could not have been easily uncovered. Some pointed helpfully to the appropriate hotel registers; others named the third parties or likely witnesses; still others described their activities in letters that could be entered in evidence. A Nova Scotia couple was married in 1916, shortly before the husband went overseas with the

Canadian Expeditionary Force. He left his wife in the care of his family in Halifax, but before long she left. By June 1918 she informed him that she was pregnant and then, after a brief correspondence, dropped from sight. Four years later she wrote to him from Toronto: 'Just a line to let you know that I am still living and doing fine. also travelling a bit Eh. Well dear this is business talk this time. Now say you remember you said if I wanted a divorce you would get it so if you have not changed your mind just write me a line right away to tell me that you will get it and as soon as I get that line from you I will write enough to get a divorce with.' The wife had met a man whom she wanted to marry. It is clear that her provision of evidence was part of a negotiated process. Her husband immediately visited a local lawyer, and then wrote to her asking for the evidence. But the wife insisted on some continuing control: 'Yes I will give you information when you send for it but I must have some proof first that the case is started you understand what I mean don't you. I do not want to be made a show of in the papers any more than you do.' She would not co-operate until she was certain that the evidence would be used in a divorce proceeding.[3]

In another case John and Elsa Martin were married in Halifax in 1911; they lived together until he was ordered to France in 1916. Sometime thereafter Elsa established a new relationship with an American naval petty officer. She deserted her family for him in 1919, just before John returned home. Elsa warned John of her impending desertion, and shortly thereafter wrote again from her new home in the United States. Elsa described at great length her newfound happiness, and in a very friendly fashion offered to buy clothes for John or their daughter at the cheaper American prices if John, a postal worker, would send the money. Elsa clearly relied on John as a link to her family of origin: 'If Mom & Pop become used to the change let me know. If they would like to hear from me I'll be glad to write.' She and her new mate had established themselves in a home, Elsa told John, and they felt that it was only fair that they pay the costs of the upcoming divorce: 'It was not right for you to have the expense & we have the benefit.' Elsa had assumed her new mate's name, but encouraged John to commence proceedings as soon as possible 'as you can imagine how I am situated.' For evidence John was instructed to examine the register of the Saint John Hotel for 29 May.[4]

The divorce process was often initially controlled by the spouses, who bargained 'in the shadow of the law,'[5] each seeking to protect his or her own interests and to meet his or her own ends. But these negotiations, while significantly influenced by the demands of the legal process, were totally outside it. The couples were taking control of divorce. What is more, this was a conscious control, and was reflected in their behaviour and their language. Couples frequently spoke as though a divorce was theirs to give rather than the state's. One defendant mother testified in 1920 that if her husband would concede custody of their daughter, 'I will give him the divorce immediately.' In 1935 a defendant husband could not understand why his wife's divorce was taking so long: 'I did not attend the court, giving her a free case, as I am willing for her to have it.' In 1939 the defendant wife of a Sudbury smelter worker was examined in Windsor, where she had cohabited for over nine years with a gas-station manager:

Q Is there any arrangement with your husband that you should get a divorce?
A I asked him once and he didn't want it. He asked me this time and I said if he wanted it he could take it. That was two months ago. I was down in Sudbury and he asked me for it and I said 'if you want it you can take it.'[6]

In this instance the decision to obtain a divorce was obviously a shared one, even though the husband had ample evidence to proceed on his own. This sense of control over divorce was reflected in co-operative behaviour that vitally affected the course of the action.

Sometimes the co-operation was born of desperation, of a desire to mend personal lives full of stress and trouble. A Halifax labourer and his wife lived together for one year before separating in 1922. They were out of touch with one another until the wife wrote to the husband in September 1926: 'I am writing to tell you every thing and you can get a Divorce as soon as you like for I give you the grounds to get one now.' She was six months pregnant and wanted a divorce immediately so that she could marry the child's father before the child was born. But the husband had his own interests to consider, and took no legal action. Six months later she again tried to induce him to seek a divorce, calling him a coward and threatening to force him to support her and her child. Not until three years later did the husband, a master mariner, commence divorce proceedings, in which his wife's letters were prime exhibits.[7] In this case the bargaining was somewhat one-sided, but the process was nevertheless controlled by the couple.

In other cases the negotiations were much more explicit and often very manipulative. Some spouses gave only conditional co-operation.

In 1939 a defendant husband in Toronto agreed to supply the names of witnesses to his adultery, provided that his wife would bear all the costs of the divorce.[8] By contrast, in a number of other cases the defendant husbands offered to pay all costs as a way of persuading their wives to seek divorce. In one instance a husband offered to pay his wife ten dollars a week, find her a permanent job, and 'make other certain provisions for me if I did not oppose this divorce.'[9] Men usually had more money than women, which meant that they had more leverage in the negotiations, but women were not without influence, although their manipulation tended to involve a few obvious areas of concern. Some offered to co-operate only if they could be assured custody of the children. In turn, women could be manipulated by the threat of publicity and the ensuing damage to their reputations: in 1929, for example, a Cape Breton Island travelling salesman coerced his wife into giving evidence and a signed admission of adultery by threatening to inform her family.[10]

Co-operation between spouses took many forms. First and foremost, it was the result that was clearly open to negotiation. This in itself could take several forms. Most obviously, the defendant spouse might agree not to contest the divorce. While the legal process took an undefended action to indicate a tacit admission of guilt, in reality many undefended actions were the result of a decision by the defendant or by both parties that a legitimate divorce was more important than public squabbling over fault and cause. In essence, they were taking the decision out of the hands of the court. Such behaviour helps to account for the large proportion of undefended divorces in this period. The state attempted to frustrate this circumvention of the adversarial process by a number of means, notably through the use of a king's proctor, but these efforts tended strongly to be unsuccessful. The absence of such an official at Ontario divorce trials, for example, meant that evidence of infringement of the 'clean hands' rule was not pursued. In one 1939 trial in Sudbury, the defendant husband testified that after he had separated from his wife she had caught a venereal disease; no one in court questioned the wife on this matter.[11] The absence of defending counsel, whether determined by the couple or by the defendant alone, could be of critical importance.

Couples could also negotiate child custody and support. Here the court had a stronger evidentiary base for interference, so that the parties could not be certain of the outcome. Nevertheless, prior negotiation helps to explain why so few of the divorces involved custody disputes or claims for alimony or child support. In one case, after almost nine years of marriage the wife of a London interior decorator deserted her husband in 1935; one year later she obtained a divorce in Nevada and remarried in New York, where she had been residing for two years. Her marriage was valid in American law, and she had nothing to gain legally by assisting in a Canadian divorce. Nevertheless, when her first husband petitioned for divorce in London, she and her new husband journeyed from Long Island to testify. In return for her co-operation, her first husband had given over custody of their son and had agreed to pay all the legal costs of the divorce.[12]

The court's role in determining custody and support was so limited that it is suggestive of most couples' intention to retain control over those matters. The small proportion of requests by female petitioners for some form of monetary support for themselves or their children has already been discussed. This may or may not mean that some form of financial settlement was worked out between the parties; it certainly means that the court was not often asked to involve itself in such matters. Similarly, most requests for custody simply asked the court to confirm an arrangement already reached by the couple and their families. In fully 88.0 per cent of the cases in which the location of the children was discussed (n = 609), the petitioner sought to confirm the status quo, by either requesting or failing to request custody. In the majority (63.3 per cent) of these cases, the petitioning mother or her relatives were given custody. But in 11.0 per cent of the cases the children were left with the defendant mother or her relatives, in 22.5 per cent with the petitioning father or his relatives, and in 3.2 per cent with the defendant father or his relatives. Thus, in only a very small proportion of the cases had the informal custody of the children not already been worked out by the couple in the circumstances of their marital breakdown.[13]

Couples could also negotiate the process itself. They could decide what evidence to use and which elements of the community would be involved in the proceeding. In one successful divorce in London, Ontario, in 1938, the co-respondent testified to the couple's negotiation as to which party to the wife's adultery should be named: '[The wife] told me three months ago she was getting a divorce, and she wanted to know if it would be all right to have me as co-defendant ... I asked her why she didn't have this fellow she was going with now as co-defendant; she figured [her husband] didn't want me, he knew where he had the goods on me, and the other fellow he was not sure about.'[14] This prior selection of the evidence by the defendant or by both spouses was very attractive. Given the continuing authority of the community and the families of the spouses, it was important to try to control or limit the social damage caused by the divorce. One of the increasingly popular ways of accomplishing this was to provide evidence of adultery without naming the third party. For example, evidence of fraudulent hotel registration as husband and wife could be easily revealed without disclosing the identity of the third party. As well, both men and women, but especially men, gave evidence of a sexual alliance so casual (prostitution, for example) that the third party's name could not reasonably be known. In 15.8 per cent of the Ontario cases (where the naming of the co-respondent was required) the petitioner avoided identifying the co-respondent.[15]

An obvious form of co-operation open especially to defendant men was the payment of all legal costs. Early in the proceedings a wife, whether plaintiff or defendant, could petition the courts (or Parliament) for an interim order requiring her husband to assume the continuing costs of her action in the case until the court made a final order as to costs at the end of the action. This was a way of attempting to ensure financially dependent wives fair access to the courts. The courts were insistent, however, that such payments by husbands be made openly through the courts. If the payments were made informally between the spouses, judges sometimes became quite upset at their apparent loss of control over the process. Any private arrangement between the spouses could be taken by the court as evidence of collusion, and was, at the very least, viewed with considerable suspicion.[16]

The most revealing form of co-operation was the 'guilty' spouse's 'confession' of adultery – a tactic that made a mockery of the adversarial process and clearly exploited the divorce process for personal ends. At times the confession could take the form of a written admission implicitly or explicitly inviting the 'innocent' spouse to take legal action. More direct, though less common, was the written confession signed in a lawyer's office before trial. In 1919, for example, after just three years of marriage, the wife of a Halifax golf instructor left her husband. Less than three months later the husband signed the following statement in the presence of the wife's lawyer: 'I acknowledge that for some time previously to my wife's leaving me in the Spring of 1919 I had been having illicit intercourse with another woman and that my wife was justified in leaving me at the time she did.' Though he provided details of the time and place of adultery, the husband declined to name the third party.[17] In another case during the Depression, an unemployed labourer wrote his own confession: 'Dear Wife, Just a few lines to tell you I have been sick, with a bad disease I have caugt from some woman I dont know who as I was with several an had I intercourse. I have been a way for five years so this is the end for us. I think it is only right to tell you as it is no fault of yours.'[18] It is difficult to read this as anything other than an open invitation to divorce. As will be seen, the courts soon began to respond to this technique by demanding corroboration in an attempt to weaken the couple's ability to control the process.

Another form of 'confession' occurred when the papers in the proceeding were served on the parties. The party being served would voluntarily tell the process server about his or her prospective divorce or current living arrangements. This hearsay information would then be repeated in court; it was particularly credible if the server was a local peace officer. On occasion, counsel for the plaintiff would instruct the peace officers directly to solicit evidence.[19]

Direct admissions were often given in testimony in pre-trial hearings or at trial. Provincial evidence statutes (except in British Columbia and Saskatchewan) specified that in divorce for adultery no one could be compelled to answer direct questions regarding his or her own adultery; in Nova Scotia until 1918 a spouse was not even competent to testify in such matters.[20] This protection could be sweeping: in a 1937 Ontario case in which the defendant wife refused to answer any questions whatsoever, the court held that her refusal was proper, since any questions put to her could tend to demonstrate that she was guilty of adultery.[21] In their testimony given under oath, most commonly in pre-trial examinations for discovery, the parties were usually advised of their rights in this regard.[22] Not all understood their rights, however. A Ukrainian-born railway foreman in northern Ontario, for example, was named co-respondent and was cautioned as to his rights at an examination for discovery in Sudbury in 1936. Without his own counsel to advise him, he was left to his own devices; when counsel for the plaintiff asked him whether he had committed adultery, he replied,

A What does 'Adultery' mean?
Q That you have slept with this woman and have had intercourse with her. If you admit it, that is your own affair.
A I just want to do what is right in the Court.

Explaining that he had seen the respondent's separation agreement and believed that it had ended her marriage, he readily admitted that he had lived with the respondent for the past three years and was continuing to do so. Both he and the respondent refused to answer questions about their sexual relationship.[23]

Some respondents were unaware of the statutory protection against self-incrimination until they were informed. In 1935 the defendant wife of a Sudbury area mine foreman was advised of her rights at her examination for discovery and then asked about her living arrangements in the eleven years since she had left her husband. She responded by asking whether she had to answer the question and offering to do so if counsel wanted her to; left to make her own choice, she declined to answer. Later she testified that a 'party' in town had contributed to her household expenses, and then debated whether she should identify him. Finally, she blurted out: 'If you want me to answer it. They all knew I was living with him as I am guilty for it. You can see it by the papers of the child's birth.'[24] While she had not planned to use the examination to reveal incriminating evidence, she was not averse to doing so once she had thought about it.

Both of these examples point to the inherently intimidating character of the legal process and its officials. Those testifying sought to please the officials, and counsel for the plaintiff took advantage of this. It is also clear that the provision of evidence under oath was not necessarily consciously planned, but rather a logical product of the couple's co-operative intent and of their shared desire for a formal dissolution of their marriage. As a result, many respondents and co-respondents chose to waive this statutory protection against self-incrimination and willingly testified to their adulterous conduct.

Some parties saw the examination for discovery as an attractive mechanism for revealing required evidence in relative privacy. A New Brunswick couple had lived together for over seventeen years in Nova Scotia, Michigan, and Ontario before the wife, Sadie Petrosky, finally deserted in 1931. Seven years later her husband brought action for divorce, and she appeared at an examination for discovery. Her husband's lawyer advised her of her rights to refuse to testify to her adultery. This led to a lengthy exchange:

A I understand perfectly what you said. It is a pretty hard proposition.
Q It is up to you.
A If I don't answer here I will have to answer some place else.
Q No. You do not have to answer any place. Mr Morton [plaintiff's counsel] may be able to prove it otherwise ...
A This thing has to go through and there is only one way Mr Morton

can get it through. It is only one way he can put that through ... I don't think you can [do it otherwise] but what I understand from Mr Petrosky [her husband] it is much easier if I came in here ... I don't want to contest this at all.

After further discussion, Sadie finally made up her mind to answer. When she was asked whether she had lived with one of the co-respondents, she replied:

A I will say, yes.
Q I don't want you to say, yes; if it is not true.
A I want it to go through. Yes; that is right.

She then supplied some details of their living arrangements, making their cohabitation clear. But when counsel pursued the matter further, Sadie sought to draw the line, although he was finally able to push her into admitting cohabitation with a second co-respondent as well.[25]

In most instances the parties to the action resented this intrusion into their private lives. Many were willing to testify to the fact of their conduct and to add a few corroborating details, but that was all. A Nova Scotia factory worker admitted at trial to having slept with the respondent on occasions; he named the place and the approximate date, but he would go no further. He quickly defended her character ('a perfect lady in every way') and then refused to provide details of their adulterous conduct: 'I don't have to tell you; I have told you enough; you don't have to tell all you know.'[26] The testimony was a means to an end as well as a matter of conforming to the subtle coercion of the legal process; but the evidence was never voyeuristic and was only rarely provided by an acquaintance or the co-respondent out of vengeance. Instead, the testimony was a device for setting oneself right with society, for assisting someone in gaining a desired divorce, and, not infrequently, for making it easier to remarry.

Co-operation could be given in other ways. In some undefended actions the defendant was nevertheless present in court. Though unwilling to contest the result, he or she was still an interested party. On occasion the presence of the defendant was convenient; in a 1927 Nova Scotia case, for example, the undefending husband was called to testify when the issue of domicile was in dispute.[27] The co-respondent might also co-operate, particularly if he or she had a continuing relationship with the defendant. Indeed, since remarriage was so often a major motivation in divorce proceedings, co-respondents could assist the defendant in achieving that end and provide supposedly untainted evidence of adultery. The legal fictions in such cases were never-ending.

Pregnancy was sometimes indisputable evidence of a woman's adultery, and a number of women took the opportunity to invite their husbands to commence divorce proceedings. A Nova Scotia railway worker had been employed in Ontario and the prairies for almost two years when his wife gave birth. She soon called on a local magistrate, presumably to start filiation proceedings, and signed a deposition as to the child's paternity. At the birth itself she openly told the attending nurse that her husband was not the baby's father.[28] In this way she manipulated community pressure to force her husband into action, a technique that tended to be most effective in small communities. In another case, the wife of a Toronto lathe operator deserted her husband in 1935, after less than a year of marriage. A year later her husband received a simple but effective letter:

> Dear Stefan,
>   You will be surprised to hear from me after such a long period of time.
>   So I might as well be briefly asking you for a divorce as I only feel that I am being fair to you after what has happened. if you have not already heard I will tell you.
>   On November 29, 1936 I gave birth to a Baby girl.
>   If you feel interested in what I have told you, you may get in touch with me at Mohawk 8803.
>   Hope to hear from you one way or another.

Though the final decision to proceed with divorce lay in this instance with the husband, the wife's initiative was important. When her husband took no action, she eventually began to live with another man, assumed his name, and registered him as the father when she gave birth to a second child in 1938. In the undefended divorce action which then ensued, both her letter and the birth registration were offered as evidence of her adultery.[29] Though the 'innocent' spouse controlled the timing of the divorce, and the state controlled the granting of the divorce, the 'guilty' spouse here and in many other cases was at least as influential in the overall process.

In the judicial sample there were twenty-two cases in which birth registration was used in this way. Most commonly, the 'guilty' wife registered her new mate as the child's father; there were also examples of the wife's leaving the space for the father's name blank (with the clear implication that the father was not her husband) and of the co-respondent's naming the defendant husband with whom she still cohabited. This use of the birth registration system becomes apparent only if the evidence entered was retained in the file. (This was not often done in proceedings in the Supreme Court of Ontario.) It is reasonable to suggest that the practice was more frequent than the numbers indicate. The co-respondent (whether officially a party to the action or not) could play a useful role in providing evidence. In most cases this too was a product of co-operation among those outside the legal system. Typically, the co-respondent expected to marry the respondent, and his or her testimony was directly or indirectly solicited by the respondent.[30]

The deliberate revealing of information was much more common in Ontario judicial divorces of the 1930s than in Nova Scotia divorces of the entire period, but whether this was a result of time or of place is unclear; 19.2 per cent of the Ontario files show that a respondent or co-respondent deliberately provided evidence, in comparison with only 6.5 per cent of the Nova Scotia files. Such figures do not necessarily represent the extent of the behaviour. Many of the files in both jurisdictions contain such small amounts of information that no accurate estimate of the real extent of this behaviour can reasonably be made. While the various techniques of co-operation were used at different times, they were all the result of an agreement between spouses that a divorce was desirable. Many spouses could reasonably count on the other spouse's co-operation in divorce proceedings. When a Port Arthur, Ontario, husband, an employee in the family lumber firm, asked the Department of Justice for a divorce in 1930, he added: 'I am almost sure there will be no hesitancy, aggression, or withholding on her part for I believe this woman is already in favor of signing off.'[31]

Lawyers, of course, willingly facilitated any agreements that furthered their clients' ends and were legally acceptable. Lawyers arranged signed confessions; occasionally, both the plaintiff's and the defendant's lawyers were present at the signing. Counsel openly solicited evidence from potential defendants. One such practitioner was G.N. Weekes of London, who was leading a public campaign for divorce reform. Disturbed by the hypocrisy and outdated character of Canadian divorce law, Weekes willingly exploited the divorce procedure; his clients showed a marked tendency to avoid naming a co-respondent, for example. At other times he openly reaped the benefit of legal loopholes. In 1937 he entered into an extensive communication with a potential defendant in the hope of gaining evidence for divorce. This case serves as an example of the lawyer's involvement and of the extent to which individuals were willing to go in manipulating the divorce process.

Grace and Geoffrey Burton were married in London, Ontario, in 1932. They resided together there for a few months before moving to England, Geoffrey's birthplace. They stayed together in England, and had a son in 1934; Geoffrey deserted in May 1935, whereupon Grace returned to Ontario with her son. Two and a half years later she consulted Weekes, having heard of her husband's liaison with another woman. Explaining the legal situation briefly in his letter to the husband, Weekes made it clear that Geoffrey's evidence was vital. 'Of course we have no proof of that [adultery] but, if you chose to be examined on oath in private and to admit it on such examination, your evidence would gain a divorce here. This would be absolutely without publicity in England and no one except you and the young lady and the official who would take your evidence, would know even that an action had been started, until I sent you a certified copy of the final decree which would entitle you to remarry. All this would be without expense to you, a good chance to get your freedom.' Weekes sent a copy of the letter to Geoffrey's sister in the hope that she would encourage her brother to co-operate. But her influence was unnecessary, as Geoffrey responded with enthusiasm. He said that he was unemployed and could not be expected to help pay any legal costs, and enclosed the name of a notary public, the name of a 'young lady that I am supposed to have committed adultery with,' and some details of their sexual liaison. If this was not enough, Geoffrey was prepared to provide any sort of evidence required; 'as I said before, I am willing to admit anything as long as it results in a divorce.' The depositions were taken and entered in evidence, the court was informed of the negotiaations between Weekes and Geoffrey, and the divorce was granted.[32]

In general there was no apparent consistency in motives for spousal co-operation. Neither one's sex nor one's 'innocence' or 'guilt' determined which spouse was the primary mover in the co-operative process. Not surprisingly, 'guilty' spouses intent on remarriage played an important role in initiating the divorce process. Vicky Becker was married in Halifax in 1931 to a mariner ten years her senior who was often at sea. Vicky soon began to go out with other men, using a girlfriend's home as a site for her adultery. Within five months of her marriage she had deserted and moved to Montreal, where she soon established herself with a local taxi driver. Despite her statements of happiness in a letter to a girlfriend, Vicky was leery of the attitude of her Nova Scotia community. Cautioning the friend to keep her whereabouts secret, she expressed her interest in getting a divorce. She delighted in the idea that her husband was unsuccessfully searching for her, but if he wanted a divorce, 'I would be on the next train for Halifax for I would like to be single again.' Her girlfriend eventually offered the letter as evidence in the divorce trial and herself gave evidence of her friend's adultery.[33]

Some couples carried their co-operation one step further by creating false evidence of adultery. As a manufacturer's agent in Regina pointed out in 1932, the existing divorce law almost invited such behaviour by artificially limiting divorce to a single ground. 'For instance, a married couple living apart under an agreement and with no intention of ever re-uniting now desirous of obtaining a proper divorce are advised that the only grounds for divorce are adultery, which means that either party must of necessity deliberately set out & commit adultery thus not only violating a moral law & creating a scene as well, all in order to be a law abiding citizen.'[34] His underlying assumption was that the law set criteria to be met, but that couples determined the result. The law's influence, though important, was indirect and potentially counterproductive. The willingness of both society and the law to draw sexual inferences from conduct that strayed beyond the boundaries of propriety made it easy to place persons of the opposite sex in circumstances from which the appropriate, if often incorrect, conclusions could be drawn. It was a simple matter to arrange for one spouse to be caught with a member of the opposite sex in a bedroom; normally the pair were at least partially undressed or together under the bedcovers. The discovery was usually made by the 'innocent' spouse or a family member together with a friend or a private detective employed as a disinterested witness. Any such arrangement was regarded as collusion by the courts, and collusion was a bar to divorce. But this did not prevent some couples from resorting to the practice.

It is difficult to determine just how many couples actually practised collusion. Certainly by the 1930s collusion was rumoured to be widespread in the Canadian divorce process. Indeed, complaints about collusion were used by the liberal divorce reformers, who were disturbed by an archaic system that forced couples to resort to fraud, to make reform more attractive. A writer in *Maclean's Magazine* suggested that collusion was 'becoming increasingly common' in the early 1930s and that several prominent lawyers admitted that many couples arranged evidence. The writer (who failed to understand the difference between collusion and the provision of existing evidence) complained about the hypocrisy of the divorce regime and the ease with which 'unprincipled' men and women were able to take advantage of the system. In such an environment, one divorce lawyer was quoted as saying, adultery was a particularly attractive ground because 'it is so easy to arrange.'[35]

A contested 1932 divorce in Toronto offers an example of collusion as a means of spousal control of the divorce process. Frank and Dorothy Renwick were married in Toronto in 1925. Both were under legal age, and their parents had not consented to the marriage. The couple lived together sporadically for five years before separating. Two years later, after Dorothy had twice taken Frank to court for non-support, he petitioned for divorce. She defended against the action, claiming that Frank had 'prevailed on me to be found in a compromising position with some man so that the Plaintiff may obtain grounds for divorce.' Because she was destitute Dorothy had agreed, and Frank and his parents had allegedly arranged for her entrapment. Dorothy had gone to the co-respondent's apartment, changed into pyjamas, and got into his bed, where Frank's father and a private detective found her. She insisted that no adultery had taken place. Frank tried to undermine Dorothy's credibility by claiming that she had frequently offered to get an American divorce if he would pay the costs.[36] In this case both spouses wanted a divorce and considered between themselves several ways in which one could be obtained; their control was very much in evidence.

One way of testing for the possible incidence of collusion is to calculate the length of time between the last specific adulterous act cited in the divorce petition and the actual filing of the petition. Presumably, couples would have been likely to commence legal action soon after the evidence was manufactured. Indeed, it is just such instances that add substance to the allegations of collusion; it is difficult to believe that anyone filing a petition on the day after the adulterous act had not had prior warning so that he or she could prepare for the subsequent legal action.

A few examples will illustrate the techniques used. Samuel Speer, a travelling salesman, had married his wife, Donna, in Toronto on 1 May 1938. Within two months Donna had become suspicious of her husband's extramarital sexual activities, and by July she felt certain enough to leave him. Six months later a private detective, hired by Donna, witnessed Samuel and a female friend spending the night together at the Ambassador Hotel on Jarvis Street in Toronto. Five days later Donna's lawyer filed her petition for divorce.[37] Some collusive petitions were as terse and limited as this; others emphasized the real causes of the marital breakdown before detailing the evidence of adultery. Helen Leswick, for example, described her husband's mean disposition, his non-support, his drinking and gambling, and his keeping company with other women before she mentioned his desertion in January 1936. They had lived apart for thirty-two months before she suddenly filed for divorce, citing evidence of his adultery two days before the filing.[38]

Such examples were not particularly common, however. Of the cases in the judicial sample for which information was available (n = 1,438), just 11.3 per cent filed the petition within a month of the most recent alleged marital misconduct. A further 21.1 per cent filed in over a month but less than a year; 11.1 per cent filed in more than a year but in less than two; 15.4 per cent between two and five years; and 5.7 per cent in six years or more. In the remaining 35.6 per cent collusion could reasonably be ruled out because the misconduct involved bigamy, a criminal conviction, or continuing cohabitation with a new partner. If a delay of less than one month between the two events is an acceptable test for collusion,[39] it was a relatively minor phenomenon, just one of several techniques used by couples to take control of the divorce process. The fact that the use of collusion tended to be centred in Toronto (57.4 per cent of the cases commenced within one month were filed in Toronto alone) helps to explain why the national media, much of which was centred in that city, began to paint collusion as a country-wide phenomenon. Not one Ontario case that meets this one-month test for collusion was defended; all such defended cases occurred in the Nova Scotia sample. Nevertheless, the belief that such collusion was widespread began to affect the conduct of a few cases by the late 1930s. In defended actions statements of defence sought to impugn allegations of adultery by pointing to the rising reputation for collusion, labelling the charges 'fictitious, untrue and purely set up by the Plaintiff for the purpose of obtaining a divorce.'[40]

In their search for ways to control divorce and to gain marital dissolutions that they believed were rightfully theirs, some persons went beyond collusion: they simply lied to the courts. This sort of conduct is difficult to detect on the basis of the court documents, but occasionally it appears. Howard Ennis, a geological engineer, had married Gloria in Sault Ste Marie, Ontario, in April 1936. They had lived in various towns in northern Ontario until early 1939. At that time Gloria asked Howard for a divorce so that she could marry James Stapleford, a local Sudbury merchant. Howard refused. Gloria left him and moved to her mother's house in Baltimore, Maryland, where she commenced divorce proceedings in May 1939. The state of Maryland had a two-year residency rule for divorce, and Gloria falsely swore an affidavit that she had been living in Baltimore since 1936; her mother corroborated her statement under oath.[41] In other cases it is clear that friends were willing to perjure themselves or to try to influence the testimony of witnesses in order to ensure the desired outcome in a divorce proceeding.[42]

When their spouses would not co-operate voluntarily and could not be coerced, some persons were so set on ending their marriages that they arranged for the spouse to be caught in a compromising situation. This practice, known as connivance, was a bar to divorce and was likely to come to light because of the 'framed' spouse's testimony. In one such instance, for example, the 'framed' wife acknowledged that a divorce would not be unwelcome 'as he never used me right nor supported me nor the children,' but she was opposed to the particular proceedings because she was threatened with the weakening of her claims to custody and support. Her husband, it turned out, had tried to pay a man to commit adultery with his wife, and admitted, 'I would not be-grudge $50.00. If I could only catch her screwing somebody.' Finally the bargain was made. The husband took an innocent witness into a field one evening, where they lay in wait at a prearranged spot. Soon a car drove up, and the wife was seen to have intercourse with the paid accomplice. The husband immediately began divorce proceedings, but when the wife complained to the attorney-general and provided evidence to support her claims of connivance, the case was halted and no divorce was granted.[43] Some individuals were obviously willing to go to extreme lengths in acting out their sense that divorce was a process that they rather than the courts ought to control.

This attitude was shared by many of the extended families of the parties. Parents, siblings, children, and other relatives were involved in expediting a divorce. Some family members were undoubtedly motivated by animosity towards the 'guilty' party who had damaged the family's reputation in the community. In a number of such cases the animus was caused not by the marital misconduct itself but by its exposure in the courts. One woman who was summoned to testify against her defendant sister-in-law commented, 'I doubt if my people would have anything to do with me, as they think it is a disgrace to go into Court or have anything to do with it.'[44]

The power of local opinion is not surprising, but what stands out is the extent of family support for the divorce process regardless of the relationship to the petitioning party. Many relatives of the petitioners testified for them in divorce actions, but so too did relatives of the defendants. This may have been an attempt by family members to dissociate themselves from immoral behaviour, but it is more likely that it was simply part of a broader process of a family's controlling its own restructuring. When a farmer's wife deserted her husband in 1914 and moved to the United States to live with a new mate, her brother visited her but said nothing to her husband; when the husband finally petitioned for divorce in 1918, however, the brother willingly testified to his sister's cohabitation; he added that his sister had mentioned her willingness to sign divorce papers whenever her husband wished. Whether the wife's family had prodded the husband into legal action is not revealed, but their desire to further the process is clear.[45] This familial support is even more apparent outside the courtroom, where there was no legal coercion requiring relatives to testify. In some cases family members – relatives of both defendants and petitioners – assisted in the service of divorce papers or in the identification of parties. At other times family members were active in pushing for divorce action, as in the case of the mother of a Truro, Nova Scotia, woman. The woman deserted her husband and gave birth to an illegitimate child before she came home to her mother. The woman signed a confession of her adultery, and the mother testified against her daughter. The local sheriff was questioned about the service of papers on the woman and her mother in the undefended action:

Q Did the wife appear anxious to get the divorce?

A She appeared anxious to get it, yes, at the time I served it ...

Q Did the mother seem anxious to get the girl a divorce?

A I thought so from her attitude.[46]

In this light the testimony of family members against their own relatives, particularly of children against their own parents, tends to take on a new cast. It was not just spouses who sought to control the divorce process and result. This was part of a long-standing impulse for private family ordering. Families and couples had long used marriage settlements, marriage contracts, legal separations, and wills as devices to control and shape family behaviour and structures; marriage settlements and contracts in particular are associated with the middle and upper classes, but there is evidence in the marriage practices of peasants and the working class to suggest that the wish to control knew no class boundaries.[47] This is certainly evident in the divorce behaviour described here.

Even those family members motivated by animus rather than co-operation were directly involved in private family ordering. Particularly in the case of the 'guilty' parties in divorce actions, families administered their own punishments – and often had done so even before the divorce action had begun. These instances tended to involve 'guilty' wives, which suggests the continuing existence of the double standard. In one case the mother and the bank manager father of a defendant wife refused further contact with their daughter after she deserted her husband and six-year old daughter in Halifax. The wife of a local fisherman was refused access to her parents' home after she deserted her husband and gave birth to an illegitimate child, although her grandfather took her in.[48] In another instance parents tried so hard to stop their married daughter from seeing another married man that the daughter left her parents' home. In a similar case, the female co-respondent was forced to leave home because of her conduct. As part of their co-operation, 'guilty' wives sometimes asked their husbands not to bother their parents with requests for information; this suggests the continuing authority of parents over their female children. The wife of a Guysborough County clerk pleaded with her husband to keep the divorce quiet 'as I would be disinherited at once you know this would kill Mamma ... I would dye a thousand times rather than for them to know I would be guilty of such an act [as adultery].'[49] Families themselves undertook enforcement of community standards of marital behaviour.

The line between family and community was not always easy to draw. The local community was often a crucial element in the informal ordering of family and marital behaviour, and violation of community standards could be punished severely. In some cases the parties feared the loss of their jobs. One major Toronto department store fired a married employee on learning of his cohabitation with another woman. In Cornwall a woman petitioned for divorce because she expected to lose her job if it was discovered that her American divorce was invalid in Canada. Some of those involved in divorce actions suffered business setbacks. In two instances male defendant doctors testified to their declining business once news of their divorce actions became public. In another case the business partner of a defendant stonemason dissolved the partnership because the defendant's misconduct was damaging his partner's reputation in the community.[50]

The community could enforce its behavioural standards in other ways. There was ample evidence, particularly in some of the smaller communities of Nova Scotia, that marital misconduct and divorce were the subject of frequent gossip. Even lovers who travelled to Halifax for their assignations could not escape detection by neighbours. Any of the parties to a divorce could bear the brunt of the gossip, but respondents and co-respondents often suffered considerable humiliation. Some were hounded out of the community; others were coerced at least temporarily into ceasing their violation of local standards. Most hotel and boarding-house keepers became incensed if they detected couples falsely registered as wife and husband; some couples were ejected, others were charged punitive rates when the deception was discovered. Landlords or landladies who were judged too tolerant of such misconduct could themselves be the subject of gossip.[51] Respondents and co-respondents sometimes sought to escape censure by moving, by changing their names, or by concealing their true identities.[52]

The 'innocent' party's reputation was often damaged by the spouse's conduct. One husband testified that he had petitioned for divorce because the alternative of supporting his wife's illegitimate child would have ruined his reputation. Another husband consented to continue living with his wife only if she would agree to move to a new area where no one knew about her adultery. After divorcing her husband, a wife was too ashamed to seek a job in her home town of Moncton, and instead sought anonymity in the big city of Halifax.[53] Those labelled by the courts as innocent victims of their spouses' behaviour were forced by their neighbours to accept some of the responsibility for that behaviour.

This community pressure on the 'innocent' party could take interesting twists. As long as the 'guilty' party's misconduct occurred quietly and out of sight of the community, there was apparently little pressure on the 'innocent' spouse. The scandal associated with a spouse's discreet infidelity was slight in comparison with the much greater scandal involved in divorce. There were a number of instances in which 'innocent' spouses tolerated a partner's misconduct and decision to cohabit with someone else, provided that this was done without publicity and in another locale. In one instance the wife of a Dartmouth merchant deserted her husband in 1891, just five months after their wedding. She remained in Nova Scotia for fifteen years before emigrating to the United States, where she 'remarried' in 1909. In 1912 she returned on holiday to Dartmouth with her new 'husband' and visited her family. Her first husband then filed for divorce. This pattern was repeated in a number of cases: only when 'guilty' spouses returned openly to the community and flaunted their deviant behaviour did the 'innocent' party file for divorce, as though forced by the local community to dissociate himself or herself from such behaviour.[54] According to John Gillis, this fits a long-standing tradition: marital misconduct was usually tolerated if it was discreet and caused no public scandal; it was the publicity of marital breakdown that justified direct intervention.[55]

Another form of community involvement was the refusal to assist a spouse seeking a divorce. Presumably in cases where the 'innocent' spouse was felt to have contributed more than usual to the marriage breakdown, neighbours declined to provide information. A Lunenburg County widower was deserted by his second wife in 1922 after less than two years of marriage. He accused his wife of physical cruelty to him and his young daughter, and of failure to prepare his meals. When he decided to seek a divorce he went from house to house trying unsuccessfully to ascertain his wife's present address. Protecting the wife, who had herself been the victim of abuse, neighbours wrote to her in Massachusetts and told her of her husband's inquiries. In such circumstances, the town thought, it was for the wife to decide whether her husband should have the information. For her part, the wife wrote a bitter letter accusing her husband of various cruelties and misconduct, returning her wedding ring, and inviting him to seek a divorce: 'So if you want to go to the law the quicker you go the better I will like it I am just as anxious to have my own name back as you are to get married. I am to much sickened of you to think about getting married to any other person they may prove out to be like yourself.'[56] As in Millie Taylor's case, it was well within the capacity of local communities to draw distinctions between various types of conduct by spouses and to alter their treatment of the spouses accordingly.

Family members could be drawn into a couple's problems by the local community. Male relatives were expected to control females. This paralleled the cuckold syndrome in which the husband was chastised for failing to control his wife. Brothers too were criticized for not regulating their sisters' behaviour, but they had little responsibility for their brothers'. In one case of persistent marital cruelty, the husband's brother interfered only indirectly by writing to the wife's father, advising him of the situation and suggesting that he act to protect his daughter. The father responded by publishing the brother's letter in a local newspaper and thus appealing to the community to condemn the husband's treatment of his wife.[57] In another case the father of a married woman who had deserted her husband, cohabited with several other men, and finally committed bigamy was subjected by counsel to severe criticism, from which he tried to distance himself:

> Q You are the father of Jane Clemens, Mrs White?
> A I was her father, yes, sir ...

Asked about his knowledge of his daughter's behaviour, he responded:

> A I didn't care what she did; she was out of my premises: I had no charge over her, and I knew she was married to Mr White.
> Q Did you care?
> A No, I didn't care what she done.
> Q I think you should be ashamed; any man would be ashamed.
> A No, I am not ashamed of anything I do.[58]

Thus the line between family and community control was often blurred.

Fear of gossip moved many persons to action. A number of parties to divorce cases made secrecy from their local community an essential factor shaping their actions. Defendants and family members were often at least partially persuaded to co-operate in a divorce action because this would avoid widespread investigation stirring up their community; co-operation would assist in an easy and relatively quiet divorce. One Napanee, Ontario, husband wrote to the minister of justice for help. His wife had deserted him and had taken up cohabitation with her uncle, who lived some twenty-five kilometres away. The husband pleaded with the minister to break up their incestuous relationship, particularly because they were planning to move back to Napanee soon. The husband offered to bear any costs incurred in saving him from humiliation in his community.[59]

Family and community thus played an important role in regulating marital behaviour and punishing misconduct. The courts accepted this parallel system of regulation with equanimity, seemingly regarding it as a secondary and complementary process that reinforced the prescriptions of the state. There was no sense of competition or incompatibility between the formal legal and the informal community systems of regulation.

But the same cannot be said for the courts' view of marital regulation by the couples themselves. With the exception of the evidentiary rule articulated in *Parry*, the judiciary consistently sought to thwart couples' attempts to control their own divorces. The structural attacks on collusion have already been discussed. Some judges certainly wished for more rigorous attacks; they suggested in their judgments that the circumstances looked suspiciously collusive and regretted their lack of resources to investigate the matter. If a couple agreed not to name the co-respondent, the court would become incensed if it became apparent that the co-respondent's identity was actually known. Here was a clear conflict over control of the divorce process. For many couples divorce was a private matter, though the state's imprimatur was required. Many couples and lawyers simply wanted to protect the reputation of third parties. But the judiciary, representing the state, insisted on setting out the broader social implications of marital misconduct and on publicly chastising the parties involved. The deliberate omission of the co-respondent's identity could result in the dismissal of the entire action.[60] Perhaps even more disconcerting, other marriages could be placed in jeopardy. In several cases co-respondents' marriages were still intact, having survived a spouse's adultery. In other cases co-respondents had since married spouses who were unaware of their pasts. In both instances the co-respondents genuinely feared that the stability of their own marriages would be undermined by the divorce actions.[61] Thus, a rigorous divorce environment that sought to reinforce marital stability in fact destabilized other marriages.

Occasionally judges demonstrated some sympathy for people in this situation. A number of cases were heard in which the co-respondent was not identified. In one trial a witness was allowed to identify the co-respondent by writing her name on a slip of paper rather than naming her publicly; in his written decision the judge referred to her as 'Jean —.' An early Ontario case may have dampened any local tendency to refrain from the naming of co-respondents, however. While the 1931 petition clearly identified two different women with whom the husband had committed adultery, counsel had asked a local judge to issue an order dispensing with the naming of the women as parties to the action. The case proceeded on this basis, only to be dismissed by the Ontario Supreme Court: the court held that the local judge had no authority to issue the order and the failure to name the women as co-respondents fatally undermined the action. The wife could renew her petition for divorce, however, and follow proper procedure next time.[62]

There was little judicial sympathy for couples' attempts to control their own divorces through the revelation of existing evidence. Rule 14 of the Ontario Matrimonial Causes Practice Rules, for example, explicitly stated that no judgment should be rendered in such cases merely upon the consent or the admissions of the parties. This rule had been held not to apply to admissions made under oath in trial testimony or in examinations for discovery.[63] By 1939 Ontario judges were willing to go further: in that year a new rule made admissions in an examination for discovery insufficient proof of a matrimonial offence; independent corroboration was henceforth required. In 1944 the Saskatchewan Court of King's Bench upheld a similar rule.[64] In Nova Scotia cases were dismissed for lack of sufficient evidence when the defendant's confession was the only proof submitted.[65]

During the early decades of the twentieth century the couple, the family, the community, and the court all attempted to regulate the divorce process specifically and marital behaviour in general. The tension between these various forces was not new and was certainly not unique to the Canadian environment. Nevertheless, it suggests the limits of the authority of the law and the interdependence of many of the mechanisms of social order in any modern community.

Finally, there can be little doubt that the entire divorce environment was shaped and coloured by social class. The class character of the ideal of the conjugal family, which formed the vital heart of the divorce environment, has already been discussed. In the opinion of the articulate middle class, deviant marital behaviour was closely associated with the working class, and opposition to divorce and marital misconduct was consistently linked with 'the better classes of society,' as one member of Parliament put it in 1930.[66] Many state and charitable programs designed to uphold the dominant familial ideal were aimed directly at the working class. In the case of the divorce process this class bias was manifested in three ways. First, the ground of adultery addressed a primary concern of the propertied middle class; other grounds, such as desertion or non-support, arguably would have addressed working-class concerns if that had been the intention of the divorce process (which it was not). Second, the use of parliamentary and judicial facilities and the insistence on cumbersome legal procedures were intimidating, and the judiciary's inherent class bias was apparent as when one judge described a defendant wife as living 'on a low social scale.'[67] Third, the cost of divorce was high, and that alone was an insurmountable barrier for many people.

The cases offer some evidence of the cost of divorce. Over the forty-year period in the Nova Scotia sample, eleven cases (between 1901 and 1926) dealing with a completed action contain some information about costs, including the cost of bringing witnesses to Halifax, the costs of the court registrar and the filing and service of the different documents, the watching counsel's fee and the lawyer's fee. Anyone filing a divorce petition was required to pay into court a deposit of $100 against costs, though occasionally this advance payment was waived. The total costs in the eleven cases ranged from a high of $479.40 in a 1901 case to a low of $90.85 in a 1905 case, with a median of $165.75.[68] If a foreign or distant jurisdiction was involved, the costs climbed. In a 1906 case in which the costs amounted to $432.85, for example, it was necessary to employ a private detective to uncover evidence ($102) and to pay for the taking of evidence on commission in the United States, which increased the court costs ($161).[69] Twice in the early years the registrar of the Nova Scotia divorce court estimated the costs of the average divorce. The expenses in undefended cases, which predominated, were normally settled between the solicitor and client without taxation through the court; in ordinary cases the costs 'should not exceed $150.00,' he claimed in 1909. Two years later, while bragging about the Nova Scotia divorce process to a local senator, the registrar put the expenses at $80 to $150. Contested divorces, he conceded, were more costly, ranging between $150 and $400. In 1925 a Nova Scotia lawyer estimated that a local divorce would cost $200.[70]

There is somewhat more extensive evidence of the costs of judicial divorce in Ontario in the 1930s. Here the sample uncovered the total costs in thirty-two cases. Overall, costs ranged from a high of $807.10 in a 1933 Toronto case to a low of $150 in a 1939 Cornwall case, though in the latter instance the figure may represent only the lawyer's charges.[71] The median costs were $241.90. Not surprisingly, uncontested divorces were less expensive. In twenty-six uncontested actions the median costs were $239.88; in six contested actions the median costs were $307.95. The average wage in Canada in 1929, before the economic impact of the depression began to be felt, was $1,200.[72] There were sound financial reasons for the couple to work out the dispute between themselves and to present the court with an uncontested case.

Parliamentary divorce was widely conceded to be much more expensive. Though the individual case files are missing, there seems little doubt that this was true. Just how expensive it was is unclear. The parliamentary fee alone was $210 in the early years; in addition, it was necessary to pay the cost of counsel, of collecting the evidence, of witnesses' travel expenses, and of the petitioner's own expenses in appearing before the Senate Divorce Committee. The figures mentioned varied considerably – from $800 to $1,500 or even $2,000.[73] The Senate Divorce Committee could and often did (as much as 40 per cent of the time in some years) waive the parliamentary fee if petitioners *in forma pauperis* established their inability to pay, but this was degrading and still left the petitioner with other costs, which the committee had no authority to waive.

In 1906 the law clerk of the Senate discussed divorce expenses in the case of one prospective petitioner. A pregnant woman in a small town in Middlesex County, Ontario, had been deserted by her husband in 1897; two years later he had apparently remarried in Africa. In 1906, having taken up housekeeping work to support her young daughter, she wrote to the prime minister seeking a divorce, explaining that she had saved some $400. The law clerk responded: if the woman petitioned the Senate to be relieved of the parliamentary fee 'and showed that you could not pay it, for want of means to do so, and because of the expense you had been put to in supporting yourself and your little girl, in getting evidence of your husband's infidelity, and in employing counsel etc., the Senate would undoubtedly excuse you from paying this $210.' The other costs had to be borne by the parties involved; 'but what you have saved ought to be more than enough to cover all your expenses in any case.'[74] His estimate appears optimistically low in this case, however, since the expense of getting evidence from Africa would have pushed the total costs much higher.

In 1926 an English woman wrote to Ottawa complaining about the charges for her 1919 divorce. She had paid $1,500 in total costs to dissolve her nineteen-year marriage; she had been living in Ottawa at the time and her husband had lived in Cochrane, Ontario, so that distance had not been an unusual factor (though their marriage had been performed in England, and that would have had to have been established). Still using her ex-husband's name, she had returned to England. Seven years later, her divorce costs still infuriated her. But it was her lawyers who took the brunt of her rage: how was it, she cried, that these '*Dirty* Canadian Solicitors could dare with such Impunity to *violate* my son's and my *own* Rights in this legal matter?'[75]

The Department of Justice received many letters from prospective divorcés who found the projected costs of the divorce process much too high. In 1913 a baker from Vonda, Saskatchewan, described his dilemma. After six years of marriage his wife had deserted him and their two young girls in Manitoba in 1907, running off with her boarder. The husband searched for his wife and then took his children back to England to be cared for by his family before returning to the prairies. He had first approached the premier of Manitoba for help in the matter; he had suggested a divorce and directed him to a lawyer. 'After putting my case to that gentleman, & hearing what it would cost, & I not being in a financial position to carry it through, had to let it drop.' At the same time he wrote to his member of Parliament, who put him in touch with the clerk of the Senate and the chairman of the Senate Divorce Committee, who assured him that he had ample grounds for divorce. Once again he was told that evidence must be taken and his witnesses must appear before the Divorce Committee in Ottawa:

> & not having the funds that is where I came up against it ... Now my dear sir, in view of all the facts I have mentioned, you as the minister of justice, is there no other ways or means for me to get out of this trouble without incurring such heavy expenses, as different lawyers I have seen in this matter, has told me that my case will cost me anyway between 1200 and 1500 dollars, if that is the case, then I will have to shoulder this burden for some time yet. perhaps you would recommend me to a lawyer in Ottawa who would carry this through for me far cheaper than a lawyer would up here in the west.[76]

His plea to the minister of justice was echoed so often that the minister soon developed a standard and exceedingly brief reply directing the suppliant to a lawyer.

Such costs were virtually prohibitive for most Canadians. 'Surely divorce in Canada should be based on grounds rather than money,' wrote one Markham, Ontario, wife who had been defrauded of her savings by her husband. Why should a divorce cost $1,000 in Canada, when one could be obtained in the United States for only $75?[77] A Hamilton, Ontario, husband pleaded for divorce law reform in 1922: 'now I have been so anchely [anxiously] waiting for the last two or three years back for this new law to be for. so that a poor man can get one for $100 or $200 with out paying $600. Now I do asks so earnsly of you to press this thing through this spring as I do not think it should take so long. as every true thinking person knows that it is badley neaded. for it is only a rich mans law now. the poore working man no matter how bad he neads on [one] cant get it.'[78] Occasionally, charitable agencies provided financial assistance for women seeking a divorce, usually in cases where such help would enable the woman to remarry and establish a stable family situation so that she no longer required public support.[79]

Clearly, the parliamentary divorce process was considerably more expensive than the judicial process. It is not surprising that the numbers of divorces rose markedly in each jurisdiction that acquired judicial divorce. Yet even judicial divorce remained costly. A 1935 Nova Scotia case illustrates the continuing problems of the poor. An English couple had married in 1925, and had had two children. The husband, a master mariner, deserted his family and emigrated to Nova Scotia. Though the wife filed for divorce in 1935, a year and a half later she was still unable to proceed with the action. She had no money to travel to Halifax to give her testimony or to pay for the taking of her evidence on commission in England; any order to have her husband pay her costs would be useless, because he was now in jail in the United States. The wife was forced to discontinue the action.[80]

The high cost of divorce in Canada could reasonably be expected to deter most members of the working class, yet working-class couples were not underrepresented among those applying for divorce (see table 17). Workers were prevalent users of the divorce process, in spite of its heavy financial demands. In the overall sample[81] – that is, for both parliamentary and judicial divorce – working-class couples made up 68.5 per cent of the total; middle-class couples made up 25.7 per cent, and farmers just 5.9 per cent. It is even more surprising that for workers there was no difference in participation rates between judicial divorce and the much more expensive parliamentary divorce. In the judicial divorce sample, workers made up 68.4 per cent of the total, compared with 68.5 per cent in the parliamentary divorces.[82] There is clear evidence of stratification in both the middle class and the working class. While the bourgeoisie, the petite bourgeoisie, and management sought divorce at a rate roughly double their numbers in the general population,[83] the behaviour of professionals was somewhat different. Professionals (such as doctors, lawyers, teachers, engineers, and accountants) were three times more likely to petition for divorce as their presence in the general population would suggest. Among workers too there were distinctly different patterns. While the rates of participation of foremen and blue-collar workers correlated directly with their numbers in the total population, white-collar workers were more than twice as likely to apply for formal divorces. Indeed, the participation rate among white-collar workers meshes well with that of the middle class, and is quite distinct from any other stratum in the working class. As might be expected, white-collar workers tended to suppress the objective reality of their class membership, and to aspire to and

TABLE 17

Percentage of divorce petitions by class, 1900–1939

Class	1900–4	1905–9	1910–17	1918–19	1920–4	1925–9	1931 census[1]	1930–4	1935–9
Bourgeoisie and petite bourgeoisie	15.0	15.9	9.1	7.0	7.1	7.7	6.8	7.1	7.2
Management	5.0	3.4	3.9	5.5	3.6	5.1		5.2	4.7
Professionals	13.3	15.9	18.3	10.9	14.4	11.2	3.9	12.8	13.9
Subtotal: middle class	33.3	35.2	31.3	23.4	25.0	24.0	10.7	25.1	25.8
White-collar	13.3	22.7	17.4	10.9	16.9	25.9	9.2	22.4	25.4
Service workers	3.3	4.6	4.8	6.3	4.1	4.5	2.9	3.9	3.5
Foremen	0.0	0.0	1.7	2.3	1.4	2.0	1.5	2.0	1.4
Skilled and semi-skilled	33.3	20.5	17.8	39.1	38.2	30.9	26.7	32.6	29.0
Unskilled	3.3	5.7	8.7	4.7	8.5	8.3	29.9	10.6	11.1
Subtotal: working class	53.3	53.4	50.4	63.3	68.9	71.5	70.1	71.6	70.4
Farmers	13.3	11.4	18.3	13.3	6.1	4.5	19.2	3.4	3.8
N	60	88	230	128	592	975	–	714	835

SOURCE: Parliamentary divorces and judicial sample of Nova Scotia and Ontario divorces, 1900–39

1 Calculated from the *Census of Canada 1931*, vol. 1, 1286–97, applying the same definition of class (as outlined in the appendix) to the data in the table of the occupational distribution of the gainfully employed

mimic the behaviour of the middle class. Unskilled workers, in contrast, were dramatically underrepresented: though they made up almost 30 per cent of the general population, they represented 11 per cent or less of Canadians obtaining divorces. Most striking of all, farmers shied away from formal divorce, and were the least likely occupational group in the country to seek divorce. The impact of class on divorce participation was neither straightforward nor simple.

Class did significantly affect the timing of the marriage breakdown and the resort to divorce. As might be expected, in the judicial sample farmers consistently showed the most conservative behaviour, taking the longest time to record marital breakdown or initiate divorce procedures. While the middle class and workers both recorded a median of 43 months between the first breakdown and the initial filing for divorce, farmers had a median of 54.5 months. Farmers reported an initial period of 97 months' cohabitation before the first recorded breakdown; the middle class had 76 months, workers 62. For the same groups the duration of the marriage at the time of the divorce petition was 180 months, 130 months, and 115 months respectively. These figures, of course, also emphasize the relative rapidity with which the working class resorted to various techniques of marriage breakdown and to the divorce process itself. Here the behaviour of white-collar spouses approximated that of the working class much more than that of the middle class.

Not surprisingly, there was some change in class and sexual participation over the forty-year period. While working-class couples made up not much more than half of the petitions in the early years of the decade (see table 17), the number of their petitions jumped markedly at the end of the First World War and climbed further in the early 1920s before levelling off between 70 and 72 per cent. Similarly, the number of middle-class petitions dropped at the end of the war, levelling off at around 25 per cent during the great increase in petitions in the 1920s and 1930s. Farmers' petitions too declined proportionately, levelling off at around 4 per cent. If this information is broken down by the sex of the petitioner, other patterns become apparent (see table 18). Among the middle class, male petitioners led the way in the first decade of the twentieth century (when the sample size is small); they were overtaken by women, particularly in the period from 1918 to 1925. This female dominance among the middle class can be understood by what has become a standard explanation of first-wave feminism: middle-class women were exploiting the paternalistic bias of the dominant familial ideal and the divorce process, and were making it serve their own ends.[84] Among the working class, female petitioners led the way for the first two decades; then men's participation climbed to a comparable level.

TABLE 18

Percentage of divorce petitions by class of husband and sex of petitioner, 1900–1939

Petitioner	1900–4	1905–9	1910–17	1918–19	1920–4	1925–9	1931 census[1]	1930–4	1935–9
Female									
Middle class	28.0	23.7	30.7	30.2	30.7	25.2	10.7	26.1	26.7
Working class	56.0	68.4	53.4	65.1	64.5	71.4	70.1	71.2	70.1
Farmers	16.0	7.9	15.9	4.7	4.8	3.4	19.2	2.8	3.2
N	25	38	88	43	251	556	–	437	559
Male									
Middle class	38.2	44.0	31.7	20.0	20.8	22.4	10.7	23.2	23.9
Working class	50.0	42.0	48.6	62.4	72.1	71.6	70.1	71.4	71.0
Farmers	11.8	14.0	19.7	17.7	7.0	6.0	19.2	4.3	5.1
N	34	50	142	85	341	419	–	280	276

SOURCE: Parliamentary divorces and judicial sample of Nova Scotia and Ontario divorces, 1900–39

1 Calculated from the *Census of Canada 1931*, vol 1, 1286–97, applying the same definition of class (as outlined in the appendix) to the data in the table of the occupational distribution of the gainfully employed

By the time the number of divorces began to rise markedly, the sex of the petitioner had become a constant factor in determining working-class divorce behaviour. Farmers consistently formed a greater proportion of the male petitioners than the female, suggesting among both women and men a stronger acceptance of a traditional hierarchy of sex in farming families.

What then is to be made of the role of social class in divorce? It is well established in other Western societies that working-class participation in divorce tended to be disproportionately high.[85] Yet in Canada this was true only of white-collar workers. This underrepresentation of workers is in itself confirmation of the overwhelming class bias of the entire divorce environment. The primary cause of their low participation rate was the high financial cost of divorce. In view of the economic situation during much of the 1920s and 1930s, it is remarkable that workers were able to participate at the rate they did. The average wage in Canada was $1,200 in 1929; the Department of Labour's estimate of the income needed to sustain the average Canadian family was $1,430.[86] Few workers would have had any disposable income, and only a very small minority of those would have had enough disposable income to afford a formal divorce. There is certainly evidence in some of the cases that spouses borrowed money from their families, particularly from their parents. Both women and workers must have been forced to rely extensively on the financial resources of others to allow them to participate in divorce at the rate that they did. This simply reinforces the well-established role of the extended family in the lives of women and workers, especially in times of crisis. It is also possible that some workers simply failed to pay the lawyers' fees after the divorce was granted, though an unpaid lawyer could have refused to file for a decree absolute. There is no evidence that failure to pay was a common phenomenon. Although it is difficult to understand how workers could have afforded even the less costly judicial divorce, it is unlikely that lawyers would have tolerated a high level of nonpayment from a sector that represented up to 70 per cent of total divorces (though it is possible that some notion of chivalry persuaded lawyers to forgo or reduce costs for female plaintiffs). In the final anaysis, any understanding of working-class underparticipation because of costs is confounded by the absence of any difference in use between judicial divorce and the far more costly parliamentary procedure.

Workers' participation in divorce reveals their familial values and attitudes. The divorce environment was the expression of a predominantly middle-class family ideal. Therefore, it might reasonably be expected to be less influential in inhibiting divorce among workers than among members of the middle class. Historians have demonstrated the vital importance of the family among the working class. Louise Tilly, Tamara Hareven, and others have argued persuasively that in the industrial economy of the late nineteenth and early twentieth centuries, workers found nuclear and extended families to be one of their few resources – indeed, their chief one. In a study of a French textile-producing city, Tilly has suggested that the conjugal family played somewhat different roles for workers and for the middle class; workers had different expectations. But when the conjugal family could not meet those broader economic or support-related expectations, it was even more essential for a worker to put aside a failed marriage in search of a more effective one.[87] This sort of reliance on family was both an expression of working-class culture and a continuing contribution to that culture. Workers actively articulated (in word and in behaviour) their own familial values and structures, which in this case necessitated finding substantial solutions to marital breakdown. The middle class may have sought divorce to protect property rights, but workers sought to form new marriages that would ensure their physical and economic survival. This class pattern can be seen in other familial behaviour. Jane Lewis, for example, has suggested that while middle-class mothers in England 'did their best to follow social prescriptions in bringing up their daughters,' for working-class mothers 'there was a greater gap between the behaviour prescribed and their own understanding of good mothering.'[88] The predominantly articulated familial structures and ideas in twentieth-century society have inevitably been those of the middle class, because that class controls the instruments of formal articulation. The working class, however, has continued to insist on its own values and needs, though always in interaction with those of the middle class, which has been successful at structurally reinforcing its ideas.

Yet formal divorce remained less common among workers than among the middle class. Led by professionals, a small proportion of the middle class was unintimidated by either the stigma or the financial costs of divorce. What is more, their participation rate was relatively steady across the forty-year period. Seemingly unaffected by changes in the economic, political, or social environment, the middle class consistently sought divorce at a relatively high rate. For the middle class, of course, divorce met some substantial economic needs. There were assets that demanded protection, marital obligations that required restatement, and inheritance rights that had to be redefined legally. Though it cannot be tested systematically with the existing evidence, logic suggests that there was a direct correlation between the value of a couple's property and the likelihood of that couple's resorting to the formal divorce process. The essential legal function of defining property ownership made divorce an institution of central importance to the middle class.

Despite the intimidating and restrictive character of the Canadian divorce environment, middle-class couples sought to assert their own autonomy. Much of the recent historical literature on the working class has depicted individuals or groups of workers struggling to assert their autonomy in an economic, political, and social environment created and dominated by a more powerful class.[89] The evidence of divorce participation suggests that this interpretation may need rethinking. At least on the individual level, which is inherent in the divorce process, the struggle for autonomy was a universal one. Members of the middle class and the working class alike sought to gain control of their own lives. The struggle for autonomy undoubtedly had different implications for members of different classes, and for each person it played a role in the continuing process of class formation. Nevertheless, it is important to recognize the existence of the individual struggle in all classes.

Farming couples clearly marched to the beat of a different drummer. Both in the divorce participation rate and in the character and timing of marriage breakdown and divorce, farming couples behaved consistently more conservatively than any other occupational group identified. Their caution and their tendency to stay together in spite of serious marital difficulties suggest a different set of expectations and values. The anecdotal evidence set out in chapter 7 makes it clear that the farming couple was an economic team, a partnership in which the labour of both spouses, though normally sex-specific, was usually interdependent and equally vital in maintaining the family farm. Most farms could not function without the unpaid labour of men, women, and children. When such economic considerations played a primary role, other criteria for judging the desirability of maintaining a marriage were dramatically reduced in importance. Beyond this, other explanations, such as demographic character or the existence of distinct informal mechanisms to handle marriage breakdown, also help to clarify the pattern of divorce in the farming population.

Formal divorce in early twentieth-century Canada was 'user controlled' by whatever means were at hand. This fact is obviously helpful in attaining an understanding of marital values and attitudes towards the law and its legitimating function. But a divorce process that was in large part controlled by the couples involved may have had an additional desirable, if accidental, result. Today divorcing couples can, to a large extent, determine their own post-divorce rights and responsibilities; the available evidence suggests that in the United States and the United Kingdom couples typically do not go to court until they have worked out matters and are ready for the court to place its imprimatur on the predetermined outcome.[90] Though they were not encouraged to do so by the legal process, Canadian couples had already gone a considerable distance in achieving such self-determination in the early twentieth century. The legal environment, however, forced couples to concentrate on meeting legal prerequisites rather than on the distribution of assets and responsibilities. None the less, current evidence indicates that there is a much higher compliance level when the settlement is mediated rather than adjudicated.[91] Therefore, in the early twentieth century compliance with family responsibilities may have been high because of the way in which couples were able to influence the process.

No class participated extensively in formal divorce in early twentieth-century Canada. The restrictiveness of the process and the hegemonic authority of the familial ideal ensured that the rate of divorce would be low. Nevertheless, a small number of couples challenged the divorce environment and asserted their own independence from legal and normative controls. They struggled to establish better lives for themselves by dissolving 'broken' marriages, usually with a view to entering into more successful remarriages that were closer to the prescribed ideal. At the same time, however, many Canadian couples used techniques outside the formal legal process in Canada to acquire what might be called an informal divorce.

9

Divorce outside the System

Self-divorce had a lengthy history among peasants and workers in Great Britain and elsewhere. Self-marriage and self-divorce were features of English plebian culture at least as early as the seventeenth century wherever the rites of the gentry or the bourgeoisie did not meet local needs. John Gillis has suggested that the popularity of marriage by consent among rural labourers was a result of the widespread mobility of workers; men moving on to work in other parishes could 'desert' their wives, and both parties were free to 'marry' a new partner. These practices had their own rituals; the consent of all parties and the presence of witnesses were essential. Edward Thompson has described the well-known practice of wife-sale in similar terms. A feature of plebeian culture, wife-sale was a public ritual by which both wife and husband could demonstrate their consent to the process and to the exchange between male spouses. The community acceptance of these practices is an important reminder of the richness and variety of familial practices and 'legal' beliefs.[1] The term 'self-divorce' is misleading in its implied absence of community or state constraints on informal divorce. The local community had always asserted its influence over informal divorce, and by the early twentieth century the state had come to play an unwittingly authoritative role in such practices.

As the plebeian culture was overwhelmed by new forces in the late eighteenth and early nineteenth centuries, proletarian culture took on similar characteristics. For example, Owenites, who adhered to the system of communistic co-operation advocated by Robert Owen, practised divorce, but only by mutual consent and with public notice. A new set of secular divorce rites drew on some of the symbolism of the earlier period. The formal return of the bride's wedding-ring was one ritual, as was the conduct of an informal 'reverse' wedding ceremony. 'Self-divorce was not done lightly,' reports Gillis, 'nor were witnesses likely to assent to the rite if a woman did not show good cause why she should be granted the status of a "grass widow." The beaten or deserted wife had the most public sympathy, but a proper "divorce" had to be very carefully managed.' Consent and some form of community involvement were crucial elements in the process, as workers sought appropriate compromises between community beliefs and the realities of individual needs. In such a culture remarriage could be achieved more easily than under state law, and bigamy charges were laid only when an original spouse decided to make trouble, in which case the community insistence on consent probably had been violated. In their own way English workers used custom and ritual to maintain essential institutions and values.[2]

Divorce by custom was altered and slowly weakened during the nineteenth century as the hegemonic power of the law increased. State and legal agencies multiplied at the local level, and the dominant beliefs and values of the middle class became more influential and authoritative. Magistrates in England were no longer willing to hear arguments based solely on custom, and the centralizing authority of the law advanced the trend towards uniformity in law and practice.[3] This led to a weakening of community controls within the working class as people were often left to fend for themselves. By the early twentieth century almost all of the folk ritual was gone, though occasionally the returning of a wedding-ring or the destruction of a marriage certificate echoed earlier rites.[4] Nevertheless, Canadians developed their own techniques to facilitate divorce outside the state system, some of which contained elements of community and state approval or acceptance while others were entirely individualist. All of these techniques – referred to here, for convenience, as informal divorce – asserted the participants' control over divorce and, for the most part, were aimed at adapting marriage and divorce practices to the realities of modern society. At the same time, informal divorce lost its distinctive class character.

The most obvious of informal technique was a foreign divorce. Though occasionally Canadians travelled to Mexico or some of the nations of Western Europe, the United States was close and accessible. By the early twentieth century many jurisdictions in the United States accepted separate female domicile, required only a limited residency, and granted divorce on a number of grounds. At one time or another Canadians travelled to almost every one of the forty-eight states for divorce, though states close to Canada were naturally visited most often. In the east, Massachusetts was a favoured site for Maritimers; central Canadians tended to head for Michigan or Illinois. Canadians from the prairie provinces travelled to the Dakotas or Minnesota, while British Columbians and some Albertans went to Washington or Oregon. California and Nevada drew people from all regions of Canada.

The disadvantages of foreign divorces were clear. The divorces were invalid in Canada; any subsequent remarriage would be considered bigamous, and prosecution, though unlikely, was certainly possible. Any American judgment regarding divorce, custody, or support simply muddied the waters if and when those issues ever reached Canadian courts. Canadians who had used the American courts carried with them an unspoken but none the less influential mark of disrepute in some circles; they had come into contact with a divorce environment that was the butt of much chauvinistic sarcasm and condemnation. As well, there is clear evidence that at least some American divorce processes were distinctly unfair to the defendant. In particular, the case could fairly easily be heard without the defendant's knowledge. While Canadian courts were rigorous in ensuring that every reasonable effort was made to get in touch with the defendant (including substitutional service of the papers on close relatives), at least some American courts readily accepted the plaintiff's claim that the defendant's whereabouts were unknown. Gloria Ennis, for example, left her husband and child in Sudbury in February 1939, and travelled to her mother's home in Maryland to get a divorce. When she told the American court that she did not know her husband's address, the judge authorized her to give notice of the proceedings by inserting a notice in a Baltimore newspaper once a week for four weeks.[5] There was a greater potential for unfairness in some American divorces, and this could have adversely affected long-term relations concerning spousal assets and responsibilities, children, family and community.

But for many couples the advantages of American divorces more than outweighed any procedural unfairness. The divorce itself was relatively inexpensive. Travel and living expenses could be high, but couples tended to control these costs by travelling to a nearby jurisdiction, establishing formal residence and then returning home to await the end of the residency period, staying with relatives in the area, or taking work in the state until the divorce was granted. Women's equal access to the courts was an obvious attraction. Grounds were also easily established: desertion, for example, was defined as a lack of co-residence for the stipulated period; cruelty was widely available as a ground and was sympathetically treated.[6]

Michigan was one of the more popular destinations. The state's divorce law was attractive to Canadians for a number of reasons. It offered considerably broader grounds for divorce than Canada – desertion for at least two years, imprisonment for at least three years, and habitual drunkenness – as well as the traditional ground of adultery, and it recognized a woman's separate domicile. Though petitioners were required to prove two years' residency in the state, from the timing of the various cases in Michigan and elsewhere it seems likely that this requirement was not effectively enforced by the courts or, more likely, that the petitioners swore false affidavits.[7] Finally, judicial divorce was available in Michigan throughout the entire period.

Many Canadians took advantage of the more liberal American process to obtain a divorce that probably would not have been available to them in Canada. American authorities did not normally report separate figures for such divorces; after all, they had been granted under the legal fiction that the applicants were American residents. Nevertheless, there are occasional suggestive figures. According to the United States Bureau of the Census, in 1922 (when there were 543 divorces in all of Canada) 1,368 divorces were granted in the United States to persons who had been married in Canada; of these, 462 were awarded in Michigan, 135 in the state of Washington, and 128 in California. While these figures represent slightly less than 1 per cent of all divorces granted in the United States, they were of major significance to Canadians. In 1928, for example, 548 Canadian couples obtained divorces in Detroit alone, a total that far exceeds the 204 divorces granted in all of Ontario in that same year. There was nothing new about this phenomenon. During the period from

1887 to 1906, Canadians were the most likely foreign group to be divorced in the United States. In that twenty-year period some 8,645 Canadian marriages were dissolved in the United States; Canadian divorces accounted for 36.9 per cent of the foreign marriages dissolved in American courts in those years, despite the fact that Canadians living in the United States constituted just 11.4 per cent of the foreign population there in 1900.[8] These figures do not include divorces obtained by Canadian emigrants who had married overseas; they do include divorces obtained by the large number of Canadians who had immigrated permanently to the United States for reasons unrelated to divorce. Nevertheless, they are indicative of a very extensive use of American divorce facilities by Canadians.

Though it was clearly a significant feature of Canadian divorce behaviour, foreign divorce was the least likely to be revealed in divorce trials in Canada. The judicial sample contains just thirty-eight instances of American divorce, while there were seventy-seven such divorces in the informal petitions. Within that small number three features stand out. First, the class participation in foreign divorce paralleled the breakdown of class use of the Canadian divorce process. Second, in 60 per cent of the American divorces in the formal petitions the spouse obtaining the divorce had remarried and remained in the United States, and 71 per cent of the persons who had obtained American divorces were still in the United States. Since permanent residence does not appear to have been characteristic of most Canadians who obtained divorces in the United States, this suggests that Canadian spouses were much more likely to take legal action concerning this divorce technique if the 'offending' partner was no longer present. In most cases where the divorcing couple remained in Canada there seems to have been at least an implicit agreement to accept the validity of the American divorce and to get on with life without bringing the Canadian legal system into the process.[9]

Third, foreign divorce was overwhelmingly a women's device. Eighty-four per cent of the American divorces cited in the formal petitions and 66.7 per cent of those cited in the informal petitions were obtained by wives. This may have been because women were less tied to jobs and were able to take the time to travel to the United States and establish residency. Women may also have been more willing to accept an American divorce as sufficient to meet their needs; men, who usually had more assets to protect, may have had more incentive to acquire a valid Canadian divorce to insulate themselves against future claims.[10]

Canadian exploitation of the American divorce process was part of a broader phenomenon within marital dissolution. A considerable number of Canadians wanted to end their marriages and sought to do so with the formal approval of the state, whose authority and sweeping responsibility were not often questioned in an era of extensive government expansion. If their own state system of divorce was unavailable or inappropriate, many Canadians nevertheless wanted the approval of some other government as a form of legitimation of the result decided on by the couple. Informal community approval was insufficient; the imprimatur of the state was required, not just because of the state's broad authority but also because divorce was beginning to be seen as a particular responsibility of the state or its judiciary. The majority of Canadian couples using American divorce systems found the foreign state's approval to be sufficient to their needs without further resort to any Canadian state process.

To what extent local communities 'accepted' American divorces is unclear. Certainly it was seen as an attractive solution by some, perhaps even more attractive than a Canadian divorce with its ensuing publicity. In one 1930 Nova Scotia case, for example, a Cape Breton Island lumberman and his wife had talked about getting a divorce for at least three years; according to her trial testimony, he asked her to 'go to the United States and get a divorce for him because he had his business to consider and also his family.' This view of the wife as a helpmate right to the end is rather ironic, but the case itself is instructive. The husband seems not to have been concerned that an American divorce would hurt his business any more than a Canadian divorce. Indeed, since he had already contracted a venereal disease from his adulterous conduct and the grounds were available for a local divorce, his stated preference for an American divorce indicates that there were some advantages to distance.[11] An experienced Guelph lawyer asserted confidently that Canadians who remarried after obtaining an invalid American divorce were widely regarded by their friends in the community as being legally married.[12]

It is also unclear to what extent Canadians understood the invalidity of American divorces. Some were well aware of it. In 1929, for example, the wife of a London, Ontario, tailor ended her four-year marriage by obtaining a divorce in Reno, Nevada. Nine years later she remarried in Detroit and took up residence there. She went out of her way to co-operate with her ex-husband's Canadian divorce action in 1939. When first asked, her mother was not surprised to hear that the Reno divorce was not valid in Canada; she commented that if her daughter was being approached 'concerning a Canadian divorce, she will only be too glad to do what she can to help.' When the solicitor served the papers on her in Detroit, she drove him to her new husband's place of work and fetched him so that he too could be served.[13] For their part, Canadian lawyers held conflicting opinions on the validity of American decrees in Canada.[14]

The use by Canadians of American divorce facilities was generally tolerated by the Canadian authorities. There was really no way of preventing Canadians from travelling south to get a divorce, and the practice served as a useful safety-valve for domestic pressure for Canadian divorce reform. The Canadian state used its appellate courts and Parliament to find American divorces invalid for Canadians, and Canadian officials spoke in similar terms.[15] Yet the authorities took no overt action against the procedure. Only when the spouses or family members found some reason to challenge the result did the issue come before Canadian courts. There was thus an implicit acceptance of marital self-determination – up to a point. That point was remarriage.

Bigamy was related to foreign divorce in several ways.[16] Obviously, since most foreign divorces were invalid in Canada, any remarriage was bigamous. Yet there is evidence that a considerable number of Canadians remarried – or, to put it in legal terms, 'went through a form of marriage' – paralleling the urge among those who had obtained foreign divorces to have their marital decisions 'legitimated' by accepted authorities. Informal, community-based cultural rituals had weakened and diffused so much that the earlier traditions of self-marriage and self-divorce were insufficient; instead, couples had to resort to the processes of the state or its agents. It was not very difficult to commit bigamy in a vast country such as Canada, and in the days before standardized government registration of individuals (through social insurance numbers, for example). It was a simple matter of leaving or being left by one's spouse and then turning to a new partner, using a religious or occasionally civil ceremony to validate the new 'marriage.' Although marriage-licence forms inquired into one's marital status, affidavits of the accuracy of the information were usually not required; many individuals made false declarations for themselves or their partner of age, parental approval, residency, or marital status. The judicial sample reveals 53 instances of bigamy (97, if one includes those who remarried after obtaining an invalid foreign divorce); among the informal petitions there were 101 bigamous marriages (or 126, including those who remarried after an invalid foreign divorce). The class distribution for those in the formal petitions was strikingly close to that for divorce applications overall: 20.8 per cent were middle-class, 70.8 per cent were working-class, and 8.3 per cent were farmers.[17]

The problem is to try to weigh these relatively small numbers against the very real constraints regarding prosecutions for bigamy. The attorney-generals in all provinces received repeated complaints from officials (local police, consular agents of foreign governments, representatives of charitable agencies) and private individuals about allegedly bigamous marriages. In 1912, for example, the clerk of the peace for Bruce County wrote the attorney-general of Ontario about a local case. Robert Boston had moved to the community in 1909, claiming to have divorced in Michigan his wife of thirty years; he soon married a local woman. Somehow suspicions arose concerning the validity of that second marriage, and the local Roman Catholic priest was 'trying to separate the pair.' The clerk charged the second wife with living in conjugal union with a married man, and called Boston as a witness. Boston testified that his first marriage was still intact, since he had signed only a separation agreement with his first wife. The clerk was uncertain about what he should do. Boston's first wife would not 'come over [from Michigan] or do anything to prosecute' Boston; the judge released the second 'wife' on her undertaking not to live with Boston; and the local church did not want Boston prosecuted since the cohabitation had now ended and he was otherwise judged to be 'a decent man.'[18] Having used informal constraints, most Canadians were willing to go no further in attacking bigamy. The attorney-general did not pursue the matter.

Instances where the first marriage had occurred in a foreign jurisdiction presented even greater difficulties for the prosecution, since the first marriage would have to be established to the satisfaction of the court and its validity proved according to the law of the local jurisdiction (this required expert testimony). There can be little doubt that at least some spouses, usually men, escaped from their marriages by emigrating. In 1926, for example, Marie Rolle received a judicial separation in Austria; she emigrated in the same year, leaving her husband and two teen-aged children behind; the following year she remarried another Austrian immigrant in the small Ontario town where they lived, and a child was soon born. Sometime in 1929 someone in the community complained to the Austrian counsul-general about the validity of the marriage, and he brought the matter to the attention of Canadian authorities. There was little doubt that Mrs Rolle had committed bigamy, said the deputy attorney-general of Ontario, but it would not be easy to prove it:

The difficulties of instituting proceedings on a charge of bigamy are the question of the proof of the Austrian marriage; that the husband to the wife's knowledge was living when the second marriage was solemnized, and that the judicial separation granted by the Austrian Courts is not a valid divorce according to the laws of Austria. Effectively to do this it would be necessary to produce the witnesses in Canada, as evidence in these cases by commission is very unsatisfactory and would not in all probability result in a conviction. Unless, therefore, the Austrian authorities are prepared to pay the expenses of the witnesses to prove the former marriage, the laws of Austria and the law touching divorce, it would be quite idle to suggest proceedings on a charge of bigamy such as this in this Province.[19]

In short, legal procedure effectively prevented the enforcement of the law in this case, and there was no apparent desire to change that procedure. In cases where foreign marriages were not a factor, there were other obstacles. When a prosecution for bigamy was contemplated in Rossland, British Columbia, the attorney-general informed local officials that they would have to bear all the costs of prosecution; he added that this was not an expense that he personally 'would feel justified in undertaking.'[20] If state authorities were unwilling to commit large sums of money for such prosecutions, aggrieved parties had to use their own resources if they hoped to pursue their complaint. As the deputy attorney-general of Ontario commented, bigamy prosecutions generally 'have not been instituted except at the instance of some person who has full knowledge of the facts.' Law officers themselves would not normally be in a position to lay charges.[21] Yet, since there was no valid marriage to be annulled, the courts were also unlikely to make a declaration of annulment regarding a bigamous marriage; the innocent spouse was left in a very ambiguous situation.[22]

There was, then, a certain amount of de facto tolerance of bigamy, both within local communities and among authorities.[23] One reason for this tolerance was that a challenge to the validity of the second marriage was often an attack on an active, functioning, 'successful' marriage, one in which children were often present. To declare the second marriage bigamous was to label the children illegitimate, to undermine if not to destroy the family, and to force the previously married spouse back into a marriage that was already dead by any but strictly legal standards. Any such prosecution was a 'no win' proposition. If the moral costs were already being paid, the social costs would rise considerably with prosecution. This attitude was shared by citizens and state officials. In one instance in 1912 two wives agreed not to charge their common husband with bigamy, 'for he had no money and we diden want our names in the papers.' The Montreal Society for the Protection of Women and Children decided in 1931 not to prosecute a local bigamist in order to preserve an otherwise stable 'marriage.'[24]

A 1911 article in the *Winnipeg Free Press* complained about divorce by consent among the Doukhobors in Yorkton, Saskatchewan. It was clear that local authorities were attempting to put an end to such 'connubial laxity.' The problem was that police investigators were unable to acquire any satisfactory evidence of divorce and subsequent remarriage, because the Doukhobors themselves sanctioned the practice and regulated it so that it conformed to local standards. In one Nova Scotia divorce trial, it was revealed that the wife of a Cumberland County farmer had deserted him after just four days of marriage, and two years later had married again in Sydney. She had lived with her first husband for so short a time that her family had been unaware of her first marriage until shortly before her second marriage, and then only because there was talk in the community. Her brother, who witnessed the second marriage, was called to account by the court for tolerating his sister's bigamy, but his testimony revealed the limits of family and community control:

Q Did you let her commit bigamy without saying anything about it?
A No, not without saying anything; I reasoned and tried all I could and told her it was wrong and all this like, but they insisted [on getting married] and of course I gave way.
Q If you knew your sister was married before, you knew she was liable to be prosecuted and she was living in adultery in your own house?
A Yes.
Q What have you to say about it?
A I have not anything to say about it at all; I am exceedingly sorry.
Q I cannot understand how a man could let his sister do this?
A Circumstances sometimes you know alters cases.[25]

The brother had recognized and fulfilled his obligation to attempt privately to prevent the bigamy, but neither he nor his family felt any duty to take the matter before a public tribunal. The woman's bigamy was revealed to the authorities only because her first husband chose to seek a divorce in 1915. Bigamy was not regarded as the most desirable marital conduct, but both family and community were willing to accept spouses' control over their own marital regimes, particularly in cases where the remarriage met local standards and conformed to the prevailing familial ideal.

That such remarriages were not infrequent is indicated by quite different types of evidence. In one instance during the First World War, for example, a soldier's wife was falsely informed in some unexplained manner that her husband had remarried in England while overseas with the Canadian Expeditionary Force. She believed the story (which suggests the common character of such conduct), and she promptly remarried, much to her first husband's chagrin when he returned.[26] Other wives all too readily believed rumours that their husbands had died, particularly during the war, and they remarried.[27] Another case demonstrates the complex tangle of marital relationships that could result. In 1915 William Smithers, a farmer, was tried in Haileybury, Ontario, for bigamy. In a letter to the minister of justice, Smithers admitted that in 1913 he had married Edith Bull, whom he believed to be a widow. They cohabited for a short time before she left Smithers to live with another man; Smithers then went to the United States 'and married a woman there who had another man & I fetched her to Canada & I lived with her & was convicted of the charge.' But at trial Edith Bull testified that she had in fact not been a widow; instead, in 1911 she had married one McDougall, whose whereabouts she did not know.[28] The trial records are not extant and the judge obviously chose not to believe these accounts; but allegedly Smithers, Bull, and the second wife (at least) had all used state processes, often involving bigamy, to bind their current marital relationship. Their activities suggest a labyrinthine pattern of 'marriage' and 'remarriage' that was difficult for the state to detect and virtually impossible to regulate.

Given the problems in prosecution and the tendency of authorities to place the onus (and often at least some of the costs) on the complaining party, the number of recorded convictions for bigamy in this period may represent only a fraction of the bigamous marriages in Canada (see table 19).[29] According to government statistics, 2,212 persons were charged with bigamy in the forty-year period under study; 81.3 per cent were convicted. Men were charged as the primary perpetrators, presumably because they were regarded as the dominant decision-makers in marriage; as well, because they were more mobile than women, they could more easily escape informal community controls. Though the law made bigamy an offence for both parties to the marriage, men were almost three times more likely than women to be charged: 74.7 per cent of all bigamy charges were laid against men. Men were also slightly more likely to be convict-

TABLE 19

Bigamy charges and convictions, 1900–1939

Years	Number charged	Number acquitted	Number convicted	Percentage convicted	Male percentage of convicted
1900–9	288	66	222	77.1	75.2
1910–19	699	121	578	82.7	73.7
1920–9	668	139	529	79.2	73.4
1930–9	557	88	469	84.2	78.7

SOURCE: Canada, *Annual Report of Statistics of Criminal Offences* (Ottawa 1901–41)

ed; 81.9 per cent of men charged were convicted, in comparison with 79.6 per cent of women.[30] The Crown was able to prove its case against 1,798 bigamous marriages over the forty-year period. Given the general reluctance to prosecute the offence (underlined by the fact that fully two-thirds of all convictions occurred in Ontario), the total number of bigamy convictions suggests that bigamy was a widespread practice across Canada at this time.

Prosecution tended to occur only when the bigamy was revealed to the state authorities in the course of other activities or when family members felt that their community reputation was threatened by the bigamy. Thus, women applying for mothers' allowances were refused when their marriages were proved to be bigamous. In one 1908 case a Vancouver solicitor approached the attorney-general on behalf of a local family. First married in 1869, a local woman had left her husband and ten children, most of whom were married and living in the area, and had recently married another Vancouverite, after first obtaining a divorce in the United States. The lawyer representing the first husband and the children took the high ground: 'It is an offence that concerns the public, and the public welfare most intimately, and the reluctance of the sons and daughters [themselves privately] to prosecute their mother, whom they think richly deserves imprisonment for the offence has suggested my writing this letter direct to you and laying the complaint before you.'[31] Where family honour, pushed by the standards of their own community, was concerned, action often ensued.

Yet even prosecution could not discourage some bigamists. One unemployed, adulterous husband, for example, had provided his wife's lawyer with information for her action. When she decided temporarily not to proceed with the divorce, the husband asked the lawyer for indirect help in facilitating the husband's bigamous remarriage, though he did not call it that. His wife, he suggested, had probably become tired of waiting and had gone off and remarried in some other town. 'If that is the case I have a very unusual request to make if you would care to play ball with me, it would make me the happiest man on earth. The idea is this, will you do me a favour and send me an official looking letter (similar to the one I have just received) stating that Mrs Burton has received her divorce and that I am quite free to remarry if I wish to. I will guarantee that it will be kept absolutely a secret.'[32] That the lawyer sarcastically rejected the proposal does nothing to alter the husband's attitude regarding real control over divorce and remarriage and the limited but crucial role of some form of state approval. In another instance, a Halifax labourer deserted his wife of three and a half years in 1929; eight months later he remarried and soon had a child by his second wife. Within four months of the second marriage he was convicted of bigamy, and a year later his first wife petitioned for divorce. His testimony at the divorce trial showed that despite the bigamy conviction he still considered himself married to his second wife:

A I have a child, and the wife which I have now, which I was up for
  bigamy; I am living with my second wife...
Q This woman you are living with is not your wife.
A She is not and she is; I went through a form of marriage.[33]

Whatever the law said, for this man even a legally invalid marriage ceremony had a powerful cultural meaning that was not invalidated by criminal process or by eighteen months' incarceration. Many bigamists confirmed the importance of the imprimatur of a state or quasi-state authority. Some argued that if a marriage licence had been issued by the state, this was a confirmation of the state's permission to remarry in circumstances where the individual lacked the legal capacity to remarry but felt that she or he had a right to do so. Others held that once the church had put its stamp of approval on a marriage, that marriage was legitimated and even guaranteed by the church.[34]

Those who committed bigamy or obtained American divorces took advantage of existing state processes. Many other couples sought to create a new state process to legitimate spousal control over marriage and divorce – the informal divorce petition. Hundreds of Canadians, usually abandoned spouses who could not afford the costs of a legal divorce, wrote to state officials seeking their direct approval of a new marital relationship. These were persons who found the existing divorce process inappropriate or inapplicable in their circumstances, most often because they lacked access or could not afford it. Instead, they approached the state for direct approval of the contemplated divorce or remarriage. The informal petitions I uncovered were addressed to a variety of officials: the local member of Parliament, the prime minister, any cabinet minister (but particularly the minister of justice), the chief justice of Canada, the Department of Justice, or even the 'Dear Government.' It is reasonable to assume that similar letters were sent to provincial officials; indeed, such petitions occasionally were forwarded to Ottawa, which had jurisdiction in divorce. The petitioners were desperate to resolve their marital situations, and they hoped that government officers would use their authority to help them do so. The petitioner and his or her spouse proposed a solution to their marital problems, but they wanted the state's approval of that solution. A forlorn wife in Sault Ste Marie wrote to the minister of justice, 'I am when all else has failed appealing to you for justice if there is any on earth at all.'[35]

There was nothing new about self-divorce. What was new was the increase in the number of people who began to ask state officials, who had no such power, to approve or facilitate the proposed marital dissolution. From an average of 4 informal petitions annually in the first decade, the number expanded rapidly in the second decade to an annual average of 27.3, peaking in 1919 at 89 and thus paralleling the surge in formal petitions. In the 1920s the average number of informal petitions climbed still higher to 37 before declining in the 1930s to 19.5 annually.[36] Only a significant change in attitudes towards the state and towards the appropriate forms of divorce and marriage can explain this sudden resort to a couple-defined system of state approval. Earlier forms of community control and support were no longer sufficient for many members of the community;[37] the state was increasingly regarded as a more appropriate source of approval. One Ontario farmer, for example, thought that because his wife's bigamy had already been established in a formal trial the federal government should issue a divorce decree without further delay. Another made a similar claim on the ground of his wife's conviction for keeping a bawdy house.[38] Such petitioners viewed the state as the appropriate institution overseeing marriage and divorce.

The letters to government officials revealed spouses' fundamental beliefs about divorce and about their own relationship to the law and the state. In some respects the petitioners were speaking not just for themselves, but also for those involved in formal divorces whose real views and attitudes were filtered and screened by the demands of the legal process and by counsel. The basic elements of the informal petitions help to clarify the insistence among most couples, in both formal and informal divorces, on controlling their marital arrangements. A 1932 petition from Prince Albert, Saskatchewan, highlights the attitudes of those seeking divorce by whatever means:

> I am asking you for permission to remarry. I understood when we came back from overseas if we found our wives had been unfaithful we were granted a free divorce. We were granted a separation by court in 1910. On account of my two boys I lost overseas I had decided to take my wife & live with her & support her when I came home from overseas but I found when I returned she had been living with another man & had 2 children by him so of course I changed my mind then & had nothing to do with her since. In regards to the lady I want to marry she has been separated from her husband in 1921 & has not been supported by him either for herself or 3 children since then & that is 12 years ago. We dont want to commit bigamy so if there is anything that can be done so we can marry, as I was informed to write to the Minister of Justice as to what to do in my case. Hoping to hear from you in the near future.[39]

Most informal petitioners believed that they had a 'right' to divorce and remarriage. Soldiers thought that right was grounded in their personal sacrifice and that they were entitled to claim reciprocity from the state and society. Other people were convinced that their marriages were invalid for reasons ranging from false declaration of ages or parental consent to coercion or deceit by the other spouse; women's claims that their husbands had married under a false name were frequent enough to suggest that this was a favoured technique among some men.[40] Some of the assertions of voidable marriages breached the bounds of credulity. One Montreal man, for example, appealed to the anti-labour attitudes of government, alleging that unnamed agents had sought revenge for his protection of life and property during the street-railway strikes in London and Montreal. These agents, he claimed, had poisoned and battered him, and tricked him into marrying one of the agents' daughters; surely such a marriage was invalid, he pleaded. One Ontario wife articulated what was implicit in many petitions. Her husband was serving a life term in a penitentiary and she was left alone to support three children: 'i think i have a right to be free to marry again if i choose.'[41] This claim to a 'right' to divorce implied that the petitioner was approaching the state as a near-equal, which made it easier for her to come close to 'negotiating' with the state. One wife, for example, offered to have her husband testify in writing to his own adultery if that would facilitate her informal divorce.[42]

The assertion of a 'right' to divorce and remarriage was linked to a second fundamental element – the appeal to justice. For these petitioners justice could involve legal principles or societal and familial ideals. In 1913 a Peterborough woman asked the governor-general to grant her a divorce since she did not have enough money to follow the normal legal procedure. The Department of Justice sent its usual unhelpful reply, advising her to consult a solicitor. Undeterred and more desperate, the woman wrote again in 1915. She had visited a lawyer, only to be informed that a divorce would cost her $1,000, which, as a deserted wife with four small children, she would never be able to afford. Detailing her husband's cruelty and non-support, she appealed to the governor-general from her 'loving mother's heart.' The woman was absolutely convinced that the state could grant her a divorce immediately if it chose to do so; 'Now you have it in your power to do this if you would,' she asserted, offering to pay any costs if and when she saved some money. Men appealed to the same domestic ideal, claiming that the young children left behind by a deserting wife needed a mother.[43] A Winnipeg wife demonstrated spousal co-operation when she told the government that she had proof of her husband's desertion and adultery; her husband, she said, wanted her to use the evidence to obtain a divorce, but she had no money. Surely this should not stand in her way?[44]

The claim to justice also had its legal elements. Another woman seeking an informal divorce in 1921 was, like many, struck by the injustice of the legal process. Her husband had twice committed bigamy, had been convicted, and was guilty of non-support; yet she was the one left on her own without the support and comfort that was possible in marriage. She was unable to understand 'why I should suffer through his misdemeaner,' particularly when she had had several offers of marriage to establish 'a happy home of my own.' What most frustrated those stranded by a spouse's desertion or non-support was the unfairness of it all. A woman writing in 1914 from Bruce, Alberta, described her husband's cruelty, non-support and desertion, and his American divorce and remarriage. Finally she had located him in British Columbia, where he lived with his second 'wife,' but the Alberta authorities refused to issue a warrant for his arrest on grounds of bigamy. Furious at her husband's apparent impunity, she threatened to follow his example: 'I am ingaget to be married in two months and will do so unless my case is taken up. At any rate I am just as free to marry as he is! Fair play is all that I am asking now will you please see that I get justice in this case.'[45] In a different case a British Columbia wife and mother was deserted by her husband; when she finally traced him to Toronto, she obtained a court order for monthly support payments, but never received any money. Although her lawyers explained that the order was unenforceable if her husband had no funds, she refused to believe that Canadian courts had no power to enforce their orders. Petitioners believed that their inability to pay heavy legal costs 'should not be a bar to [their] obtaining justice,' as one Hamilton resident put it in 1915. Often enough it was not clear exactly how the government was expected to respond to the sorry tale of marital woe, but the anticipated result was perfectly apparent: 'all i am Asking is for you to Give me Justus And freedom,' wrote one returned soldier.[46]

A third element implicit or explicit in many informal petitions was an appeal to a long-standing plebeian belief that after seven years' separation a marriage was automatically dissolved and the spouses had a right to remarry.[47] Given the frequency with which the 'rule' was mentioned in both formal and informal divorce petitions, the notion obviously had widespread currency among English- and French-speaking Canadians. Belief in the 'rule' had weakened enough, however, that many petitioners wrote the government seeking confirmation of its validity. The terms of the 'rule' were somewhat fuzzy. Though most had heard that seven years was the stipulated length of separation required, others were uncertain about the precise number of years. Was it correct that this law of separation, as a Saint John wife called it, allowed her to remarry without a divorce when she had been separated for eight years without support or knowledge of her husband's whereabouts? A Victoria, British Columbia, woman expressed her understanding of the rule succinctly: 'I understand the Dominion laws are such that if a husband neglects his wife for seven years that the marriage is null.' A Regina draughtsman's wife had deserted in 1908 and received a North Dakota divorce in 1910. 'Is there any law,' he asked in 1916, 'that provides that when the time of separation has extended for a period of seven years that an annulment of the marriage bonds is granted the injured party?'[48] Some had heard that in addition to the separation, it was necessary to assert lack of knowledge of the spouse's whereabouts; that is, all contact between the spouses had to have ceased. Some women believed that there must be an absence of support payments from their husbands during the period. In short, in its various forms the 'rule' required a de facto end to the marriage. Most had heard that after seven years' absence a marriage was automatically dissolved without any formal state action, though some felt that some forms might have to be filled out or a certificate obtained. A few thought it would give them grounds for a formal divorce action.

Various authorities for the rule were cited by petitioners. A Toronto woman inferred the rule from other government regulations: she had heard that the Department of the Interior had informed a Saskatchewan woman whose husband had left her on an unpatented homestead that if in seven years' time he was still absent and not heard from, she could claim patent on the land if the homestead regulations had all been met; the department's reply 'seemed to give the understanding that after that period she would also have the right to marry again.' Others inferred the rule from their understanding of the law on presumption of death: 'Isn't there a law here that after so many years [twelve] absence a person is the same as dead?' asked a Waterford, Ontario woman who was interested in 'getting my freedom.'[49] Indeed, section 308 of the Criminal Code implied acceptance of the rule in its statement that persons would not be prosecuted for bigamy if they remarried after the previous spouse had been continually absent for the past seven years and the spouse's existence was unknown to the remaining wife or husband during that period. Less formal authority was also cited. A Montreal woman claimed to have seen a statement in the *Gazette* that the government granted permission to remarry after seven years' separation. Two Romanian immigrants had been given permission by the bishop of the Romanian Oriental Greek Catholic church to marry 'after a term of five years had elapsed,' since the woman's husband had deserted without a trace.[50]

The government's replies to these queries occasionally lent some credence to the rule. For example, a Vancouver woman reported, 'Now we have been told by different people that the marriage would be annulled after a lapse of seven years.' Since the costs put a formal divorce beyond reach and it was too expensive to consult an attorney, she asked the government to confirm the rule and to explain the appropriate procedure. As it did on occasion, the Department of Justice said that there was no such legal rule, but that the bigamy section of the Criminal Code did tolerate a second marriage in such circumstances.[51] When a deserted wife in Vancouver inquired about a divorce from her husband who had been missing for eleven years, a solicitor in the provincial attorney-general's office replied, 'Personally, I may point out to you that if your husband has been continuously absent for seven years and you have not heard from him or known him to be alive at any time during the seven years then a presumption of his death arises and you are free to marry again without incurring a prosecution for bigamy. In such a case no divorce is required.'[52] Thus, the seven-year rule was based on a mixture of formal and informal authority.

The appeal of the seven-year rule was considerable. It was seen by most people as a cheap alternative to divorce rather than a means to divorce. As one wife put it in 1925, after ten years' separation from her bigamist husband, 'As far as divorce is concerned I cannot think of it for I am no millionaires daughter, and I have to look out for myself.' The seven-year rule would enable her to remarry so as to provide for her old age.[53] Moreover, the rule put control of this form of divorce in the hands of the participants. Indeed, in serving to confirm the spousal control of this type of informal divorce, the rule implicitly condoned and legitimated spousal control of formal divorce. This explains the occasional self-justifying reference to the rule even in formal divorce petitions.[54] Yet despite all the reports of the existence of such a rule, all of these people sought confirmation 'from the *proper authorities*,' as one writer put it in 1923.[55]

A fourth element that was common to many of the petitions was the belief that the writer's behaviour ought to be and was law-abiding – a popular version of the clean (or at least cleaner) hands concept. Some of these statements were simply attempts by the petitioners to ingratiate themselves with state authorities. But others seemed genuinely to seek the approval of the community through the state. Lacking access to the existing legal apparatus, such petitioners appealed to the idea of operating within the parameters of state approval on behalf of the community. A brother, for example, described the plight of his married sister in Alberta. She had been deserted by her husband, who had since left for Australia. Now she had found a prospective new husband, and they were 'both anxious to live according to the laws (both written & otherwise) of the country.' A divorce was essential, but she could not afford a parliamentary petition.[56] Some petitioners – a deserted wife in one locale, a deserted husband in another – turned to the state for 'written permission' to remarry, despite the alleged encouragement of their families or communities simply to assume the 'right' to form a new marital arrangement.[57]

The great majority of these informal petitioners sought one of two things. Many wanted information about the law and procedure concerning marriage, divorce, and remarriage.[58] Though the petitioners' marriages had already broken down, either the solution to that breakdown was still being sought or the petitioners were seeking 'official' validation of a solution already adopted. The marital situations described covered a broad spectrum of behaviour and problems, but all the petitioners shared a desire for valid and reliable legal information on marital matters. Many simply sought basic information, such as the grounds, costs, or procedures of divorce, and they usually provided at least minimal details about their marriages. An Alberta wife who had suffered from her husband's desertion and non-support, for example, described her situation from her point of view, and asked: 'Now in such circumstances as this, does not the law of Canada grant a divorce? Also what moves must I make to get one? And what will the cost be? And how long will it take till I may receive the same. Kindly tell me too if a divorce received in the States would be recognised in Canada' (a question asked by many).[59]

Most of these petitioners turned to Ottawa because they could not afford to seek help from local lawyers, whose fees were consistently regarded as prohibitive. The petitioners felt strongly that inability to pay should not be a bar to divorce or to access to the legal system. Direct resort to the state was merely a substitute means to 'justice' and remarriage. 'I write you regarding the cheapest way ... of getting a divorce,' said a Saskatchewan working woman 'of limited means.' A deserted wife in the Alberta foothills wrote: 'I want to know just what a divorce will cost me. and where I will have to go to get it ... but remember as I tell you I am working supporting 3 children I can not put up a great amount of money or lose any time So please. advise me the cheapest way the nearest way and the quickest way.'[60]

If such approaches seem naïve, it is important to remember just how uncommon divorce was. Many lawyers throughout Canada had little or no knowledge of or experience in handling divorce cases until the number of divorces began to expand at the end of the First World War. In 1920, for example, the Windsor, Ontario, law firm of Furlong and Company wrote the Department of Justice on behalf of a woman whose husband had been incarcerated for life: 'She now has an opportunity to marry again and secure a good home for herself and the children and we understand there is a permit which can be given by some Department of the Government allowing her to do so.'[61] The belief in state authority and the vagueness about divorce law thus permeated a considerable spectrum of Canadian society.

Like the members of the Windsor law firm, many petitioners believed that the government's authority in the area of marriage and divorce was so sweeping and so immediate that its officials could deal directly with individual marital problems. This could be done in one of two ways: either by issuing a divorce by return mail, or by granting permission to remarry. There is a plethora of examples of those who believed with the Windsor firm (and with Harriet McGill, quoted in the introduction) that the state could simply issue a 'remarriage permit.' 'I am writing for a permit to remarry,' began one petition in 1917 from an Alberta husband who had not heard from his wife for almost nine years. Belief in the availability of remarriage permits was widespread, if ill-defined. One mother, seeking to protect her daughter from a married man she judged undesirable, pleaded with the government not to grant the man a remarriage permit.[62] A London, Ontario, woman implicitly appealed to the seven-year rule in her request. Having raised her five children by herself after her husband deserted her, she wrote to the prime minister after thirteen years of single motherhood: 'If at any time I saw an opportunity of getting a good home for my old age could you suply me with a clear paper so I would be protected from my hubson, from the Laws of the land.'[63]

Though the term 'permit' implies an official document, other petitioners simply asked for a letter stating that they could marry again. 'If you can't grant me permission to remarry,' wrote one deserted wife in 1918, could she force her father or her father-in-law to support her child? One Toronto husband, who described himself as a 'Colored Musician,' had already asked the minister of justice 'to alow me the pleasure of taking another wife'; when he did not receive an affirmative reply, he wrote to the governor-general in 1902 for permission to marry the woman to whom he was already engaged. A fifty-year-old Ontario farmer expressed the same wish to the governor-general: 'As man to man I would ask & beg your consent, that I give some deserving woman the protection of my name & home in exchange for a housekeeper and helpmeet & companion.'[64] A Central European immigrant in Edmonton, whose wife had deserted him and obtained an American divorce, even went so far as to seek government permission in 1912 to hire a housekeeper, clearly aware that he had not yet breached any legal or community standards and anxious to maintain his standing. Similarly, a Galician immigrant in Oshawa, who claimed a spotless record with the law, wanted to know how long he had to wait 'to get me a permission for second marriage.' A London, Ontario, veteran waited for the seven-year rule to take effect before he applied for permission to remarry. He had been overseas when his wife took up with another man; he stopped her allowance and severed relations with her. He then turned to another woman, whom he sent out to Canada at the end of the war; they lived together thereafter, and had two children. Finally, in 1927, after his wife had been gone for ten years, he wrote for permission to marry the woman so as 'to legalize' his children.[65]

Other petitioners were deterred from using the formal divorce process solely by costs.[66] Their belief in their 'right' to approach the state was strong. Indeed, many took an immediate divorce for granted, and made the request merely to facilitate a remarriage already planned. A thirty-year-old Montreal wife, married just nine months earlier and deserted after eight weeks, sought a divorce; she had already received an annulment from her church. Unable to pay for a 'regular' divorce, she pleaded in 1909 for government help because 'I have a chance to get married and be happy the rest of my days to a very good man.' A Calgary wife had suffered through her husband's drinking, adultery, and non-support, and now in 1920 'I have a chance of getting married to a nice young Christian Fellow if I only had the divorce so I was wondering if you would be so kind as to let me have it.'[67] Many were struck by the injustice of the process of seeking a divorce when their spouses ignored that step in Canada, taking remarriage totally into their own hands.

For others, remarriage was not an issue. A Toronto woman simply 'wanted her freedom,' in the commonly used and evocative phrase. She had no intention of remarrying, 'for I have no thought of placing myself in any such trouble again I have learned a good lesson and learned it well and I do not care for any other man and never will.' After briefly describing her past married life, a Kitchener woman simply asked that the government send her 'a paper to prove I am free from him.'[68] This urge to end finally and demonstrably an unhappy situation was underlined effectively by a northern Ontario woman, who described her married life as twenty-five years of 'poverty, starvation, and slavery.' She asked the government for separation or divorce papers, 'or can I go by my maiden name? for if I could go by my maiden name it would be worth to me as much as separation papers.'[69]

Resort to state approval, even if informal, was a major phenomenon among Canadians seeking marital dissolution in the early twentieth century. But many others were willing to settle their own problems and make their own arrangements without the approval of the authorities. Desertion, cohabitation, and common law relationships all played a significant role in the lives of Canadians in this period. A Toronto wife, for example, described a seven-year marital odyssey that had involved complete self-control of marriage and divorce combined with occasional resort to the community and to the state. Married in 1906 at age sixteen, she lived with her husband for almost two and a half 'miserable' years before he deserted. She then went home to her father, and eventually heard reports that in Peterborough her husband was passing off another woman as his wife. The Toronto wife sent a letter of complaint to the local police, and her husband was allegedly arrested. A year later reports were received that her husband was now living with another woman in northern Ontario. In 1912 her husband returned to Toronto and tried to resume relations with his first wife; after she refused, he took up cohabitation with another woman there. At this point, the wife sought to define her own end to the marriage. She and her husband 'drew up a mutual agreement' stating that he would never bother her again and that she was free to remarry; the agreement was witnessed by two friends – a form of community approval. Her husband had repeatedly defined his own marital arrangements by establishing at least three serial relationships in addition to his formal marriage and then drawing up an agreement to terminate that marriage. But his wife hesitated. Several months after signing the agreement, she appealed to the state for a divorce; she had no money, but was willing 'to give half my life' to be free of her husband.[70] It is these techniques of self-divorce outside any appeal to state approval that must finally be examined.

Many adult Canadians at some point in their lives resorted to extralegal marital solutions and arrangements. There is no effective way of establishing the numbers involved, but there are indications that they were considerable.[71] State forms of legitimation were not always available or wanted. For some people community controls and approval were sufficient; others were satisfied to act independently, and such behaviour was tolerated within certain limits. The details are revealed only occasionally in the divorce documents, but there can be no doubt about the behaviour itself. Here, where the numbers are most difficult to establish, the working class participated most frequently. While desertion, cohabitation, and common-law marriages were found among all classes, the indirect evidence suggests strongly that these techniques of self-divorce were used mostly by workers. Without much property to protect or inheritance rights to secure, working-class men and women sought marriages that met their own immediate needs and expectations. This behaviour is

confirmed by contemporary observers. Public discussions of desertion and cohabitation assumed that workers more than any other
group engaged in such practices, and often offered descriptive evidence to support this belief. While my analysis of this behaviour is
constrained by the evidence in the divorce documents, the extent and
the class character of desertion and cohabitation should not be
underestimated.

Desertion was a common phenomenon among married Canadians.
The term is a flexible one: in some cases there was a straightforward
abandonment of the marriage by one spouse, but in other cases it
was difficult to determine which spouse had actually deserted because each spouse had her or his own opinion as to where the
marriage was (or ought to be) located. In some instances the desertion depended on one's perspective. The state recognized this: the
deserted wives' maintenance acts of several provinces, for example,
provided that where a wife left her husband because of his cruelty
or failure to support her, it was the husband who had deserted the
marriage. That is, desertion was not so much the physical act of
leaving a spouse as it was the act of abandoning one's marital obligations and proper role. The law and its formal and informal enforcement agencies were concerned not simply with the serious
social problems that often involved increased demands on the local
welfare purse, but also with the violation of the dominant familial
ideal.

The distinction between desertion and migration is particularly
imprecise. Physical mobility was a significant characteristic of
nineteenth- and early twentieth-century Western society, particularly
in North America, where there were vast stretches of territory to be
developed and exploited. When one spouse wanted to move and the
other spouse did not, which spouse deserted the other? Most men,
not unexpectedly, felt that it was the wife's duty to go wherever the
husband decided; large numbers of women probably would have
agreed, even if reluctantly, and there are many accounts of the
hardships suffered by wives in these circumstances.[72] The informal
petitions contained twenty-three instances of a wife's refusal to
migrate with her husband, and just one of a husband's refusal. At
some point, however, this parting of the spouses went beyond a basic
disagreement about location (and perhaps about spousal dominance)
to involve a deliberate use of migration to end a marital relationship.
This technique was used largely by men who immigrated to Canada
or moved to another district in order to sever their links with their
spouses. While some such actions were clearly premeditated, others

simply occurred as a result of separation and exposure to potential new partners.

A Toronto woman in 1918 gave one detailed example of desertion through migration. Her husband had emigrated from Scotland in 1911, expecting to send for her in a year's time. She stayed in her father's home for that year and the next; she received no money from her husband, although he wrote frequently. 'I naturally thought he was saving it up for a home for me, as he wrote every week and told me I would get a home and everything else when I came out. When Father died and I got things settled up, I paid my own way out to Toronto to join my husband. He met me at the Station and took me to furnished lodgings. I was not many weeks with him, when I found out he had been staying with another woman, and she had a family to him passing her off as his wife, although not married to her.'[73] Seemingly without premeditation, the man had immigrated to Canada and soon found himself seeking the companionship and support of a woman. Perhaps unable to afford his wife's passage or perhaps merely preferring a new mate, he readily took up cohabitation, and he and his new 'wife' lived in the community as a married couple. Others clearly intended to desert, and simply used migration as a way of putting distance between themselves and their family obligations.[74]

Desertion was the single largest complaint by women and men in the informal petitions. While men had deserted in 260 instances and women in 166, simple adultery (excluding foreign divorce or bigamy) was alleged for just 53 men and 109 women. Men may have been more likely to desert, but women made considerable use of the technique. By its very nature, of course, desertion tended not to involve spousal co-operation, and in this sense was distinguishable from mutually agreed-upon separation. Many petitioners simply stated that they had separated from their spouses; given the extent to which I argue that spouses did make this sort of mutual decision about their marriages, such separation is not defined here as desertion. What courts and charitable agencies perceived to be desertion may have been mere separation from the couples' point of view; only later, when it became financially or legally advantageous, might the wife agree to define the breakdown in terms of desertion.

Later studies have shown that desertion tends to be a serial phenomenon; that is, the deserter repeatedly uses desertion as a solution to marital problems.[75] For example, Ulrica Kant married a farm labourer, Clarence Kant, in Grey County, Ontario, in February 1914. After they had lived together for five months, Ulrica left her husband

and returned to her parents' home. Some three years later the couple resumed cohabitation and, except for Clarence's absence overseas for a year, remained together in London, Flint (Michigan), and Kitchener until 1923, when Ulrica again left her husband. After two and half years' separation, they lived together for seven months before Ulrica left again in May 1926. Thereafter, they cohabited for one week in April 1928 and one week in May 1934. When Ulrica was not with her husband, she resided with her parents, first in Grey County and then in Kitchener.[76] The marriage continued for some twenty years, yet the spouses were apart more often than they were together; the consistent solution to their marital problems was for one of them to leave home for extended periods of time.

As Ulrica Kant's experience demonstrates, the parents' home remained a sanctuary for women throughout their adult lives. This was recognized by both husband and wife, and is illustrated by the frequency with which male deserters left their wives in the care of the wives' parents before deserting. Just as pregnant single women often relied on the family of origin for support,[77] abandoned wives were often expected by husbands and community to fall back on their parents. One Meaford, Ontario, woman lived with her husband for nine years, most recently in North Dakota, before returning with him to her home town in 1912. Not long thereafter he deserted her, taking up cohabitation with another local woman and refusing to support his wife and children. When local authorities finally put pressure on the husband to assist his family, he simply left town. In 1917 he wrote to his wife, telling her that he wanted to remarry and asking that she sign some separation papers; local authorities responded by bringing him back and obtaining a court order for support, 'but after a few days he was gone. I have never seen him since,' the wife wrote thirteen years later.[78] The husband, from his perspective, had fulfilled his obligations by bringing his wife and children back to her family and community. No amount of legal or community pressure could force him to accept an obligation he no longer acknowledged. He insisted on controlling his own marital status, yet he asked his wife to endorse an end to the marriage by signing some form of separation paper.

While migration to the wife's family was often a prelude to a husband's desertion, at other times husbands simply sent their wives back to their parents before desertion. A Quebec wife, for example, complained that her husband had asked her 'to go back to her father's home until he can earn more money, and can make a better home for her etc.' But once he had transferred his obligations to the wife's father, the husband told her that he wanted a divorce.[79] This man's appeal to his role as provider points to another standard device employed by deserting husbands: relying on their status as bread-winners to justify a search for new job opportunities, husbands would leave, only to disappear without sending the promised support to their wives.[80]

Not infrequently linked with desertion was cohabitation with a new partner in what is popularly referred to as a common law marriage.[81] Indeed, the term was used by some persons to give their conjugal relationship an aura of legitimacy. There are a number of indications that extramarital cohabitation was a common phenomenon in early twentieth-century Canada. In the informal petitions, 93 wives and 44 husbands were clearly accused of such behaviour; in the formal petitions the comparable figures are 203 and 187. A 1919 correspondent urged the government to carry out its proposed divorce reforms; without such legislation, 'there will be a great many living as man & wife who is not man & wife.' Once again, this behaviour was linked by many with the working class and with certain ethnic groups.[82]

During the First World War the Canadian bureaucracy fully faced for perhaps the first time the complex and varied marital relationships that actually existed in the country. The Canadian Patriotic Fund undertook to support the wives and children of enlisting soldiers, paying them a 'separation allowance.' The fund regulations at first called for proof of the wife's marital status and of the children's paternity, but as Sir Herbert Ames, the head of the fund, reported, it was soon discovered that there were 'hundreds and hundreds of such [cohabiting] families.'

> It was found necessary at the very beginning of the war to say that where such a case had existed, they would pay the separation allowance and pay it to the de facto wife, to the woman with whom the man was living, to the woman and children whom he was accustomed to support, whom he had to leave when he enlisted and went overseas ... A pledge was made by the military authorities to that man that that woman would be regarded as his wife, and the same pledge was made and kept by the Patriotic Fund.

While deploring the morality of such relationships, Ames called on the state to recognize the reality of their existence. From his point of view, cohabitation was imposed on women by married men; if these women and their children were to be protected by the state, the government must accept that hundreds of Canadians had developed stable relationships outside the institution of marriage.[83] For Ames, cohabitation retained enough of the central features of the ideal of the conjugal family to warrant protection and support by the state. Parliament was persuaded to accept the commitments made to cohabiting couples during the war, and enshrined them in the 1919 Pension Act.[84]

The 1927 case of Ted Broadhead, a Hamilton house painter, is a good example of a cohabitation arrangement. His 'wife,' Clara Fitzpatrick, had married George Fitzpatrick in 1906, but he soon 'left her and went to the United States and has not been seen or heard from since.' In 1908 Ted 'took [Clara] to live with' him, and they established a stable union. They eventually had six children; when Ted went overseas, Clara and the children received Ted's pay and allowance 'the same as if we were married,' because Ted had made a declaration before a justice of the peace as to his support for his family. By 1926 the couple went to a local magistrate who approved of their plan to marry; a local cleric interviewed both them and the magistrate before performing the ceremony.[85] A cohabiting relationship that conformed in most respects to the dominant familial ideal had been condoned by the state and, after eighteen years, had received the imprimatur of both state and church.

But others were not so certain as Sir Herbert Ames that cohabitation should be condoned. Canadian courts consistently declined to protect cohabiting partners from one another. Marital obligations and rights were not created, contracts between the two parties were not enforceable, and assets were not recoverable.[86] Nor was the government happy with the monetary obligations or the morality condoned by the military pension act. In the midst of the depression of the 1930s the federal government mounted a serious challenge to informal marriages. The government's action is evidence both of their widespread existence and of the reluctance of many Canadians to accept such marital behaviour.

The state's attitude was manifested in the policies of the Board of Pension Commissioners as part of an overall aim to lower their costs in the depths of the depression. One way of reducing claims was to challenge the marital status of the claimants; if a 'marriage' was proved invalid, payments to the veteran would be reduced and payments to dependent wives and children reduced or cancelled. Beginning early in 1933, almost 77,000 cases were investigated, and many pensions were cancelled or reduced. In the first nine months of the investigation, pensions had been reduced or cancelled in some

2,467 cases; 168 of these reductions were based on the invalidity of the marriage. Pensioners appearing in disputes before the board were now required to bring their marriage certificates, their children's birth certificates, and divorce decrees or death certificates for former spouses. The opposition defence critic, James Ralston, offered the House of Commons examples of the board's decisions early in 1934. Several of his constituents had lost some or all of their pensions because the board had arbitrarily declared their marriages invalid. In one case the board had found a marriage bigamous and the children thus illegitimate. In a second case a married woman had 'remarried' in 1901, seventeen years after being deserted by her husband, in the belief that he was dead; her second 'husband' was informed that he had no claim to married benefits, since his marriage was invalid. In a third case an amputee had been deserted by his wife before the war; having unsuccessfully searched for her for fifteen years and having obtained a court order of presumption of death, he had remarried, only to be told by the board that his second marriage was invalid.[87] In response to opposition complaints, the government agreed that the Pension Board should obtain a legal opinion in all cases where a marriage might be considered invalid. Within a month the Department of Justice estimated that some 570 such cases would be reviewed. According to the minister, the cases ran the full gamut of the techniques by which couples sought to control their own marital status. In the majority of the cases, as Ralston put it, the couple had lived together as husband and wife and had been recognized by their community as such; they had 'discharged the duties and responsibilities of married life, taking care of the children and the man supporting the woman.'[88] Ralston's sympathetic attitude, undoubtedly politically motivated, was clearly based on the couples' strong tendency to conform to the ideal of the conjugal family, even though they had taken control of their own marital status.

The prevalence of cohabitation is suggested by other state responses. In 1936, when the Manitoba Deserted Wives' Maintenance Act was amended to recognize the rights of common law wives, the legislature not only acknowledged the prevalence of such cohabitation, but also acted to bring these 'marriages' closer to the prevailing ideal. Just as they had during the First World War, government officials soon found themselves dealing with complex marital situations as they attempted to apply regulations to soldiers' dependents in 1940. Officials soon faced the problem of determining whether common law wives qualified for support and whether the validity of marriages should be closely examined. One anglophone officer reported the problems with Acadian soldiers from the New Brunswick north shore: 'The Paymaster of this Unit was up against a very difficult proposition, as a number of the men were recruited from illiterate French Canadians, where large families are the vogue, the registering of deaths and births means nothing to them, and common law wives are frequent.' In one instance the deaths of a 'married' soldier's two previous wives had never been recorded and were not listed in any church burial documents. Army authorities decided to accept the man's statutory declaration of their deaths and the validity of his current marriage, but unofficially they were highly sceptical.[89] Not long after the war had begun, officials found themselves required to draw up regulations accepting common law wives as dependents, albeit under restricted circumstances.[90] A similar problem arose for the officials who administered old age pensions.[91]

There were a number of variations in cohabiting relationships and several couple-controlled techniques for inducing acceptance by the community. In some instances the title of housekeeper was assigned to the woman in the hope that the neutral term would imply social distance; in other cases true employment had evolved into a conjugal relationship. Frequently the couple (or the married spouse) spread rumours of widowhood or of an American divorce and subsequent remarriage. Sometimes families assisted in these deceptions. For example, after several years of desertion and non-support the sister of a Saskatchewan man wrote his wife, telling her that he had died and implicitly encouraging her to consider the marriage ended. Some couples made mutual consent the pivotal element in self-divorce, and signed their own separation papers declaring that they were no longer married. Individual spouses followed the same practice of making a formal written declaration, but without the partner's participation. Others simply passed themselves off as married and referred to themselves as 'Mr and Mrs Jones.'[92]

Indeed, naming practices were a particularly authoritative and symbolic device. At times cohabitation could be disguised by the informal adoption of a single family name. A deserting wife in northern Ontario who took up residence with a new male companion adopted his family name as a way of gaining acceptance in the local community. The taking of a common name – the husband's – was recognized as a symbol of marital commitment and stability, of an implied acceptance of gender roles, and of the creation of a new and united entity. Equally, separating couples often used naming practices to emphasize the split. When a woman from northern Ontario asked the government for an informal divorce or for permission to revert to her maiden name, she made it clear that the latter device was as important to her as the former. A Vancouver husband whose wife had deserted him and their children not only wanted the government to send him a divorce ('Some day maybe under the common law, as it is supposed to be today, the permanent officials can hand out the application blanks for Divorce as they do under the Vital Statistics'), but also wanted an order issued barring his wife from using his name.[93]

The extent to which cohabiting relationships were tolerated and regulated in various communities is unclear. Certainly there was a good deal of middle-class pressure to use the law to attack such behaviour; the attacks usually were directed against the working class and specific ethnic groups. Nevertheless, some persons openly used such terms as 'common law wife.' The spousal and community rules by which cohabiting arrangements were regulated are not clear. To an undiscovered extent they undoubtedly varied in different places and among different groups. At least some persons found cohabitation more acceptable for unmarried persons. A farmer's wife of twenty years had left her husband to live with another Nova Scotian in Chelsea, Massachusetts; when her new partner learned that she was married and that her husband was petitioning for divorce, the man immediately left her, rejecting any possibility of remarriage. Family approval seems to have been important. For example, when Harriet McGill, a deserted Saskatchewan wife, appealed for permission to remarry, she cited her mother's attitude: 'My mother says for us to get married and we were also advised in Winnipeg to get married.' The family's approval was just as important as the advice from the unidentified person in Winnipeg.[94]

Even in self-divorce couples responded to the rules and rituals of state, community, and family. Earlier forms of proletarian marital rituals and beliefs were becoming increasingly attenuated within Canadian society as a whole. For many Canadians seeking marital dissolution, the approval of family or community was no longer sufficient; the power and authority of the state occupied a much more prominent place in the culture of early twentieth-century Canada.[95] This suggests a partial explanation for the rise in the number of formal divorces in the early twentieth century. Increasingly, informal (or non-state) divorce processes were abandoned, and spouses turned to the state as the most authoritative and powerful body in contemporary society. While family and community opinion still exerted considerable influence, for many couples their authority was an inadequate sanction for the dissolution of a marriage. State processes were increasingly incorporated into the validation of individual divorces. Yet that process of validation remained a complex one, combining the power, authority, and beliefs of individual, family, community, and state.[96] The use of the legitimating authority of the state in informal divorce knew no class boundaries, though the meaning of the behaviour and the values behind it may not have been the same for all classes. None the less, all elements of the society, either implicitly or explicitly, recognized and accepted the power and the cultural authority of the state, and the hegemony of the ideal of the conjugal family remained pervasive in all its aspects. The adoption of various techniques of self-divorce generally reflected an acceptance of that ideal and a striving for its fulfilment.

10

Conclusion

The Canadian divorce environment developed its own distinctive symmetry. Shaped and articulated in defence of a particular construction of the family, the law and the process of divorce were reshaped by users in a way that subverted many of the law's immediate aims. Divorce law might thus be seen to be unsuccessful from the point of view of many of its defenders; despite the relatively low number of divorces in Canada in comparison with other Western societies, the divorce environment had after all failed to prevent a massive increase in the rate of formal divorce in the country. But even though the immediate goal of marital stability was not totally realized, the broader goal of enforcing the dominant ideal of the conjugal family was achieved.

Although it would take many years before leading Canadians realized the implications of this behaviour, the suppression of divorce had always been simply a means to an end: it discouraged the questioning of many ideas basic to Canadian society – ideas of class and gender, of religion, of ethnicity and nationalism – that were wrapped up in the prevailing familial ideal. The problem in the first half of the twentieth century was that the existing divorce environment had become an end in itself. Once it was realized that divorce did not challenge the basic tenets of the familial ideal, divorce appeared less threatening; substantive reform and easier access became first tolerable and then acceptable. Husbands and wives showed so much persistence and ingenuity in circumventing the restrictive divorce law that policy-makers were forced to rethink their ideas about divorce and the ideal of the family. This rethinking eventually led not only to meaningful divorce reform but to a more open and multifaceted family ideology. In the process the centrality of the metaphor of the family was reduced, leading to a more open perspective and an environment of inquiry regarding divorce and the family.

It took reformers, legislators, and clerics several decades to discover what was implicit in the behaviour and often explicit in the appeals and statements of early twentieth-century divorcees. Idealized marriage was a fine goal (albeit one that gradually changed over time as the rights and needs of women came to the fore), but individual marriages sometimes could not be saved. Where reform could not work, an end to the marriage was for many the obvious answer, so that they could get on with their lives, seeking a new marital relationship to sustain them physically, socially, and emotionally. The cry for divorce or remarriage on the individual level was in most cases not a rejection of marriage in general, but rather a rejection of an individual marriage. In 1918 a deserted prairie wife spoke for many when she told the minister of justice about her past problems and her hopes for the future:

in 1906 I married a man by the name of Michael John O'Neil, believing him too be a good man. after we were married a month he deserted the army, and went too the states, and i went too him but soon found he was a bad man still i lived with him he was arrested for housebreaking but it was decided he was insane from heavy drinking so he was send too the aslum. I got him out afrer six months, and took him too Toronto but he was always getting in too jail I work out and kept myself and him most of the time in 1912 he married wife number 2 two but he got out of that after i had talk too the girl ... when Mr O'Neil was release from Kingston pen. he went too Hamilton Ont he wrote me from their saying that he had join the army and wanted me too come back and live with him ... but i had decided never to live with him again. he had threaten my life so many times that I coulden trust him any more thats over 2 years ago now and i haven heard from him since I have tried too find him since but can get no trace I heard he was married befor he married me but cannot prove it. but i thought if i could find out were he was and get a office too go with me he might own up too it if it were so and if he had been married before that would clear me I saw his name in two different newspapers that he had been killed at the front but their was no address, it might of been another man by the same name. could i marry again bleiveing him too be dead or must i prove his death before i marry again. their are plenty that think it would be all right but I want too be sure. if I can't, I understand that it cost a thousand dollar too get a divorse is that the least one can be got for. I have read in the papers that it is too be made easy for soldiers too divorse their wifes that haven been true while they were away. I feel justified in asking you why not make it easier for good women of our country that have been deceived in too marrying bad men too get a dovorse from such racals as the one i married prove too be. their are plenty of men in this westren country were canadian women are so scrase, would be glad too get good wifes and give them good homes and make their lifes happy and would also rear families that the country would be proud of in the comeing years.[1]

This reaffirmation of marriage in the midst of marriage breakdown is a cliché in studies of divorce, but it is none the less true. The individual lives and marriages depicted in this study bear witness to the powerful desire among Canadians of all classes for marriages that met the individual needs of each spouse.

Those needs were as varied as the participants, and are the bane of family historians searching for patterns to analyse and discuss. Those needs have been examined elsewhere and are not the subject of this study.[2] But almost as varied were the techniques used by people who wanted to escape from unsatisfactory marriages. In their sometimes desperate search for a marriage that met their demands and expectations, individual Canadians adopted a fascinating array of techniques and mechanisms to attain the desired end. The complexity and richness of their marital histories offers a new perspective to our understanding of their past. While formal divorce was relatively new and still rare among early twentieth-century Canadians, other forms of divorce and remarriage were age-old and traditional. In early twentieth-century Canada those older forms and traditions were subjected to changing pressures and demands, and were adapted to meet the circumstances of a new age. State-approved facilities and techniques replaced older and less formal communitarian methods. Though the rising number of formal divorces in Canada in this period was fundamentally disturbing to many, it is possible that the growing divorce rate simply reflected a shift from informal (and thus uncounted) techniques to a formal and very public process. The state and the legal process played an increasingly prominent role in divorce and remarriage, but it was not necessarily the role that legislators and jurists had envisioned. Couples seeking divorce used the law in their own ways and for their own ends. In the current language of the historical discipline, women, men, workers, and the bourgeoisie took their history into their own hands, at least in part. They shaped their own marriages and divorces, and in doing so ultimately shaped the law and the institution.

There is a lesson in this about the power and the role of law, certainly the role of family law. Though most articulate observers in the first two or three decades of the twentieth century would not have agreed, today few doubt that there are distinct limits to the power of the law; there are many areas of human behaviour that the law cannot effectively direct. For Canadians the most public and explicit declaration of this was Pierre Trudeau's assertion that 'the state has no business in the bedrooms of the nation.'[3] It is appropriate that it was Trudeau who brought in the first general divorce law in Canadian history. That law has now evolved to the point at which consensual divorce is fully recognized. The history of early twentieth-century divorce in Canada suggests that such a system is both appropriate and desirable.

At the same time, however, our current law is not neutral with regard to family form, structure, or roles. Like the divorce environment discussed in this study, family law is based on a particular view of appropriate familial and spousal behaviour. Whether this is desirable or even avoidable is debatable, but it must be recognized. Early twentieth-century divorce law played its role in articulating, promoting, and defending the prevailing ideal of the family. The law and the process were exploited by those seeking divorce, and the law was somewhat unsuccessful in preventing marital dissolution but effective in supporting the ideology of the family. The law is a powerful instrument, not just in its individual effect but in its broader cultural influence.

In spite of (or perhaps because of) the relative absence of divorce law reform in this period, that law played a central role in contemporary society. The continual debate about reform, the limited statutory changes, and the broader legal environment regulating divorce all had important indirect (or extralegal) results. David

Sugarman has commented that 'law is much more than a directly
coercive behavioural injunction.' It also includes, in the words of R.S.
Summers, 'educational efforts, rewards and other incentives, symbolic deployment of legal forms, publicity (favourable or unfavour-
able), continuous supervision, public signs and signals,' and much
more.[4] Law is a major means of organizing and expressing beliefs
and social relationships. Law combined with familial ideals is a
particularly powerful force. Family is at the heart of much of Western
culture: it speaks to social structure and values, gender roles and
relationships, and physical, economic, and emotional support systems. The ideal of the family is a way of conceptualizing social relationships. In combination with the law, the family is an influential
'mode of organizing beliefs and values'; both the family and the law
'carry and reproduce ideology within a particular social formation.'[5]
The law relating to family structure 'actively regulates the behaviour
of family members and through a variety of methods encourages
marriage and reproduces the "social relations between the sexes." '[6]

The absence of significant divorce reform is suggestive of the
centrality of the ideal of the conjugal family and of the supportive role
of the law. Family solidarity was so central to the belief system of the
leaders of Canadian society that significant change in the divorce law
could not easily be tolerated. The idea of the child-producing family
and of the lifelong, sexually exclusive marriage was fundamental to
social reproduction, economic organization, gender relations, and
sexual morality. Any change in laws affecting marriage or the conjugal family in any basic way would almost inevitably come slowly.
Indeed, Canada was not unique in the Western world in the relative
absence of change in early twentieth-century family law.[7]

Yet the divorce environment was not completely static. Fundamental changes in Canadian urban society were reflected in urban
divorce behaviour, and in many areas of everyday life new behavioural standards were articulated. In the 1920s and 1930s new attitudes towards various aspects of family life gained strength and
public notice. It became increasingly socially acceptable to limit
family size. Children were sent to school for longer periods, and the
use of corporal punishment as a means of discipline was falling into
disfavour. A new materialistic ethos was beginning to gain popular
acceptance, particularly among young adults and city dwellers,
precisely those people who most frequently divorced. None of this
was unique to Canada; these changes were occurring in both Europe
and the United States. Canada's openness to external cultural influences, particularly in the age of radio, movies, and mass-market

magazines, ensured that these new ideas would play an important role here.

The new material goods of the 1920s and 1930s, such as automobiles and radios, as well as the new forms of leisure and cultural expression, such as jazz and new dance steps and new dress styles, gave expression to and were part of these new values and attitudes. The expansive scope of activities and goods available to the urban young opened new opportunities and gave great vitality to the new values. Individualism, self-gratification, and personal freedom were key elements in this changing society. Movies and advertising spread the word of a new life-style in which consumption of material goods (particularly the ownership of a car) was proof of individual freedom, seductive sexuality was admired, and drinking alcohol was no longer a sin but an expression of sophistication and authority. New forms of socially sanctioned leisure facilitated the expression and the spread of these new values.[8]

Such broad societal changes were reflected in the patterns of Canadian divorce. If the law was changing very little, the use of the formal process escalated dramatically towards the end of the second decade of the century. To judge from the timing of the informal petitions, the use of informal divorce expanded at approximately the same time. Even the restrictive character of formal divorce could not fully suppress elements of change. By the 1930s some judges were saying that a couple would be better off divorced than married. In a 1933 case where the evidence was insufficient to sustain allegations of adultery, Justice R.H. Graham of the Nova Scotia Supreme Court commented, 'The parties are hopelessly estranged. They have not lived together for years. It is a case where each would be better off if their marriage were dissolved, and for that reason I regret that I have to dismiss the petition.' Similarly, in 1932 Justice Logie of the Supreme Court of Ontario, expressed his discomfort in dismissing a petition: 'I regret the result. The parties can never live together again, and if the matter had rested in my discretion I would have granted the divorce.'[9] Nova Scotia jurists in the late 1930s began to mitigate their findings of 'guilt' and 'innocence.' Where wives were judged guilty of a marital offence warranting a divorce, their husbands were nevertheless required to provide for their support if the wives would otherwise be left poverty-stricken.[10] Such a point of view, if not unthinkable, had certainly been unacceptable among such social arbiters at the turn of the century. But the extent of the change should not be exaggerated, nor should the continuing social and familial trauma associated with divorce be minimized.

The evidence uncovered in this study suggests that social class, while it was vital in constructing the contemporary Canadian divorce process, played a complex role in divorce behaviour; the reader should bear in mind, however, that the trial records showed only occupation – often vaguely described – as an indicator of class. Despite that limitation, the cases revealed striking similarities in divorce behaviour among members of the middle and working classes. Individuals in both classes sought consistently to control the divorce process and to manipulate it as best they could to serve their own needs. While members of the middle class used formal divorce much more frequently than workers did, the latter were nevertheless exceptionally active in seeking divorce, given the barriers inhibiting their participation. Divorce probably met quite different needs for members of the two classes, and there is clear evidence that their pre-divorce marital behaviour was significantly dissimilar. At the same time, the evidence suggests that youth and urban residence were equally influential in determining participation in divorce; the importance of these two factors is confirmed in the general literature for the period. Gender was probably the single most important variable in the divorce environment and in the degree of participation by the sexes.

The relative consistency and rigidity of the Canadian divorce environment was in part a product of the dominant familial ideal. It follows that within that divorce environment, as within that ideal, married women were physically, culturally, and economically constrained in their options and opportunities. Indeed, in a whole range of fundamental legal issues in the early twentieth century there was virtually no law reform favouring married women in any important way. Nevertheless, as Veronica Strong-Boag has argued, married women in this period 'were far from being without resources.'[11] One of the most striking aspects of Canadian divorce in the early twentieth century is the way in which Canadian women asserted their own rights and sought to meet their own needs in marriage and family. Women were not just token participants in the formal and informal divorce process; they were not simply 'allowed' by their husbands to act as the 'innocent' party in a divorce action. Women made many of their own choices, and sought both formal and informal solutions to their marital problems.

These women were not radical and were not challenging the basic ideals of marriage. They were simply trying to find practical solutions to commonplace problems. An Ottawa wife who had been deserted for six years poured out her sorry story in the midst of the 1938 debate over extending the grounds for divorce, defending marriage while seeking an answer to her own problems:

> For twenty years I sank my own individuality to cater to the wants and whims of a selfish man who traded on my love, and conception of my duty as a wife. Now I want to be *legally* free from him so that I can enjoy once more the things every normal woman is entitled to, social contacts without fear of meddlesome gossipy tongues that no woman in my position is ever free from. Widening the grounds for divorce will not make divorce more general, or weaken the bonds of matrimony. In spite of my own unhappy experience I still believe that marriage is the ideal state, regardless of the increasing divorce rate. The fault lies with the human beings who undertake it rather than with the institution.[12]

She spoke for many women in her situation, regardless of class. They were not passive victims of their husbands and the divorce environment; they sought change, sometimes at the general level as in this case, more often on an individual basis. But always they, like the much larger number of women in stable marriages, were actively designing and carrying out strategies to defend their views of women's rights and position and to enhance their own lives. Such actions on the part of those women who sought marital dissolution is suggestive of the activities of the much larger number of married women in making their marriages work in ways more appropriate to their needs and perceptions.

The family is the social space 'where the two sexes define their differences and power relations,'[13] and is much more fundamental to men's and women's lives and personal power than some of the more public battlegrounds. Without denying – indeed, while emphasizing – the central role of such public processes as the law in constructing such issues, there is clear evidence of the undoubted power of women in shaping their own marital history. Marriage and family are based on an exchange of power and authority; while in the early twentieth century that exchange undoubtedly favoured men, women were not without influence. Many women were willing to use their power where necesssary, even to the point of ending an undesirable marriage, to protect themselves and their interests and to open up the possibility of a better future. Thus, while marital roles do not seem to have been much contested, power certainly was.

In this context divorce can and should be viewed as a process, not just as an event. For formal (and often for informal) divorces, the legal system was simply the site of the struggle for power. The process of confrontation informed and shaped ideas of class and gender for those involved. Confrontation between spouses played a fundamental part in informing and structuring attitudes towards gender, marriage, and family. Confrontation with outside authority – with the law, the state, the church, the community, or the extended family – did the same. But confrontations with outside authority were also part of the continuing process of class formation. Thus, marital dissolution was of great importance on several different levels for early twentieth-century Canadians: for the participants, it transformed their marital status and family structure and shaped their values and identity; for the community, it helped to confirm and reinforce the ideal of the conjugal family.

Appendix:

Social Class and Occupation

The concept of social class is basic to this study. It is vital to an understanding of the composition and motivations of the reformers and public officials who sought to create and maintain a particular social and legal environment regarding marriage and divorce. It is equally vital to an understanding of the responses by couples and families, both individually and in groups. But the use of class as a basic interpretive tool raised two crucial problems. First, I had to come to grips with the class structure in rather precise terms. Second, I had to use occupation as an indicator of an individual's class membership. Social class is an objective phenomenon and has a material basis. Class membership is determined by and reflected in a number of factors, both tangible and intangible: one's class is not merely a subjective phenomenon. Class is a fundamental reality classically defined by several major elements: its place in a historical system of social production; one's relation to the means of production; one's role in the social organization of labour; and the mode of acquiring and the size of one's share of the social wealth.

The major classes as defined above are two. In this study I refer to the bourgeoisie as the middle class; this reflects the common, liberal North American usage. This middle class is not homogeneous: it is stratified, though not necessarily on a hierarchical basis. For the purposes of this study, I defined those strata in such a way as to make the data useful and to allow other investigators to substitute their own perceptions of the class structure:

1 self-employed (i.e., the bourgeoisie and petite bourgeoisie other than professionals or farmers);
2 professionals;
3 management.

The working class was subdivided into the following strata:

4 foremen / supervisors / superintendents;
5 lower-level white-collar workers;
6 service workers;
7 skilled and semi-skilled manual workers;
8 unskilled manual workers.

The strata are not self-contained; the boundaries between each stratum are blurred.

A worker who controls neither the means of production nor the means of administration is a member of the working class. It matters not whether this worker is employed in a 'blue-collar' or 'white-collar' occupation;[1] the wage-labour characteristic and the direct and relatively complete control of his work and his work environment by others clearly indicate his working-class membership. It is thus important to distinguish between management and lower-level white-collar workers, who are members of different classes.

The minor class of the petite bourgeoisie occupies an intermediate position between the middle class as defined here and the working class. Traditionally defined as owners of their means of production and as dependent for a substantial portion of their income on their own and / or family labour, this class is best represented by farmers; I have subdivided the class into

9 farmers, and
10 other members of the petite bourgeoisie (coded within the self-employed).

The petite bourgeoisie is the least distinct group. In the same way that members of this class have traditionally vacillated between the working class and the middle class, the occupations associated with the class are vague. Those men coded as farmers include not simply independent, self-employed, owner-occupier farmers. Also included (particularly in the sample from Nova Scotia) are a number of marginal farmers who supplemented their income, usually through some form of wage labour (such as lumbering, farm labouring, fishing, or carpentering). Because of the blurring of class position for this particular occupation, I have treated farmers as a separate group in the calculations and in the discussion. Skilled or semi-skilled craftsmen, such as electricians, can of course be members of the petite bourgeoisie or of the working class; there is no way to ascertain the class membership of such men without additional information. Where such information was lacking (that is, in the majority of such cases), they were coded as working-class. Thus, a bias in the coding underrepresents the petite bourgeoisie.

The only consistently present and useful indicator of an individual's class membership and position was his occupation. It is important to emphasize that there is much more to the idea of social class than mere occupation; one's employment is not the equivalent of one's class position, and occupation is not a substitute for class. It is fair, however, to use occupation as representative of social class.[2]

Several scales or methods of classification have already been developed by historians and sociologists as the basis for socio-historical investigations and analyses far more intense than the one I have attempted here. Some of these, such as the Blishen scale, have been rejected because of their ideological approach. Others have been judged inappropriate because of the quality of information (about each individual) they presume; Gérard Bouchard and Christian Pouyez, for example, have developed a potentially very useful classification scale for Canadian historians, but its effective use depends on much more detailed information about each individual than was available in this study.[3]

An attractive feature of using the data on the husband's occupation is that the information was provided directly and without apparent external constraint by the individuals involved. That is, there were no apparent prescribed categories confining or defining the description of employment. Individuals were free to choose the job description they thought most accurate. This is true whether the information appears in parliamentary divorce proceedings, on marriage licences, or in private correspondence. The person's description of himself as a 'labourer,' a 'dog fancier,' or a 'gentleman' is indicative of a sense of self and of class membership.

However, an occupational description does not always clearly indicate a class position. Terms such as 'labourer' or 'ticket agent' cause no problem. But what of 'barber'? Does the term describe an itinerant barber wandering through small towns and countryside looking for individual heads of hair to cut, or perhaps a semi-skilled worker in a small city shop? Or does it suggest a petit bourgeois small businessman operating his own shop (and perhaps even employing others)? Though there are several possible methods of dealing with this problem, I chose to employ a bias against coding individuals as petit bourgeois and to code them as either middle-class or working-class, as seemed appropriate in each case.

An important characteristic of the data being discussed here is that the information was almost always very limited. A one-word description of an occupation is not a definitive representation of social class. It would have been possible to uncover further information on many of the workers discussed here. A search of assessment records or city directories, for example, might have removed some of the ambiguity surrounding a 'barber,' provided that records for an individual could have been uncovered. But this research was not practicable. This study covers all of Canada, and neither the time nor the money for a detailed study of so many individuals was available. It was therefore necessary to interpret the information in as revealing a way as possible, without distorting or misusing it. I chose to accept the occupational descriptions at face value. I also tried to guard against imputing too much precision to those descriptions.

Normally, only the husband's occupation was recorded. Given the gender-related constraints on women's employment in the early twentieth century, information on a wife's occupation is arguably less revealing of her class position. For these two reasons I decided to use only the man's occupation as an indicator of the class position of both spouses. This equation of a wife's class with that of her husband undoubtedly creates problems, only some of which are obviated by the inclusion of white-collar and blue-collar work within the definition of the working class.[4]

archives was an excellent facility in which to work. According to the Dominion Bureau of Statistics, during the period from 1900 to 1940 there were some 973 divorces in Nova Scotia, but they were very unevenly divided. As in the rest of Canada, the number of divorces rose rapidly beginning in 1918. There were 136 divorces from 1900 to 1917 inclusive, and 837 from 1918 to 1940. To compare these two periods, I examined the entire population of divorces for the first period and a sample (generated by a random-numbers table) from the second period. The case records varied considerably in their completeness. There were more case files than there were actual divorces, but it was often impossible to determine whether any one divorce had ended in a final decree. I chose to treat all the files in the same way, on the basis that the marriage was at least in serious trouble and that at least one spouse was turning to the divorce process for a solution. The total sample for Nova Scotia was 797 cases: 199 cases were all those initiated between 1900 and 1917 inclusive; a further 598 cases represented a 50 per cent sample of the cases filed after 1917.

For the second group of judicial divorces I could have chosen cases from Alberta, Saskatchewan, Manitoba or Ontario. I chose Ontario because it was the only province that had had a significant number of parliamentary divorces before judicial divorce was adopted in 1930, and the trial cases were readily accessible at the Archives of Ontario. But the Ontario cases had their own peculiar problems. First, divorce applications were heard not by a separate court (as they were in Nova Scotia and New Brunswick), but by the Supreme Court of Ontario. The cases were filed among all the others heard by that court in the course of its busy trial schedule. What was worse, the Supreme Court of Ontario held its trials in each county seat in the province, and the cases were grouped by county. It was far too cumbersome to create a random sample of each of the counties, so I created a judgment sample of eight counties reflecting the rural-urban, commercial-industrial, ethnic, and religious diversity of the province. For six counties – Bruce (16), Dundas-Glengarry (14), Grey (27), Huron (16), Sudbury (67), and Wellington (34) – I examined the total population of cases filed from 1930 to 1939, producing 174 cases; for Middlesex I examined a similarly generated random sample of 193 (of 499 cases). Having thus ensured that diverse elements of the province were represented, I then turned to York, for which there were so many case records that I selected a further 376 (of 2,439) by a random-numbers table. The records of the Department of the At-torney-General contained 60 cases for 1930 during the few months when procedural rules required that the attorney-general be named a defendant party in each divorce case; since these cases represented a geographically diverse group from within the jurisdiction I included them in the Ontario sample, ensuring that there was no duplication of cases already coded. The total Ontario sample was 803 cases.

The final source was uncovered by traditional methods. While researching the records of the Department of Justice, I systematically watched for files concerning divorce. Near the turn of the century occasional files began to appear; in subsequent years the numbers of files grew larger and larger until by the end of the First World War the files were bulging. The files were fascinating (especially when compared with the records of the Supreme Court). Desperate, frustrated spouses had written to some distant, anonymous official describing the often pathetic details of their marriages. They asked in very personal terms for help (usually for a divorce), and after approximately 1908 (and only rarely before then) they received (for good reasons in law, but also for impersonal bureaucratic reasons) no help at all; they were almost always simply told to consult a lawyer, even though many of the letter-writers had already made it clear that they were too poor to afford legal counsel.

Here was a group of spouses who had sought unconventional solutions to their marital breakdowns. They offered an attractive comparison to regular divorce cases. Unfortunately, much of the material was anecdotal, and very little information was quantifiable (for purposes of comparison with the divorces). Nevertheless, the writers provided the information that *they* thought was important, revealing much about marriage breakdown, about informal techniques for dissolution, and about popular attitudes towards divorce.

These informal petitions for divorce to the Department of Justice were supplemented with a small number of similar letters found in the personal papers of leading politicians. I investigated the papers of all prime ministers, justice ministers, and members of the Supreme Court of Canada, and of some members of Parliament. In total there were 851 such divorce petitions. Letters that simply inquired in a non-specific manner about Canadian divorce laws were not included, nor were letters that discussed divorce or divorce law outside the context of a specific marriage, though there were also many of these.

A condition of research access to the archival trial cases of both Nova Scotia and Ontario was that the identity of the individuals involved not be revealed. I have used fictitious names, but the social characteristics of the individuals have not been altered. Since the

Notes

ABBREVIATIONS

AC   Appeal Cases
AO   Archives of Ontario
BCR   British Columbia Reports
CCC   Canadian Criminal Cases
DLR   Dominion Law Reports
NAC   National Archives of Canada
NBR   New Brunswick Reports
OLR   Ontario Law Reports
OR   Ontario Reports
OWN   Ontario Weekly Notes
P.   Law Reports, Probate, Divorce, and Admiralty Division
PABC   Public Archives of British Columbia
PANS   Public Archives of Nova Scotia
Sask LR   Saskatchewan Law Reports
SCR   Supreme Court Reports
WLR   Western Law Reports
WWR   Western Weekly Reports

1 Introduction

1 There is no evidence that John Taylor was charged with bigamy; this is suggestive of the many-layered character of the legal environment and of the varied application of the law. This topic is discussed in later chapters.

2 PANS, RG 39 D, files C-242A and C-242B

3 NAC, RG 13, A2, #495/1922

4 E.P. Thompson, *The Poverty of Theory and Other Essays* (New York 1978), 96

5 R.W. Gordon, 'Critical Legal Histories,' *Stanford Law Review* 36 (1984), 109

6 M. Poster, *Critical Theory of the Family* (New York 1978), 143; C. Smart and J. Brophy, eds, *Women-in-Law: Explorations in Law, Family and Sexuality* (London 1985)

7 A. McLaren and A.T. McLaren, *The Bedroom and the State: The Changing Practices and Politics of Contraception and Abortion in Canada, 1880–1980* (Toronto 1986); G. Kinsman, *The Regulation of Desire: Sexuality in Canada* (Montreal 1987)

8 K. Thomas, 'The Double Standard,' *Journal of the History of Ideas* 20 (1959), 209–10

9 E. Lapointe (Liberal, Quebec East) in Canada, House of Commons, *Debates*, 1930, at 1947

10 *Canada Year Book 1921* (Ottawa 1922), 825

11 For two recent discussions of these changes, see E.T. May, *Great Expectations: Marriage and Divorce in Post-Victorian America* (Chicago 1980), and R.W. Griswold, *Family and Divorce in California, 1850–1890: Victorian Illusions and Everyday Realities* (Albany, 1982).

12 This is unfortunate, for a number of studies have established that ethnicity is an important variable in family behaviour. See, for example, J. Bodnar, *Lives of Their Own: Blacks, Italians, and Poles in Pittsburgh, 1900–1960* (Urbana, Ill. 1982), and V.Y. McLaughlin, 'Patterns of Work and Family Organization: Buffalo's Italians,' in T.K. Rabb and R.I. Rotberg, eds, *The Family in History: Interdisciplinary Essays* (New York 1971), 111–26.

13 See, for example, J.M. Beck, 'The Canadian Parliament and Divorce,' *Canadian Journal of Economics and Political Science* 23 (1957), 298–305; R. Pike, 'Legal Access and the Incidence of Divorce in Canada: A Sociohistorical Analysis,' *Canadian Review of Sociology and Anthropology* 12 (1975), 122–3.

2 The Family and Canadian Public Culture

1 The following discussion has benefited from a very considerable liter-

ature, including M. Barrett, *Women's Oppression Today: Problems in Marxist Feminist Analysis* (London 1980); M. Barrett and M. McIntosh, *The Anti-Social Family* (London 1982); F.E. Olsen, 'The Family and the Market: A Study of Ideology and Legal Reform,' *Harvard Law Review* 96 (1983), 1497–1578; and C. Smart, *The Ties That Bind: Law, Marriage and the Reproduction of Patriarchal Relations* (London 1984).

2　G.S. Holmested, 'The Marriage Laws of Canada,' *Canadian Law Review* 2 (1903), 527

3　For a discussion of weddings in the 1920s, see S. Morton, 'The June Bride as the Working-Class Bride: Getting Married in the North End of Halifax in the 1920s,' paper presented to the Canadian Historial Association Annual Meeting, Laval University, 1989.

4　The Church of England in Canada issued a revised version of the *Book of Common Prayer* in 1918, and it is from this version that the information is taken. The bride, in fact, twice promised to 'obey' her husband. According to one Protestant minister, there was already pressure from some couples to omit the word 'obey' from the vows. See I.D. Lyttle, 'Marrying and Giving in Marriage,' *Canadian Magazine* 63 (1924), 220–1.

5　F.F. Moore, 'The True Wife,' *Canadian Magazine* 53 (1919), 195–203. For a similar example in a contemporary novel, see the depiction of Cynthia Elton in P. Child, *God's Sparrows* (London 1937).

6　See, for example, R. Cook and W. Mitchinson, eds, *The Proper Sphere: Woman's Place in Canadian Society* (Toronto 1976), and B. Welter, 'The Cult of True Womanhood: 1820–1860,' in M. Gordon, ed., *The American Family in Social-Historical Perspective* (New York 1983), 372–92.

7　For a recent analysis of the power of this view of women's nature and role in Quebec, see A. Lévesque, *La norme et les déviates: des femmes au Québec pendant l'entre-deux-guerres* (Montreal 1989). For a general discussion of the female world of work in the home, see V. Strong-Boag, 'Keeping House in God's Country: Canadian Women at Work in the Home,' in C. Heron and R. Storey, eds, *On the Job: Confronting the Labour Process in Canada* (Kingston 1986), 126–51.

8　J.H. Thompson (with A. Seager), *Canada 1922–1939: Decades of Discord* (Toronto 1985), 152

9　M. Vipond, 'The Image of Women in Mass Circulation Magazines in the 1920s,' in S.M. Trofimenkoff and A. Prentice, eds, *The Neglected Majority: Essays in Canadian Women's History* (Toronto 1977), 116–24; S.J. Wilson, 'The Changing Image of Women in Candian Mass Circulating Magazines, 1930–1970,' *Atlantis* 2 (2) (1977), 33–44

10　*Canadian Magazine* 35 (1910), 89

11　B. Light and J. Parr, eds, *Canadian Women on the Move 1867–1920* (Toronto 1983), 152–3; L. Oren, 'The Welfare of Women in Laboring

Families: England, 1860–1950,' in M. Hartman and L.W. Banner, eds, *Clio's Consciousness Raised* (New York 1974), 226–44

12 'A Plea for Woman Suffrage in Canada,' *Canadian Magazine* 29 (1907), 151–2

13 *Canadian Magazine* 29 (1907), 475

14 NAC, Canadian Federation of University Women, vol. 18, file 'Resolutions – Status of Women'; Manitoba Welfare Supervision Board, *Report on the Problem of Family Desertion in Manitoba* (Winnipeg 1931), 19–22

15 C. Lasch, *A Haven in a Heartless World: The Family Beseiged* (New York 1977)

16 C.L. Bacchi, *Liberation Deferred? The Ideas of the English-Canadian Suffragists, 1877–1918* (Toronto 1982)

17 Dr J.M. Ewing, in *Proceedings of the Sixth Canadian Conference on Social Work* (n.p. 1938), 83

18 NAC, Canadian Council on Social Development, vol. 51, file 456, 1936–47, 'Family Protection To-day.' See also A. Ravenhill, *The Place and Purpose of Family Life*, bulletin no. 35, Department of Agriculture (Victoria 1911), and Lévesque, *La norme et les déviantes*, passim.

19 See, for example, V. Strong-Boag, *The Parliament of Women: The National Council of Women of Canada 1893–1929* (Ottawa 1976), 296, and Light and Parr, *On the Move*, 146–7.

20 See, for example, *The New Outlook*, 1 October 1937, 887.

21 London (Ontario) Children's Aid Society, *Annual Report of 1906* (London 1906), 33

22 M. McIntosh, 'The State and the Oppression of Women,' in A. Kuhn and A. Wolpe, eds, *Feminism and Materialism* (London 1978), 255

23 Barrett and McIntosh, *Anti-Social Family*, 26

24 V. Strong-Boag, 'Working Women and the State: The Case of Canada, 1889–1945,' *Atlantis* 6 (2) (1981), 1–9; J. Ursel, 'The State and the Maintenance of Patriarchy: A Case Study of Family, Labour and Welfare Legislation in Canada,' in J. Dickinson and B. Russell, eds, *Family, Economy and State: The Social Reproduction Process under Capitalism* (Toronto 1986), 164, 168; R.R. Pierson, 'Gender and the Unemployment Insurance Debates in Canada, 1934–1940,' *Labour/Le Travail* 25 (1990), 77–103. As used here, the term 'reproduction' refers to the production of human life, involving three processes: procreation, socialization, and daily maintenance.

25 V. Strong-Boag, ' "Wages for Housework": Mothers' Allowances and the Beginnings of Social Security in Canada,' *Journal of Canadian Studies* 14 (1979), 24–34; AO, RG 4, C-3, #3106/1922, #1247/1927; Canadian Welfare Council, *Mothers' Allowances: Comparative Analysis* (Ottawa

1936); J. Haddad and S. Milton, 'The Construction of Gender Roles in Social Policy: Mothers' Allowances and Day Care in Ontario before World War II,' *Canadian Women's Studies* 7 (1986), 68–70

26 D.J. Hall, *Clifford Sifton: The Lonely Eminence, 1901–1929* (Vancouver 1985), 300; J.H. Perry, *Taxes, Tariffs, and Subsidies: A History of Canadian Fiscal Development*, vol. 1 (Toronto 1955), 158; J.L. Granatstein and J.M. Hitsman, *Broken Promises: A History of Conscription in Canada* (Toronto 1977), 84; D. Morton and G. Wright, *Winning the Second Battle: Canadian Veterans and the Return to Civilian Life, 1915–1930* (Toronto 1987), 53 and passim; C.A. Cavanaugh, 'The Women's Movement in Alberta as Seen through the Campaign for Dower Rights, 1909–1928,' MA thesis (University of Alberta 1986); M. Hobbs and R.R. Pierson, ' "When Is a Kitchen Not a Kitchen?" ' *Canadian Women's Studies* 7 (1986), 71–6

27 D.L. Barker, 'The Regulation of Marriage: Repressive Benevolence,' in G. Littlejohn et al., eds, *Power and the State* (London 1978), 239–66; J.D. Payne and M.P. Downs, 'Permanent Alimony,' *Western Ontario Law Review* 9 (1970), 5–9; N. Basch, *In the Eyes of the Law: Women, Marriage, and Property in Nineteenth-Century New York* (Ithaca 1982), 15–25

28 On the world of female paid labour, there are a number of useful works; but see especially V. Strong-Boag, 'The Girl of the New Day: Canadian Working Women in the 1920s,' *Labour / Le Travailleur* 4 (1979), 131–64, and M. Steedman, 'Skill and Gender in the Canadian Clothing Industry, 1890–1940,' in Heron and Storey, eds, *On the Job*, 152–76.

29 Thompson and Seager, *Canada 1922–1939*, 149–51

30 B.D. Palmer, *Working-Class Experience: The Rise and Reconstitution of Canadian Labour, 1800–1980* (Toronto 1983), 192

31 Strong-Boag, 'Working Women,' 5

32 *National Home Monthly*, April 1935, 23. V. Strong-Boag, *The New Day Recalled: Lives of Girls and Women in English Canada, 1919–1939* (Toronto 1987) effectively uses advertising to make this point.

33 E. Pleck, *Domestic Tyranny: The Making of Social Policy against Family Violence from Colonial Times to the Present* (New York 1987), 7

34 L.C. Halem, *Divorce Reform: Changing Legal and Social Perspectives* (New York 1980)

35 The central place of divorce in the development of family sociology in this period in the United States is discussed in R.L. Howard, *A Social History of American Family Sociology, 1865–1940* (Westport, Conn. 1981).

36 London (Ontario) Children's Aid Society, *Annual Report of 1919* (London 1919), 2–3. See also Howard, *Family Sociology*, 46–7.

37 L. Pélland, 'Divorce,' *La Revue du Droit* 17 (1938), 10
38 T.C.L. Ketchum, 'The New Brunswick Divorce Court,' *Canadian Magazine* 43 (1914), 486
39 *Canada Law Journal* 46 (1910), 637
40 Reprinted in *Canada Law Journal* 53 (1917), 189
41 Toronto *Globe*, 26 April 1928; 25 February 1929; 16 April 1929; 17 April 1929; 20 April 1929
42 *Canada Law Journal* 46 (1910), 638; ibid., 47 (1911), 716–18
43 PANS, RG 39, file C-59B. Much of the rest of this material comes from anonymous interviews, but on Foster see P.B. Waite, *The Man from Halifax: Sir John Thompson, Prime Minister* (Toronto 1985), 391. On Harris, see 'Lawren Harris: Journey towards the Light,' Canadian Broadcasting Corporation, 1986. On the role of such stigma in the family, see C.D. Bryant, 'The Concealment of Stigma and Deviancy as a Family Function,' in C.D. Bryant and J.G. Wells, eds, *Deviancy and the Family* (Philadelphia 1973), 391–7, and A.C. Cain and I. Fast, 'The Legacy of Suicide,' ibid., 227–34.
44 *Canada Law Journal* 49 (1913), 153–4
45 See, for example, *Fortnightly Law Journal* 6 (1937), 233, and C.S. McKee, 'The Law of Divorce,' *Canada Law Journal* 108 (1922), 229–30.
46 'J.H.' in Toronto *Globe*, 15 March 1901
47 *Calgary Herald*, 12 July 1919
48 *Vancouver Sun*, 18 April 1929
49 Montreal *Star*, 16 April 1929. On the importance of the north in Canadian nationalism see C. Berger, *The Sense of Power: Studies in the Ideas of Canadian Imperialism, 1867–1914* (Toronto 1970).
50 Dominion Bureau of Statistics, *Divorces in Canada 1923* (Ottawa 1924), 1, *Divorces in Canada 1924*, 1, and *Divorces in Canada 1932*, 1
51 T.D. Williams, in Canadian Conference on Social Work, *Proceedings of the First Annual Meetings* (Montreal 1928), 49
52 C. Whitton, *Canadian Cavalcade 1920–1935* (Ottawa 1935), 27; NAC, C. Whitton Papers, vol. 19, file 'Social Legislation in Canada – 1929,' 30–1
53 See, for example, B. Thomson, 'Parliamentary Divorce in Canada,' *Canadian Law Times* 39 (1919), 253–63; C.S. McKee, 'The Law of Divorce in Canada,' *Canada Law Journal* 108 (1922), 211–15; *Fortnightly Law Journal* 4 (1934), 130; and H.L. Cartwright, *Law and Practice of Divorce in Ontario* (Toronto 1932)
54 See, for example, *Fortnightly Law Journal* 8 (1938), 33.
55 See, for example, E.F. Raney, *Marriage and Divorce Laws of Canada* (Toronto 1914), 3–5, and *Fortnightly Law Journal* 1 (1932), 245.
56 H. Bourassa, *Le divorce: aspects constitutionels et politiques* (Montreal 1930); Rev. M.C. Forest, *Divorce* (Ottawa 1921); Rev. J.J. O'Gorman,

Divorce in Canada: An Appeal to Protestants (Toronto 1920); NAC, La Fédération des femmes Canadiennes-français, 5, file 'Divorce 1921'

57 *The Doctrine and Discipline of the Methodist Church, 1906* (Toronto 1907), 26–7; *Baptist Year Book 1919 for Ontario and Quebec and Western Canada* (Toronto 1920), 223; *The United Baptist Year Book 1921* (Truro 1921), 114. I am grateful to G.A. Rawlyk for bringing this latter information to my attention.

58 In 1930, for example, when two minor divorce reforms were being debated in Parliament, Cardinal Rouleau issued a pastoral letter attacking divorce; see Lévesque, *La norme et les déviantes*, 46.

59 On the social gospel, see R. Allen, *The Social Passion: Religion and Social Reform in Canada 1914–28* (Toronto 1971).

60 *Social Welfare* 1 (1919), 209

61 *Social Welfare* 2 (1920), 137

62 *Social Welfare* 3 (1921), 149–50, 158–60

63 See, for example: *Social Welfare* 5 (1923), 134, and 6 (1924), 123.

64 *Social Welfare* 18 (1939), 62

65 United Church of Canada, *Record of Proceedings of the Fifth General Council* (Toronto 1932), 276–86; *The New Outlook*, 5 February 1930, 127, and 26 February 1930, 204

66 Bacchi, *Liberation Deferred?* 64–6

67 C. Houston and W.J. Smyth, *The Orange Order in Nineteenth-Century Ontario* (Toronto 1980), 13

68 J.C. Hopkins, *The Canadian Annual Review of Public Affairs 1909* (Toronto 1910), 13

69 Bacchi, *Liberation Deferred?* 11–12

70 See, for example, *Report of the Tenth Annual Meeting of the National Council of Women of Canada* (Toronto 1903), 94–6; NAC, National Council of Women of Canada (hereinafter NCWC), vol. 66, file 'Criminal Code Amendments, 1896–1922,' 'Further Recommendations on Divorce'; *The Year Book of the NCWC 1919–1920*, 90; ibid., *1920*, 63, 125, 166, 172, 211; ibid., *1936*, 63; and Strong-Boag, *Parliament of Women*, 358.

71 See, for example, *Fortnightly Law Journal* 3 (1934), 171, 203, 219, and *The Year Book of the NCWC 1929*, 46–7.

72 *Canadian Law Times* 25 (1905), 527

73 Walton, 'Divorce in Canada and the United States,' 595

74 H. Dobson, 'Coming Gales and the Marriage Bond,' *Social Welfare* 11 (1929), 110–11

75 'The Marriage Pattern,' *Social Welfare* 12 (1930), 143

76 E. Thomas, 'Christian Marriage,' *Social Welfare* 14 (1932), 165–6, 179

77 Ibid., 166

78 *Social Welfare* 15 (1935), 95

79 See, for example, Walton, 'Divorce in Canada and the United States,' 583.
80 'Divorce and Remarriage,' *Social Welfare* 15 (1935), 110–11
81 A. Horstman, *Victorian Divorce* (New York 1985), 56–62
82 On Weekes, see G.N. Weekes, *Divorce and Matrimonial Causes Act* (London, Ont. 1938); NAC, A. Meighen Papers, #95842-3, Weekes to Meighen, London, 25 March 1936; and NAC, J.S. Woodsworth Papers, Weekes to J.S. Woodsworth, London, 10 December 1938. The defenders of the existing system were able to employ such established groups as the Catholic Women's League of Canada or la Fédération des femmes canadiennes-françaises as vehicles for the lobbying of politicians.
83 In 1943 a Gallup poll of Canadians reflected their general unwillingness to support significant change in the divorce regime. In response to the question 'In your opinion is it too easy to get a divorce in this country, or not easy enough?' the following results were tabulated:

	Canada overall	Roman Catholic	Non-Roman Catholic	French-Canadian	English-Canadian
Too easy	27%	42%	20%	42%	23%
Too hard	24	17	27	18	26
About right	32	25	36	25	34
Undecided	17	16	17	15	17
	100%	100%	100%	100%	100%

While the sex of the respondent made no substantial difference in the answers given, older Canadians were more inclined to feel that divorce was too easy. See Canadian Institute of Public Opinion, Public Opinion News Service Release, ballot 119–5, 14 July 1943. See also Canadian Youth Com-mission, *Youth, Marriage and the Family* (Toronto 1948), xi.

3 Divorce Legislation

1 W.E. Raney in *Canada Law Journal* 51 (1915), 86
2 See Province of Canada, *Parliamentary Debates on the Subject of the Confederation of the British North American Provinces* (Quebec 1865), 577–9, 776–82; Canada, House of Commons, *Debates*, 1929, 1573. While 'marriage and divorce' were consistently projected to be within federal jurisdiction, 'solemnization of marriage' did not appear among the list of provincial responsibilities until the 1866 resolutions of the London Conference; see Canada, Senate, *Report Relating to the Enactment of the British North America Act, 1867* (Ottawa 1961), annex 4, 63.

3 England, 20 & 21 Vict., c. 85

4 New Brunswick, 23 & 24 Vict., c. 37; Nova Scotia, 29 & 30 Vict., c. 3. The Nova Scotia legislature first exercised its authority in this field in 1758. For details of this early colonial activity in the Maritimes, see H.T. Kingdon, *Divorce and Re-marriage: Historical Evidence* (Montreal [189?]), 101–7, and C.B. Backhouse, ' "Pure Patriarchy": Nineteenth-Century Canadian Marriage,' *McGill Law Journal* 31 (1986), 266–71.

5 Backhouse, ' "Pure Patriarchy," ' 270–1

6 This desire for uniform law was not limited to divorce; see section 94 of the British North America Act.

7 *Watts* v *Watts*, [1908] AC 573; PEI (1835), 5 & 6 Wm. IV, c. 10

8 Canada, House of Commons, *Debates*, 1901, 1417; ibid., 1919, 3773, 3780; Canada, Senate, *Debates*, 1920, 178

9 From 1868 to 1882 there was an average of 4.7 divorces annually; from 1883 to 1899 there was an average of 11.8: *Canada Year Book 1921* (Ottawa 1922), 825.

10 B.M. Britton (Liberal, Kingston) in Canada, House of Commons, *Debates*, 1901, 1413

11 W.F. Maclean (Conservative, York East) and Laurier (Liberal, Quebec East) in Canada, House of Commons, *Debates*, 1901, 1422–3. See also R. Phillips, *Putting Asunder: A History of Divorce in Western Society* (Cambridge 1988), 465.

12 Canada, House of Commons, *Debates*, 1902, 4122; ibid., 1903, 573

13 Ibid., 1902, 4122; ibid., 1906, 5444 (debating a divorce for Sir Hugh Allan's niece) and 5459; ibid., 1911, 8975 (debating a divorce for Sir William Mackenzie's daughter); ibid., 1919, 3775; ibid., 1929, 3574; ibid., 1930, 945; ibid., 1935, 2950; ibid., 1938, 1947; ibid., 1939, 3989; Senate, *Debates*, 1934, 502–3; NAC, W.L.M. King Papers, MG 26 J2, vol. 2, file D-6100. The courts were dubious about the quality of judicial work in parliamentary divorces. In *Upper* v *Upper*, [1933] OR 1, the Ontario Court of Appeal held that a 1928 alimony decision was not overtaken by the Senate's decision to award a divorce to the husband, because courts decide on legal issues while Parliament decides on the basis of expediency.

14 Charlton's career shows how ideologically complex were the issues related to family reform. While Charlton pushed for a limited liberal reform in divorce process, he also supported the raising of the age of consent and the criminalization of the dissemination of birth control information.

15 D. Tisdale (Conservative, Norfolk South) in Canada, House of Commons, *Debates*, 1903, 578

16 Finance Minister W.S. Fielding, ibid., 587

17 See, for example, ibid., 1905, 6376–7; ibid., 1906, 5438, 6036–7, 6047–

8; and ibid., 1917, 5503, 5903, 5908.

18 E.A. Lancaster (Conservative, Lincoln), ibid., 1906, 6357

19 H.J. Cloran (Liberal, Ontario) in Canada, Senate, *Debates*, 1905, 107

20 Ibid., 1906, 495–512; ibid., 1907–8, 722–3

21 Senator Cloran introduced similar bills in 1909 and 1913.

22 *Walker* v *Walker* (1917), 35 DLR 207 (Man. KB); (1918), 39 DLR 731 (Man. CA); [1919] AC 947 at 953 (JCPC), and *Board* v *Board*, (1918) 41 DLR 286, [1919] AC 956 (JCPC)

23 J. English, *The Decline of Politics* (Toronto 1977); J.H. Thompson, *The Harvests of War* (Toronto 1978)

24 Canada, House of Commons, *Debates*, 1918, 2065–6; J.M. Beck, 'The Canadian Parliament and Divorce,' *Canadian Journal of Economics and Political Science* 23 (1957), 300. Borden intimated as early as 1917 that divorce reform was being considered; see Canada, House of Commons, *Debates*, 1917, 5903.

25 NAC, Sir R. Borden Popers, #54636–9, 54643–4, 54517–19, 54672–3; A. Meighen Papers, #6207, Meighen to Mrs R.W. Reford, Ottawa, 26 October 1918; NAC, RG 13, A2, #462/1921, E.L. Newcombe to Pvt S. Cherry, Ottawa, 11 March 1919

26 Canada, House of Commons, *Debates*, 1919, 1662

27 Ibid., 3781–2

28 Ibid., 3777. See also, for example, G. Lynch-Staunton in Canada, Senate, *Debates*, 1920, 175.

29 Sir H.B. Ames (Conservative Unionist, Montreal St Antoine) and D.L. Redman (Conservative Unionist, Calgary East) in Canada, House of Commons, *Debates*, 1919, 3778, 3781

30 Ibid., 1920, 134

31 Committee of the Family (of the SSCC), *Some Aspects of the Divorce Situation As It Affects Canada: A Report Prepared for the Use of the Committee 1921–22* (Toronto 1922) 37–8

32 A. Trahan (Liberal, Nicolet) in Canada, House of Commons, *Debates*, 1921, 228

33 Canada, Senate, *Debates*, 1923, 105

34 C.A. Fournier (Liberal, Bellechasse) in Canada, House of Commons, *Debates*, 1925, 553

35 Ibid., 576

36 Ibid., 3870–1, 3883–4

37 Canada, 15 & 16 George V, c. 41

38 R.R. Pierson, 'Gender and the Unemployment Insurance Debates in Canada, 1934–1940,' *Labour/Le Travail* 25 (1990), 84–5

39 A representative example is the vote on second reading, approving the bill in principle. Regionally, the votes were: British Columbia and the

West, 48 yes, 3 no, 6 absent; Ontario, 44 yes, 14 no, 20 absent; Quebec, 3 yes 41 no, 17 absent; Maritimes, 14 yes, 10 no, 7 absent. The voting by party was: Conservatives, 31 yes, 3 no; Liberals, 24 yes, 60 no; Progressives, 48 yes, 4 no; Independents, 6 yes, 1 no. By religion the voting was Baptist, 5 yes; Church of England, 15 yes, 4 no; Congregationalist, 2 yes, 1 no; Methodist, 24 yes, 4 no; Presbyterian, 46 yes, 7 no; Roman Catholic, 1 yes, 51 no; United Church, 4 yes; other, 8 yes, 1 no; unknown, 3 yes. See Canada, House of Commons, *Debates*, 1925, 576. (The party and religious affiliations were calculated using *The Canadian Parliamentary Guide, 1925.*)

40 In British law, every child at birth acquired a domicile of origin which was the domicile of the child's parents; when the child reached the age of majority, the domicile of origin could be replaced by a domicile of choice. The determination of domicile was a matter of law and involved the weighing of various evidence; the most important involved the intention of a person to adopt a particular place as a permanent home.

41 Women's leaders were disturbed by one of the more public results of this legal rule: a Canadian-born woman who married a landed immigrant automatically adopted her husband's citizenship and lost her own Canadian citizenship.

42 H.H. Stevens (Conservative, Vancouver Centre) and L.J. Ladner (Conservative, Vancouver South) in Canada, House of Commons, *Debates*, 1929, 1861–2

43 J-F. Pouliot (Liberal, Témiscouata), ibid., 2701; see also Canada, Senate, *Debates*, 1929, 369–70. In case these arguments failed to persuade his colleagues, Pouliot also raised that old Canadian standby, 'provincial rights'; he claimed that any federal legislation regarding domicile was an invasion of provincial jurisdiction over property and civil rights; see Canada, House of Commons, *Debates*, 1929, 2927.

44 Ibid., 2931, 3126–7

45 L. McMeans (Conservative, Manitoba) in Canada, Senate, *Debates*, 1929, 355, 376

46 E. Lapointe (Liberal, Quebec East) in Canada, House of Commons, *Debates*, 1930, 1947

47 There was only one recorded vote; on third reading the bill passed by a vote of 74 to 47. See ibid., 2041.

48 Canada (1930), 20 & 21 George V, c. 15

49 Canada, House of Commons, *Debates*, 1921, 3769; ibid., 1926, 4201

50 Ibid., 1927, 667, 1331, 1363, 1469, 1956, 2095, 2099

51 Ibid., 1957

52 Canada, Senate, *Debates*, 1928, 672–3

53 Canada, House of Commons, *Debates*, 1928, 2464–9

54 Ibid., 2571–3
55 A cabinet committee (L. Cannon, R. Dandurand, J.C. Elliott, W.D. Euler, R. Forke, and J.L. Ralston) was struck on 29 November 1929 to study the question of divorce legislation; see NAC, W.L.M. King Papers, MG 26 J4, #C52544.
56 Ibid., reel C 2309, #147288, Dandurand to King, Montreal, 4 February 1930; ibid., #136891, Dandurand to L. Cannon, Montreal, 23 December 1929; ibid., #136892, King to Dandurand, Ottawa, 31 January 1930; ibid., King diary, 28 January 1930. Beck, 'Parliament and Divorce,' 302–3 gives a useful summary of the 1928–30 debate in the House.
57 Canada (1930), 20 & 21 George V, c. 14
58 One other statute, passed in 1937 (1 George VI, c. 4), facilitated appeals to the British Columbia Supreme Court in divorce cases.
59 Canada, Senate, *Debates*, 1938, 88; House of Commons, *Debates*, 3849
60 F.E. Olsen, 'The Family and the Market: a Study of Ideology and Legal Reform') *Harvard Law Review* 96 (1983), 1512, 1540; C. Smart, *The Ties That Bind* (London 1984), 28–32. For a similar example in Canadian society at this time, see Pierson, 'Gender and the Unemployment Insurance Debates,' 77–103.
61 Canada, Senate, *Debates*, 1938, 88
62 See, for example, E.A. Accampo, *Industrialization, Family Life and Class Relations: Saint-Chamond, 1815–1914* (Berkeley 1988); L. Gordon, *Heroes of Their Own Lives: The Politics and History of Family Violence: Boston, 1880–1980* (New York 1988).
63 Canada, House of Commons, *Debates*, 1930, 561; Senate, *Debates*, 1928, 82
64 Phillips, *Putting Asunder*, 480, 494–5

4 The Judiciary

1 G.O.W. Mueller, 'Inquiry into the State of a Divorceless Society,' *University of Pittsburgh Law Review* 18 (1957), 545–78; M. Rheinstein, *Marriage Stability, Divorce, and the Law* (Chicago 1972)
2 Michael Grossberg, *Governing the Hearth: Law and the Family in Nineteenth-Century America* (Chapel Hill 1985)
3 Constance Backhouse, 'Shifting Patterns of Nineteenth Century Custody Law,' in D.H. Flaherty, ed., *Essays in the History of Canadian Law*, vol. 1 (Toronto 1981), 211–48; 'Nineteenth-Century Canadian Rape Law, 1800–92,' in Flaherty, ed., *Essays in the History of Canadian Law*, vol. 2 (Toronto 1983), 200–47; 'Involuntary Motherhood: Abortion, Birth Control and the Law in Nineteenth-Century Canada,' *Windsor Year-*

book of *Access to Justice* 3 (1983), 61–130; 'Desperate Women and Compassionate Courts: Infanticide in Nineteenth-Century Canada,' *University of Toronto Law Journal* 34 (1984), 447–78; ' "Pure Patriarchy": Nineteenth-Century Canadian Marriage,' *McGill Law Journal* 31 (1986), 264–312; 'The Tort of Seduction: Fathers and Daughters in Nineteenth-Century Canada,' *Dalhousie Law Journal* 10 (1986), 45–80; 'Married Women's Property Law in Nineteenth-Century Canada,' *Law and History Review* 6 (1988), 211–57. See also A. Sachs, 'The Myth of Male Protectiveness and the Legal Subordination of Women,' in C. Smart and B. Smart, eds, *Women, Sexuality and Social Control* (London 1978), 27–40.

4 T.G. Mathers, *A Summary of the Law of Divorce* (Winnipeg 1920), 3
5 *Le Mesurier* v *Le Mesurier*, [1895] AC 517 (JCPC)
6 (1901), 1 OLR 629 (Ont. SC), 2 OLR 249 (Ont. CA)
7 (1914) 6 WWR 1231, 20 BCR 34 (BCSC)
8 See, for example, *Adams* v *Adams* (1901), 11 WLR 358, 14 BCR 301 (BCSC); *Boyle* v *Boyle*, [1925] 1 WWR 829 (Man. KB); *Breen* v *Breen*, [1929] 2 WWR 345, [1929] 4 DLR 649 (Man. KB).
9 *Kalenczuk* v *Kalenczuk*, [1920] 2 WWR 415, 13 Sask. LR 262, 52 DLR 406 (Sask. CA)
10 *Thornback* v *Thornback and Thomson*, [1923] 4 DLR 810, 1 CBR 879 (Yukon Terr. Ct). See also *Coleman* v *Coleman*, [1919] 3 WWR 490 (Alta. SC); *Chaisson* v *Chaisson* (1920), 53 DLR 360 (Div. & Matr. Causes Ct); and counsel's brief in PANS, RG 39 D, file D-95. Plaintiff's counsel in another case at this time also raised the possibility of making deserted wives an exception to the rule of domicile; see *Marriaggi* v *Marriaggi*, [1923] 3 WWR 849, [1923] 4 DLR 463 (Man. KB).
11 *Payn* v *Payn*, [1924] 3 WWR 111, [1924] 3 DLR 1006 (Alta. SC)
12 [1920] 2 WWR 714, (1920) 55 DLR 386, (1920), 15 *Alberta Law Reports* 400 (Alta. SC). See also *Swift* v *Swift*, [1920] 3 WWR 874 (1920), 55 DLR 393 (Alta. SC).
13 [1923] 4 DLR 366 (Alta. CA). The trial judge commented that if he had had jurisdiction, he would have granted a divorce on grounds of cruelty, desertion, and adultery; however, he felt bound by the rule of united domicile.
14 *Attorney-General for Alberta* v *Cook*, [1926] AC 444 (JCPC)
15 [1929] 2 DLR 546 (Sask. KB), [1930] 1 WWR 173, (1930) 24 Sask. LR 234, (1930) 4 DLR 736 (Sask. CA)
16 [1928] 3 WWR 291 (Sask. KB), [1930] 1 WWR 189, (1930), 24 Sask. LR 250, [1930] 3 DLR 522 (Sask. CA). See also *Lauritson* v *Lauritson* (1932), 41 OWN 274 (Ont. SC), where deportation to his native land of a hus-

band, who had been convicted of the criminal offence of having carnal knowledge of a minor female, was insufficient to relinquish a domicile of choice.

17 The legal community in general was beginning to argue in favour of the limited new principle found in this legislation. Not only were the courts expressing their support, but so too were counsel. In December 1928 counsel for the female plaintiff in a Nova Scotia divorce case contended that a subsequent change in domicile by the husband ought not to deprive the court of jurisdiction in his earlier marital misconduct: 'It will be noted that the [claim to] jurisdiction is founded not on the ground that the wife may have a domicile separate from that of her husband but that the husband, even if he had acquired a new domicile, cannot allege it for the purpose of divesting the Court of jurisdiction to give relief to the injured wife' (PANS, RG 39 D, file D-95). The conservative character of counsel's argument matched the conservative nature of the courts' attitude and the limited changes that legislators were willing to contemplate.

18 *Jolly* v *Jolly*, [1940] 2 WWR 148, (1940), 55 BCR 61, [1940] 2 DLR 759 (BCCA)

19 [1941] 1 WWR 535 (Sask. KB), [1941] 2 WWR 489, [1941] 3 DLR 578 (Sask. CA)

20 The National Council of Women of Canada, for example, began to discuss and lobby for reform at both the national and local levels: see, for example, the published reports of the annual meetings of 1922 (p 110), 1924 (pp 30, 80), 1926 (p 97), 1929 (p 47), and 1930 (pp 83–4).

21 *Stephens* v *Falchi*, [1938] SCR 354

22 This distinguished two recent cases (*McLeod* v *Attorney-General for New South Wales*, [1891] AC 455 (JCPC); *R.* v *Plowman* (1894), 25 OR 656 (Ont. SC)) and re-established the situation that had existed before 1891; see *R.* v *McQuiggan* (1853), 2 LCR 340 (Que. QB); *R.* v *Brierly* (1887), 14 OR 525 (Ont. Ch.)

23 *In re Criminal Code Sections relating to Bigamy* (1897), 27 SCR 461, at 481

24 *Armitage* v *The Attorney-General, Gillig* v *Gillig*, [1906] P. 135 (PDA); *Bater* v *Bater*, [1906] P. 209 (CA)

25 Canada, House of Commons, *Debates*, 1887, 1017–28; 50 & 51 Vict., c. 127. 'The Validity in Ontario of Foreign Decrees of Divorce,' *Fortnightly Law Journal* 7 (1938), 247–8, surveys the facts in a number of cases over the forty-year period.

26 (1907), 14 OLR 434 (Ont. CA)

27 [1924] 3 WWR 578, [1924] 4 DLR 835 (Man. KB)

28 See, for example, *Holmes* v *Holmes*, [1927] 2 DLR 979 (Alta. SC); *MacDonald* v *Nash*, [1929] 2 WWR 84, [1929] 4 DLR 1051 (Man. KB);

Drake v *MacLaren*, [1929] 2 WWR 87, [1929] 3 DLR 159 (Alta. SC)

29 (1925) 58 NSR 65, [1925] 2 DLR 256 (NSSC).

30 [1927] 2 DLR 655 (BCSC)

31 [1938] 1 WWR 885, (1938) 53 BCR 13, [1938] 3 DLR 379 (BCSC)

32 Ontario and Alberta courts had held that a party who invoked and submitted to the jurisdiction of a foreign court was precluded from setting up want of jurisdiction even by way of defence, although the decree was one that the Canadian court might not recognize; see *In Re Williams and the Ancient Order of United Workmen* (1907), 14 OLR 482 (Ont. Div. Ct); *Detro* v *Detro* (1918), 70 DLR 61 (Alta. SC).

33 A.W. Mewett and M. Manning, *Criminal Law* (Toronto 1978), 483

34 RSC 1906, c 146, section 307

35 *R.* v *Haugen*, [1923] 2 WWR 709 (Sask. CA). See also *R.* v *Tolson*,(1889), 23 QBD 168, and *R.* v *Sellars* (1905), 9 CCC 153 (Co. J. Crim. Ct.).

36 See also *R.* v *Bleiler*, (1912) 1 DLR 878 (Alta. SC); *R.* v *Simard* (1931), 37 RLNS 167, (1931) 56 CCC 269 (Ct Sess. P.); *R.* v *Morgan* (1942), 16 MPR 335, (1942), 78 CCC 129, [1942] 4 DLR 321 (NSCA).

37 *R.* v *Brinkley* (1907), 14 OLR 434, at 455 (Ont. CA)

38 *R.* v *Woods* (1903), 6 OLR 41, [1903] 2 OWR 338, (1903), 7 CCC 226 (Ont. CA)

39 Canada (1953–4), 2 & 3 Eliz. II, c 51, section 240 (4); 'Conflict of Laws as to Nullity and Divorce,' [1932] 4 DLR 1

40 [1924] 4 DLR 951, at 953 (NBCA)

41 *A.* v *B.* (1906), 3 WLR 113 (Man. KB)

42 (1921), 49 OLR 15 (Ont. CA)

43 *Leboeuf* v *Leboeuf*, [1928] 1 WWR 423 (Alta. CA); *Sylvester* v *Sylvester* (1920), 18 OWN 363 (Ont. Div. Ct)

44 *M.* v *M.*, [1933] OWN 116 (Ont. SC)

45 *Einfield* v *Einfield and Einfield*, [1939] 1 WWR 1 (Man. KB); *Edmonds* v *Edmonds* (1912), 1 WWR 989 (BCSC); *Gowdy* v *Gowdy*, [1933] 1 WWR 379 (Man. KB); *Roberts* v *Roberts*, [1927] 1 WWR 993 (Alta. SC)

46 *Hoskin* v *Hoskin*, [1940] OWN 283 (Ont. SC)

47 [1926] 2 WWR 185 (Sask. CA)

48 *Lasko* v *Lasko and Miller*, [1935] 3 WWR 363 (Sask. KB)

49 *Sanborn* v *Sanborn et al.*, [1928] 1 WWR 78 (Sask. KB)

50 *Stacey* v *Stacey*, [1927] 1 WWR 821 (Alta. SC). Cf *Albert* v *Albert et al.*, [1934] OWN 407 (Ont. CA).

51 *Jasper* v *Jasper et al.*, [1934] OWN 411 (Ont. SC); *Wens* v *Wens*, [1939] 3 WWR 606 (Man. KB); *Paulin* v *Paulin and Martin*, [1937] 1 WWR 753 (Sask. KB), [1938] 1 WWR 261 (Sask. CA)

52 PANS, RG 39 D, file B-157

53 *Gordon* v *Gordon and Watt*, [1935] 2 WWR 419 (Sask. CA)

54 *Paulin* v *Paulin and Martin*, [1937] 1 WWR 753

55 [1928] 1 WWR 383. See also, for example, *Monaghan* v *Monaghan*, [1931] 2 WWR 1.

56 *Fitz Randolph* v *Fitz Randolph* (1918), 41 DLR 739. That a criterion such as social class could operate to the advantage of the working class was demonstrated in an unreported judgment of Justice R.H. Graham of the Nova Scotia divorce court (PANS, RG 39 D, file D-14). Graham declined to infer adultery from the conduct of an elderly couple (a retired sixty-nine-year-old painter and his fifty-six-year-old housekeeper), stating, 'Age and narrow means leave little place for passion.'

57 *Evans* v *Evans* (1790), 1 Hag. Con. 35, 161 ER 466 at 467 (P. & D.). Backhouse considers related nineteenth-century jurisprudence in ' "Pure Patriarchy," ' 303–11.

58 J.M. Biggs, *The Concept of Matrimonial Cruelty* (London 1962), 20, 51

59 A.J. Hammerton, 'Victorian Marriage and the Law of Matrimonial Cruelty,' paper presented to the Law and History Conference, LaTrobe University, May 1987; R.L. Griswold, 'The Evolution of the Doctrine of Mental Cruelty in Victorian American Divorce, 1790–1900,' *Journal of Social History* 20 (1986–7), 112–48. For a fuller development, see J.G. Snell, 'Marital Cruelty: Women and the Nova Scotia Divorce Court, 1900–1939,' *Acadiensis* 18 (1988), 3–32.

60 Biggs, *Cruelty*, 7–9

61 Sex of petitioner is not very revealing, since at all times cases involving cruelty were disproportionately initiated by wives. Social class was reported too infrequently in these cases for any useful discussion. No region or province differs markedly from the general patterns.

62 *Reynolds* v *Reynolds* (1905), 6 OWR 782 (Ont. SC)

63 *McIlwain* v *McIlwain* (1915–16), 35 OLR 532 (Ont. Div. Ct)

64 *Jones* v *Jones et al.*, [1925] 1 WWR 449 (Sask. KB). Cf *Dorset* v *Dorset* (1921), 57 DLR 636 (Man. KB).

65 See, for example, *Keweluk* v *Keweluk*, [1923] 2 WWR 78 (Sask. CA); *Walker* v *Walker* (1922), 21 OWN 170 (Ont. SC); *Brizard* v *Brizard* (1914), 5 WWR 1160 (Man. KB); *Payne* v *Payne* (1905), 10 OLR 742 (Ont. Div. Ct); and *Lofthouse* v *Lofthouse* (1908), 12 OWR 140 (Ont. SC).

66 16 OWN 358 (Ont. SC). See also, for example, *Bailey* v *Bailey* (1919), 45 OLR 59 (Ont. CA); *Hummell* v *Hummell* (1908), 11 OWR 113 (Ont. SC); and *Connolley* v *Connolley*, [1925] 2 WWR 426 (Sask. KB). Cf *Lovell* v *Lovell* (1907), 13 OLR 569 (Ont. CA); *Munshaw* v *Munshaw* (1923), 25 OWN 18 (Ont. SC); *Jones* v *Jones*, [1925] 1 WWR 449 (Sask. KB); and *McKieran* v *McKieran*, [1926] 1 WWR 199 (Man. CA).

67 *Denning* v *Denning* (1922–3), 53 OLR 130 (Ont. SC). See also, for example, *Whimbey* v *Whimbey* (1919), 45 OLR 228 (Ont. CA); *Cesale* v

Cesale (1920), 54 NSR 91 (NSCA); and *Burnfiel* v *Burnfiel,* [1925] 2 WWR 629 (Sask. KB).

68 *Cowie* v *Cowie* (1910), 15 OWR 771 (Ont. CA)
69 See, for example, *Lovell* v *Lovell* (1906), 11 OLR 547 (Ont. Div. Ct), 13 OLR 569 (Ont. CA); *McIlwain* v *McIlwain* (1915–16), 35 OLR 532 (Ont. Div. Ct); and *Bailey* v *Bailey* (1919), 45 OLR 59 (Ont. CA).
70 See Graham's unreported judgment in a divorce petition on ground of cruelty (PANS, RG 39 D, file C-448): 'The parties seem to be unalterably alienated, and I would grant a decree if the evidence permitted.' However, the evidence of physical and mental abuse had not clearly injured the wife's health and thus did not constitute legal cruelty.
71 Graham Parker discusses the role of discretionary justice in 'Canadian Legal Culture,' in L.A. Knafla, ed., *Law and Justice in a New Land: Essays in Western Canadian Legal History* (Toronto 1986), 23–4. Though jury trials were possible under rules in most jurisdictions, no evidence of their use was uncovered in the divorce records examined.
72 G.B. Baker, 'The Reconstitution of Upper Canadian Legal Thought in the Late-Victorian Empire,' *Law and History Review*, 3 (1985), 275.
73 Grossberg, *Governing the Hearth*, passim

5 The Role of the State

1 G.L. Savage, 'Divorce and the Law in England and France Prior to the First World War' *Journal of Social History* 21 (1988), 499-513
2 The parliamentary rules changed somewhat over time: unless otherwise specified, the discussion here represents a synthesis of those rules. The rules are set out and discussed in J.A. Gemmill, *The Practice of the Parliament of Canada upon Bills of Divorce* (Toronto 1889); R.R. Evans, *The Law and Practice Relating to Divorce and Other Matrimonial Causes* (Montreal 1923); and F.D. Hogg, *Parliamentary Divorce Practice in Canada* (Toronto 1925).
3 PANS, RG 39 D, file D-14
4 G.L. Savage, 'The Divorce Court and the Queen's – King's Proctor: Legal Patriarchy and the Sanctity of Marriage in England, 1861–1937,' Canadian Historical Association, *Historical Papers 1989*, 210–27
5 PANS, RG 39 D, files C-216, C-292, D-301, D-534, D-550, and D-615
6 Savage, 'Divorce and the Law,' 506, states that in England the king's proctor intervened in fewer than 10 per cent of the cases, a figure that would still be considerably higher than those in the provinces other than Nova Scotia, though no precise figures can be calculated.
7 Gemmill, *Practice of Parliament upon Divorce*, 105, 122; NAC, W.L.M. King Papers, MG 26 J1, #128293–4

8 AO, RG 4, C-3, #2932/1930, R.V. Sinclair to W.H. Price, Ottawa, 25 November 1931, passim; PABC, GR 1323, D-67-11, deputy attorney-general to F.C. Wade, Victoria, 22 May 1920

9 AO, RG 4, C-3, #3072/1930, E. Bayly to Rowan, Parkinson, Gardiner, and Willis, Toronto, 12 November 1931; ibid., #3185/1927, E. Bayly to T.M. Costello, Toronto, 24 January 1928; A. Horstmann, *Victorian Divorce* (New York 1985), 102. According to Horstmann, at the end of the nineteenth century the queen's proctor stopped about 5 per cent of English divorce suits.

10 AO, RG 4, C-3, #2518/1930; ibid., #735/1932; ibid., #1064/1932

11 Ibid., #3185/1927; ibid., #3210/1930; ibid., #293/1932; Ontario (1927), 17 Geo. V c. 47, section 36

12 *Alberta Gazette* 1919, 694; *Elkowech v Elkowech and King's Proctor*, [1925] 3 WWR 705 (Alta. CA); *Sherman v King's Proctor*, [1936] 2 WWR 152 (Alta. CA); W.K. Bowker, 'Procedure in Divorce Actions in Alberta,' *Alberta Law Quarterly* 3 (1938), 62; *Vancouver Sun*, 8 June 1925, 16

13 *Keslering v Keslering and Attorney-General*, [1921] 2 WWR 967 (Sask. CA); W.K. Power, *The Law and Practice Relating to Divorce* (Toronto 1948), 93

14 British Columbia adopted legislation in 1945 authorizing the attorney-general to intervene in divorce cases; see W.K. Power, *The Law and Practice Relating to Divorce and Other Matrimonial Causes in Canada* (Calgary 1948), 93.

15 AO, RG 4, C-3, #1283/1933; #2932/1930; #710/1933

16 Article 186 of the Code civil shares with common law the intention to rule out mutual consent as a ground for altering marital status.

17 In instances where the petitioner had committed some such marital offence, she or he could admit and explain the offence at the beginning of the proceeding and beg the exercise of the court's discretion on behalf of the petitioner. Though not common, the procedure is reminiscent of the role of discretion in eighteenth-century English criminal law, as discussed by D. Hay, 'Property, Authority and the Criminal Law,' in D. Hay et al., eds, *Albion's Fatal Tree: Crime and Society in Eighteenth-Century England* (New York 1977), 16–63.

18 Bowker, 'Procedure in Alberta,' 53; *1925 Supreme Court Rules* (Victoria 1925), 373–83

19 *Re DeMille*, [1926] 2 WWR 148, [1926] 3 DLR 140 (Alta. SC in Chambers)

20 *Re Coots* (1910), 1 OWN 807 (Ont. SC); *Re Sell*, [1924] 4 DLR 1115 (Ont. SC in Chambers); *Re Bull*, [1934] OWN 284 (Ont. SC); *Re Irvin*, [1940] 4 DLR 736 (Ont. SC). In 1950 the Ontario Marriage Act (c. 42, section 11) was amended to allow applications for declarations of presumed death.

21 *Re Irvin*, [1940] 4 DLR 736 (Ont. SC)

22 *In re Carlson* (1923), 32 BCR 24 (BCSC in Chambers); *In re Ball* (1923), 34 BCR 162 (BCSC in Chambers); *In re Jelfs*, [1925] 1 WWR 735 (Alta. SC in Chambers); *Re Debray*, [1943] 4 DLR 103 (BCSC)

23 *Re Tomes*, [1927] 2 DLR 864 (Man. KB); *Re Deloli*, [1929] 3 DLR 763 (Man. KB); *Re Morgan*, [1939] 3 DLR 142 (Man. CA)

24 Ibid.

25 RSNB 1877, c. 145, section 3; *R.* v *Strong* (1915), 43 NBR 190 (NBCA); *R.* v *Akerly* (1918), 46 NBR 195 (NBCA); *Ex Parte Belyea* (1918), 45 NBR 308 (NBSC in Chambers); *R.* v *Foster* (1934–5), 8 MPR 10 (NBCA)

26 *R* v *Harris* (1906), 11 CCC 254 (Sess. P.); *R.* v *Tolhurst, R.* v *Wright*, [1937] OR 570, 63 CCC 319 (Ont. CA)

27 J.G. Snell, ' "The White Life for Two": The Defence of Marriage and Sexual Morality in Canada, 1890–1914,' *Histoire sociale* 16 (1983), 119–22

28 NAC, RG 13, A2, vol. 212, #767, Rev. C.F. Mackinnon to [C.J. Doherty], Sydney Mines, NS, 2 May 1918

29 See, for example, NAC, RG 13, A2, vol. 184, #324; vol. 200, #389; vol. 214, #1378; vol. 250, #1511/1920; vol. 257, #657/1921; vol. 266, #416/1922; vol. 270, #1390; vol. 296, #562/1925; #835/1927; and NAC, Sir W. Laurier papers, #202504.

30 AO, RG 4, C-3, #1122/1915. See also #1119/1915 and #1126/1915; AO, RG 22 (London) SCO, #301/1931; RSO 1914, c. 231, section 2(h); RSC 1927, c. 108, section 30; G. Parker, 'The Legal Regulation of Sexual Activity and the Protection of Females,' *Osgoode Hall Law Journal* 21 (1983), 231–2.

31 Canada (1918), 8 & 9 Geo. V, c. 16, section 1; (1933), 23 & 24 Geo. V, c. 53, section 3; (1935), 25 & 26 Geo. V, c. 36

32 Parker, 'Regulation of Sexual Activity,' 232–5

33 D.E. Chunn, 'Regulating the Poor in Ontario: From Police Courts to Family Courts,' *Canadian Journal of Family Law* 6 (1987), 101

34 Snell, ' "White Life," ' 122–3

35 NAC, RG 13, A2, vol. 201, #516, W.A. Duncan to W.J. Bowser, New Westminster, BC, 17 March 1916. See also vol. 250, #1511; vol. 319, #273; vol. 320, #631; and L. Gordon, *Heroes of Their Own Lives* (New York 1988), 100.

36 SBC 1901, c. 18; SS 1910–11, c. 14; RSM 1900, c. 28; SNB 1926, c. 11; SNS 1941, c. 8. See also S.R. Fodden, 'The Deserted Wives and Children's Maintenance Act,' in H.T.G. Andrews, ed., *Family Law in the Family Courts* (Toronto 1973), 15–53.

37 SBC 1919, c. 19, section 3(2); *Brown* v *Brown*, [1924] 3 WWR 94 (BCSC in Chambers)

38 C.A. Cavanaugh, 'The Women's Movement in Alberta as Seen through the Campaign for Dower Rights 1909–1928,' MA thesis (University of

Alberta 1986); RSBC 1920, c. 94

39 *Brown* v *Brown*, [1924] 3 WWR 94 (BCSC in Chambers)

40 *Schwab* v *Schwab*, [1929] 3 WWR 188 (Sask. Dist. Ct); *Jackman* v *Jackman*, [1923] 3 DLR 798 (BCCA)

41 *Re Hanlan* (1921), 50 OLR 20 (Ont. SC in Chambers); see also *Gagen* v *Gagen*, [1934] 3 WWR 84 (BCCA).

42 See, for example, AO, RG 4, C-3, #2996/1927; #957/1925; #1661/1921.

43 Manitoba Welfare Supervision Board *Report on the Problem of Family Desertion in Manitoba* (Winnipeg 1931), 15. Cf NAC, Canadian Council on Social Development Papers, vol. 57, file 489 (1957–9).

44 AO, RG 4, C-3, #2712/1930, E. Bayly to Judge E. Reynolds, Toronto, 1 November 1930. Police officers felt the same way; see NAC, Papers of the Montreal Society for the Protection of Women and Children, vol. 10, minutes of case conferences 1931–40, 21 September 1932.

45 PABC, GR 1323, file D-67-1; AO, RG 4, C-3, #1661/1921, #2996/1927; NAC, RG 29, vol. 992, file 499-3-7, part 4

46 McGill University Archives, Montreal Council for Social Agencies, box 19, file 10, E.F. O'Neill, *Survey of the Protestant and Non-Sectarian Relief Giving Organizations of Montreal* (Montreal 1924), 2–3; box 18, file 244, 'Manual Outlining the Policy and Functions of the Society,' January 1939

47 Box 18, file 244, 'Manual Outlining the Policy and Functions of the Society,' January 1939

48 NAC, RG 13, A2, #1151/1920, V. Barre to C.J. Doherty, Montreal, 23 June 1920

49 Montreal Council of Social Agencies, *Welfare Work in Montreal in 1933* (Montreal 1934), 147–52

50 *Welfare Work in Montreal in 1929* (n.p., n.d.), 113

51 NAC, Papers of the Montreal Society for the Protection of Women and Children, vol. 10, G.B. Clarke, 'Domestic Relations and Problems of Child Dependency: A Study of Broken Homes,' 7–8

52 Except where otherwise cited, this information can be found in an extended version in J.G. Snell and C.C. Abeele, 'Regulating Nuptiality: Restricting Access to Marriage in Early Twentieth Century English-Speaking Canada,' *Canadian Historical Review* 69 (1988), 466–89. See also A. McLaren, *Our Own Master Race: Eugenics in Canada, 1885–1945* (Toronto 1990), and J.G. Snell, 'The International Border as a Factor in Family Behaviour: A Historical Case Study,' *Ontario History* 81 (1989), 290–6.

53 Clarke, 'Broken Homes,' 7

54 McLaren, *Our Own Master Race*, 75

55 Quoted in J.G. Snell, 'Courts of Domestic Relations: A Study of Early

Twentieth-Century Judicial Reform in Canada,' *Windsor Yearbook of Access to Justice* 6 (1986), 36–44. See also Chunn, 'Regulating the Poor in Ontario,' 85–102.

56 D.B. Harkness, *Courts of Domestic Relations: Duties, Methods and Services of Such Courts: Are they Needed in Canada?* (Ottawa 1924), 2–4; E. Pleck, *Domestic Tyranny: The Making of Social Policy against Family Violence from Colonial Times to the Present* (New York 1987), 125–44

57 NAC, Canadian Council on Social Development, vol. 50, file 455, 'Family Courts 1935–49,' Judge R.S. Hosking to Miss J.I. Wall, Toronto, 4 September 1935

58 D.E. Chunn, 'Family Courts and the Dependent Poor in Ontario, 1920–1945: Intended and Unintended Consequences of Reform,' paper presented to the Canadian Historical Association Annual Meeting, Vancouver, June 1983, table III

59 AO, RG 4, C-3, 1929, #1917, Judge H.S. Mott to W.H. Price, Toronto, 17 May 1929, passim

60 AO, RG 4, C-3, 1934, #824, I.A. Humphries to H.A. Burbidge, Toronto, 23 February 1934

61 Ibid., H.A. Burbidge to W.H. Price, Hamilton, 17 February 1934; 23 February 1934; Chunn, 'Regulating the Poor,' 90–100. A recognizance established a court-ordered obligation for a person – in this case, an obligation to appear before a domestic relations court, thus giving that court considerable power to expand its authority and to include in a formal (or more often an informal) hearing parties who were often unwilling participants.

62 PANS, RG 39 D, C-270, C-431, D-359; NAC, RG 13, A2, vol. 138, #931; AO, RG 4, C-3, #1812/1932

63 G. Marquis, 'Police Social Service in Early Twentieth-Century Toronto' (unpublished)

64 NAC, RG 13, A2, vol. 160, #237. See also vol. 293, #2036.

65 *Sherman* v *King's Proctor,* [1936] 2 WWR 152 (Alta. CA)

66 NAC, RG 18, vol. 1545, file 127-04, report from Knee Hill Creek, NWT, 17 June 1904

67 Ibid., vol. 1682, file 135/12, part 4, A.P. Sherwood to the acting comptroller, Ottawa, 6 December 1912

68 Ibid., part 3, Staff Sergeant D.G. Quinn to officer commanding, Swift Current, 10 October 1912

69 Ibid., vol. 1545, file 127-04, report of Cpl H. Lett, Estevan, 29 September 1904

70 J. Donzelot, *The Policing of Families* (New York 1979); C. Lasch, *Haven in a Heartless World: The Family Besieged* (New York 1977)

71 I. Minor, 'Working-Class Women and Matrimonial Law Reform, 1890–

1914,' in D.E. Martin and D. Rubinstein, eds, *Ideology and the Labour Movement* (London 1979), 111, 120

72 J.R. Gillis, *For Better, for Worse: British Marriages, 1600 to the Present* (New York 1985), 239

6 The Demography of Marriage and Divorce

1 Ellen Gee has produced detailed historical analyses of Canadian nuptiality and fertility; unless otherwise indicated, the information in the following section is taken from her work: 'Fertility and Marriage Patterns in Canada: 1851–1971,' PhD thesis (University of British Columbia 1978); 'Early Canadian Fertility Transition: A Components Analysis of Census Data,' *Canadian Studies in Population* 6 (1979), 23–32; 'Female Marriage Patterns in Canada: Changes and Differentials,' *Journal of Comparative Family Studies* 11 (1980), 457–73; 'Marriage in Nineteenth-Century Canada,' *Canadian Review of Sociology and Anthropology* 19 (1982), 311–25; 'The Life Course of Canadian Women: An Historical and Demographic Analysis,' *Social Indicators Research* 18 (1986), 263–83. See also W. Mertens, 'Canadian Nuptiality Patterns: 1911–1961,' *Canadian Studies in Population* 3 (1976), 57–71.

2 The singulate mean age at marriage is a summary statistic that provides an estimate of the average age at first marriage for those in the population who marry.

3 'Female Marriage Patterns,' 460

4 D.C. McKie, B. Prentice, and P. Reed, *Divorce: Law and the Family in Canada* (Ottawa 1983), 83–7

5 This is not to dispute the argument of Marta Danylewycz, who in *Taking the Veil: An Alternative to Marriage, Motherhood, and Spinsterhood in Quebec, 1840–1920* (Toronto 1987) points out that a small but not insignificant number of females found satisfactory alternatives to marriage.

6 Gee, 'Fertility and Marriage Patterns,' 186; the comparison is between males aged 17½ to 47½ and females aged 20 to 49.

7 Ibid., 194; the comparison is between males aged 22½ to 27½ and females aged 20 to 24.

8 Gee, 'Female Marriage Patterns,' 463, compares unmarried (single, divorced, or widowed) males aged 22½ to 37½ with unmarried females aged 20 to 34.

9 See also I.I. Reddy and P. Krishnan, 'Ethnic Differentials in Age at First Marriage, Canada 1961,' *Journal of Comparative Family Studies* 7 (1976), 55–63; L. Tepperman, 'Ethnic Variations in Marriage and Fertility: Canada, 1871,' *Canadian Review of Sociology and Anthropology* 11 (1974) 324–43.

10 See, for example, J.S. Moir, 'Canadian Protestant Reaction to the *Ne Temere* Decree,' Canadian Catholic Historical Association, *Study Sessions* 48 (1981), 78–90; and R.D. Lambert and J.E. Curtis, 'Québécois and English Canadian Opposition to Racial and Religious Intermarriage, 1963–1983,' *Canadian Ethnic Studies* 16 (1984), 30–46.

11 D.M. Heer, 'The Trend in Interfaith Marriages in Canada: 1922–1957,' *American Sociological Review* 27 (1962), 245–50; D.M. Heer and C.A. Hubay Jr, 'The Trend of Interfaith Marriages in Canada: 1922–1972,' in S.P. Wakil, ed., *Marriage, Family and Society: Canadian Perspectives* (Toronto 1975), 85–96; *Canada Year Book 1943–44* (Ottawa 1944), 155–6; L. Ferretti, 'Marriage et cadre de vie familiale dans une paroisse ouvriere montréalaise: Sainte-Brigide, 1900–1914,' *Revue d'histoire de l'amérique française* 39 (1985–6), 238–41

12 J.R. Gillis, *For Better, for Worse: British Marriages, 1600 to the Present* (New York 1985)

13 The general fertility rate is the ratio of live births per 1,000 women of childbearing age (15 to 49) in the population.

14 J. Henripin, *Trends and Factors of Fertility in Canada* (Ottawa 1972), 30. See also G. Bouchard, 'Family Structures and Geographic Mobility at Laterière, 1851–1935,' *Journal of Family History* 2 (1977), 353. The total fertility rate is the sum of the age-specific fertility rates over the whole range of reproductive ages for a particular year.

15 J. Légaré, 'Demographic Highlights on Fertility Decline in Canadian Marriage Cohorts,' *Canadian Review of Sociology and Anthropology* 11 (1974), 293

16 On birth control in Canada, see A. McLaren and A. Tigar McLaren, *The Bedroom and the State: The Changing Practices and Politics of Contraception and Abortion in Canada, 1880–1980* (Toronto 1986); A. Lévesque, *La norme et les déviantes: des femmes au Québec pendant l'entre-deux-guerres* (Montreal 1989), 97–114.

17 A.J. Pelletier, F.D. Thompson, and A. Rochon, *The Canadian Family*, census monograph no. 7 (Ottawa 1942), 27

18 For a comparison with post-1968 divorces in Canada, see McKie et al., *Divorce*, 87–9.

19 W.P. Ward, 'Unwed Motherhood in Nineteenth-Century English Canada,' Canadian Historical Association, *Historical Papers 1981*, 39; the rates ranged from a low of 7.1 to a high of 19.0.

20 F.F. Furstenburg Jr, 'Premarital Pregnancy and Marital Instability,' *Journal of Social Issuess* 32 (1976), 67–83. For the calculation of pregnancy at marriage, the standard test of birth not more than 7½ months later was employed. It is likely that the figures in table 4 underestimate the actual number of divorcing women who were pregnant

at marriage; parents could avoid the stigma by being vague about a child's age or by falsifying a child's age.

21 Using a T-test, the following characteristics were also tested: petitioner, defence, and duration of marriage at time of divorce petition. Length of initial cohabitation was significant to .001.

22 AO, RG 22 (Owen Sound) SCO, #783/1938

23 See, for example, AO, RG 22 (Toronto) SCO, #3338/1933.

24 AO, RG 22 (Cornwall) SCO, #34/1939

25 PANS, RG 39 D, files D-385, D-421, D-423, D-508, D-590

26 Ibid., file D-289. Graham is quoted in the transcript of testimony as saying, 'I wish there was some way to horse whip you.' In the end the young man grudgingly agreed to marry the woman, commenting, 'I will have to eventually I suppose.'

27 See, for example, S.E. Palmer, 'Reasons for Marriage Breakdown: A Case Study in Southwestern Ontario,' Journal of Comparative Family Studies 2 (1971), 252-3; A.-M. Ambert, Divorce in Canada (Don Mills 1980), 75-8.

28 Denominational membership did not always determine the location of the wedding ceremony. For clandestine weddings couples naturally sought churches (of their own or a different denomination) in which they were strangers. Nevertheless, there is clearly some correlation between church membership and location of weddings, and for lack of a more accurate indicator location of wedding is here used as an indicator of church membership.

29 T.P. Monahan and W.P. Kephart, 'Divorce and Desertion by Religious and Mixed-Religious Groups,' American Journal of Sociology 59 (1953-4), 454-65

30 R. Phillips, Putting Asunder: A History of Divorce in Western Society (Cambridge 1988), 277

31 F.A. Dahms, Population Migration and the Elderly: Ontario 1971-1981 (Guelph 1987), 2

32 G.L. Savage, 'The Operation of the 1857 Divorce Act, 1860-1910: A Research Note,' Journal of Social History 16 (1983), 108-9; Phillips, Putting Asunder, 516-25

33 NAC, RG 13, A2, #462/1921, soldier to C.J. Doherty, St Thomas, Ont. (late September 1919)

34 See, for example, ibid., Elliot, David, and Mailhiot to E.L. Newcombe, Montreal, 4 December 1918; A.C. McArthur to the minister of justice, Calgary, 17 March 1919; L.G. Johnson to the minister of justice, Newton Hyde, England, 9 March 1919; NAC, A. Meighen Papers, #6205, E. Reford to A. Meighen, Montreal, 25 October 1918; and NAC, RG 24, vol. 439, file HQ 54-21-1-133, Hunter and Hunter to the Department of the Militia, Toronto, 28 August 1918.

35 The same was true in England; see Phillips, *Putting Asunder*, 522.
36 The differences, therefore, between the data included in table 7 and that in the Dominion Bureau of Statistics bulletins are that the former includes all petitioners (not just those who were successful) and those who sought 'informal' divorces (as described in the Note on Sources).
37 Calculated from Dominion Bureau of Statistics, *Divorces in Canada* (Ottawa 1923–1940)
38 Dominion Bureau of Statistics, *Divorces in Canada, 1933* (Ottawa 1934), 4
39 Ambert, *Divorce*, 34; Statistics Canada, *Vital Statistics* II, *Marriages and Divorces, 1985* (Ottawa 1986), table 1
40 Although most studies calculate the duration of the marriage from the wedding to the time of dissolution, I have used a different basis. Delays in courtroom procedures or arbitrary obstruction in Parliament were but two of many ways in which additional time could be added to the official length of a marriage. The insistence on a separate application for a final decree sometimes led to considerable delay in the formal dissolution of the marriage. Instances were found in the Ontario sample, for example, of a petitioner's being unaware of the need for this second application; some petitioners waited over a decade before seeking a decree absolute. Therefore, I date the duration of the marriage from the wedding to the point of first formal application for divorce, on the ground that the latter time reflects more accurately the point at which the petitioner was no longer willing to maintain the official status of the union. Ambert (*Divorce*, 35) refers to this as 'the age at which the *real* divorce (that is the emotional and physical divorce ...) occurs.' This dating has an added advantage: while the actual time of dissolution was not clear in many of the cases, the timing of the resort to the divorce process was almost always apparent for the judicial divorces.
41 Ambert, *Divorce*, 35–6; *Vital Statistics*, vol. 2: *Marriage and Divorce, 1985*, table 1. See also Phillips, *Putting Asunder*, 278.
42 Kephart, 'Duration,' 288
43 Phillips, *Putting Asunder*, 270
44 Dependency was defined as under 16 years of age for both sexes.
45 See, for example, McLaren and McLaren, *The Bedroom and the State*; N.J. Davis, 'Childless and Single-Childed Women in Early Twentieth-Century America,' *Journal of Family Issues* 3 (1982), 431–58; and J. Blake, 'Coercive Pronatalism and American Population Policy,' in R. Parke Jr and C.F. Westoff, eds, *Aspects of Population Growth Policy* (Washington 1972), 81–109.
46 For figures on the number of dependent children in post-1968 divorces, see McKie et al., *Divorce*, 96.
47 Dominion Bureau of Statistics, *Divorces in Canada, 1940* (Ottawa 1941), 1, 3

48	For judicial petitions, n = 1602; for unofficial petitions, n = 673
49	In recording complaints for analysis, up to five grievances could be recorded for each case, and these were recorded by the sex of the alleged perpetrator.
50	E.T. May, *Great Expectations: Marriage and Divorce in Post-Victorian America* (Chicago 1980), chapter 8; Ambert, *Divorce*, 69–71
51	J. Kelly, 'Divorce: The Adult Perspective,' in A. Skolnick and J. Skolnick, eds, *Family in Transition* (Toronto 1986), 315–16; S. Albrecht and P. Junz, 'The Decision to Divorce: A Social Exchange Perspective,' in L. Cargan, ed, *Marriage and Family: Coping with Change* (Belmont, Calif. 1985), 302; W.J. Goode, *Women in Divorce* (New York 1956), chapter 10

7 The Role of Gender

1	M.G. Cohen, *Women's Work, Markets, and Economic Development in Nineteenth-Century Ontario* (Toronto 1988); E.L. Silverman, *The Last Best West: Women on the Alberta Frontier 1880–1930* (Montreal 1984)
2	NAC, RG 13, A2, #90/1931, farmer to H. Guthrie, Formosa, Ont., 7 December 1931
3	PANS, RG 39 D, file C-408
4	Ibid., file C-236; AO, RG 22 (London) SCO, #2031/1936 and #2429/1937; *Karch* v *Karch*, [1912] 4 DLR 250
5	PANS, RG 39 D, file C-270
6	AO, RG 22 (Owen Sound) SCO, #562/1935
7	Ibid. (London) SCO, #2371/1937
8	PANS, RG 39 D, files B-11, B-32, B-54, B-168
9	R.L. Griswold, *Family and Divorce in California, 1850–1890* (Albany 1982)
10	PANS, RG 39 D, file B-4
11	NAC, RG 13, A2, #528/1918, farmer to the Privy Council, Birdsholm, Alta. (late February 1918)
12	J.E. Hodgetts et al., *The Biography of an Institution: The Civil Service Commission of Canada, 1908–1967* (Montreal 1972), 484–7; and see, for example, NAC, R.B. Bennett Papers, #126470–3, Mrs W. McManus to Bennett, Smith Falls, Ont., 3 January and 27 May 1931.
13	A. Prentice et al., *Canadian Women: A History* (Toronto 1988), 218–39
14	B. Bradbury, 'Pigs, Cows, and Boarders: Non-Wage Forms of Survival among Montreal Families, 1861–91,' *Labour / Le Travail* 14 (1984), 9–46
15	AO, RG 22 (Sudbury) SCO, #7/1936
16	Ibid. See also, for example, PANS, RG 39 D, file C-406.
17	AO, RG 22 (London) SCO, #2391/1937
18	PANS, RG 39 D, files B-61, D-283; NAC, RG 13, A2, #90/1934. See also,

for example, A. Kojder, 'Women and the Polish Alliance of Canada,' in J. Burnet, ed., *Looking into My Sister's Eyes* (Toronto 1986), 103, and L. Davidoff and C. Hall, *Family Fortunes: Men and Women of the English Middle Class, 1780–1850* (Chicago 1987), 390–1.

19 NAC, RG 13, A2, #677/1921

20 L. Gordon, *Heroes of Their Own Lives* (New York 1988), 97

21 PANS, RG 39 D, file C-43. See also, for example, files C-17, C-262, and C-359.

22 Ibid., file D-380

23 Ibid., file B-58

24 See, for example, NAC, RG 13, A2, #1507/1919.

25 PANS, RG 39 D, file C-377. See also, for example, files D-283 and D-353.

26 AO, RG 22 (Toronto) SCO, #55/1939, and (London) SCO, #315/1931

27 See, for example, Davidoff and Hall, *Family Fortunes*, 209–13; N. Davies, ' "Patriarchy from the Grave": Family Relations in 19th Century New Brunswick Wills,' *Acadiensis* 13 (1984), 91–100.

28 PANS, RG 39 D, file C-340

29 Ibid., file D-669

30 Ibid., file D-533

31 See, for example, ibid., file B-38.

32 AO, RG 22 (Cornwall) SCO, #2/1933

33 PANS, RG 39 D, file D-441. See also file D-581. Only occasionally did the two female parties to an action find common ground against a male who had deceived them both; see, for example, AO, RG 22 (Toronto) SCO, #3120/1938.

34 AO, RG 22 (Toronto) SCO, #3856/1932

35 PANS, RG 39 D, file C-218

36 Ibid., file C-80

37 Canada, House of Commons, *Debates*, 1905, 6275–89, 6347–77

38 Ibid., 6364

39 Ibid., 1917, 5499–500, 5908–9; 1929, 1569–70; 1935, 2949

40 PANS, RG 39 D, file B-17

41 Ibid., file B-84. See also file D-625.

42 Ibid., files B-67, B-190, C-89, C-499, D-122, D-138, D-505, D-608; AO, RG 22 (Owen Sound) SCO, #242/1932 and #610/1936

43 Griswold, *Family and Divorce in California*; PANS, RG 39 D, file B-124

44 AO, RG 22 (London) SCO, #3370/1939

45 Ibid., #2031/1936 and #2429/1937

46 PANS, RG 39 D, file D-118; AO, RG 22 (Toronto) SCO, #1753/1938

47 AO, RG 4, C-3, #2399/1930. See also, N. Basch, 'Relief in the Premises: Divorce as a Woman's Remedy in New York and Indiana, 1815–1870,' *Law and History Review*, 8 (1990), 15.

48 PANS, RG 39 D, file D-376

49 Ibid., file B-171

50 Ibid., files C-314, C-376

51 Ibid., file D-182

52 N. Basch, 'The Emerging Legal History of Women in the United States: Property, Divorce, and the Constitution,' *Signs* 12 (1986), 102

53 See also, for example, M. McCallum, 'Keeping Women in Their Place: The Minimum Wage in Canada, 1910–1925,' *Labour / Le Travail* 17 (1986), 55.

54 PANS, RG 39 D, file B-38½

55 W.J. Goode, *Women in Divorce* (New York 1956, 1965); J. Kelly, 'Divorce: The Adult Perspective,' in A. Skolnick and J. Skolnick, eds, *Family in Transition* (Toronto 1986), 308–12

56 Of a total of 1,572 cases in the judicial sample that gave evidence of spousal behaviour, 51.5 per cent listed at least one of these informal divorce techniques prior to formal proceedings.

57 PANS, RG 39 D, file B-76

58 Ibid., files B-68, D-107, D-358, D-723; AO, RG 22 (Owen Sound) SCO, #35/1937; (Toronto) SCO, #3856/1932; (Guelph) SCO, #26/1939; NAC, RG 13, A2, #945/1912, #458/1913, #462/1922, letter of 26 October 1921. Husbands, of course, were equally capable of selling off assets at the point of desertion, and certainly did so. However, household effects and furniture were regarded by some couples as the wife's property, since they were part of the domestic sphere; see PANS, RG 39 D, file C-218.

59 PANS, RG 39 D, file B-68

60 Ibid., files D-199, D-80

61 Ibid., file D-216

62 Ibid., file D-130

63 Ibid., file C-82

64 See, for example, AO, RG 22 (London) SCO, #3373/1939.

65 PANS, RG 39 D, file C-1

66 Ibid., file B-124½

67 Ibid., file B-142

68 Ibid., files B-4, C-153

69 Ibid., file D-302

70 Ibid., file B-40

71 NAC, RG 13, A2, #462 / 1922, letter of 29 January 1922

72 PANS, RG 39 D, files D-320, D-221

73 Ibid., file D-644; see also, for example, files B-109 and D-402.

74 Basch, 'Relief in the Premises,' 15. The costs of divorce were considerable and in reality wives would not necessarily be able to force their husbands to bear those costs; therefore, it is possible that the women

petitioning for divorce represent a disproportionately self-sufficient segment of the married female population.

75 N.F. Cott, 'Divorce and the Changing Status of Women in Eighteenth-Century Massachusetts,' *William and Mary Quarterly*, 3d series, 33 (1976), 586–614; M. Grossberg, *Governing the Hearth: Law and the Family in Nineteenth-Century America* (Chapel Hill 1985); L. Kerber, *Women of the Republic: Intellect and Ideology in Revolutionary America* (Chapel Hill 1980), 174 and passim

76 V. Strong-Boag, 'Pulling in Double Harness or Hauling a Double Load: Women, Work and Feminism on the Canadian Prairie,' *Journal of Canadian Studies* 21 (1986), 32–52

77 NAC, Sir J.R. Gowan Papers, reel M 1897, Lord Dufferin to J.R. Gowan, Clandeboye, Ireland, 10 November 1900

8 Making the Divorce Process Work

1 [1926] 2 WWR 185 (Sask. CA)

2 AO, RG 22 (Guelph) SCO, #61/1934

3 PANS, RG 39 D, file C-335

4 Ibid., file C-119

5 R.H. Mnookin and L. Kornhauser, 'Bargaining in the Shadow of the Law: The Case of Divorce,' *Yale Law Journal* 88 (1979), 950–7

6 PANS, RG 39 D, files C-176, D-340; AO, RG 22 (Sudbury) SCO, #49/1939

7 PANS, RG 39 D, file D-174

8 AO, RG 22 (Toronto) SCO, #755/1939

9 Ibid., RG 4, C-3, #2518/1930

10 PANS, RG 39 D, file D-112

11 AO, RG 22 (Sudbury) SCO, #72/1939

12 Ibid., (London) SCO, #2243/1936

13 For similar evidence in a more modern process, see I. Thèry, 'The Interest of the Child and the Regulation of the Post-Divorce Family,' in C. Smart and S. Sevenhuijsen, eds, *Child Custody and the Politics of Gender* (London 1989), 87.

14 AO, RG 22 (London) SCO, #2800/1938

15 Here, n = 793.

16 See, for example, PANS, RG 39 D, files D-376 and D-590.

17 Ibid., file C-141

18 Ibid., file D-391

19 See, for example, ibid., file D-57.

20 See, for example, RSNS 1900, c. 163, section 36; SNS 1923, c. 225, section 38; Ontario (1909) 9 Edw. VII, c. 43, section 8.

21 *Pascoe* v *Pascoe*, [1937] OWN 645 (Ont. SC)

22 Failure to inform the respondents of their rights did not, however, render their testimony inadmissible; see *Elliott* v *Elliott and Cook*, [1933] OR 206 (Ont. SC).

23 AO, RG 22 (Sudbury) SCO, #8/1936

24 Ibid., #21, #35/1935

25 Ibid., #27/1938

26 PANS, RG 39 D, file C-242. See also, for example, file B-27 and AO, RG 22 (London) SCO, #1555/1934.

27 PANS, RG 39 D, file D-34

28 Ibid., file C-271

29 AO, RG 22 (Toronto) SCO, #2529/1938

30 See, for example, PANS, RG 39 D, file C-359. Only those co-respondents who had a continuing cohabiting relationship with the respondents were considered in this discussion of 'marital' co-operation.

31 PAC, RG 13, A2, #90/1930

32 AO, RG 22 (London) SCO, #2774/1938

33 PANS, RG 39 D, file D-315

34 NAC, RG 13, A2, #90/1934, letter of 26 February 1932

35 D.M. Sanders, 'Are We Honest about Divorce?' *Maclean's Magazine* 1 March 1932

36 AO, RG 22 (Toronto) SCO, #368/1932

37 Ibid., #260/1939

38 Ibid., #2418/1938

39 Changing the one-month test to 'less than two months' would raise the figure to 15.4 per cent; changing it to 'less than three months' would raise the figure to 17.6 per cent. While the one-month test is by no means foolproof, a disproportionately high number of these cases were uncontested – 90.1 per cent. Women were slightly more likely to be the petitioners in these cases than in the other cases; 71 per cent of the petitioners were women.

40 See, for example, AO, RG 22 (London) SCO, #1981/1935, #1983/1935

41 Ibid., (Sudbury) SCO, #73/1939

42 See, for example, ibid., RG 4, C-3, #3053/1930.

43 Ibid., C-3, #3942/1934

44 PANS, RG 39 D, file C-59B

45 Ibid., file C-70

46 Ibid., file C-418

47 J.R. Gillis, *For Better, for Worse: British Marriages, 1600 to the Present* (New York 1985)

48 PANS, RG 39 D, files C-119 and C-395

49 Ibid., file B-7. See also, for example, AO, RG 22 (London) SCO, #775/

1933 and #2774/1938, and (Toronto) SCO, #1333 and #1343/1932, #3302/ 1932, and #2703/1936.

50 AO, RG 22 (Cornwall) SCO, #32/1936, and (Toronto) SCO, #4471/1934; PANS, RG 39 D, files C-292, C-448, C-205

51 PANS, RG 39 D, files B-22, B-111, D-315, D-555; AO, RG 4, C-3, #4813/ 1930, and RG 22 (Goderich) SCO, #6/1931

52 See, for example, PANS, RG 39 D, files 61, C-100.

53 Ibid., files C-218, C-227, C-430

54 Ibid., files B-140, B-149, B-154, C-423, D-628, D-630, D-652

55 Gillis, *For Better, for Worse*, 78–9; see also R. Phillips, *Putting Asunder: A History of Divorce in Western Society* (Cambridge 1988), 349–50.

56 PANS, RG 39 D, file C-338. See also, for example, files B-32 and C-288.

57 PANS, RG 39 D, files B-161, D-20. The newspaper letter is reprinted in Snell, 'Marital Cruelty,' *Acadiensis* 18 (1988), 15–16.

58 PANS, RG 39 D, file B-145

59 NAC, RG 13, A2, #2006/1920

60 See, for example, PANS, RG 39 D, file D-434.

61 See, for example, AO, RG 22 (Sudbury) SCO, #35/1933, and (London) SCO, #2612/1937; PANS, RG 39 D, files C-169A, C-335, D-225.

62 AO, RG 22 (London) SCO, #51/1931

63 *Elliott* v *Elliott and Cook*, [1933] OR 206

64 *Fortnightly Law Journal* 15 February 1939, 210, 1 July 1939, 39; D.C. Disberry, 'Evidence by Admissions in Divorce Actions,' *Saskatchewan Bar Review* 9 (1944), 4–9

65 See, for example, PANS, RG 39 D, file D-569.

66 J.E. Sinclair (Liberal, Queen's, PEI) in Canada, House of Commons, *Debates*, 1930, 726

67 PANS, RG 39 D, file D-589

68 Ibid., files 63, B-4, B-40. In file C-304 the total costs were taxed at $140.40 – $64.70 for plaintiff's counsel, $1 for the commissioner, $22 for the registrar, $3 for the service of the citation on the defendant, $1 for the crier, $19.20 for witness fees, $9.50 for a court stenographer, and $20 for the watching counsel.

69 PANS, RG 39 D, file B-55

70 Ibid., miscellaneous file, memorandum by W.L. Barss, Halifax, 28 January 1909; ibid., W.L. Barss to W. Ross, Halifax, 23 January 1911; NAC, RG 13, A2, #31/1925, letter of 3 March 1925

71 AO, RG 22 (Toronto) SCO, #2514/1933, and (Cornwall) SCO, #36 / 1939. In the Cornwall case counsel claimed $345 for his efforts, but the judge ordered that $150 be paid; whether this was for all costs or only the lawyer's fees is unclear.

72 J.H. Thompson (with A. Seager), *Canada, 1922–1939: Decades of Discord* (Toronto 1985), 138

73 See, for example, NAC, RG 13, A2, #1574/1907, #1153/1913, #1248/1913, #1518/1916, and #1271/1917.

74 NAC, Sir W. Laurier Papers, #110049–55

75 NAC, RG 13, A2, #31/1926; (1919), 9 & 10 Geo. V, c. 151

76 NAC, RG 13, A2, #1153/1913

77 Ibid., #462/1922, letter of 4 May 1919

78 Ibid., #765/1922

79 See, for example, NAC, Montreal Society for the Protection of Women and Children, 10, 19 December 1934 and 20 March 1935.

80 PANS, RG 39 D, file D-451

81 Occupational information was available for 89.6 per cent of these divorces.

82 For the middle class the participation rate was 23.4 per cent in judicial divorce and 27.1 per cent in parliamentary divorce; for farmers the comparable figures were 8.2 per cent and 4.4 per cent respectively.

83 For comparative purposes, the 1931 census population was selected for two major reasons. First, the occupational data is presented in a manner very similar to the coding used for divorce petitioners. Second, the timing of the data is closest to the middle of the timing of the divorce petitions, since most petitions were presented in the period from 1918 to 1939.

84 C.N. Degler, *At Odds: Women and the Family in America from the Revolution to the Present* (New York 1980); V. Strong-Boag, 'Nellie McLung,' in Strong-Boag and A.C. Fellmen, eds, *Rethinking Canada: The Promise of Women's History* (Toronto 1986)

85 This disproportionate use of the divorce process by the working class is confirmed by other studies; see R. Griswold, *Family and Divorce in California, 1850–1890* (Albany 1982), 25, and W.J. Goode, *After Divorce* (Glencoe, Ill. 1956), 44.

86 Thompson and Seager, *Canada, 1922–1939*, 138

87 L.A. Tilly, 'Rich and Poor in a French Textile City,' in L.A. Moch, ed., *Essays on the Family and Historical Change* (College Station, Tex. 1983), 65–90; T.K. Hareven, *Family Time and Industrial Time: The Relationship between the Family and Work in a New England Industrial Community* (Cambridge 1982)

88 J. Lewis, ed., *Labour and Love: Women's Experience of Home and Family, 1850–1940* (Oxford 1986), 14

89 R.Q. Gray, *The Labour Aristocracy in Victorian Edinburgh* (Oxford 1976); S. Eisenstein, *Give Us Bread but Give Us Roses* (London 1983)

90 Mnookin and Kornhauser, 'Bargaining in the Shadow,' 950–1

91 C.A. McEwen and R.J. Maiman, 'The Relative Significance of Disputing Forum and Dispute Characteristics for Outcome and Compliance,' *Law and Society Review* 20 (1986), 445–6

9 Divorce outside the System

1 J.R. Gillis, *For Better, for Worse: British Marriages, 1600 to the Present* (Oxford 1985), 98–100, 199, 212–17; E.P. Thompson, 'Wife-Sale,' paper presented to McMaster University, Hamilton, Ontario, 17 March 1988; R. Phillips, *Putting Asunder: A History of Divorce in Western Society* (Cambridge 1988), 289–302

2 Gillis, *For Better, for Worse*, 209–12, 217–19, 225–7, 246. While the parameters and details of such informal marriage and divorce remain unexamined for eighteenth- and nineteenth-century British North America, there is little doubt of their existence throughout that period. For an example of wife-sale in the 1860s, see J. Fingard, 'Jailbirds in Mid-Victorian Halifax,' in R.C. Macleod, ed., *Lawful Authority: Readings on the History of Criminal Justice in Canada* (Toronto 1988), 74–5.

3 Gillis, *For Better, for Worse*, 217

4 Wedding-rings were also used as pledges of future marriage by those seeking divorce. See, for example, AO, RG 22 (Sudbury) SCO, #56/1938.

5 Ibid., #73/1939. See also, for example, ibid. (Toronto) SCO, #1095/1932; NAC, RG 13, A2, #462/1922, letter of 19 August 1919.

6 Although legal aid societies assisted those seeking divorce in some American cities, this was not true in such favoured sites as Boston, Detroit or Chicago; see E. Pleck, *Domestic Tyranny: The Making of Social Policy against Family Violence from Colonial Times to the Present* (New York 1987), 141.

7 *Howell's Annotated Statutes of the State of Michigan* (Chicago 1913), c. 309, the Divorce Act, sections 11453–11503; *Compiled Laws of the State of Michigan 1929*, c. 245, Divorce Act, sections 12723–12787

8 United States, Bureau of the Census, *Marriage and Divorce, 1923* (Washington 1925), 24, 60–1; ibid., *Marriage and Divorce 1867–1906* (Washington 1909), 35; Canada, House of Commons, *Debates*, 1928, 380. See also Phillips, *Putting Asunder*, 438, 474.

9 The total number and the comparable figures – 29.2 per cent and 50.0 per cent respectively – among the American divorces in the informal petitions tends to confirm this. Of the 115 total American divorces, 7.8 per cent returned to Canada after the divorce; 16.5 per cent remarried in the United States before returning to Canada; 22.7 per cent remained in the United States without any evidence of remarriage; 34.7 per cent

remarried in the United States and remained there; 7.8 per cent remarried in Canada; and in 10.4 per cent of the divorces no further information was provided.

10 See, for example, NAC, RG 13, A2, #462/1922, letter of 31 July 1919.
11 PANS, RG 39 D, file D-154
12 Canada, House of Commons, *Debates,* 1934, 1784
13 AO, RG 22 (London) SCO, #3373/1939
14 See, for example, NAC, RG 13, A2, #1546/1918, #2361/1919.
15 See, for example, University of Western Ontario, D. Mills Papers, box 4287, Letterbook 1900–1, 293.
16 Phillips, *Putting Asunder,* 296–302, discusses the place of bigamy in the history of informal divorce.
17 This class distribution may, however, be dictated by the data base; since the data concerning class is here a product of the divorce process, it is not surprising that the findings for class reflect the class character of the broader divorce process. In contrast, police-generated criminal statistics concerning bigamy certainly depicted bigamists as sharing characteristics associated with the working class (for example, lower levels of schooling).
18 AO, RG 4, C-3, #1020/1912. See also, for example, PABC, GR 1323, #6714-4-12.
19 AO, RG 4, C-3, #3137/1930. See also, for example, ibid., #2488/1925, #289/1936.
20 PABC, GR 1323, #6714-4-12. See also, for example, NAC, RG 13, A2, #1585/1913, #1907/1922.
21 NAC, RG 13, A2, #1575/1925, E. Bayly to W.S. Edwards, Toronto, 18 February 1926; ibid., #360/1926
22 AO, RG 4, C-3, #2488/1925, #75/1927
23 Phillips, *Putting Asunder,* 370
24 NAC, RG 13, A2, #625/1918; NAC, Montreal Society for the Protection of Women and Children, Casebooks, 16 November 1931
25 PANS, RG 39 D, file B-161
26 Ibid., file C-39. See also, for example, NAC, RG 24, vol. 2049, file HQ 54-27-1-21, part 1; NAC, R.B. Bennett Papers, reel M-1264, #326763 and #326898.
27 See, for example, NAC, RG 13, A2, #94/1919.
28 Ibid., #903/1916
29 The published statistics for criminal prosecutions in Canada are notoriously weak in this time period, being vulnerable to irregular reporting procedures and to very subjective and inadequate criteria. The recorded social characteristics of the convicted are especially problematic. Nevertheless, the reports surely represent a minimum number

of prosecutions and convictions, and the associated information is at least suggestive.

30 An alternative hypothesis is that bigamy was a particularly male technique, and that wives tended not to be charged because they had no prior knowledge of their husbands' previous marriages. An investigation of bigamy cases at the trial level would be necessary to resolve this issue.

31 D. Guest, *The Emergence of Social Security in Canada* (Vancouver 1980), 60; PABC, GR 429, #1793/1908. See also, for example, NAC, RG 13, A2, #488/1900, #1195/1909, #1341/1914, #2013/1920, #90/1931, letter of 7 February 1929.

32 AO, RG 22 (London) SCO, #2774/1938

33 PANS, RG 39 D, file D-201

34 See, for example, NAC, RG 13, A2, #657/1916, #903/1916; W.O. Weyrauch, 'Informal Marriage and Common Law Marriage,' in R. Slovenko, ed., *Sexual Behaviour and the Law* (Springfield, Ill. 1965), 298.

35 NAC, RG 13, A2, #1201/1920

36 It may well be that the decline in the 1930s is simply a product of major changes in the filing and file retention systems of the Justice Department; in the early 1930s there is a dramatic drop in the number of files in many areas of the department's activities.

37 Social class was not an important factor in determining participation in this informal petitioning process. The various classes were represented almost exactly in proportion to their numbers in the total population (see table 17); 71.7 per cent of marriages were working-class, in an impressive 56.9 per cent husbands were skilled or semi-skilled workers, in 17.7 per cent the husbands were farmers, and just 10.6 per cent were middle-class (n = 283; occupation was reported in 33.3 per cent of the 851 informal petitions coded).

38 NAC, RG 13, A2, #252/1919, #267/1919

39 Ibid., #90/1934, letter of 11 February 1932

40 Ibid., #1575/1918, #2340/1918, #364/1930

41 Ibid., #1861/1914, #1610/1918

42 Ibid., #141/1920

43 Ibid., #620/1909, #798/1915, #564/1917

44 Ibid., #1223/1921

45 Ibid., #1559/1921, #1341/1914

46 Ibid., #167/1921, #348/1915, #2343/1918

47 Gillis, *For Better, for Worse*, 99; Phillips, *Putting Asunder*, 298, 370

48 NAC, RG 13, A2, #934/1919, #762/1915, #866/1916

49 Ibid., #49/1917, #90/1931, letter of 23 October 1931

50 Ibid., #1734/1919, #877/1912

51 See, for example, ibid., #2867/1919, #2186/1922. See also *Trudeau* v *R.* (1935), 58 Que. KB 14, 63 CCC 206 (Que. CA).
52 PABC, GR 1323, D-67-8, 11 February 1920
53 NAC, RG 24, vol. 439, file HQ 54-21-1-133, letter of 25 June 1925
54 See, for example, PANS, RG 39 D, files C-59A, C-242A; AO, RG 22 (Owen Sound) SCO, #137/1931.
55 NAC, RG 13, A2, #28/1923, letter of 18 October 1923
56 Ibid., #2833/1919
57 Ibid., #495/1922, #31/1928, letter of 16 February 1927
58 Of the informal petitioners, 34.8 per cent sought information.
59 NAC, RG 13, A2, #412/1910
60 Ibid., #141/1920, #1606/1922
61 Ibid., #227/1920
62 Ibid., #1414/1917, #31/1925, letter of 17 May 1926, #28/1923, letter of 26 May 1924; 13.8 per cent of the informal petitioners asked for permission to remarry.
63 Ibid., #90/1931, letter of 14 September 1931
64 Ibid., #2289/1918, #826/1902, #849/1906
65 Ibid., #1474/1912, #28/1923, letter of late October 1923, #31/1925, letter of 31 January 1927
66 Of the informal petitioners, 56.4 per cent sought a direct divorce. As well, 13.2 per cent of the petitioners urged the state to punish the offending spouse for their conduct.
67 NAC, RG 13, A2, #620/1909, #707/1920, #1559/1921
68 Ibid., #806/1915, #876/1916, #1966/1918
69 Ibid., #28/1923, letter of 19 May 1923
70 Ibid., #1497/1913
71 A.-M. Ambert, *Divorce in Canada* (Toronto 1980), 26; Phillips, *Putting Asunder*, 280; L. Gordon, *Heroes of Their Own Lives* (New York 1988), 91
72 See, for example, M. Hiemstra, *Gully Farm* (Toronto 1955), and L. Petroff, 'Macedonian Women in Toronto,' in J. Burnet, ed., *Looking into My Sister's Eyes* (Toronto 1986), 128.
73 NAC, RG 13, A2, #2729/1918
74 L. Amey, 'History of the Amey/MacBeth Family,' unpublished, 1983
75 NAC, Canadian Council on Social Development, vol. 58, file 489 (1957–60), *Family Desertion: Its Causes, Effects and Recommendations for Dealing with It* (Ottawa 1960)
76 AO, RG 22 (Goderich) SCO, #33/1935
77 W.P. Ward, 'Unwed Motherhood in Nineteenth-Century English Canada,' Canadian Historical Association *Historical Papers, 1981*, 46-48; L. Fee, 'Women on Trial: Serious Female Crime in the Assize Court in Ontario, 1880–1930,' MA thesis (University of Guelph 1988), 46

78 NAC, RG 13, A2, #90/1931, letter of 7 July 1930
79 Ibid., #1548/1917, #1057/1921
80 See, for example, NAC, RG 13, A2, #412/1910.
81 A 1950s study of desertion found that common law marriages made up
    19.1 per cent of desertion cases. See NAC, Canadian Council on Social
    Development, vol. 58, file 489 (1957–60), M. Rogers to N. Cragg, Winni-
    peg, 19 December 1958.
82 NAC, RG 13, A2, #462/1922, letter of 5 May 1919. See, for example, AO,
    RG 4, C-3, #289/1909.
83 Canada, House of Commons, *Debates*, 1919, 4277–8. I would like to
    thank Glenn Wright for bringing this reference to my attention.
84 Canada, 9 & 10 Geo. V, c. 43, section 33(3)
85 NAC, RG 13, A2, #699/1927. Interestingly, Ted's concern in writing the
    minister of justice was to try to legitimate his children, since their birth
    registrations had falsely indicated that George Fitzpatrick was the father
    'to cover the shame as it was then.' For another example, see J. Sangster,
    Dreams of Equality: Women on the Canadian Left, 1920–1950 (Toronto
    1989), 254 n92.
86 See, for example, *Rosentzweig* v *Swartz*, [1937] 3 DLR 256 (Man. KB);
    Petschl v *Bucki*, [1926] 3 WWR 598 (Alta. SC); *Frere* v *Shields*, [1939] 2
    WWR 396 (Sask. CA); *Pepperas* v *Le Duc* (1913), 4 OWN 1208 (Ont. SC);
    Stockholder v *Stockholder*, [1934] 1 WWR 365 (Man. KB); *Re Sheran*,
    (1906) 4 Terr. LR 83 (NWTSC).
87 Canada, House of Commons, *Debates*, 1934, 526–7, 537, 1778–9, 1787–9
88 Ibid., 1784, 1788, 2829–30; NAC, R.B. Bennett Papers, reel M-1259,
    #319579–719; ibid., reel M-1264, #326768–70 and #326797–800
89 NAC, RG 24, vol. 2076, file HQ 54-275-11, part 2, Major G.F. Furlong to
    director of pay services, Saint John, NB, 17 September 1940
90 Ibid., part 1. The common law relationship required corroboration from
    neighbours and friends; neither party could be validly married; the
    couple had to have lived together in a conjugal relationship for at least
    a year prior to enlistment and to have represented themselves to the
    community as man and wife. The woman was eligible for a dependent's
    allowance if the relationship met these tests and if she was 'not com-
    monly regarded as a loose character' and had been regularly supported
    by the soldier involved.
91 NAC, RG 29, vol. 128, #208-2-3, part 2, V.D. McElary to J.W. MacFarlane,
    Toronto, 8 June 1940; Ibid., vol. 140, #208-5-7, part 2, W.C. Mills to J.W.
    MacFarlane, Regina, Sask., 19 March 1940; Ibid., vol. 155, #208-7-4, part
    3, Proceedings of the Interprovincial Advisory Board, 12 January 1948,
    66–8
92 AO, RG 22 (London) SCO, #1672/1935; AO, RG 4, C-3, #3252/1930;

PANS, RG 39 D, files C-52, C-242A; NAC, RG 13, A2, #495/1922, #218/ 1927; Gillis, *For Better, for Worse*, 236

93 NAC, RG 13, A2, #31/1928, letter of 12 June 1928. Some women preferred to disguise their divorced status by continuing to use their married names.

94 PANS, RG 39 D, file B-65; NAC, RG 13, A2, #495/1922

95 See, for example, D. Owram, *The Government Generation: Canadian Intellectuals and the State 1900–1945* (Toronto 1986).

96 'Community,' of course, refers not simply to geographical location, but also to social groupings around such central forces as religion or ethnicity.

10 Conclusion

1 NAC, RG 13, A2, #625/1918

2 See R.L. Griswold, *Family and Divorce in California, 1850–1890: Victorian Illusions and Everyday Realities* (Albany 1982), and E.T. May, *Great Expectations: Marriage and Divorce in Post-Victorian America* (Chicago 1980).

3 A. McLaren and A.T. McLaren, *The Bedroom and the State: The Changing Practices and Politics of Contraception and Abortion in Canada, 1880–1980* (Toronto 1986), 9

4 D. Sugarman, 'Theory and Practice in Law and History,' in B. Fryer et al., eds, *Law, State and Society* (London 1981), 82

5 R.Q. Gray, *The Labour Aristocracy in Victorian Edinburgh* (Oxford 1976), 5

6 C. Smart, *The Ties That Bind: Law, Marriage and the Reproduction of Patriarchal Relations* (London 1984), 101; M.B. Sussman, 'Law and Legal Systems: The Family Connection,' in S.K. Steinmetz, ed., *Family and Support Systems across the Life Span* (New York 1988), 11–34

7 M.A. Glendon, *State, Law and Family: Family Law in Transition in the United States and Western Europe* (New York 1977)

8 N.H. Clark, *Deliver Us from Evil: An Interpretation of American Prohibition* (New York 1976), 152–216; J.H. Thompson (with A. Seager), *Canada, 1922–1939: Decades of Discord* (Toronto 1985), 138–92

9 PANS, RG 39 D, file D-253; AO, RG 4, C-3, #1064/1932. See also PANS, RG 39 D, files D-310 and D-434.

10 Ibid., files D-395, D-402, D-419, D-429, D-432, D-574, D-638, D-671

11 V. Strong-Boag, *The New Day Recalled: Lives of Girls and Women in English Canada, 1919–1939* (Toronto 1987), 218

12 NAC, A Meighen Papers, #095911–16, 29 March 1938

13 M. Poster, *Critical Theory of the Family* (New York 1978), 143

Appendix: Social Class and Occupation

1 Michael Katz et al. include 'business employees (largely clerks …)' among the 'business class' in their two-class model of society; such a grouping in the early twentieth century seems to me incorrect. See M.B. Katz, M.J. Doucet, and M.J. Stern, *The Social Organization of Early Industrial Capitalism* (Cambridge 1982) 44.

2 This problem is discussed by Michael Katz in 'Occupational Classification in History,' *Journal of Interdisciplinary History* 3 (1972), 63–88.

3 'Les Catégories socio-professionelles: une nouvelle grille de classement,' *Labour / Le Travail*, 15 (Spring 1985), 145–63

4 M. Barrett, *Women's Oppression Today* (London 1980), 124–5, 129–30; J. Acker, 'Women and Social Stratification: A Case of Intellectual Sexism,' *American Journal of Sociology* 78 (1973), 936–45; E. Garnsey, 'Women's Work and Theories of Class Stratification,' *Sociology* 12 (1978), 223–43

Index

abortion 7, 174
adultery 11, 22, 33–4, 41–3, 46, 49–50, 57–9, 63, 68, 73, 109, 111–14, 122–3, 128, 152–6, 168–9, 173, 192, 197–8, 201, 250; aggravated 59–61, 64, 71, 91, 99; examples of 55, 78, 85–6, 92–4, 98–9, 125, 159, 163, 167, 169, 171, 173–4, 177–9, 186, 193–7, 199–201, 203, 205–6, 209–10, 212, 241, 247, 287 n13, 290 n56; in the courts 91–7
age of consent 283 n14
alcoholism 39, 96–7, 108, 112–14, 122–3, 126, 152, 154–5, 170, 206, 229, 247
alimony 25, 29, 78, 86, 97–9, 108, 158, 167, 177, 179, 188–9, 195, 283

n13. *See also* support
Allan, Sir Hugh 283 n13
Ames, Sir Herbert 252–3, 284 n29
Anglicans 142, 285 n39
annulment 15, 41, 70–1, 86, 107, 234, 242, 247
artificial insemination 92–4

Babineau v *Babineau* 91
Baptist church 41
Baptists 141, 285 n39
Becker, Vicky (pseud.) 203–4
bestiality 91
bigamy 58–9, 73, 83, 110, 153–5, 183–4, 188, 206, 227–8, 232–8, 243, 308 n17; examples of 3–4, 81, 84, 89–90, 188, 192, 210, 212, 239–42,